Henry Duke of Glocester
borne at Otlandes the eight
of July 1640

KING CHARLES I WITH HIS THREE SONS

KING CHARLES
and
KING PYM
1637-1643

KING CHARLES
and
KING PYM
1637-1643

by

Esmé Wingfield-Stratford, D.Sc.

"When all its work is done, the lie shall rot;
The truth is great and shall prevail,
When none cares whether it prevail or not."

COVENTRY PATMORE

GREENWOOD PRESS PUBLISHERS
WESTPORT, CONNECTICUT

Library of Congress Cataloging in Publication Data

Wingfield-Stratford, Esme Cecil, 1882–
  King Charles and King Pym, 1637-1643.

  Reprint of the 1949 ed. published by Hollis & Carter,
London.
  Bibliography: p.
  Includes index.
  1. Charles I, King of Great Britain, 1600-1649.
2. Pym, John, 1584-1643. 3. Great Britain--History
--Charles I, 1625-1649. I. Title.
DA396.A2W495 1975   941.06'2'0924 [B]   74-31870
ISBN 0-8371-7948-3

To

ERNEST SHORT

amicitiæ causa

Originally published in 1949 by Hollis & Carter, London

Reprinted with the permission of B. Wingfield-Stratford

Reprinted in 1975 by Greenwood Press,
a division of Williamhouse-Regency Inc.

Library of Congress Catalog Card Number 74-31870

ISBN 0-8371-7948-3

Printed in the United States of America

CONTENTS

Prologue

1 THE GENESIS OF A MYTH   3
2 AN UNCROWNED KING IN THE MAKING   8

I Transfer of Sovereignty

1 THE BOOK   19
2 THE COVENANT   25
3 FARCE ON THE BORDER   32
4 STRAFFORD TO THE RESCUE   39
5 THE SHORT PARLIAMENT   45
6 "THE BLUE BONNETS ARE OVER THE BORDER"   53
7 CONQUEST AND BLACKMAIL   61
8 PYM STRIKES FIRST   66
9 REIGN OF TERROR   74
10 REVOLUTION BY LAW   78
11 THE GREAT REFUSAL   80
12 TRIAL AND NO TRIAL   87
13 PLOT AND PROPAGANDA   95
14 SUPREME ACCEPTANCE   104
15 PYM'S MASTERSTROKE   112
16 BILLS FOR SIGNATURE   116

II Double Surrender

1 LONDON COMES TO WHITEHALL   123
2 THE BELEAGUERED PALACE   128
3 LODGINGS AT WESTMINSTER   129
4 THE MAN AT THE COUNCIL BOARD   132
5 THE CONSCIENCE OF THE KING   137
6 THE LAST TURN OF THE SCREW   142
7 DIVINE IMPERATIVE, HUMAN VETO   146
8 ROYAL DEATH-WARRANT   150
9 "LIKE A GENTLEMAN AND A CHRISTIAN"   153

III *Check to King Pym*

1 STRANGLEHOLD 159
2 WHOSE END IS DESTRUCTION 162
3 A LITTLE CLOUD 166
4 AN OPPOSITION IN BEING 170
5 PARALYSIS OF SOVEREIGNTY 172
6 UNDERMINING THE THRONE 176
7 TERROR BY LEGISLATION 181
8 THE ATTACK ON THE CHURCH 186
9 THE CONVERSION OF EDWARD HYDE 188
10 WRECKERS WHO WOULD NOT GOVERN 193
11 A QUEEN ON THE RACK 197
12 PYM MEETS HIS MATCH 203
13 THE KING GOES NORTH 209
14 PARLIAMENTARY FIASCO 215

IV *Checkmate to King Charles*

1 SCOTTISH TRAGEDY 221
2 OFFENSIVE WITHOUT LIMIT 227
3 CATASTROPHE IN IRELAND 232
4 PROPAGANDA BARRAGE 239
5 REVOLUTIONARY MANIFESTO 242
6 REMONSTRANCE AND COUNTER-REMONSTRANCE 247
7 THE KING'S HOMECOMING 250
8 THE MOB COMES BACK TO WESTMINSTER 254
9 THE KING'S HAND IS FORCED 260
10 INDICTMENT FOR TREASON 263
11 SUICIDE BY COMPULSION 271
12 FLIGHT FROM WHITEHALL 279
13 DRIFTING TO WAR 283
14 "BY GOD ! NOT FOR AN HOUR !" 285
15 DECISIVE HESITATION 288
16 *Dieu et Mon Droit!* 293

V *Appeal to the Country*

1 THE PREDETERMINED ISSUE 301
2 PRINCE RUPERT SETS THE PACE 305
3 THE KING TAKES THE OFFENSIVE 310

CONTENTS

4 AMATEUR ARMIES CLASH AT EDGEHILL 318
5 THE THRUST FOR LONDON AND THE UNFOUGHT DECISION 329
6 CAVALIER GRAND STRATEGY 335
7 "YOUR SHE MAJESTY GENERALISSIMA" 339
8 A RAID AND ITS SEQUEL 342
9 CAVALIER ZENITH 348
10 "GIVE US THAT DOG PYM !" 352
11 THE CAMPAIGN OF NEWBURY 356
12 KING PYM PLEDGES HIS COUNTRY 363

VI *8th of December, 1643* 371

APPENDIX : A NOTE ON SOURCES 383
INDEX 389

ILLUSTRATIONS

KING CHARLES I WITH HIS THREE SONS FRONTISPIECE

EDWARD HYDE, EARL OF CLARENDON facing page 214

LUCIUS, VISCOUNT FALKLAND 214

QUEEN HENRIETTA MARIA 215

KING CHARLES I IN ARMOUR—from a painting by Van Dyck 230

JOHN PYM : "A DAMNABLE TREASON" 231

OLIVER CROMWELL—from a painting by Robert Walker 346

PRINCE RUPERT—from a miniature by John Hoskins 346

JOHN HAMPDEN : (inset) HAMPDEN BEING CARRIED, MORTALLY WOUNDED, FROM CHALGROVE FIELD 347

SIR JACOB ASTLEY 354

KING CHARLES I ON HORSEBACK—from a Van Dyck sketch 355

MAPS

PLAN OF WHITEHALL 124

THE CAMPAIGN OF EDGEHILL and the King's advance to Oxford 312

PRELIMINARIES OF EDGEHILL, 23rd October, 1642 318

BATTLE OF EDGEHILL, 1st Phase : Royal Offensive 321

BATTLE OF EDGEHILL, 2nd Phase : Roundhead Counter-offensive 323

BATTLE OF EDGEHILL, *Final phase*   327

THE KING'S ADVANCE ON LONDON *and*
projected Roundhead pincer movement   334

CAVALIER STRATEGY OF *1643 showing the King's*
plan for the encirclement of London and his ring of
strong posts round Oxford   338

RUPERT'S MARCH TO CHALGROVE FIELD   346

THE RELIEF OF GLOUCESTER *and the march to*
Newbury   359

THE FIRST BATTLE OF NEWBURY   360

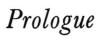

Prologue

I

THE GENESIS OF A MYTH

I HAVE tried, in this volume, to set down the story of the six years that elapsed between the fatally misguided attempt of Charles I and Archbishop Laud to impose a new Prayer Book on the Church of Scotland, and the death of John Pym at the end of 1643.

It can safely be said that no other six-year period of British history—except that which precisely corresponds to it in time during the Twentieth Century—is of such vital significance or dramatic interest. And yet about none, in historic times, is the truth less known.

This may appear a hard saying in view of the innumerable histories, biographies, essays and text books in which that story has been, and continues to be told, and of the vast amount of labour that has been devoted to the unearthing of every scrap of evidence that can possibly throw light on the royal tragedy of which it comprises the central and climacteric agony. It is a story of which even the most sketchily educated person is firmly, and even passionately convinced that he knows all that is essential of the plot, the leading characters, and the moral. And indeed it is a moot point whether the imaginary events and characters that have been planted on the common consciousness of the nation are not facts of history at least as significant as those that actually happened. The original Hamlet, if he ever existed at all, is a person of infinitesimal importance compared to the imaginary Prince, the depths of whose reality no critic has yet succeeded in plumbing. And so it may be plausibly maintained that the great drama, or melodrama of popular liberties entitled *The Tyrant versus the Patriots*, and created by such mighty masters as Macaulay, Gardiner, and Green, is a national asset too precious at this, of all times, to be taken to pieces and forced into a pedantic conformity to fact.

To think thus may be wrong, but it is neither ridiculous nor contemptible. Every great civilization has been built on faith, and faith cannot be assimilated neat, in creeds and abstract dogmas. It needs something on which the imagination can fasten, some myth or epic or gospel—what journalists call a story. To provide that story has been the function of the classic historians, ever since history became an art. And it needs an almost super-human additional effort of faith to grasp and act upon the assumption that the true story is under all circumstances the best story ; that it is an unconditional obligation laid on the historian to seek and ensue the truth regardless of every other consideration, patriotic or otherwise ; and that in so doing he will be serving the cause of his country, and mankind, better than if he had allowed patriotic or moral bias to predetermine his manipulation of the facts.

British historians, unlike the state stooges who perform that office in Totalitarian countries, have indeed seldom failed to honour, with all their conscience, the obligation laid on witnesses in the courts to tell the whole truth, and nothing but the truth. But it used to be said of one of the most representative of Englishmen, Mr Gladstone, that he was in the habit of following his conscience as the driver follows the horse. Beneath the conscience of the truth-seeker, and behind it, there is the subconscience of the patriot, the moralist, and even of the party politician. The historian is still performing his time-honoured function of national myth maker all the more efficiently because he is propagating the myth, not with his tongue in an official cheek, but with what he himself believes to be a passionate and impartial candour.

Thus it comes about that to the understanding reader, historical classics are apt to throw more light upon the historian himself, and his age, than the past that they profess to record. For an age is best known by what it chooses to believe. Taken literally, the myth may be a story in the nursery sense, but it is also the truth in cipher, if we can only decode it.

And whether we like it or not, it is hopeless to think of getting on with the true story until we have come to some sort of understanding of the myth. For otherwise we shall find ourselves in the humiliating case of grown ups, who attempt to foist their own version of one of the familiar fairy stories upon a juvenile audience, that breaks in upon every sentence with, "But that isn't right," or "That's not what Auntie told us."

The current myth about King Charles, that of *The Tyrant*

versus the Patriots, is not the original version. For at least a century after the Restoration, the nation was obsessed by the horror of military rule, that had been seared into its soul during the Protectorate of Cromwell. It therefore demanded a drama in which the usurping commander should play the part of arch villain and the King that of his innocent victim. The Parliamentary chiefs, the Frankensteins who had generated the monster, were kept out of the limelight. Their apotheosis would have been plainly inconsistent with that of King Charles ; their denigration would have involved that of their political heirs, the rich oligarchs who after the Glorious Revolution of 1689, lorded it over King and people alike.

But a time came when the red coat of the British soldier inspired confidence rather than fear, and when the prestige of monarchy was declining towards the mud bottom level it reached under the sons of George III : and this, when not only in England, but in much of Europe and America, the British way of ordered freedom had become the object of unstinted panegyric. The British had begun to feel themselves a constitutionally chosen people. And such a state of mind emphatically demanded a legend to support it, a myth of the founding and founders of this highly specialized liberty which, it was agreed by all except a diminishing band of high and dry reactionaries, had been consummated in 1689 by a Dutch William the Conqueror.

But the task of turning this good, but unprepossessing European, into the saviour hero of a nation that he had disliked almost as much as it had detested him, and of making a heroic epic out of a crook drama and spy story in which all the leading characters were engaged in double and treble crossing King, country and one another, proved beyond the genius even of a Macaulay to do convincingly. So it became necessary to look further back to a time of unequivocally heroic deeds, and characters cast in a proportionally generous mould.

Such a time was not far to seek. A great constitutional struggle transferred from the Parliament House to the field, and culminating in a deed that struck and shocked the British imagination more than any other on historic record, the trial of a King by his own subjects, and his execution in front of his own palace !

It was easy to see the form that the reconstructed legend of this time would now take. It was to be a drama of Parliamentary liberties. The King must obviously be retained as the most conspicuous character ; but since he had admittedly been at loggerheads with each one of his five Parliaments, he must be changed from Charles the Martyr to Charles the Tyrant, and his sentence represented as substantially just, if a little irregular in form. But what was to be done about a hero ? Cromwell, however much he might be exalted in the capacity of Parliamentary commander and vindicated in that of regicide, had dealt with Parliament in a way that put him out of the running for the part of hero. And it was an unfortunate fact that with the exception of Cromwell, all the most obviously impressive and commanding figures happened to be on the wrong side ; Strafford among the statesmen, Laud and Juxon among the Churchmen, Prince Rupert among the soldiers, and last, but not least, the Royal Martyr himself. Who could be put up to hold a candle against these ? There was Pym, of course, who rightly understood, might have challenged the highest place of all in point of sheer political genius ; but it was genius of a kind worse than useless for the sort of legend required ; and consequently, since the legend had got to be put across somehow, and this simply could not be done without a sympathetic hero, the want was supplied by the invention and apotheosis of a John Hampden, who had as much and as little connection with the millionaire* politician who had borne that name in real life, as the Hamlet of Shakespeare with his Viking original.

This naturally entailed a proportionate lowering, or as the word now is, debunking, of the chief reputations on the other side. Strafford had to become a sort of stage tyrant, the bold, bad, black-browed villain of melodrama ; Laud a "ridiculous old bigot "; Rupert a headstrong young fool. And most essential of all, the King himself had to be degraded from his status of Royal Martyr, to what he is described as being in his own death sentence :

"A tyrant, traitor, murderer, and enemy of the good people of this country."

The low-souled King may have been as imaginary a creation as the high-souled Patriot, but the one was necessary to the other, and both to the legend.

The other characters fall as naturally into their places, as the teams in a schoolboy pick-up behind their respective skippers : the friends of freedom on the right hand, the minions of tyranny

---

* I mean of course an enormously rich man, the equivalent of the modern millionaire. There were few, if any, actual fortunes in those days of seven figures sterling.

on the left. For there is nothing like honest to God melodrama for capturing the popular imagination.

And this particular myth is so impregnably fixed in the national subconsciousness, that to question it is to engender a heat that has to be experienced to be believed. For everyone knows, or thinks he knows, that the good fight for British liberty was fought and won by the Parliament men—those simple and stainless patriots—against a perfidious despot. Their reputations are felt to be part of our democⅰatic heritage. He who goes about to suggest a rather different explanation of their proceedings and to demand a retrial of the case from A to Z, is felt to be a reactionary fifth columnist, more fit to be suppressed than argued with.

But with those who have the patience to listen, it may be pleaded that such melodrama travesty works out, in the long run, hardly less unfairly for its selected heroes and paragons, than for its villains and buffoons. The real Hampden, little as we know about him, seems to have cut a more forceful and interesting figure than the patriot dummy, or Bowdlerized John Bull, that has been dressed up in his name to resemble nothing on earth— least of all the formidable and secretive personage whose power we can feel, but the exact course of whose proceedings is to this day enveloped in the mystery in which he deliberately sought to involve it.

But the imaginary Hampden has at least the advantage of having become so wholly a figure of symbolic mythology that, like the joker in cards, he can be played to any heroic or human value whatever. People accept him as they do the flag and the person of the Sovereign, or as St Athanasius did the Trinity, as something that, though not entirely comprehensible, ought in all things to be worshipped. But the far greater figure of John Pym has never come alive at all. The idea of him as a high-souled and rather naïve idealist is too palpably at variance with the known facts of his career to be assimilated, even if swallowed. Consequently to the plain man, he remains a sort of constitutional abstraction, or, at the most human, signifies the gloating expression and goat's beard of a crudely etched portrait.

Parliament itself, though it has found room in its precincts for a statue of Cromwell, has even more conspicuously forgotten to match it with one of Pym. And what is hardly less significant is that while the imaginary Hampden never fails to be accorded the fervent, or reverential prefix of his Christian name, the Johnning of Pym is a ceremony commonly dispensed with. And how many of all those who have feasted their eyes on the Banqueting House at Whitehall and the Houses of Parliament, have spared a glance at St Margaret's churchyard* for his sake? That, whether we regard him as the man who saved, or the man who came within an ace of destroying, Parliamentary government in England, seems niggardly measure to accord to the great Commoner who came to be called King.

2

AN UNCROWNED KING IN THE MAKING

JOHN Pym was already in his 47th or 48th year, which was more venerable by contemporary than it would be by modern reckoning, when he commenced his association with the political-financial group of which he soon came to be the virtual controller, and which in ten years' time he would have forged into an instrument powerful enough to overturn the whole fabric of church and state. He had come to this task with a reputation, built up in successive Parliaments, that was solid rather than brilliant. There was nothing of the glamour attaching to his personality that invested such leadership as that of Wentworth and Eliot. His fellow-members knew him as "the Ox". He was massive and deliberate and shaggy; never in a hurry, never put out of his stride, always shambling unimpressively on in a straight line ahead, and somehow, in the long run, leaving behind his more mettlesome competitors.

Pym was not called the Ox for nothing. Of all characters in history there is none that provides the up-to-date biographer with less opportunity for imparting what is called the human touch. Even the stories that have clung to his name of a secret addiction to gallantry have never been indubitably proven—the same sort of scandal used to be propagated about Gladstone. If he had a private life at all, or personal feelings, hardly the faintest hint survives of them. We do not even know for certain the year in which he was born, and very little about his family, except that they appear to have been small Somerset squires; we know that

* Where his remains lie buried in a nameless pit, after their expulsion from the Abbey at the Restoration.

he went up to what is now Pembroke College, Oxford, and that he went down without taking a degree ; that he was admitted to the Middle Temple, but never called to the bar ; that he entered into government service and—what is a great deal more significant—took shelter under the patronage of the Earl of Bedford, the head of the most powerful and purse-proud of all those upstart Houses which had founded their fortunes on the plunder of the monasteries, and had gone on expanding them ever since. It was through this connection that he got jobbed into the well-paid receivership of three Wessex shires.* At some unknown date about this time he married an equally unknown lady (except for her name, and even the exact form of that is a little uncertain) and having, with his usual industrious application, caused her to produce nine children, proceeded to bury her in a year we know, 1620, after which, having committed his estate into the hands of trustees,† he devoted himself with austere concentration to the career of a self-made politician. Even so, in such mists of obscurity is his life, up to middle age, enveloped, that it is to this day keenly disputed whether, as *The Dictionary of National Biography* asserts, he had sat in King James's abortive Parliament of 1614. If he did, no record has survived of his having taken any part in its brief proceedings. Which is no more than we should have expected, for it is not characteristic of the Ox to be quick off the starting line.

Mr Pym emerges into the light of history in the fateful year 1621, when—no doubt not without some aid and comfort from his exalted patron—he was returned to the third Parliament of James's reign as member for the petty borough of Calne in Wiltshire, one of those counties of which he held the receivership. He had now achieved something like that detachment from private ties which had enabled great celibate Church-statesmen like Wolsey and Richelieu to harness the impersonal devotion of sainthood to ends the most mundane pursued by ways the most devious. We search in vain among all the records of his activities for anything that gives us the least clue to a personal bias. His friendships—if we can call them that—are exclusively business or political. Never, as far as we know, did he evince more kindness or tenderness or pity for any living creature than a chess player

---

*See especially *John Pym*, by S. Reed Brett.

† Though not without the power to resume it, which he seems to have exercised when he wanted to realize all he could to gamble away in the Providence Island speculation. See S. Reed Brett, *op. cit.*, p. xxvi.

may be presumed to have for the pieces on the board. And it must be added that he was apparently as devoid of hate as of love. Though as ruthless as the tide, he was never sadistic or vindictive ; never resorted to emotional stimulants, holy or otherwise, in order to reconcile his conscience to any necessary move in the game. It was not a matter of conscience but simply of calculation what pressure it was necessary to exert, or what opposition to liquidate. And it must be acknowledged that he was by nature economical, even of injury. Only in the last resort did he proceed to violence. He preferred to confront an opponent with so hopeless a situation as to leave him no choice except between capitulation and suicide. Only where that opponent threatened to destroy Mr Pym, did it become a case of "stone dead hath no fellow", or of plunging the whole country into a blood bath. And Mr Pym, though far from being a man of blood, was still less a man to take chances where his own safety was concerned. He had nothing of the soldier in his composition, and though he could play his hand with iron nerve when occasion demanded, he preferred to gamble on certainties. We might even—from the one or two occasions on which he ever betrayed agitation—suspect that physically he was inclined to be timid.

Almost the first notice we have of his activities in Parliament gives us a flashlight on the man. It is of his intervention, already recorded, in the almost incredible debate on the torture to be inflicted, illegally, on a harmless old Catholic lawyer in the Fleet Prison who was supposed to have let fall some disrespectful remark about the Princess Palatine. It was characteristic of Mr Pym to have cut in with one of those practical suggestions that are the surest foundations of a new member's career. His business instinct having apprised him of the extreme improbability of an inmate of the Fleet having a thousand pounds to pay, he thoughtfully suggested a whipping for the old gentleman in default of payment. Having made his point he was probably quite unconcerned whether the suggestion should bear fruit or no.

Which in fact it did not ; thanks largely to the equally characteristic intervention of young Prince Charles, also making his maiden appearance in politics, to get at least the physical part of the monstrous sentence remitted.* It was not the last time that the Tyrant and the Great Parliamentarian would be found on the opposite sides of the same quarrel.

* See *Charles, King of England*, pp. 68-9.

By such modest increments Pym went on adding to his weight in the House. His rise had nothing in common with that of the men who in successive Parliaments had forged to the front and achieved a supremacy as brief as it was dazzling. He had none of the magnetic brilliance of Eliot, or of the statesmanlike sweep of Wentworth. He attempted no dramatic coup nor purple patch of oratory. But with his indefatigable industry and power of detailed application, he soon became more versed than any other member in the already highly specialized technique of conducting the multifarious business of the House. His name appears on the lists of innumerable committees, and eventually it would seem as if it were unthinkable for any important business to be transacted without Mr Pym's massive assistance in the essential spadework. And in the course of these arduous but uninspiring activities he was acquiring not only a knowledge of, but a touch upon, the House of Commons, such as no member had probably ever approached before, or would surpass afterwards. In any given project he knew just how far he could go, and the way to go about it.

Most of all in the main project of building up his own career. It was here that he differed from the other Parliamentary leaders, who sought to compass the loftiest ends by the quickest means. That was not the way of the Ox. The next step was enough for Mr Pym, and he never took it unless he was quite sure of his footing.

From the first he seems to have resolved to build up his reputation in connection with some strictly limited field of activity. Mr Pym's choice of such a field shows how remarkably he had anticipated the technique of the Totalitarian masters of our own time. For he instinctively realized that the surest way to the control of human beings in the mass is to prepare their minds and wills by the intoxication of a common hatred, and a hatred quickened by fear. Nor was an intelligence like Pym's likely to hesitate long about the choice of an object. If only by that recent orgy of sadistic Papophobia on the part of his fellow-members, the Catholics must have been as plainly indicated to him as the Jews to Hitler—all the more because, as with anti-Semitism in modern Germany, there was just enough substratum of truth in the anti-Catholic case to render it plausible. The Catholic peril had been no imaginary one in the days of Elizabeth, and if it was out of date now, it was because the clash of nationalist interests on the Continent had, for an indefinite time to come, put out of practical possibility the reunion of Europe under the spiritual empire of Rome, by the sword of a Catholic Caesar. But out of date it certainly was, and the minority of devoted Catholics that still lingered on in England was far too anxious to be left in peace to go seeking for trouble by Fifth Column activities. And the King, heretic though he was, received no more devoted loyalty in the hour of his direst need, than from the old Catholic families of his realm.

But this did not in any way diminish the value of the Catholic bogey as a propaganda stimulus, and nobody knew better how to work it than Mr Pym. There is no need to suspect him of any sort of fanaticism. If Pym had any religious feelings at all, he kept them, like his other feelings, locked in his own bosom. He specialized on the religious issue for strictly, and indeed frankly political motives. Throughout his Parliamentary career his weight was behind every measure of general or individual persecution ; he worked up into a grievance every attempt by the Crown to temper with mercy the application of the ferocious code that sentenced priests to be disembowelled alive for ministering to their flocks—he did this without malice and without bigotry, as part of a very complicated game, in the opening stages of which the persecution line was indicated as the most promising.

But having settled on persecution as his speciality, Pym had no reason to limit its scope to Catholics. It was characteristic of his technique to be gradually and cautiously expansive. The original line, like a railway, comes to a junction from which it fans out in more than one direction. From Catholic baiting it was an easy step to the persecution of all those elements in the Church of England that failed to come up to the hundred-per-cent Geneva standard of Protestantism. Nothing could bring more grist to the political mill than to start a heresy hunt after some indiscreet divine who, in the course of one of those pious polemics that were as popular then as they are unreadable now, had betrayed himself into the utterance of sentiments that could be quoted as Romanist. For it was characteristic of Pym's step by step methods to found the Anglican phobia on the Catholic phobia. The Catholic Fifth Column was supposed to be linked with an Arminian—or as we should call it, "High"—Sixth Column, inside the Church, which in its turn, had backing in the high places—and perhaps even the highest—of the State.

For inevitably, sooner or later, there must come a third stage in this grimly expansive advance. First the Catholics; next the Church, and after that—the Throne. Had Pym foreseen this from the first? Had it entered into his original calculations that an offensive against the Church, if pushed home, was bound to develop into one against the Crown, in the course of which it would be necessary—a matter of life or death—to subvert the whole constitutional fabric on which the sovereignty of the Crown reposed ; to overpower the law and even to destroy that very institution of representative government in the name of which these proceedings would be ostensibly undertaken? Did he look further and envisage the possibility of having to enforce revolution by civil war, or even, in the last resort, to push the offensive against the Crown to its total conclusion ?

It would be tempting to imagine the master player of the political game as having plotted out its whole course in advance ; but it is a temptation that—except by the writer of historical fiction—must be resisted. Pym was indeed an adept in the art of foreseeing his opponent's moves and planning his own to circumvent them, but that he ever got beyond or above this, there is not the remotest reason to believe. He was, as far as we can judge by his utterances and actions, a politician pure and simple, without any vision beyond the horizon of the moment. His very strength may have been due to this entire concentration upon the next few steps, this refusal to concern himself with anything except the next main point to be scored in the game.

But whose game ? That of Parliament ? Or the Deity ? Or the Earl of Bedford ? By what political philosophy was Mr Pym inspired ? What were his principles ? What master plan of statesmanship was he pursuing ? Assuming that he were to remove all opposition from his path and get the whole power of the state into his hands—as in the event he so narrowly missed doing—what use did he aspire to make of it ?

To these questions one can search in vain through the few depressing relics that have survived of his speeches—monotonous thuds of a pile driver hammering some crude debating point into the skull of his audience—for the clue to an answer. But if you could have got him in a moment of entire confidence, he might perhaps have put it aside with a quotation from the Psalms : "I do not exercise myself in great matters that are too high for me.

My time," he might have added, "is fully enough occupied with more practical matters."

And so he went on, in these five Parliaments of the sixteen-twenties, at his ox-like gait, clinging to his own chosen line of religious intolerance and heresy hunting, but by imperceptible stages causing the offensive on the alleged Romanizers in the Church to develop into one on the Head of the State, by whom the High Anglican element in the Church was tolerated, if not actively favoured. But even here, he acted with characteristic caution. In the last stages of Charles's third Parliament, he was too cautious to mix himself up with the nakedly seditious ebullitions of Eliot and his wild men. He faded discreetly into the background of the proceedings leading up to the final riot, in which he bore no ostensible part. Consequently he escaped scot free from the retribution that fell like an extinguisher on Eliot.

A question for which we have not the material for a definite answer—though we can draw what inference we please from the fact that from the beginning of the reign he sat for Tavistock, the membership for which was virtually in the gift of the Earl of Bedford—is, at what point and to what extent during this opening phase did Pym come to be associated with that powerful and plutocratic group of which he afterwards came to be the moving spirit?

We can, however, date the revolutionary conspiracy of which Pym was the organizing genius from the formation of the Providence Island Company, with himself as Secretary, on the 4th of December, 1630. It is true that the Company itself was a bubble, and the project a mare's nest. But it was out of the closely knit and highly capitalized junta that constituted its directorate that Pym was able to forge a political instrument with which his peculiar genius could arm itself powerfully enough to overturn the existing order and plunge the whole country into bloody chaos.

But not quite powerful enough, as it proved, to bring order out of chaos—such a new order as Pym and his confederates designed to impose on the country. For to talk of these men as authentic champions of Parliament is to beg the whole question, in view of the unquestionable fact that Pym's greatest achievement was to have destroyed Parliamentary, in the sense of representative, government in England—or at any rate to have suspended it indefinitely by the passing, through a combination of chicanery and terrorism, of what we should now call an Enabling Act, whose effect was to cut off Parliament from its constituents, and to turn it into an assembly that he at least designed to be one of his own Yes-men.

From the King's assent to that Act, which was forced upon him simultaneously with that for the butchering of his minister, Strafford, the reign of King Pym may be said to commence. From thenceforth, for the thirty months that Pym has still to live, the contest can indeed be legitimately regarded as a duel between two mighty antagonists, or, in principle, as I shall hope to show, between constitutional monarchy and a revolutionary conspiracy, long hatched and elaborately organized, to subject everything in Church and State to the unfettered domination of a plutocratic minority.

After Pym's death, a second revolution begins to engulf the first, and now it is no longer a tyranny of the purse, but of the sword that usurps the sovereignty of England, and confronts her lawful Sovereign with the choice between becoming its accomplice or its victim. And thus the curtain goes down on the drama of *King Charles and King Pym*, and the stage is set for that of *King Charles the Martyr*.

One concluding and necessary word, the only one of a personal nature I shall presume to speak. What I have written is not in the service of any party or sect or cause, but what, after examining all I can find of the evidence, has seemed to me to be the truth. I do not happen to be any of the things that blasphemers of the current myth are commonly labelled as being. Though, as I trust, a Catholic, in the sense of the Creed, I have no right to the prefix Anglo or Roman ; I am a Conservative, in that I deem the thing of all others worth conserving to be liberty, and have from the first totally abhorred and rejected all forms and shirt-colours of Totalitarianism, Fascibolshevism, and Hitlinism ; and I have never been able to take quite seriously the picturesque neo-Jacobite cult of the white rose and the House of Stuart that for all I know may still have its devotees in drawing rooms.

If I may be permitted to make my humble request to the reader, it is that he will endeavour to clear his mind of all pre-possessions or pronouncements, however authoritative, and judge the case, as I have tried to do, on the facts alone, so far as they can be ascertained, and with the sole determination to follow the truth wherever it may lead.

I

Transfer of Sovereignty

I

THE BOOK

FOR the eleven years after the dissolution—just in time—of his third Parliament, Charles I had governed England virtually as his own Prime Minister, and on the exiguous peace time income that the law allowed him. As he had required no extra money for taxation, he had been able to put off indefinitely the summoning of another Parliament. In this he was formally justified, according to the existing constitution, even as reinforced by the recently granted Petition of Right.

For eight of these years there had seemed no reason to anticipate any change or catastrophe. England had continued to present the spectacle, in a distracted Europe, of an island of peaceful prosperity, and there was every apparent prospect of this happy state of things being indefinitely prolonged. And yet, there was something about this very prosperity too reminiscent of one of those enchanted gardens of Fairyland, that a word or a false step will cause to vanish into bare wilderness.

The word, in this case, was War. Charles was able to scrape along from year to year, and even to improve his position, on the sole condition of his remaining at peace with his neighbours, and his subjects. Military force he had none to speak of, nor could he afford to have it. A determined riot of the London mob would probably have been more than he could have found means to cope with.

But then, this limiting condition of his power was one with which it did not appear to be too hard to comply. A country with no land frontiers and adequate sea power is able to deny itself, at a pinch, the luxury of an army. Charles had provided, though by a dangerous straining of his prerogative rights, for the second of these conditions, and the first appeared to have been provided for him by nature. Great Britain was an island.

Yes—but would it be always possible to think in terms of

Great Britain? Men yet in middle age could remember the time when England had been no island Power, but had shared a land frontier with a jealous neighbour, who could usually be relied upon to stab her in the back when she was involved in hostilities overseas. Since the Crowns of England and Scotland had been united in the same person, men had ceased to think of Scotland as a potential enemy, and of the Border as a theatre of chronic hostilities. Scotland had been left to her own devices, and few Englishmen knew or cared greatly what these devices might be. But Parliament had seen to it that the union of Crowns should be no union of nations, and the fierce spirit of Scottish independence smouldered on unquenched.

What was there to prevent those fires waking into a blaze of open hostility, and England returning to her age-long condition of a land power, with a frontier to be defended and the need of an army to defend it? Simply and solely the refusal of any sane monarch to allow his double kingdom to be divided against itself. But this was only a guarantee on the assumption that the monarch was in effective control of both realms. How if one of them should become divided against the monarch himself, and take its destinies into its own hands? In such a situation a state of war develops automatically, for if the King lacks the support of a standing army, he will find himself compelled to rely on such forces as he can raise in his presumably loyal kingdom to cope with the rebellion of the other.

Such a necessity would bring Charles face to face with ruin. It would compel him to raise an army and fight a land war, for which it was beyond his power to provide the sinews. Had he been capable of appreciating these elementary facts, that seem so obvious in the light of the event, he would have realized that it was a life and death matter for him to maintain a quiet, and reasonably contented, Scotland. And indeed there seemed no reason for thinking that Scotland was likely to be anything else. Since King James had accomplished his great work of reducing Church and State in that country to some reasonable semblance of order, it had settled down quietly enough, and there had been no serious attempt to upset the existing regime. The great chiefs ruled their clans with the power of little kings, and the ministers in the parishes exercised a tyranny over their congregations more minute and searching than that of any King. It may not have been an ideal or very efficient state system, but it suited the

Scottish nature, and, if left alone, appeared likely to go on running itself indefinitely.

It is true that an episcopal superstructure had been imposed on the Kirk, but the Bishops were little more than dignified figureheads, and being canny Scots, they did not invite trouble by attempting to assert their authority against the Calvinist extremism of the congregations. Even when King James allowed his theological enthusiasm so far to outrun his native shrewdness as to impose some dangerously ritualistic articles, or regulations, they prudently refrained from combating the resistance with which the attempt to enforce them was spontaneously greeted, and tacitly connived at their reduction to dead letters. James might say what he liked, but it did not much matter so long as the ministers continued to do what they liked—and James was too fond of a quiet life to kick with any vigour against the pricks.

But Charles had nothing of that worldly wisdom that is prepared to tolerate things as they are, rather than to invite trouble by straining after perfection, and he had at his side that little bustling enthusiast, Archbishop Laud, with his fatal itch for setting right whatever he saw anywhere amiss. The royal way to ruin, beyond the Border, was paved throughout with the noblest intentions. It was none the less tragically direct.

It began with what in itself was a just and moderate measure, designed to secure fair play for the Kirk against the nobles who were gorged with its loot, and that of the old Catholic Church that it had superseded. This Edict of Revocation did not attempt to make the spoilers disgorge their spoil, as happened when the Emperor was ill-advised enough to undertake a similar task in Germany. It merely insisted on their obtaining regular titles, at a moderate fee, for their own or their fathers' irregularly gotten lands, and of undertaking, in practice, obligations to endow the Kirk that even they did not deny in theory. The passing of this measure obtained the King no gratitude from the Kirk that it benefited, but it had been enough to rekindle the spirit of anarchic disloyalty that was traditional in the Scottish nobility. The wealthy lords were touched in their most sensitive spot, and did not know when they might be touched again.

The next step in the way of suicide was to stir up against the Crown all the uncompromising fanaticism of the national Kirk. The hold of that formidable organization on the affections of the

Scottish people is something that even to-day it is hard to understand. Its effect was to set up in every parish an inquisitorial discipline from which the Christian spirit of love and tenderness was ruthlessly eliminated, whose God was as much a figure of terror as the devils of Benin or Fiji, that waged ruthless war on all forms of mirth and enjoyment, however innocent, and under whose auspices the life of any poor old woman might at any time be brought to an end with tortures worthy of a Red Indian village. But it is beyond all doubt that this yoke was accepted, if not exactly with cheerfulness—which in itself was a sin—at any rate with a stern assurance of its necessity for salvation. In spite of sermons lasting for hours on end, and the gowk's stool of repentance, nothing can be more certain than that the Scottish congregations were solid behind the grimmest of their ministers, and that they were ready to go to all lengths, even to war and martyrdom, for the faith that was in them.

Any statesman who had the remotest comprehension of the realities of Scottish life, would have avoided, above all other things, coming into direct collision with a spirit that, once aroused, would be that of Scotland itself, or at any rate of the Lowland and more civilized part of it. But Charles, though he loved the country of his birth, had not visited it since his infancy, and to him it was practically unknown ; nor were the Scottish courtiers, whom he delighted to honour, the men to enlighten his ignorance. As for Laud, he was something worse than merely ignorant—like another great Oxonian, where Church matters were concerned, whatever there was to know he knew it, and what he didn't know wasn't knowledge.

It was not till he had been on the throne eight years, that Charles was able to fulfil his long cherished ambition of visiting his Northern Kingdom, in order to be crowned King of Scotland ; a tactful and gracious act in itself, and one that was rewarded by an exhibition of devoted loyalty as he made his state progress through the long, filthy street that was the backbone of Edinburgh. But unfortunately he had brought Laud, then Bishop of London, in his train, and the little man was busily peering about, taking stock of everything that he saw.

Laud's life work was to realize the beauty of holiness, and not even the devoutest imagination could have discovered much beauty in the peculiar type of holiness cultivated by the Kirk, which positively prided itself on its lack of outward adornment or seemly ritual. The slovenliness and disorder of which Laud was labouring to purge the English Church were rampant and aggravated in that of Scotland. To a mind like Laud's, with its old-maidish itch for putting things in their places, the desire to effect a grand tidying and smartening up of this shocking state of things was compulsive. It was true that even when, in the same year, he became Primate, the shortcomings of the Kirk were in no sense his business. Scotland is no part of the province of Canterbury. But Laud was one of those people who cannot endure to leave things out of their places, even in somebody else's house.

It was in this spirit that he and, for that matter, Charles himself, approached the problem of the Kirk. They had no other desire than to impart beauty and order to the service of God, and they were incapable of seeing how such a desire could be a stumbling-block of offence.

But to the uncompromising Calvinists of the Kirk, the matter presented itself in a very different light. To them the very idea of an ordered ritual smacked of Popery, and the Scotch were so completely obsessed with the No-Popery mania, that it was possible for Clarendon to write of "their whole religion consisting in an entire detestation of Popery, in believing the Pope to be Antichrist, and hating perfectly the persons of all papists, and I doubt of all others who did not hate them."

Under these circumstances, Charles and Laud, on the one hand, and the Kirk, on the other, were bound to be at cross purposes. The attempt to impose from above the beauty of holiness was viewed in the light of a desperate conspiracy to bring back the Babylonian bondage, from which God's elect had emerged into whatever sort of freedom they enjoyed under the dictation of their ministers. And there was another feature of this new counter-Reformation that was almost equally offensive. It was imposed from above, by authority, and that not even a Scottish authority. Now the Kirk, whatever else it may have been, was intensely democratic in its organization, and national in its spirit. What was practically a High Church Anglican drive, was exquisitely calculated to outrage every feeling and prejudice in the Scottish-Calvinist nature.

Charles and Laud were making just such a blunder as that which, in a later age, was to precipitate the Indian Mutiny. The new discipline and ceremonial that they sought to impose upon the Kirk was resented as fiercely as the attempt to force greased cartridges on the Hindu and Moslem sepoys. And, to complete the parallel, the grievance of the cartridges was capable of being worked up and exploited by enemies of the existing regime, whose motives were not religious at all. For Charles's government had already, by its Edict of Revocation, rendered itself obnoxious to the most powerful interest in the country, and the Scottish magnates were well versed in the arts of conspiracy.

In entire ignorance of the risks involved, and equal innocence of any sinister intention, the King, urged on by Laud, kept giving fresh turns to the screw. The Scottish bishoprics were filled, as they fell vacant, not with moderates of the old type, but with High Church zealots. A series of new canons was forced upon the Kirk, that to the suspicious minds of its devotees spelt sheer Romanization. And the culminating outrage was the attempt to impose a new prayer-book, or rather the old Anglican prayer-book, with modifications of a ritualistic tendency, under pains and penalties, upon every minister and congregation in the country. It was an act of as sheer madness as the requiring of Hindus to bite cow's fat. And yet it does not appear to have struck its authors in any other light than that of a straightforward attempt to introduce sweetness and order where they were so palpably lacking. Much pains were spent in giving the finishing touches to the new book. Even the printing was to be appropriately beautiful. It was King Charles's gift to his Scottish people, and he no doubt expected it to be received in the spirit in which it was conferred. That to them it would constitute a declaration of war was the last thing he could have suspected.

The many delays in imparting the finishing touches to the book, had given time for resentment to accumulate and resistance to be organized. Exactly what part the discontented nobles had in fomenting passions that were, in themselves, spontaneous, is to this day uncertain.

What we do know is that the first attempt to conduct service according to the new book precipitated an explosion. On the 23rd of July, 1637, the Dean of the newly-created diocese of Edinburgh, in the Cathedral Church of St Giles, began to read the service out of the new book. There were a large number of women among the congregation, and the Edinburgh viragoes had a formidable reputation. But on this occasion there is some reason for suspecting the most militant of the lassies to have been prentice lads in skirts. In any case, the whole affair was certainly organized in advance, and the service had no sooner started than it became a riot, in which the Dean and Bishop were in no small danger from a bombardment of stools. Even when the magistrates had succeeded in clearing the church of the most active demonstrators, the service was continued to an accompaniment of noises off and crashing glass. And when it was over, the officiating clergy were lucky to get home with their lives.

It is from this incident that we have to date the final act in the tragedy of King Charles. Nothing now, it appears, can prevent his destiny from moving to its mortal conclusion, in front of the palace at Whitehall. It is like a stone dislodged from the mountain top, that moves slowly at first, but gradually acquires momentum, until its downward progress becomes irresistible. The flag of revolt had been hoisted, and the King had no force at his disposal to prevent revolt from developing into revolution.

2

THE COVENANT

DURING the eleven and a half years that were left him, after the riot at St Giles's Church, King Charles must sometimes have felt like a man in a prolonged nightmare, one of these atrocious dreams where nothing ever goes right, and where the dreamer finds that he has no strength in his limbs to resist or escape the horrors that close upon him.

Looking back upon it, even now, it is difficult to say with assurance, that if at any given point of this time, Charles had been wise enough to act differently in such and such a way, he would have retrieved his fortunes or averted his doom—without, that is to say, the shameful surrender of that which he esteemed dearer than life. Once the stone of destiny had gathered momentum on its downward course, it is doubtful whether any human effort could have stopped it short of the bottom.

The best chance of all would have been in the first stages, when it had barely begun to move, and seemed hesitating on the brink of a plunge. If the King had been capable of appreciating the true significance of that Edinburgh riot, it is possible that a great gesture of concession, such as Elizabeth might have made, might have retrieved the loyalty that had been so exuberant at his Scottish coronation. This would certainly have involved the scrapping of the new prayer-book and probably of the canons that had preceded it. It would also have entailed the cancelling of the Edict of Revocation.

Even so, it is by no means certain, and perhaps not probable, that he could have got off so easily. The indignation of the Kirk, that had at last boiled over, had been simmering for a long time. A surrender of the Crown to the first show of violence might well have served as a stimulus for further and unlimited demands. Nothing might have sufficed but for the whole episcopal structure to be swept away, and for the sovereignty of the Kirk to supersede, in effect, that of the Crown. And we must remember that we are not dealing with a mere spontaneous outburst of emotion. There is every reason to suspect careful and calculated organization behind every move in the revolutionary game. The disgruntled nobles had no wish to encourage an accommodating spirit among those humbler brethren who trembled for the integrity of their Protestant principles.

But, whether it might have succeeded or not, there was not the least chance of the experiment in concession being made with that promptitude which alone would have given it a chance of success. The mind of Charles was not swift to adapt itself to a new situation ; his essentially critical and balancing intelligence wanted time before striking out a line of decisive action. Nor did it occur to him to attach any ominous or tragic significance to the news from Edinburgh, still less to dream of allowing his authority to be openly flouted by a handful of termagants. "I mean to be obeyed" was what he said, a curiously exact anticipation of his successor, George III's, "Rebels must be made to obey," after the Boston Tea Party.

But George at least would have an army on the spot to enforce obedience, whereas Charles was without any force to speak of for the backing of his will. It would not matter how much he meant to be obeyed, if his Scottish subjects decided not to obey him. He was utterly dependent on their goodwill, and on the inertia of habit that keeps men submissive to established authority.

But this was more than neutralized by the discipline of self-help that is the strength of Calvinism. Every congregation, under that system of militant democracy, was a self-sufficient unit, capable, at a pinch, of functioning independently, and electing its own representatives to the superior group, or Presbytery, which again furnished delegates for the supreme body of all, the General Assembly. It was a complete framework of democratic or, one might almost say, of soviet government, within the body of the State, and inspired with a conviction of its divine right to impose its own spiritual and political will upon every rival authority, including that of "God's silly vassal," as one of its divines had characterized the King.

Three generations of Calvinism had been enough to develop in the people of the Scottish Lowlands the habit and faculty of political self-help. Once let the soul of the Kirk be moved to its depths, and it would be the most natural thing in the world for its sons to take their salvation into their own hands, and work it out, not in fear and trembling, but with business-like efficiency.

It is of agelong experience that the first thing needful for a successful revolution is some symbolic object of hate—the imaginary figure of the capitalist or the Jew, the aristocrat or the infidel. For the devout Lowlander of the seventeenth century, this necessary target was provided by the Church of Rome, and all the more scope was afforded for imaginative denigration by the very remoteness of the danger. In spite of the fact that the old faith had been as good as wiped out of the Lowlands, the hand of Rome was detected in every attempt to depart from the strictest Calvinist orthodoxy, and the Pope was transformed into as ever-present a bogey as Satan himself.

When, at that memorable service at St Giles's, the Bishop had ascended the pulpit in a plucky attempt to pacify the congregation, he had been greeted—amongst other uncomplimentary epithets —with shrieks of "A Pape ! a Pape !" One of those amiable ladies, who had expressed a wish to cut the Bishop's windpipe, and had been told that a worse man might after all come into his place, had promptly replied,

"Na ! When Cardinal Beaton was sticked, we had never another cardinal sin syne !"

It was such a spirit that was now loose, an anti-papal frenzy in which the King was only involved, as it were, by accident. The series of High Church pinpricks, exacerbated by organized propaganda, had created a terror of a conspiracy, headed by the Bishops, to restore the Mass and the priesthood, and plunge back the whole country into the Babylonian woe. God's Kirk was in

danger—who was on the Lord's side ? If not the King, so much
the worse for monarchy ! The elect of the Lord would go forward
in *His* strength—alone !

Of these forces Charles was abysmally ignorant. It is hard to
blame him. Unlike his father, he had never had direct experience
of the Scottish spirit, and he had few reliable sources of information. There was hardly anybody on whose wisdom or candour
he could rely for a truthful account of the real state of things.
Even those of the Scottish leading men who were not positively
disloyal to him, were mostly lukewarm, or hedging for their own
safety. In framing his Scottish policy, Charles was like a man
without eyes.

It is not to be wondered at, under the circumstances, that he
fumbled that policy hopelessly. He endeavoured to assert an
authority that he had no means of enforcing. He even tried to
bring Edinburgh to its senses by depriving it of the Council and
Court of Session, and thereby two of its principal sources of
income. He ordered the arrest of the ringleaders in the riot ;
the expulsion of strangers from the town. The only result was
another and worse riot, with which the Council was powerless
to cope, and which had to be appeased by invoking the aid and
authority of the very strangers it was proposed to expel.

The King's government had practically ceased to function,
and a new, revolutionary control of the country was organized.
By the end of the year this control was vested in four committees,
or tables, of nobles, gentry, burgesses and ministers, and these
were supported by a representative assembly of commissioners.

Early in the next year, a still more decisive step was taken.
It was with the object of enlisting the support of the whole people
that a Covenant, or bond of union, based on a similar manifesto
of 1580, but with some very emphatic additions, was drawn up
for every Scotsman of goodwill to sign, as signed it was, amid
manifestations of extraordinary enthusiasm, throughout the
greater part of the Lowlands. The length and prolixity of this
famous document are such as to make one wonder how many of
the signatories can have actually read and digested it. It starts by
working up a perfect frenzy of abuse, defiance, and abjuration of
the Roman Antichrist, coupled with detestation of "all his vain
allegories, rites, signs, and traditions," and then, after citing
interminable precedents, comes down to brass tacks with a
solemn undertaking to maintain the purity of the reformed

religion against all sorts of papistical innovations, not omitting the unconscious humour, customary in all anti-monarchial documents of this time, of protesting an entire loyalty and devotion to the King's Majesty. What all this verbiage boils down to, is an uncompromising determination to sweep away the King's whole superstructure of Church government, and set up, in the teeth of his authority, and above it, an undiluted Presbyterian theocracy.

The signing of this Covenant killed the last chance there may have been of the King's differences with his Scottish subjects being resolved by any means short of surrendering all but the name of sovereignty over the ancestral kingdom of his House. The spirit of an anti-papal crusade had been aroused, a spirit all the more formidable in its unreasoning strength, because it was directed against an invisible and largely imaginary foe. It was significant enough that some of the Covenanters should have written their names in their own blood—it was of even greater significance that some among them should have come in arms to sign. In such a mood of collective panic and hatred as had now been engendered, it was not likely that this, more than any other crusade, would confine itself within the limits of the law, or that anything but superior force would keep it from its objective.

And yet the inevitable catastrophe developed with deceptive slowness. All through that year, 1638, the situation in Scotland went on steadily deteriorating, but as yet there was no open appeal to the sword. Even after the news of the Covenant had arrived, Charles appears to have been quietly confident of his ability to control the situation, to judge at least by his reply to the frightened Queen, bidding her not to alarm herself, and assuring her that when he wished, he could reduce his subjects to obedience as usual.*

There were others, however, who had a truer intuition of how the land lay. One of these was the King's fool, Archie Armstrong. It was only in the technical sense that there was anything of the fool about Archie ; he was one of those sardonic and malicious jesters of whom Rigoletto is a type, he is believed to have started life as a sheep-thief on the Border, and, having done extremely well for himself during his tenure of office, ended up rather worse than he had begun, as a skinflint usurer. One of the

* Reported by the Venetian Secretary, Zonca, in a dispatch of the 9th of April, 1638.

principal targets of this fellow's envenomed quips had been
Archbishop Laud. The ex-border-thief was quick to realize, from
the first signs of resistance, how hopelessly His Grace had upset
his own, and his master's, apple-cart. Imagining, from long
impunity, that the privilege of the bells would cover any outrage,
he took the earliest opportunity of shouting at Laud, "Wha's
the feule noo ?" He also appears to have railed at the venerable
prelate as a monk, a rogue, and a traitor. This was going a little
too far, and Laud very properly complained to the King, who had
Archie kicked, literally, out of his Court. This ceremony of
farewell might have been supplemented by a sound thrashing,
had not Laud, with his customary humanity, interposed his good
offices.

But Archie had been only too right in his estimate of the
situation. The Archbishop's move had exposed not only himself
to capture, but the King to checkmate. Too late—and Charles
was always a move too late in this game—it dawned upon His
Majesty that, in order to avert a complete *débâcle*, concessions,
that a few months ago would have seemed unthinkable, must be
stomached. The prayer-book might have to go, the new canons,
the ecclesiastical court of High Commission, even the Articles
of Perth, that had been part of his father's Kirk settlement.

It would have given the best chance, even now, if the King
could have gone to Edinburgh in person. But he decided to
delegate his authority, and this to about the most unfortunate
person he could possibly have chosen, the Marquis of Hamilton.
There was some surprise about this choice, as Hamilton had
never escaped the suspicion of harbouring designs on the throne.
But Charles, with that unshakable loyalty of his to those to whom
he had once given his trust, refused to regard his cousin in the
light even of a possible traitor. And in this he was right to the
extent that Hamilton had no stomach for calculated and deliberate treason ; he was even fond of Charles after his fashion, and
eventually laid down his life for him courageously enough. But
behind his merely physical courage, there was no moral stamina ;
he had all the unreliability, all the defensive cunning, of a weak
nature. It was a weakness aggravated by anxiety for the great
possessions he had inherited in both countries, and which it was
his instinct to safeguard by having a foot in every party that was
likely to be in power.

That was the case now. As the King's Commissioner, Hamilton

played his part with ostensible loyalty, but with a secret determination to reinsure the main chance by conduct for which the language of modern gangsterdom provides a more appropriate term than the old-fashioned treason. He double-crossed his master, by going behind his back with the Covenanters, and assuring them—there is good reason to believe—"as a kindly Scotsman," that they had only to go on with courage and resolution to carry whatever they pleased ; but that if they fainted or gave ground in the least, they were undone.

Under these circumstances it is hardly to be wondered at that Hamilton's mission, or rather, his three missions—for he returned twice for instructions to London—were worse than a failure. But this is not to say that, even if he had been as loyal as Wentworth and as astute as Pym, he could possibly have achieved success. The flood of Covenanting nationalism was rising too rapidly to be kept within bounds by any improvised embankments. Nor was Charles prepared to empower his plenipotentiary to offer that prompt and unconditional surrender of the points in dispute that had now become the sole alternative to a decision by force. He qualified ; he bargained—even the prayer book and the canons he at first proposed merely to insist upon no further than the law allowed.

Hamilton, to whom this, or any, religious issue was a matter of perfect indifference, and to whom the rights of the Crown were, at best, of secondary concern, was at least sincere in his desire to fix up a little arrangement that should satisfy everybody, and redound to his own credit as an honest broker. Since the Covenanters were not likely to toe the line, his disinterested advice was that Charles should oblige. But the King replied, with perfect truth, that as long as the Covenant held good, he would have no more power than a Doge of Venice, "which," said he, "I would die rather than suffer." And in this he had the support of an abler and more faithful counsellor than Hamilton, for Wentworth, writing from Ireland, was urging the King to grasp the nettle, and to crush, instead of parleying with, treasonable conspiracy. Excellent advice in the abstract, had not Charles been faced with a similar necessity to that of the King who sitteth down and consulteth first whether he be able with ten thousand to meet him that cometh against him with twenty thousand.

And so matters drifted, until the King was induced to concede the calling of a Kirk Assembly in the autumn, to be followed by a Scottish Parliament in the spring. The Assembly met in the cathedral of Glasgow, and it was evident, from the first, that its task was one of uncompromising revolution, and that so far from acknowledging the authority of the bishops, it intended to sit in judgment on them as delinquents. There was nothing for it but for the unfortunate Hamilton, driven desperate, to declare the Assembly dissolved in the King's name. The delegates continued to sit, and, without further ado, proceeded to make a clean sweep of book, canons, articles, and bishops. Presbyterian government was set up on lines of naked Calvinism, and every minister who failed to conform to its most exacting standards was marked down for expulsion.

Such flaming defiance no King could be expected to brook. Even if Charles could have bowed his neck to the yoke and submitted to the virtual abdication of his authority in Scotland, it was not thinkable that the matter could end there. Such an utter shattering of his prestige would make his position in England impossible. What could he do but unsheathe the sword in the hope, however forlorn, of vindicating the law that he was sworn to uphold, and the rights that had descended to him from his ancestors?

3

FARCE ON THE BORDER

IT was now for the first time that Charles began to show signs of the mental strain that was to go on increasing through the long-drawn nightmare of his remaining years. It was observed, during that summer, while Hamilton was playing his double game in Scotland, that the King had ceased to attend the tennis court, and that even his beloved hunting was cut down to a minimum.

As yet there were no visible signs of disturbance in the calm surface of English life. The peace and prosperity that had reigned, now, for nine years, continued outwardly unbroken. There was no open challenge to constituted authority in Church or State. Those who had an eye to penetrate beneath the surface did indeed divine ominous portents. As early as January, 1637, we find that invaluable observer, the Venetian Ambassador, writing of prominent personages plotting in secret to bring back Parliaments, to root out innovations in the Church, and even to depose the Primate—His Excellency having evidently got wind of the Broughton and similar caballings. But so long as the King could go on paying his way, and the ordinary citizen paying his, the malcontents were never likely to obtain a fulcrum for levering up the throne.

Now, however, the one thing that could, and must, bring the whole edifice of Kingly government toppling in ruins, was coming to pass. Very slowly, but unmistakably, the writing on the wall was becoming decipherable, and the word was War. By the year's end it stood out in vast lettering, for all to read. Whatever forms of loyal verbiage it might be expedient to employ, the plain truth of the matter was that Scotland, having defied her King, was now beginning to arm against him. Most ominous of all, was the fact that the most powerful man in Scotland, as well as the shrewdest and least scrupulous, the Earl of Argyll, had come in on what his squint eyes perceived to be the winning side. And Argyll, though an abject coward, could order, if he dared not lead, 5,000 warriors of his Clan Campbell into the field.

King Charles had also begun to arm—with what reluctance we can imagine—against that part of his own dominions that had always been nearest to his heart. But now he must have begun to experience to the full that nightmare feeling of having no power in his limbs to strike or to flee. He had, ever since those disastrous military experiences of the Buckingham time, framed all his plans on the assumption of a sea-protected realm without frontiers, that could afford to dispense with an army. Except for the local trained bands, or militia, he had nothing, not even a regiment of guards, with which to wage an offensive war. An army, even if it could be recruited, would need to have its training, equipment, and staff improvised, practically out of nothing, before it would be fit to take the field. And this would not only take time, but, since, as Henry VII's minister, Dudley, had very truly observed, "war is a marvellous great consumer of treasure and riches," a great deal more money than Charles, who had much ado to balance his accounts in time of profoundest peace, could hope to lay hands on.

As it happened, at this particular juncture, the Treasury was more than usually depleted. Several items of extraordinary expenditure had taken toll of what little cash in hand was normally available. To add to his other troubles, Charles had been the most unwilling recipient of a visit from the French Queen Dowager, Marie de Medici. That incurable intriguer, of whose presence Richelieu had relieved France, and whom exile had reduced pretty nearly to her last sou, had the bright idea of quartering herself in luxury on her son-in-law. Charles was appalled at the idea, and did his polite best to decline the honour, but when a woman of Marie's chin and disposition has made up her mind, it takes a sterner nature than that of Charles to put her off. Her reply was to take ship for England, suite and all, and give His Majesty the choice of driving her from his ports, or making the best of a bad business. Being Charles and not Richelieu, he chose the latter, and, putting his feelings in his pocket, gave her St James's Palace, and received her with royal and lavish hospitality. Even poor Henriette had not been able to refrain from sighing, "*Adieu, ma liberté!*" But it was after all "*maman*," and Henriette was the most dutiful of daughters.

This visit, which the guest had every intention of prolonging *sine die*, was about as awkward a thing as could have happened to Charles at this particular juncture. It was not only that it put a new and considerable strain on his already overstrained finances, a strain increased by the shameless rapacity of the large suite that the Queen Dowager had imported with her, but that her presence in England caused grave offence to Richelieu, at the very time when it was all important to keep on the right side of him and of France. And the presence of this Catholic colony, which fully shared its mistress's love of intrigue for its own sake, was a new and powerful irritant of the anti-papal phobia that was endemic in London, and served to redouble the hatred and suspicion that was already focused on the Catholic Queen of England.

But this was not the only source of financial leakage. As if one mistress intriguer had not been enough, that now considerably ripened beauty, the Duchesse de Chevreuse, had turned up again in England, and her entertainment likewise had figured on the debit side of the treasury account. And finally Charles, whose loyalty to his sister and her cause had not diminished now that she had been six years a widow, had made a free gift of what was then the not inconsiderable sum of £30,000 to her eldest son, the Palatine claimant, who was, in due course, to show his gratitude by betraying him.

The cupboard was therefore more than usually bare when its contents were most needed. By what means was a King without an army and without funds to raise an expeditionary force for Scotland ? It was easy to say "call a Parliament," but it would have been optimistic indeed to imagine that that body would be ready to provide, for the crushing of an ostensibly anti-episcopal crusade, the funds it had formerly refused for a popular war with Spain, or for the relief of the brethren at Rochelle.

Charles was therefore put to desperate shifts to scrape together enough to provide himself with even the semblance of an army. He was driven back upon the fatal expedient of selling not only honours, but offices, such as the Mastership of the Rolls. Money was borrowed to the last limit in anticipation of the revenue. Everybody who could be touched or begged for money was tried —the clergy, the Catholics, the City—with exiguous results. Henriette even hit upon the curiously modern device of starting a subscription among the ladies of England, to show their loyalty to the King. But it seemed as if feminine loyalty had no cash value whatever.

The King's mind, always fertile in precedents, hit upon what seemed one solution of the difficulty, in a summons to his nobility to rally to his standard, with their retainers. It was a revival of the long obsolete feudal host, that even the early Plantagenets had found unworkable. But it might have had some measure of success if the King could only have counted upon the support of a loyal nobility. But the titled magnates were honeycombed with disaffection ; the King's policy of holding the scales even between all classes of his subjects had not been calculated to enhance his popularity among the promoters of oligarchy. Two of the opposition leaders, Lords Saye and Brooke, returned a flat refusal to the summons. The rest, however, either made a formal show o compliance, or else pleaded inability, on one ground or another, to serve in person, and sought to compound for it by a grudging dole of money.

Meanwhile, the enemy was going about his task in a very different spirit. The covenanting enthusiasm was sweeping everything before it in Scotland. An invaluable nucleus for an army, and particularly in the commissioned ranks, was formed by the numerous soldiers of fortune who had seen service in Germany. One of these, a little, crooked, illiterate man, called Alexander Leslie, had already, in the service of Gustavus Adolphus, won a

European reputation by having turned back the mighty Wallen-stein, then on the flood tide of success, from the gates of Stralsund. Upon him the office of commander-in-chief naturally devolved, and a better man could not have been found to make an army out of this raw material of Jehovah-drunken crusaders. Like Oliver Cromwell, he knew how to enlist religion in the service of discipline, and the voice of the preacher was as loud in the camp as that of the drill-sergeant. Both at morning and evening rose the sounds of psalm-singing, praying, and scripture reading, mingled, it is true, with a certain amount of regrettable language from imperfectly regenerated elements. Calvinism was, in itself, one of the most powerful systems of discipline ever devised by man.

Meanwhile the King's motley host, consisting of local militias and the followings of various noblemen, was beginning to arrive, in driblets, up North. A very different spirit informed it from that of Leslie's army. Except for the militia of the Northern counties, among whom the cry of the Scots on the Border could revive the fighting spirit of centuries, there was no more enthusiasm in the service than there was discipline. Some of them were more of a terror to peaceful civilians on the march than they were ever likely to be to the enemy in the field—the Essex contingent, in particular, distinguished itself by robbing, plundering, and even murdering, all along the route.

To oppose Leslie as commander-in-chief, Charles had selected the Earl of Arundel, a personage whose two main interests in life were the assertion of his own dignity, and the collection of works of art, of which he was hardly less of a connoisseur than the King himself. Unfortunately he had never seen a shot fired, and the vulgar business of war appealed to him so little, that when, subsequently, it started in England, he quietly packed up and betook himself to the more congenial atmosphere of Italy. His subordinate commanders were the water-fly Holland, whose presidency of that same Providence Island Company of which John Pym was treasurer might have rendered his loyalty as suspect as his competence, and the Earl of Essex, who within three short years would be the rebel generalissimo in England. The one soldier among the lot capable of looking Leslie in the face, was Sir Jacob Astley, a veteran of Elizabeth's Dutch wars, who, as sergeant-major of the army, was responsible for licking it into some sort of military shape, and found the task rather beyond the genius that even he possessed as a trainer of troops.

Nevertheless, it was a formidable enough force on paper ; an expected 30,000, whose very numbers would make it more than ever impossible to pay, equip, or provision with decent adequacy. The plan of campaign had been worked out on the most grandiose scale. The fullest use was to be made of sea-power. Lord Antrim, from Ireland, was to make a descent upon Argyll's country. Meanwhile Hamilton, on board the ship-money fleet, was to throw 5,000 men into Aberdeen, the one important place in the Lowlands that stood out against the Covenant ; these would join hands with the Marquis of Huntly and his following of Gordon clansmen, thus forming one claw of the pincers of which the King's army, advancing by the East coast, was to be the other. To complete the picture, the fleet would return South and blockade the coast, possibly seizing Leith.

It was all what Haig would have described as "theoretical rubbish." The English garrison could not be weakened in Ireland without risking all the horrors of a Catholic rebellion, and it would have been asking for worse than defeat to entrust it to such slippery hands as those of its self-proposed commander. And long before Charles could get his army together, Leslie, with the aid of the young Marquis of Montrose, had cleared up the situation in the North by occupying Aberdeen, and bringing Huntly, who under the promise of a safe return, had been lured into their clutches, a perhaps not wholly unwilling prisoner, to Edinburgh. As for Hamilton, he found Leith too tough a nut to crack, and therefore brought his troops to reinforce the main army at Berwick.

The game would therefore have to be fought out between Charles himself, who reached his advanced base at Berwick on the 28th of May, and Leslie, whose headquarters were at Dunglass, a safe distance away to the North. Had Charles been an uncompromising fighting leader, it is just conceivable that he might have whipped up enough enthusiasm in his army to compensate for its lack of training, and that, by seizing the priceless advantage of the initiative, he might have launched an attack that would have opened his path to Edinburgh. It was, at any rate, the one chance he had, and therefore worth trying.

But Charles, though he was to show himself, in after years, a brave and not unskilful commander, was the last person to drive home a brutal offensive. Even now, he had no heart in this unnatural war against his own subjects ; he still trusted that a way might be found of avoiding bloodshed. He had warned the

Scots to keep a distance of ten miles from the Border, and the warning had been respected. The last thing that Leslie wanted to do was to arouse the hitherto dormant patriotism of the English ; a waiting game, against an opponent who could not afford to wait, was plainly called for.

It was Charles who made the first move by pushing forward a column to the town of Duns, which it entered without opposition, and where Arundel had the congenial task of reading a proclamation to a predominantly feminine audience. Having accomplished this piece of work, the column was presently withdrawn.

Leslie's reply to this blow in the air, which relieved him of the ten miles' prohibition, was to push forward a force to Kelso, twenty miles up the Tweed from Charles's camp outside Berwick, thus threatening the English communications with the South. The King pushed out Holland with a strong force of all arms, to dislodge them. That commander looked at the Scottish position and convinced himself that it was too strong to attack, especially as the heat of a gruelling day seems to have been too much for an infantry unversed in march discipline. Clarendon, no mean authority, believes that he was the victim of a carefully arranged bluff. Anyhow, having parleyed with the enemy instead of fighting them, he made the best of his way back to camp, only too glad that Leslie, out of deliberate policy, did not offer to molest him.

After this, it was hopeless to think of an offensive. The last embers of fighting spirit had been stamped out of the King's army by Holland's fiasco. Even if there had been no enemy, it must soon have gone to pieces of its own accord. Disease had broken out in the camp, and the soldiers were busily occupied in picking out of their clothes what they politely called Covenanters. Provisions were short, and beer at prohibitive prices ; the springs of pay were running dry. If Leslie had chosen to take full military advantage of the position, he might have had the King at his mercy. But the Scots were as yet too much afraid of provoking the vengeance of a united England, to push matters à outrance, and Charles must have accounted himself lucky, under the circumstances, to find them ready to discuss terms that would at least save his face.

In these negotiations, the King figured in a new and hitherto unsuspected light. When the Scottish delegates had duly assembled in Arundel's tent, they were surprised by the sudden entrance of His Majesty, who proceeded to take entire charge of his own case, and proved capable, single-handed, of more than holding his own, point by point, day after day, against such formidable debating opponents as a committee of Scotsmen. It was a talent that he was to display even more conspicuously on a later occasion.

The treaty itself was on the surface a triumph of pacific reasonableness. Forces were to be disbanded, His Majesty's fortresses handed back, the Tables dissolved, an amnesty granted on both sides, and another General Assembly convened, that the King, God willing, would honour with his presence. If the goodwill to peace had informed this settlement, it might well have been that discussion would have taken the place of force, and that the Kirk, having purged itself of the last traces of ritualistic domination would have adjusted its relations with the Crown on a new footing. And then that tragic destiny of the King, which had begun to slide, like a stone, towards the abyss, might have been caught, as it were, on a ledge, and come to rest, still not so far below the summit.

But without goodwill, or good faith, the treaty would have settled nothing and done nothing, except to gain time for revolutionary designs to ripen—and that not in Scotland only. In spite of the apparent check, the stone had not ceased to move, and the slope was beginning to steepen.

4

STRAFFORD TO THE RESCUE

CHARLES had not even left Berwick before he was forced to realize that the Scottish leaders had not the least intention of honouring the Treaty in the spirit, or more of it than they found convenient in the letter. As any other honourable man would have been, he was furious to discover that, with a promptitude at least highly creditable to the Edinburgh printers, a garbled account of the negotiations was put into circulation, in which concessions were put into his mouth that he had never dreamed of making. "Why do you use me thus?" he had complained to one of the lords who had been in negotiation with him, and he had the libel burned, in England, by the public hangman.

But it was not only of words that the King had to complain. News from Edinburgh soon made it clear that at least the nucleus of the Covenanting army remained in being, and the renewed riots that broke out there, in which the Lord Treasurer was mobbed and his staff broken, showed what a spirit was in the ascendent. Charles, in a last hope of getting things amicably settled, sent for fourteen of the Scottish leaders to confer with him. Only six of them condescended to obey the summons. After this it is not surprising that his projected visit to Edinburgh was abandoned, and that he returned South to London.

After this the revolution in Scotland went forward unchecked. First the Assembly confirmed all the work of its predecessor, whose legality Charles had refused to recognise, in a root and branch destruction of episcopal rule ; and the Parliament followed up the work in the political sphere by voting legislation that would have destroyed the power of the Crown in the State almost as completely as the Assembly had done in the Church. There could be no doubt that unless the King was prepared tamely to capitulate to these demands, the Scots would try to enforce them at the sword's point.

That was bad enough, but worse was to follow. For the Covenanting leaders were plotting the revival of what had been a perpetual menace to England in the days of a divided Britain, the alliance between France and Scotland ; nor did they see anything incongruous with an anti-popery crusade in seeking aid from a Catholic nation and a Cardinal of the Roman Church. A letter, that fell into the King's hands, was prepared—though it would not appear to have been actually delivered—addressed to King Louis in the style of *au roy*, which, as its signatories must have been well aware, implied the acknowledgment of the addressee as their Sovereign. Moreover, the two Scottish commissioners who arrived in London in December took the opportunity of approaching the French Ambassador, with an offer to conclude no peace with the King in which the Scottish-French alliance was not explicitly recognized.

There was, as a matter of fact, no danger of such an alliance materializing under the auspices of Richelieu, who had his hands too busy on the Continent to lust after fresh commitments. Britain, in her present state, could be trusted to eliminate herself as a disturbing factor from his European calculations, without any special effort of France, and economy of effort was part of

Richelieu's technique. But it is the will and not the opportunity that makes the traitor, and the discovery that his Scottish subjects would not stick at calling in the foreigner, or bartering their allegiance to a foreign King, must have revealed to Charles, as nothing else could, how all things were crumbling beneath his feet. To what quarter was he to look for support ? Not to his army —the army that had proved a broken reed in his hands. Not to his nobility, whose loyalty, where it existed, was at best luke-warm. Not with any confidence to a public opinion infected with Puritan propaganda, and proportionately biased in favour of the Covenanters. Besides all which, he must at least have suspected the existence of an organized group of irreconcilables, watching every turn of the situation, and biding the hour, that would surely come, when the Lord, or the enemy at the gates, should have delivered the monarchy into their hands.

Two incidents that occurred during this Autumn showed the depth of utter impotence to which rebellion north, and disloyalty south of the Border, had reduced the King's government. A huge but ill-found fleet, the last of the great Spanish Armadas, after having had its feathers plucked in the Channel by the redoubtable Dutch Admiral, Tromp, had taken refuge, under the protection of the British fleet, in the King's roadstead of the Downs. There lay all three fleets, while Charles, driven desperate for want of money, was conducting an undignified auction of British support to the highest bidder. At last, when a sea fog lay over the anchor-age, one October morning, Tromp decided to end the business in his own way. The English Admiral heard the sounds of a terrific cannonade—it was impossible to tell who had begun it, and even if it had been possible to have taken effective action under such conditions, his orders were not definite enough to warrant it. In an hour it was all over ; the last surviving units of Spanish sea power were in full flight for Dunkirk, and the Armada, as an armada, had ceased to exist. Never had British sovereignty of the sea been so contemptuously flouted.

This same Autumn, King Charles's nephew and protégé, Charles Louis, eldest son of the late Elector Palatine, and the present claimant, set sail from these same Downs, at his uncle's instigation, in order to seize the command, left vacant by the death of Duke Bernhard of Saxe Weimar, of the Protestant army on the Rhine. Like Charles, on a previous occasion, he proposed to pass through France incognito. But this time there was no question of turning the blind eye. Richelieu, who intended to secure that army as a piece in the French game, showed what he thought of both uncle and nephew, by having the young man arrested, and put out of harm's way in the fortress prison of Vincennes.

Thus beset, it was but natural that Charles should have bethought him of the man whose strength and loyalty inspired confidence in his ability to master this, as he had every other, crisis. It was at the end of July that Charles sent a brief note from Berwick to the Lord Deputy Wentworth, which concluded with the words, "Come when you will, ye shall be welcome to your assured friend, Charles R." This letter was soon followed by one from the Queen, who now at last, in the hour of need, had become "*votre bien bonne amie*" to this stern, unpliable man to whom, in the past, she had vouchsafed nothing but the pinpricks of petty intrigue. "He is ugly," she confided long afterwards to her friend, Mme de Motteville, "but agreeable, and has the finest hands in the world."

By September, Wentworth had crossed the sea and was at Charles's side. It was the supreme opportunity for which he had long waited. His administration of the North had been an outstanding, that of Ireland a miraculous, success. And now at last, with his Sovereign's full confidence, he was as much in control as any minister could be, of the government of England. If he was called upon to grapple with overwhelming difficulties, that was no more than he had been doing, with success, ever since he had entered the King's service. He seems to have had no doubt of his ability to pilot the ship of state through the storm that was now plainly impending. Gladly would she respond to the firm and expert hand that now grasped the helm, after the timid and uncertain guidance that had brought her so near to a lee shore.

But here he suffered from the strong man's infirmity of irrational optimism, the faith that all difficulties must yield to the unconquerable will. And there was a vein of moral idealism in the man, that caused him to take too hopeful a view of average human nature. Incapable, himself, of baseness, he counted on an answering nobility in those whom he aspired to lead. Most of all, he had faith in the great soul of his fellow Englishman. The essence of this new policy that he had come to put into force was to take England herself into her Sovereign's confidence. Let the

King take the plunge from which he had hesitated so long ; let him boldly summon Parliament, and throw himself and the country upon its support against the now undisguised menace of this alien folk in arms against its own, and England's Sovereign. When that damning draft of the letter *"au roy"* came to hand, it provided him with a case that, to so loyal a mind, appeared overwhelming. Whatever differences Englishmen might have among themselves, it was surely inconceivable that they would fail to unite, as one man, behind their Sovereign, against treason so black, and aggression so naked.

For Wentworth was not the apostate that his former associates saw in him. Never, for a moment, had he ceased to be at heart a Parliament man. But he believed in a Parliament working in harmonious and loyal co-operation with the King's government. The mere fact that the King stood high above all classes, rendered his government national in a sense that one nominated by the dominant faction in Parliament could never be. And for that very reason it was as important to preserve the prerogative of the one as the privilege of the other.

It was not so much a question of constitutional form, as of the informing spirit. Wentworth's ideal was that of a patriotic Sovereign resting on the support of a willing nation, and of Parliament as that nation's mouthpiece, and the vehicle of its loyalty. That Parliament should be in a state of chronic sedition, and that its whole energies should be devoted to a war of political extermination against the Head of the State, was, in his view, the supreme evil that could possibly befall a nation. With the like of Hampden and Pym he had no patience—such mere wreckers, as he accounted them, ought to be whipped into their senses.

Of the present crisis his appreciation was characteristically simple. That the King should tamely surrender to the most outrageous demands of the Scottish rebels, seemed to him unthinkable. No one realized better, that there was not even safety in such a course. The Covenant, as he put it, spread too far—its unresisted triumph in Scotland would lead to a similar collapse of constituted authority in England. Wentworth was no advocate of the strong hand for its own sake ; he would have the King ready to listen to the desires of his Scottish subjects, and even to meet them half way, if that way was the way of loyalty. But to rebellion in arms, and to traitors in league with the foreigner, he would concede nothing but blows.

At the same time, such a farce as had been enacted that summer on the Border was a thing he never wished to see repeated. An ill-found, dispirited army, under such leadership as that of Arundel and Holland, would never stand up to the host of the Lord and Alexander Leslie. And yet the wealth and man power of a united England would be overwhelmingly able to account for the utmost that Scotland could put into the field. The whole problem was, how to put that wealth and man power at the King's disposal. And it was, like all the major problems of statesmanship, to be solved in terms, not of the law, but of the spirit. Let the King enlist the willing loyalty of the nation, and nothing could withstand either. Let him fail in that, and then— God help him !

That was why Wentworth was resolved to stake all on the calling of a Parliament. He knew—none better—what had been the spirit informing that body earlier in the reign, a spirit not of loyalty but of incipient revolution. And yet—was it possible that the gentlemen of England would stand coldly by to see their King betrayed and their country invaded ? That they would see in this necessity no more than an opportunity for political blackmail ? He thought more nobly of human, or at least of English, nature. Being what he was, he could think no otherwise.

And then there was that superb confidence of his in his own power to dominate and inspire. It was no Buckingham, this time, to whom the King had confided the shaping of his policy ; there would be no more muddling of the nation's affairs or squandering of its money on madcap adventures. Things would be different now.

It was one of those pieces of sheer bad luck, that do really make it seem as if some curse had been put on Charles at his birth, that at this crisis of his fortunes, the man on whom all depended should have had his powers impaired by sickness. When the King's call for help reached him, the Lord Deputy had become so much a martyr to his old enemy, the gout, as hardly to be able to stand.

"It is no time to complain now," he had written in his reply, "... I trust in God that he hath not given your Majesty so just a cause, nor me so good a heart, to take my legs from me in such a conjuncture of your affairs as this is, and however these should, yet I will hope a litter may supply the defect."

This unconquerable spirit was no doubt capable of rising

superior to bodily infirmity, and yet the judgment and temper of a man racked with gout could hardly fail to suffer—even if it were to an imperceptible degree. And there was always the chance of physical prostration in the hour of supreme emergency.

It was in January that the King gave Wentworth the proof of his confidence that he had so long delayed. He invested him with the Earldom of Strafford, and at the same time promoted him from Lord Deputy to Lord Lieutenant of Ireland.

Along with these titles, the new Earl had also asked for, and obtained, the Barony of Raby, vacant since Elizabeth's reign. Now it so happened that a certain Sir Harry Vane, who next month was jobbed by the Queen and Hamilton into a Secretaryship of State for which he was in every way unfitted, had for some time had his eye on this self-same Barony for himself. Strafford was not the man to notice trifles of this description, but in Vane's little soul it rankled and became a deadly grievance, for which, if he ever got an opportunity, he would take a deadly revenge.

5

THE SHORT PARLIAMENT

GREAT was the rejoicing in the country when it was known that at long last the King was going to summon a Parliament to Westminster. But any credit that he might have got for this determination to throw himself upon the loyalty of the people, to whom his rule had brought all these years of prosperity, was neutralized by rumours, started none knew how, that this apparent confidence was but the mask for a diabolical plot to raise funds for an army that would be employed to put England under the heel of an armed tyranny. It is the first we hear of a suggestion put about by King Charles's opponents on every possible occasion until the time of his death, that if he were ever allowed to exercise a King's right to command the armed forces of his realm, he would use them for the precise purpose for which, ironically enough, they were eventually employed by the men who did him to death.

Rumours of this kind do not generate themselves spontaneously. When in 1914 it got about, among the Indian troops destined for

France, that this was a cunning plot of the Sahibs to take them out to sea and sink them, and the adjutant of a Baluchi regiment was actually murdered at the embarkation dock—it was known to be the work of enemy agents. And one cannot help sensing, in this story of the decline and fall of Charles I, the existence, even if we cannot expose all its ramifications, of a no less skilfully organized propaganda, by which the popular mind was kept in a state of perpetually inflamed suspicion about the monarchy and its intentions. It was never the intention of the extremist leaders that the King should have a fair chance of putting his case before his subjects, or their representatives in Parliament. A counter-vailing bias to any incipient loyalty must at all costs be created in advance.

This would be a task requiring no little skill, for the crisis was one that might well have induced the majority of newly-elected members to rally round their King in an access of spontaneous patriotism. The first words that he addressed to them from the throne were as impressive as they were undeniable.

"There was never a King that had more great and weighty cause to call his people together than myself."

It was glaringly evident, by this time, that the Scots had no intention of honouring the treaty they had concluded with the King, and that they were preparing to take the field in greater strength than ever. And the King was able, through the mouth of the Lord Keeper Finch, to show how impossible it was for him to raise or maintain an army without special taxation. And to conclude that first day's proceedings, the King bade Finch produce the intercepted letter to Louis. If that did not convince them of the greatness and urgency of the need, nothing would.

Most of them were probably undecided themselves what line to take. They were after all, as yet, only a mob, and, like all mobs, easily stampeded. If they had had a Strafford among them, it is conceivable that he might have ruffled up their spirits, and persuaded them to contribute to the King's support as enthusiastically as the Irish Parliament, under his eye, had done a month before. But Strafford had gone to another place, and the King's cause had no one to plead it whose advocacy was likely to kindle any responsive fires. And the opposition, which for years had been waiting for this opportunity, had no longer, as in previous years, to be improvised in each successive Parliament, and to discover its own leaders, but was ready formed by the team work of a highly organized nucleus of wealthy conspirators, who had perfected their technique in the intimacy of speculative finance, and included, if not perhaps a statesman, at least such past masters of political tactics as Pym and Hampden.

Parliament had met on Monday the 13th of April. It was not till the following Thursday that the House settled down to its serious business, with a full dress debate on the state of the nation. The ice was broken—the expression is Clarendon's*—by the Recorder of Colchester, Sir Harbottle Grimston, who, tacitly ignoring the King's appeal, delivered himself of a portentous oration—it was probably the supreme moment of a hitherto obscure life—in which Magna Charta, the Petition of Right, the Plagues of Egypt, the words of Ezra, and much beside, are cited to show that the only subject worthy of the House's consideration is the eternal one of grievances. He was followed by that veteran agitator, Seymour, and several other members, primed up with petitions of grievances from various counties. It was only on the second day of the debate that John Pym, having no doubt judged the House to be warmed up to the right condition of suggestibility, rose in his place to make his grand bid for the leadership that had once been Eliot's.

A greater contrast could not be imagined. Eliot had been all fire ; he had infected the House, as an actor his audience, with the passion of his part. If he had ever had a nickname, it might have been Barak—lightning—just as Strafford seems a living thunder-cloud. But the nickname that actually fastened on to Pym, and that brings his whole personality before us, is "the Ox." He was one of those solid and stolid individuals who never seem in a hurry or capable of getting violently excited about anything, and who, if they have feelings, keep them locked up in some secret place far beyond the reach of human appeal. But for all this he had a plodding, reserved strength, that rendered him a more formidable opponent, in the long run, than the brilliant Eliot ; and to guide it, a calculating coolness of judgment, that prevented him from ever taking a false or premature step. His ends were strictly practical and mundane, but, though he could bide his time with inexhaustible patience, nothing could ever turn him aside from their pursuit. His very strength as a politician lay largely in the fact that he never aspired to be anything more.

* Used by him, inaccurately, of Pym.

Of his capacity or even ambition for constructive statesmanship, his career affords not the faintest evidence. He could undermine, thwart, destroy, as no other man of his time, but when he had done his worst—he had not done. He must kill where he had crippled, and plod to the end of every furrow, because it was not within the nature of the "Ox" to do otherwise.

There is a legend that, like so many historical myths, is more significant than fact, to the effect that when Wentworth had quitted the Parliamentary opposition for the King's service, Pym had remarked, "You may quit us, but I will never quit you so long as your head is on." It was not like the "Ox" to have let fall so theatrical an indiscretion, but the originator of the story seems to have been a successful thought reader. There need have been no question of anything so human as malice—it was a matter of sheer calculation that for Pym to succeed, Wentworth, as the chief prop of the throne, would have to be removed.

Long speeches had not yet come into fashion, and it was no small tribute to Pym's confidence in himself that he should have trusted his unemotional, yet weighty, periods to hold the attention of the House for two hours on end. He indulged in a bare minimum of rhetorical flourishes, beyond informing Parliament that it was to the Commonwealth what the soul was to the body, a statement unlikely to be disputed by his audience, but whose practical implication it would be easier to guess than deduce. His two hours were barely enough for the task he had set himself, which was the ordered and classified recital of all the accumulated grievances of the last eleven years. The art of this memorable speech, which though one of the dullest to read, must have been among the most effective ever delivered, was in its calculated restraint ; this elderly, thick-set man was apparently only bent on cataloguing, item by item, the heads of an indictment against the Crown, under the three main groupings of violated liberties, of religious innovations, and arbitrary taxation. The very monotony of the recital must have contributed to its impressiveness—it must have seemed as if the list of the nation's wrongs were never coming to an end : Catholics unpersecuted, Popery running riot in the Church, naval construction financed, depopulation of the countryside by the rich interfered with, patents granted, nuisances abated by administrative action, customs collected, Parliament intermitted, rich men mulcted of petty sums, and so on, and on, and on, winding up with a proposal to embody the whole list in a grand remonstrance to be presented by both Houses to the King, by way of an implied ultimatum.

Pym's speech was decisive. Its effect was to ruin irretrievably the King's, and Strafford's, purpose of throwing themselves on the loyalty of Parliament in a national crisis. Before Pym had got up, there might have been still a chance ; but by the time he had sat down, he had put the King in the dock as the only public enemy worth considering—it is needless to say that he threw in the most fervent expressions of loyalty. The Scottish mobilization, the Border open to invasion, the rebel plot to call in the foreigner —these things were forgotten. The House had come together for one purpose alone, and that was to overturn the existing order in Church and State. How drastically would transpire later— revolution is a medicine that the English digestion can only assimilate in carefully graduated doses.

Unless the King were prepared to make a surrender that would be no more final than ploughing waist deep into a quick-sand, the days of this Parliament were numbered. It was on the Tuesday of the next week that the King, finding nothing done to meet the emergency, summoned both Houses to his presence and caused the Lord Keeper to make an urgent, an almost desperate appeal—the army was on the march ; the cost of it at least £100,000 a month :

"It is not a great and ample supply ... that His Majesty doth now expect ; but it is such a supply as without which the charge will be lost and the design frustrated."

He might as well have appealed to stones. The only effect of his words was that the House resolved that until their own liberties and those of the Kingdom were cleared, they knew not whether they had anything to give or no. In other words, the troops might starve and the country lie naked to invasion, until the whole vast catalogue of Mr Pym's demands, and any others that might subsequently be tacked on to them, had been conceded by the Crown in due legal form.

Charles might as well have dissolved Parliament at once, for all the good he could possibly have expected to derive from it. But Strafford was at his side, and Strafford was not prepared to give up even now. A great gesture of conciliation might yet have its effect. Only let them vote the bare minimum necessary for maintaining the army on the Border, and the King would sacrifice his right to levy funds for the navy. This, unless he were to leave his shores unprotected, would henceforth, even in time of peace, put him at the mercy of Parliament.

It was an heroic bid for conciliation, and one that might well have been successful had the choice depended on the spontaneous feeling of the House, the majority of whose members were certainly sincere in their professions of loyalty. But since that speech of Pym's, the Commons had passed, like a hypnotized subject, under a control that had no intention of allowing them to come to terms with the King.

Nothing was more easy than to nip any attempt at conciliation in the bud. The King had scored a dubious point by an appeal to the Lords, a majority of whom had enough left of the tradition of loyalty to vote that the relief of his present necessity ought to come before the ventilation of grievances. This was immediately pounced upon by the Commons as a breach of privilege, and their determination to concentrate on grievances and nothing else was proportionately hardened.

It only too soon became apparent that the sacrifice of the navy was not enough, even for a start. The Commons were going to have the army too ; to deny the King what even the Petition of Right had left him—the time-honoured right of calling out the county militias for the defence of the realm, and of levying coat and conduct money for their support. It had come to this, that in response to his urgent appeal for help against invasion, his Faithful Commons were about to present him, in lieu of money, with a modest request that he should strip himself, and the country, naked to the enemy.

There was but one step that the Commons were capable of taking beyond this, and there is every reason to believe that they were on the verge of taking it. This was openly to declare themselves on the enemy's side, and require that instead of fighting at all, the King should yield and submit to whatever terms the rebels might choose to impose on him or, in Parliamentary language, be reconciled to his Scottish subjects. The effect of such a request on the troops, and the country at large, could easily be imagined, and if, as seems probable, the King had got wind that it was about to be made, the only resource he had left was to forestall it by a prompt dissolution.

But if he were driven to this desperate expedient, it was essential that he should make it clear to his people that he had exhausted every resource for conciliation, and that he was driven in his own defence, and the nation's, to forestall what amounted to a treason-able conspiracy—for indeed the opposition leaders were now acting in collusion with the Scottish commissioners in London.

But even the poor consolation of demonstrating himself in the right was denied to the King. He was of too simple and un-suspicious a nature to be versed in the arts of propaganda, and there is only too good reason for believing that the atmosphere of treachery, by which he was surrounded, had permeated to his own Council Chamber. What exactly took place behind the scenes will never be cleared up, but there can be no reasonable doubt that the new Secretary, Vane, was—to gain some private ends—playing a deliberately losing game with his master's cards.

It had become imperatively necessary to bring matters to a head. The guns of Edinburgh Castle had boomed out the first shots in the new war, against siege works that the rebels had begun to throw up opposite the gate—four of them had been killed. If the country was to be saved from actual invasion by the formidable and well-appointed army that Leslie was certain to bring back to the Border, there was not a moment to lose. Hastily the Council cast up an estimate of the King's requirements ; Vane pressed for a minimum of twelve subsidies, or about £840,000, to be spread over three years—certainly not a penny more than would be needed, especially as with the abandonment of ship-money, it would have to serve for naval as well as military needs, but a staggering demand to present all at once to a House that had just indicated its intention of postponing any sort of contri-bution for what must, at best, be a lengthy period of adjusting grievances.

Strafford, whom nothing could cure of his trust in the assembly that had once responded to his leadership, was passionately opposed to such a categorical demand. He would have the King throw himself unreservedly, without bargaining or conditions—except those that he himself freely offered to concede in the abandonment of ship-money—upon the loyal affection of his Commons. He would have him gratefully accept half the number of subsidies for a start—no doubt in the faith that once the English army had begun to fight its way to Edinburgh, it would prove unthinkable to let it perish for lack of support. Heart could call to heart ; generosity would breed generosity.

It would appear that Strafford prevailed so far as to get the

King to lower his minimum from twelve to eight subsidies ; it is certain that, in spite of this, Vane went down to the House next day, and, in his ministerial capacity, demanded the whole twelve. What sort of a mandate, if any, he had wheedled out of the King —and by what means—we can only conjecture.

The error—if we can use a term so innocent—proved fatal. This time it was not Pym who struck the decisive blow for the opposition. On the second day of a debate that had hitherto swayed uncertainly, Hampden—a popular hero on account of his lawsuit—rose to make one of his rare, but usually decisive, interventions, with the bland proposal to take Vane at his word, and vote whether to give the whole twelve subsidies, or nothing at all. The super-subtle politician must have foreseen that this would have the effect of forcing a blank negative, and thus ruling out all chance of the compromise that might at least have postponed a final breach between King and Commons.

It was in vain that one of the rising lights of the Bar, Edward Hyde, striving in good faith to avert the catastrophe, moved a counter-proposal to take the vote on the simple question of whether a supply should be granted at all, without specifying the amount. There was a confused scene ; Hyde's proposal was so obviously sensible that it seemed—to judge, at any rate, by his own account—as if, in spite of Hampden's immense prestige, he were about to carry the House with him ; when Vane rose again to make the brutal declaration that if they were to vote anything less than the full amount demanded, the King would refuse to accept it.

Even so, the debate was adjourned, from sheer exhaustion, at the then unusually late hour of five, without a vote having been taken. But there was no hope now of the compromise on which Vane had slammed the door half closed by Hampden. Not that, even if it had remained open, a penny of cash would have come through it for the King's war chest. The sacrifice of the navy was a mere *hors d'œuvre* to the Gargantuan banquet of surrenders that the opposition leaders intended to have served to their order, before there could be any question of settling the bill.

The hurried dissolution of Parliament, that followed next day, was inevitable. The King's hand was forced by the trump card that Pym was about to produce from his sleeve ; for the very next day it had been arranged by the opposition wirepullers, that he should bring forward this motion advocating acceptance of the enemy terms,* and he was quite capable of getting it carried. What Vane had done was to make it appear, in the eyes of the nation, as if the King had been wholly the aggressor, and had acted like a spoilt child in a fit of temper. Even Hyde could so far misconceive the situation as to write, long afterwards :

"It could never be hoped that more sober and dispassionate men would ever meet together in that place, or fewer who brought ill purposes with them ; nor could any man imagine what offence they had given which put the King to that resolution."

If that could be the considered judgment of the great Royalist historian, how must the matter have appeared to the average Englishman of the time, biased as he was by his Puritan leanings and a ceaseless propaganda in favour of Parliament against the King ?

A cynic might maintain that the one thing worse than being in the wrong, is to put yourself in the wrong in the eyes of the world. That was just what Charles, with the help of his Secretary of State, had succeeded in doing. If the effect of Pym's speech had been to put him in an invisible dock, the effect of his own tongue-tiedness, and the rascally counsel he had briefed, had prevented him from putting his irrefutable case to the jury, or even from letting it be realized that he had a case at all.

No wonder that a grim joy sat on the faces of the opposition leaders, and that the saturnine St John, after the House had broken up, was observed to smile for the only time on record.

"All is well," he remarked, "and things must be worse before they can be better."

The worse, in fact, the better ! Satan himself, speaking through the mouth of Milton, could not have expressed it with greater candour.

6

"THE BLUE BONNETS ARE OVER THE BORDER"

"TRIED all ways, and refused always."

Such had been Archbishop Laud's despairing verdict on the situation. Now that, within three short weeks, and without its having granted a penny, Parliament had been dissolved, the

* D.N.B., John Pym.

King's position had become about as hopeless as anything in this uncertain world can well be. Not only was he more than ever without the men or the means to defend his realm against the coming invasion, but behind whatever apology for an army he could muster on the Border, his home front had broken. The opposition propaganda swept the country ; few people hesitated to put the whole blame for the breakdown on the King's shoulders, or those of the evil counsellors who were supposed to be advising him.

Popular feeling had been worked up to a boiling point of excitement, and the extremist organizers did not intend to let it cool. With significant promptitude, the next day after the dissolution, London was placarded with notices inciting the mob to "hunt William the Fox"—or Laud—for breaking Parliament, and this was quickly translated into an appeal to rise and sack his palace. Nothing loth, a mob of apprentices and other rowdies marched up with a drum beating at their head, and would probably have made an end of the old man, if he had not been warned in time, and taken refuge, across the river, in Whitehall. Other placards now appeared, to the effect that he should be followed up and murdered there ; that the Queen Mother's residence at St James's should be attacked ; nor were even the King and Queen spared. "A Palace to Let" was what some prophetic wag wrote up about Whitehall.

But the citizens who composed the Trained Bands had not been worked up to the point of abandoning the Capital to mob law and bloody revolution, and they turned out, dutifully enough, in what we should now call the capacity of special constables. The ringleaders of the riot were laid by the heels, tried for treason, and punished with exemplary severity. But the revolutionary flood was rising unchecked, and it was of little avail to skim such casual flecks of foam from the surface. It was more to the point that when Pym's papers were seized upon, nothing in the way of evidence could be found against him. He was too old a hand to be caught in that way.

But it was not only the prentices and journeymen of the London streets that the spirit of anarchic violence had possessed. The very detachments of troops that were on their way to the Northern front, were little better than so many mobs of desperadoes let loose on the countryside. They were worse than undisciplined—they were actively mutinous. Their own officers went in terror of them, and with good reason. There was one particularly brutal murder of a lieutenant, who had struck back with his sword, when a mutinous drummer had attacked him on parade with a drumstick. Another officer, of the Devon contingent, was murdered on the mere suspicion of Catholic tendencies. The men demonstrated their Protestantism, not to speak of their sympathy with the enemy, by tearing up altar rails, dragging Communion tables into the middle of churches, and sometimes scaring the parson out of the parish. It was no wonder that poor old Sir Jacob Astley described the new arrivals up north as the arch knaves of the country, and the Governor of Newcastle as men fit for Bridewell and Bedlam, of whom, anticipating a remark of Wellington's, he professed to be in greater fear than he was of the enemy, with the devil to boot.

What made it worse was that the Petition of Right had debarred the officers from exercising any coercive authority, except in flat defiance of the law and hope of a royal pardon. Nor could even the key position of Newcastle be put into a proper state of defence, for fear of infringing the rights of its citizens.

And last, and worst of all, the King was without the means— or anything approaching them—of maintaining an army or fighting a campaign.

It would have been difficult for any ordinary eye to detect the least gleam of hope within the compass of the horizon, but it would have taken more than this to daunt the great heart of Strafford. He had staked everything on the support of Parliament, and that support had failed. But on the very day of the dissolution, he told the Council that he was as confident as anything under heaven that Scotland could not hold out for five months. "One summer," he said, "well employed, will do it." There must be no half measures, no scruples on nice points of law, but a swift and ruthless offensive, supported by the army that Strafford was at last prepared to bring to His Majesty's support from Ireland. No doubt he trusted to his own compelling will to overcome all obstacles, and infuse some of his own spirit into the men.

But it was not to be. The hand that seemed determined to strike down any chance that King Charles might have had of evading his destiny, now intervened. To the gout that had already crippled Strafford, was added dysentery. When every hour counted, and all was crumbling to ruin around the throne, the man upon whose genius and decision the last forlorn hope depended, was lying helpless on his bed. He had rallied a little, when the King came to visit him. With that passionate loyalty of his, he had insisted on getting up to receive His Majesty with due honour. Pleurisy had supervened, and it seemed as if the end had come. But the indomitable will fought him back to life, and during June, though in bed, he was keeping his secretary busy. It was not however till July that he was back in his place at the Council Board.

His absence had been disastrous to his master's cause. No one among his colleagues had the power, few the hope, and not all the will, for surmounting the crisis. They let matters drift, while the enemy, without and within the gates, was acting with swiftness and decision. Even in Ireland, nothing was done now that the strong control was relaxed. The expeditionary force, with which Strafford had been confident of bringing Scotland back to its allegiance, never left Ireland.

Meanwhile events were moving rapidly to a climax in Scotland. Leslie's first business, as it had been in the previous year, was to secure the country in his rear. The unfortunate Aberdeen was again occupied, and its inhabitants forced to sign the Covenant. And Argyll, who had taken to himself a commission for upholding the Lord's cause against certain of his fellow chieftains, the hereditary rivals of his clan, having first secured the person of the most formidable of them by a characteristic act of treachery, proceeded to lead his 5,000 Campbells burning, looting, killing, and torturing, far and wide through Highland glens and the Lowlands of Forfarshire.

This being satisfactorily accomplished, the interest shifted to the main theatre of war upon the Border. But this time there was no question of holding the soil of England inviolate. Leslie was no longer haunted by fear of the dormant patriotism of England taking fire and consuming him.

He was well aware that contact had been established between the chiefs of the rebellion and the opposition leaders in England, and that at least the most influential of the Patriots could safely be relied on to act in collusion with an invading army, whose presence on English soil would have the effect of putting the Crown at their mercy. While Leslie's army had been in course of mobilization, certain of the leading opposition peers had been approached for an assurance of their support in advance ; the go-between on the English side being Lord Savile, a Yorkshire magnate, whose father had been a bitter enemy of Strafford's and who had himself been imprisoned by Star Chamber for robbing his own sister of property left her in trust under their father's will, by terrorizing the trustee with a naked dagger—not to speak of the subornation of witnesses in the subsequent proceedings. This not untypical martyr of Star Chamber tyranny was excellently qualified for the task of promoting treasonable conspiracy. His fellow peers, Warwick, Bedford, Mandeville, Essex, and Brooke, had written to assure the Scots of their support, within the limits of the law. This was not enough for the purposes of invasion, the promise of support behind the lines must be unqualified. And sure enough the promise arrived to specification, and with signatures complete—the amiable Savile having got over the little difficulty by forging the lot.*

It was in confidence, then, of being able, with impunity, to go to all the lengths of military violence against the King, that Leslie now took the field. The resources of Scotland were available without stint for the support of his army, until such time as he was able to help himself to those of England. Meanwhile the King, with the defence on his hands of the far richer country, was starving in the midst of plenty. In his desperate need for money to keep his army from dissolving, he canvassed one sordid and desperate expedient after another. In vain and repeatedly did he apply for a loan to the financial magnates of the city—it was rumoured that Strafford, in his indignation, had talked of hanging up one or two disloyal aldermen. A beginning was made of the universal war practice of modern governments, that of inflation, or, as it was then called, debasing the currency, but this, in the absence of a credit economy, proved too great an outrage on public sentiment to be persisted in. Vain and undignified efforts were made to get money on loan from Spain, France, and even the Pope. An advance of £50,000 was, indeed, obtained from the East India Company, who extracted the monstrous usury of 16 per cent for it, and the City was at last got to advance a driblet of £40,000, in order to prevent the King from appropriating the bullion entrusted by foreigners to the safe keeping of the Tower. But this was ludicrously inadequate to meet the requirements of the army—and default on pay day had already resulted in mutiny.

* They took it in strangely—and, one is almost tempted to add, suspiciously—good part, when Savile ingenuously owned up to his little stratagem. May it not be that he who wills the end sometimes winks at the means?

Nevertheless, it is the amazing fact that Juxon, by heroic efforts, did succeed in raising enough money for the King to carry on with, after a fashion, as long as the campaign lasted, and even to provide a depot of munitions at Hull that, two years later, was destined to be of priceless service to the rebel forces in Yorkshire.* But if money had been never so plentiful, it could not have availed where the spirit was lacking in the men.

If Strafford had been dictator, and in health, it is just conceivable that his own uncompromising spirit might have triumphed over all obstacles, and inspired the King's forces to hack through to some sort of victory. With the invader at the gates, and the defence paralized, it is no time to stand on niceties of constitutional procedure—the King's duty to keep his realm inviolate may not only justify, but even compel him, to employ any means that lie to his hand. But Charles was the last man to lend himself to such methods. His rational and sensitive nature had an aversion that was almost physical from the way of violence, the brutal short cut past the notice boards of law. He could only hesitate and fumble with the profoundly distasteful expedients that grim necessity forced upon him, and thus ensure his reaping the odium without the profit.

One thing he could do, which was to go up north and take his place at the head of his army. His chances of putting heart into it would have been better if he could have gone up with a full pay chest. It was the 23rd of August by the time he arrived at the headquarters base at York. But by that time the Blue Bonnets— that being the uniform head-dress of the invading army—had already been three days over the Border, and were marching without opposition through the whole length of Northumberland. It was the Earl of that county, the head of the Percies, who had been appointed Commander-in-Chief, the incompetent trio of the previous year having been got rid of. But Northumberland had no heart in the business and, no doubt to his own great relief, had eased himself of the burden by going sick, leaving the command to devolve upon Strafford. It was only four days after the King that Strafford was able to leave London ; but the exertion of travelling prostrated him with a return of his illness at the end of the first stage. Indomitable still, he fought it down, and, jolting agonizingly over the ruts and potholes of the Great North Road, arrived somehow at York on the 27th, where he instantly

* F. C. Dietz, *English Public Finance* 1558-1641, p. 287.

proceeded to address the assembled gentry of his native shire, who had been grumbling and petitioning about the billeting of soldiers, and furthering every difficulty in the way of the King's service :

"We are all bound," he thundered at them, "to attend His Majesty in this service, in case of invasion ; I say it again, we are bound unto it by the common law of England, by the law of nature, and the law of reason, and you are no better than beasts if you refuse. ..."

But the effort had been too much for him ; chafing as he was with eagerness to take charge at the front, he collapsed again, and could only send an urgent command to Lord Conway, who was in command at Newcastle, not to abandon another foot of ground to the enemy, but hold out on the line of the Tyne while the King rushed up all available troops to his support.

But whatever chance Strafford might have had of infusing his own high courage into the defence, events had forestalled. The very next day, the 28th, the issue was decided beyond hope of appeal.

Lord Conway, at Newcastle, was at least a soldier, and had seen service at Rhé ; but he appears to have fallen into the mood of despairing inertia that had begun to infect even the most loyal spirits. He made his dispositions, more with the hope of saving his own honour than of stopping Leslie. That wily veteran had no idea of knocking his head against the Northern defences of Newcastle, especially as he was aware that, owing to civic obstruction, these hardly existed on the Southern side. He therefore resolved to threaten the garrison in reverse by fording the Tyne at Newburn, four miles above the city, and where the wooded hills, on the North, came close down to the still tidal river.

To oppose this, Conway had detached a wholly inadequate force, which threw up a couple of hastily constructed field works on the low ground by the river—mere targets for a plunging fire from the heights opposite. Leslie had a numerous artillery, and had learnt in Germany all there was to know about its use. Accordingly, as soon as the tide had sunk, and after he had tested the determination of the English to stand their ground, he opened, from the concealed positions in which he had sited his batteries, a concentrated bombardment to which the few English guns could make no effective reply.

The raw levies in the redoubts were not of the stuff to stand still and be shot at. In one of them, Colonel Lunsford's, they were grousing lustily at having to do day duty after standing to arms all night ; and when a ball, crashing through the breast-work, accounted for three or four of them, they had had enough of it, and bolted. The other redoubt, which now got the benefit of the whole concentration, did not last much longer. And then, with its drums thundering out the new Scottish march, the Covenanting host forded the river, horse and foot, in overwhelming force. There was one solitary attempt to retrieve the honour of the English arms, when twelve squadrons of cavalry, which included a fair proportion of gentlemen of the roystering, cavalier type, flung themselves upon the Scottish life guards, and even forced them to give ground—but numbers told, and, leaving their commanders prisoners, the cavalry were soon joining in the general rout, and throwing away their arms for the careful Scots to collect.

Conway was at least wise enough not to let himself be trapped in what was practically an open town, and soon the whole army —such of it as remained under orders—was streaming along the road southward, not stopping even at Durham, whence the Bishop and clergy fled for their lives. Strafford, at the news of the defeat, dragged himself from his sick bed and hastened to meet the fleeing rabble that he had come to command. Then at last, though he took charge with all his masterful energy, the horror of black despair clouded his spirit. Writing to his cousin and friend, George Radcliffe, about the general cowardice, panic, and disaffection around him—"none sensible of his dishonour"— he speaks of himself as "here alone to fight with all these evils, without anyone to help. God of his goodness deliver me out of this, the greatest evil of my life."

There was now added to his bodily crosses one more agonizing than any—the stone. It was no wonder that in his physical and mental agony, the control that he had hitherto maintained over that terrific energy should at times have been strained beyond breaking point ; that he should have enforced martial discipline with draconic severity, and even sought to have a gallows erected in front of every regimental headquarters.* At one moment there flashed through his brain a dreadful project for banishing all Scottish settlers from Ulster. It was no more than the half delirious irritation of an overtaxed mind—but Strafford, as the principal

* *Strafford*, by C. V. Wedgewood, pp. 254-5.

support of a tottering throne, was now marked down for destruction, and every angry outburst was good for the propaganda that was being worked up against him. The nickname had been fastened on him of Black Tom the Tyrant ; his, like Buckingham's, was being translated into a symbolic figure, a grievance of grievances.

7

CONQUEST AND BLACKMAIL

AFTER the rout at Newburn, not even Strafford could hope to retrieve the military situation with the whipped, mutinous, unpaid mob that was the army of England. It was no longer a question of driving out the invaders, but of whether it would be possible to stop Leslie if he chose to come on and make for a London, whose mob had greeted the news of his success with undisguised delight. Gustavus's old Field Marshal played his cards with a skill that argued him as expert a politician as a soldier. He advanced, without hurry or opposition, to the line of the Tees, and there, with Northumberland and Durham in his occupation, he sat down. He fully realized that his main strength lay, not so much in his own army, as in the collusion of the King's enemies in England, and in their ability to maintain the control that they had established over popular sentiment.

Accordingly the Blue Bonnets received strict orders to be on their best behaviour. They paid for what they took, and scrupulously refrained, on their march, from any sort of casual outrage, or indiscriminate looting. When Newcastle was occupied, care was taken that there should be no interruption of London's all important coal supply.

But if the inhabitants of the two counties harboured the illusion that a Scottish occupation was no more than a visit of friendly customers, they were not long in being undeceived. Whatever Leslie may have pretended, it was not like the Scottish nation to maintain an army of occupation out of its own exiguous resources, when the thing could be done by living at compulsory free commons on their hosts. The word plunder had been introduced into the language by Leslie's veterans of the German wars;

but it is not the way of a Scot to waste his enemy's substance with riotous looting, when it is more profitable to relieve him decently and in order. The process started by making fair game of property belonging to Catholics, to the Bishopric of Durham, and anyone suspect of imperfect sympathy with the cause of Christ and His Covenant, and by the gutting of houses left vacant by people who had run away. Such preliminary takings, however, went but a little way towards satisfying the requirements of a hungry army. To these the whole population—devout or otherwise—must be made to contribute, by that system of unrepresentative taxation that is known as military levy. This was a screw to which successive turns could be given as long as there was a penny or a scrap of food left to squeeze—and bitter was the cry set up, too late, in petitions to the King for help, by the people of Northumberland and Durham.

But this was only a beginning, and the Scots had no intention of confining themselves to the exploitation of the two shires of which they were in actual, physical control. Their army, encamped on English soil, constituted a threat to the whole country. At any moment Leslie might cross the Tees as he had crossed the Tyne, and brush King Charles's militia from his path as he had done at Newburn. It would then be open to him to collect the money, that Parliament had denied to the King, from Yorkshire, from the Midlands, from London itself. There were really only two things to choose from—to fight it out, or to pay ransom, in the form of allowing England to be taxed, as she had not been taxed within living memory, to maintain a foreign army on her own soil, and on its own terms.

It might have been imagined that the mere idea of England's being subject to such unheard of extortion and humiliation, would have aroused whatever there was of latent patriotism in her soul ; that the whole nation would have rallied in its wrath to its King's standard, resolved never to lay down its arms until the last of these insolent blackmailers had been chased from her soil, and that standard had been planted again on the castle of Edinburgh. It was the last hope that had fired Strafford's mind when he had heard of the defeat.

But it was not destined to materialize. The fact was that a Scottish army of occupation, fastened on to the country like a leech, was, from the point of view of the nobleman and politicians who had long been plotting revolution, a veritable godsend, the crowning mercy that put the game into their hands. For consider what it meant. So long as the Scots remained encamped in the North, their demand for blackmail constituted a steady drain on the resources of the country, far beyond the capacity of the now bankrupt exchequer to supply. It could only be met by taxation, and taxation could only be granted by Parliament—a Parliament that the revolutionaries were certain of controlling. And then would come *their* opportunity of exacting blackmail, ruthless and unlimited, from the Crown. For once let Charles boggle at conceding any terms they liked to exact, and stoppage of supplies would bring the Covenanting army southward, with nothing to stop it until the Blue Bonnets had mounted guard over Whitehall.

The success of this plan demanded that the Scots should be kept in occupation of English soil, until the Crown had been so completely humbled and stripped of power as to render such aid superfluous. It would never have done to have taken the obvious course of buying off the invaders with a lump sum, after making the best terms possible. Like the surgeons of those days, though with less disinterested motives, the opposition consultants insisted upon treating their patient's malady by a course of daily bleeding, indefinitely prolonged.

It was of course necessary to keep the patient from raising unseasonable objections—but that, under the circumstances, was not as difficult as it might have seemed. We have already seen how public opinion could be reconciled to the most flagrant outrages, if only the aggressor could be represented as a Calvinist and a brother. Men who had turned a blind eye to extortion and even massacre, when practised by Dutchmen, were not likely to be more censorious at indirect pressure from the apostles of Christ and His Covenant, who were constantly represented to them as fired by the same holy zeal as themselves, for the same spiritual ends.

Besides, it is the first and simplest trick of the propagandist's repertoire, to divert popular indignation from a concrete and present injury, to one that is either hypothetical or imaginary. The man in the London street was less concerned with the Scottish army, that was about to rifle his pockets with a freedom un-dreamed of by the most arbitrary of Sovereigns, than with the Popish army that, according to one horrific yarn, Black Tom was importing from Ireland to make England safe for tyranny, or with the Spanish army that was supposed to be on the point of landing in Ireland itself, and wiping out every Protestant in it. The very present tyranny of a rapacious invader was nothing accounted of—the men who were conspiring to foist it on their own country, were equally capable of foisting on their country-men a version of the facts to justify it, a melodrama in which Strafford, backed by Laud, was the arch villain, and the Scots noble deliverers, to whom no one would grudge any trifling commission they might see fit to charge for services so indispensable.

In the years to come no word was destined to more monstrous abuse than "Treason." But if we are to attach any meaning to it at all, it can hardly be denied that, both legally and morally, the collusion—which not even their staunchest apologists deny— of the opposition chiefs with the Scots, and their deliberate and most successful use of the military occupation to bring the King to his knees, constituted treason in the highest degree, treason so flagrant that nobody could fail to realize it, once the whole truth came to light. And the consciousness of this, in such acute minds as those of Pym and Hampden, becomes a factor of the utmost importance in the struggle that is about to develop. For now they must have felt that their very lives depended on the utter des-truction of the King's power and of those who upheld it—once let him cease to be at their mercy, and he could be relied upon to call them to a terrible account. "Even Christ," as Alfred the Great had remarked in legislating on treason, "could not forgive Judas," and few of his fellow monarchs of later time would take a less prejudiced view.

The collapse of the army had put the control of the situation completely into the hands of the opposition chiefs—even Strafford was powerless to withstand them. On the very day of Newburn, a petition had been presented signed by a dozen peers, including those—with the exception of Savile—who had already been in negotiation with the enemy, but of which the real joint authors were Pym, Hampden and St John. This not only contained the usual list of grievances and demand for another Parliament, but also one for the condign punishment of obnoxious ministers— the hunt was up for the blood of Strafford. The Scots quickly returned the pass, by a petition in which they made it their business to demand the assembly of an English Parliament— the collusion was now undisguised.

But in the ruin of his cause, the King no longer had the heart, even if he had the power, to stem the current. He seems to have thought that the best thing to do would be to leave the men who were most in sympathy with the victorious enemy, to get such terms out of them as they could be persuaded to grant. He had tried to spin out time by summoning the Lords, without the Commons, to York. Sixteen of them were appointed to meet the Scottish commissioners at Ripon, including nearly all the opposition chiefs, not excepting the forger Savile, but with a leaven of moderates like the invincibly loyal Bristol,* to whose presence it is perhaps due that a successful attempt was made to beat down the Scots from the vast fee that they originally demanded for the honour of their company on English soil. The whole negotiation resolved itself into a haggle with a blackmailer, by a corrupt attorney who, though he may have scaled down the rate of payment, was determined, for purposes of his own, to keep his client under the harrow. It was agreed that the Scots should stop on indefinitely, and should be entitled to an indemnity of £850 per diem, chargeable to His Majesty's account. The effect of this was to break the back of the royal finances. Neither Juxon nor anybody else could have hoped to raise the money unless Parliament would consent to put the screw on the English taxpayer. There was therefore nothing for it but to summon a new Parliament as soon as possible. This with the Scottish army held in reserve by the opposition, and public opinion thoroughly worked up against a beaten and humiliated monarchy—for after all there is nothing that fails like failure—was tantamount to putting the King and his ministers utterly at the mercy of men who dared not, even if they would, be merciful.

Substitute the Tees for the Rhine, England for Germany, and the Scots for the Allies, and you have a situation not altogether dissimilar from that of the Peace of Versailles—if we can imagine the Kaiser to have remained on the throne, and that a revolutionary faction in Germany, having first engineered the defeat of their own army in the field, had negotiated the terms with a view to prolonging the occupation indefinitely and compelling His Imperial Majesty to find money for reparations, with an invasion of the Ruhr or Berlin to follow in case of default ; thus making him helplessly dependent upon the good offices of the party dominant in the Reichstag, until such time as the sovereignty of the Empire had been irrevocably transferred to the

* Rushworth's addition of his name to the signatories of the previous petition is apparently his own invention.

hands of its chiefs. To complete the parallel, we have only to suppose the French, or leading Ally Government, to have been of the same ideological complexion as that of the party in question, and that even while the country was being bled white for reparations, an intensive propaganda was being conducted to induce the German Michael to regard the occupying army in the light of disinterested co-workers against tyranny.

The parallel only fails when, for a neurotic War Lord, we substitute a Sovereign so different in personality and record as King Charles.

8

PYM STRIKES FIRST

MR. PYM was a portly personage—ill-natured gossip had even described him as a belly-god—and it was at some considerable sacrifice of personal convenience that during the forty days that intervened between the issue of writs and the polling, he hoisted himself into an unaccustomed saddle to ride, with Hampden, from constituency to constituency, on the first recorded electioneering campaign in English history, But with such issues at stake, he must have accounted the game well worth the candle.

To such cautious strategists—and two more consummate masters of political warfare history does not record—the very assurance of victory was reason for making that assurance doubly sure. And besides, an element of danger had entered into the situation. There are always risks, present or deferred, attaching to the employment of treason, risks that may become acute when the facts are in possession of so incalculable an opponent as Strafford. As long as he was at large, there was no saying what he would do—or when. One must, at any cost of aching joints and saddle-soreness, make sure of a House of Commons warranted to respond obediently to opposition control.

Greater success could not have crowned their labours. The new House of Commons was as intransigent in its composition as the voters could make it. It was observed that the members had come together in a mood of strange exaltation—those who had talked of moderation in the last Parliament had now thrown it to the winds ; "Thorough" might have been their watchword, but in a very different sense from that of Strafford and Laud. "They must now," said Pym, "be of another temper than they were the last Parliament. They must not only sweep the house clean below but must pull down all cobwebs ... by removing grievances, and pulling up the causes of them by the roots, if all men would do their duties." According to Mr Pym's definition, he had as much reason as Nelson himself to expect that every man would do his duty.

For now he had not only the Commons behind him—or would have as soon as in his slow way, so different from Eliot's, he had established his hold on them—but he had two allies of even greater strength on whom he could fall back in an emergency. One was the Scottish army, which he could hold, like a loaded pistol, at the King's head. The other was the ever-present menace, to a practically unarmed monarchy, of the London mob. How formidable that menace had become, recent events had revealed. Less than a fortnight before Parliament met, a mob sacked the Court of High Commission, and even Star Chamber dared not lift a finger to punish them. Pym was the first of English politicians to have grasped the art of employing mob violence scientifically, of keeping it perpetually simmering, so that at any required moment it could be made to boil over.

The first debates showed unmistakably the way things were going. Pym, with his inevitable preliminary catalogue of grievances, was merely the leader of a chorus, all competing with each other in denouncing first this, and then that, iniquity of the administration ; or, more ominously still, calling for vengeance on the persons supposed to be responsible. There was not a dissenting, scarcely a moderating voice. It was hardly possible to speak of these sittings as debates—the only difference was in extremes of denunciation. It was evident this time that a final reckoning was about to be demanded from the Crown.

A more ideal state of things, from the opposition standpoint, could not be imagined. The skill with which that organized group had played a none too scrupulous game, and with which they had exploited every favourable development of the situation, might have moved the admiration of a Machiavelli. The real testing time was now at hand, when it would be revealed whether they were good for anything except mere destruction. Had they a programme of constructive reform, a vision of an England spiritually reborn and enjoying a new lease of prosperity in the sunshine of freedom ? or could it really be that their statesmanship was limited—once they had got the King down—to bludgeoning the life out of him, or, at best, of leaving him so hopelessly crippled as to be as good as dead politically? It would soon be seen.

Certain it was that Pym meant to leave no means unemployed for the consolidation of his power. He had taken lodgings in a small court, at the back of Westminster Hall, where he, Hampden, and one or two kindred spirits, clubbed together to keep open table for anyone they thought worth nobbling. Even now, it is worth noting, Pym who, though comfortably off, was no Crœsus like Hampden, had retained his aristocratic patron the Earl of Bedford, head of the most acquisitive and consistently successful of all the *nouveaux riches* Houses that had founded their fortunes on the loot of the Church, and among whose multitudinous pickings was the Borough of Tavistock, for which Pym continued to sit as Member. The reigning Earl had been engaged in financing the vast operation of draining the East Anglian Fens, and though the company had come to the end of its resources with its contract unfulfilled, it had managed to get the Crown to buy it out with the gift of lands whose annual rental amounted to some 60 per cent of its exhausted capital*—no bad bargain, one would have thought, though more had been expected. Bedford was the recognized leader of the extreme Protestantism that had proved so lucrative an investment to the Russells, and the worthy ancestor of a line of Whig magnates—a favourable specimen, be it said, for he was of all the opposition leaders the one most averse from extreme courses, though incapable of acting as an effective brake upon so much stronger a personality as that of Pym.

Hardly a week had passed in the life of this longest of all Parliaments, before the decisive issue had been joined, and decided, between the Crown and its enemies. In the otherwise hopeless situation to which he was reduced, the King had still the support of Strafford, now more than ever, in his loneliness and defeat, so conspicuously the dominating figure, that it seemed possible to rely upon the sole force of his genius to turn back the revolutionary flood in full spate.

Strafford at York had struggled to the last against accepting

* See Welsford, *The Strength of England*, pp. 335-7, 345

the shameful terms of surrender to the Scots. When he had been finally overborne, and the King was on the point of taking his departure to London, Strafford had earnestly pleaded to stay at his post as commander-in-chief of the still undisbanded army. With his clear-sighted appreciation of fact, he saw that by going to London he would be walking into a trap. He knew the men with whom he had to deal. It had been evident, for some time, that they meant to have him ; and once in their clutches there would be no escape. Here, at York, he would be in the midst of his troops, and free, at a pinch, to retire to his Lieutenancy of Ireland.

But Charles, in the dire strait to which he was reduced, felt the need of him at his side. It is easy in the light of the event to tax him with indifference to the sacrifice of his most loyal servant. But he had not that X-ray vision that pierces through the form to the heart of Things—and to how few mortals is that vision granted ! It is hard to blame him for not having appreciated, with an insight that three centuries of history have failed to confer, the nature of the forces that had him in their grip. He felt now, as inwardly as he felt on the scaffold, that he had a good cause on his side ; and he still believed that these subjects of his, who had never ceased to overwhelm him with their professions of loyalty, would at least be amenable to conviction, now, of all times, when the refusal of support to their King had laid their country under the proud foot, and grasping hand, of a conqueror. He would appear to have harboured, even at this eleventh hour, the illusion that the Parliamentary leaders, who gloried in the name of patriot, would make their first business, as he put it in his opening speech, "the safety and security of the Kingdom," which, he added, consisted first in "chasing out of rebels," and secondly, in a full and hearty redress of grievances—a fair basis, if any could be, for a reasonable settlement.

What he did not understand was the ruthless and organized intransigence of that little group of men who had the real control of Parliament, and that the very last thing these men wanted, was either to get rid of the invaders (they were in fact, highly incensed at his even daring to call them rebels), or to co-operate, on any terms with him. They had their own programme of upper class revolution—and the first, and indispensable, item of this programme, was the destruction of the one man capable of withstanding it.

Strafford, who had had better opportunities than his master of sizing up Pym and his friends, realized this with uncanny intuition. But it was hidden from Charles, when he continued to press Strafford to join him in London ; and when he gave him, as he did, his kingly word that Parliament should not touch a hair of his head, he had not the faintest doubt of his ability to fulfil it. What new and unheard of means of pressure would be brought to bear on him, he had as yet no suspicion.

And there were other voices at his elbow. Even now it is beyond our power to unravel the web of treachery and intrigue that was being spun round the throne ; but with far more reason than Cromwell, might Charles have breathed the prayer, "The Lord deliver me from thee, Sir Harry Vane !"* And to reinforce his pleadings were those of the incurably crooked Hamilton.

With Strafford, there could be no question of refusal. His Sovereign needed him, and that was enough. Only recently he had brought himself to death's door with pleurisy, merely in order to greet that Sovereign with due deference. Now there was, as he must have realized, scarcely one chance in a thousand of his ever coming back, if he once took the London road. But on that one chance he was prepared to gamble. Only first he asked the boon of paying one last visit to his Yorkshire home. Thence, having refreshed his spirit with three days of peace, he set forth, sick and in pain as he still was, to look death in the face.

But it was in no spirit of fatalistic resignation. Whatever the odds, he would still dominate the lists, as if in the assurance of victory. He had formed a plan of characteristic boldness. He would not wait for Pym and his friends to strike ; but, seizing the initiative, he would expose, before his fellow Peers, and in sight of the whole nation, the black treason of which they were guilty, in conspiring with the King's enemies to lay England under tribute.

It was a desperate plan ; one that we can hardly imagine, under the most favourable circumstances, to have succeeded. That the Peers, some of whom Strafford intended to unmask as ringleaders in the conspiracy and few of whom were more than lukewarm in opposing the Scots, would under any circumstances have given a fair hearing to such an arraignment, is hardly conceivable. The tide was flowing too strongly in favour of the

* Of the father, of course, in this case.

opposition to be turned back by mere fact or argument. But if Strafford was the fool who was charging a windmill, the miller, as Chesterton might have put it, was a knave—and was afraid. It would have been disconcerting, to say the least of it, for the Patriots to be suddenly changed from the accusing to accused party, and that on an indictment to which they had no more convincing answer than "Off with his head !" The cynical disingenuousness of arraigning Strafford on an unplausible *tu quoque* might have been too much for the Peers, or even the country, to stomach. There are limits to all things—especially in England.

Mr Pym had intended to go about the necessary business of annihilating his old comrade, with his customary deliberation. In one or more of his first speeches he would appear to have singled out Strafford by name as what might be best described, in the vivid American phrase, as "Public Enemy number one." But with Strafford out of his clutches at York, it was necessary to proceed with extreme caution—to pounce prematurely might ruin the whole design. It was accordingly decided to attack him where he was believed to be most vulnerable—through his Irish administration.

All the corrupt adventurers on whom his hand had lain so heavily, were back again in power—and they were thirsting to be even with him. The disreputable Mountnorris had turned up to pour his grievances into willing ears ; an even more shady individual—if that were possible—Sir John Clotworthy, had also turned up with an even more formidable list. A Commons' sub-committee was accordingly appointed for the congenial task of raking up whatever mud of Irish scandal might be supposed capable of sticking to the Lord Lieutenant. It was Pym's tactics that he should be thoroughly discredited before any attempt was made to clinch the matter by a formal indictment. So long as Strafford was away at York, and therefore unable to speak for himself, there was no occasion for hurry.

But now everything was changed by his sudden arrival in London, within a week of the opening of Parliament. The astounding boldness of the move was in itself cause for alarm. That he should have thrust his head into the lion's mouth, simply because he was told to do it, was not likely to have suggested itself to such an intelligence as Pym's. He had presumably come on his own initiative, and because he saw the chance of snatching a winning advantage—perhaps of effecting some sort of a *coup d'état*. Luckily the Court was honeycombed with treachery, and Pym had eyes and ears everywhere. He was soon informed of the line that the Earl meant to take, and he realized at once the necessity of shutting his mouth, at all costs. Pym could act quickly when he saw occasion.

But not quickly enough, if Strafford had taken full advantage of the surprise. It was a question of hours, and not even Pym could have prevented him from getting in his blow, if, on the morning of the 11th of November, he had risen in his place in the Lords to thunder that accusation of treason that Pym and his associates had so much reason to dread. But something held him back, and we can only conjecture that it was the King. It was like Charles to wish to consider the situation in all its aspects before sanctioning what would certainly be twisted into declaration of war on the new Parliament. And it was like Strafford to throw away his last chance of life, rather than act against his Sovereign's expressed wishes. It may, on the other hand, have been his sickness that prevented him from taking advantage of those lost hours. What is unthinkable is that the delay can have been due to any vacillation of his.

It would take more than eight days for Pym to establish that virtual autocracy of his over the Commons that procured him the nickname of King. However urgent the need, he would have to prepare his ground before launching his decisive attack. All that morning the Commons were being worked up into a state of raging panic. The most tried and effective stimuli were applied at full pressure. The never failing scare of a Popish plot ; the supposed machinations of the Queen ; plot of Black Tom to terrorize the City by military force ... it so happened that the King had arranged to review some troops who were about to be discharged from duty at the Tower, proof enough that the worst was about to happen. At the normal end of a morning's sitting, Pym decided that his moment had come—it would indeed have been unsafe to delay longer. He moved to have the House closed and the members kept virtual prisoners. Then, with all the eloquence he could command, he proceeded to denounce Strafford as an apostate, a traitor, and the greatest promoter of tyranny that any age had produced, not forgetting to throw in an insinuation that his private morals were no better than they should be. The chorus of denigration was now fairly started, and the only difficulty was to get from words to deeds before Strafford forestalled them.

He, it would appear, had got wind of the danger, and went to the King in a supreme effort to end the hesitation and procure for himself a free hand. He was successful ; but while he was pleading, the last sands had run out of the glass. The first fruits of the locked door debate had been the appointment of a committee of seven, including Pym, Hampden, and St John, to collect the necessary evidence for an impeachment. But no one knew better than Pym that the delay implied in this procedure would give time for the launching, against himself, of a charge based on evidence that needed no muck rake for its accumulation. It had, in fact, already been secretly decided to impeach Strafford without delay for high treason, and Pym had got the House into such a condition of excitement that they were ready to follow him without regard for consistency. Only one voice was raised in protest, that of the gentle and accomplished Lord Falkland. Falkland was no friend of Strafford, but he had the instincts of a great gentleman, and the cynical indecency of arraigning a man for treason, before they had even satisfied themselves that there was a case against him, moved him to shocked protest. But Pym swept him aside, urging with unusual, and probably flustered, candour, that by getting their victim safely shut up, they would debar him from access to His Majesty, and that they could take what time they liked about collecting evidence.

At about three o'clock, Strafford, having at last obtained the free hand he sought, came down to the Lords to look, as he said, his accusers in the face, and—we can hardly doubt—to become the accuser himself. But as he strode up to take his place in the House, he was greeted with cries of "Withdraw ! Withdraw !" which we may suspect to have been most emphatic of all from those opposition chiefs at whom the thunderbolt was to have been launched. Pym had been only just in time in coming to the Bar of the Lords with an accusation of High Treason, and various other crimes—the grounds of which would be specified later— against the Earl of Strafford, in the name of the Commons of England. In vain did the accused man plead that he might have his liberty until some guilt should be made to appear. He had seen the last of liberty.

And as Black Tom was driven off, through a frigidly hostile crowd, to the safe custody of the Tower, Mr Pym must have heaved a great sigh of relief. The Ox had been hustled into a momentary gallop that did not agree with his constitution. And now the customary pace could be resumed, deliberate but unrelenting.

9

REIGN OF TERROR

PYM—who may perhaps have taken his cue from that intuitive expert in practical psychology, Hampden, had rightly divined the decisive importance of isolating Charles from Strafford. To a Prince who shared with Hamlet, however much he may have differed from him in other ways, his habit of spinning out indefinitely the combining and balancing processes that are the mid work of the brain between sense and will, the marriage with a mind so tempestuously will-driven as that of Strafford, formed in very truth a union with a better, or at any rate, a missing half. It had been in no spirit of vain caprice that Charles had summoned Strafford to his aid from York. It was more like the cry of a drowning man.

Now that the great minister was torn from his side—though he was still able to correspond with him in his captivity—the King was, but for the love of his wife, in the grip of a loneliness more frightful than that of any prisoner in solitary confinement or castaway on a desert island ; the articulate loneliness of a nightmare, filled with voices talking treason in the language of loyalty, darkening counsel and concealing thought. It was the deliberate purpose of his now triumphant enemies to remove from his side every human being on whom he could possibly depend ; to create such a reign of terror that no one would dare, for his life, to render him faithful service or to give him honest advice.

After Strafford, the next Minister marked down for destruction was Secretary Windebank, who had, by his master's orders, intervened on several occasions to save priests and Jesuit fathers from martyrdom. He very sensibly did not wait to be impeached for so unforgivable a crime, but made his escape, in one of the King's ships, overseas, whither he was followed, a fortnight later, by Lord Keeper Finch, who for eleven years had been marked down for vengeance, owing to his refusal as Speaker, to be party to the act of riotous defiance that had closed the life of Charles's third Parliament. And on the 18th of December, Archbishop Laud who was not the man to run away under any circumstances, was put under arrest in his own palace, though it was not till the beginning of March that he was taken, through a mob howling for his blood, to join Strafford in the Tower, there to be cast aside without trial, a helpless, infirm old man, for more than three and a half years, before his enemies could find leisure for the formalities preliminary to butchering him.

In this same month of December, as if public calamities had not been enough, a terrible private grief fell upon Charles and Henriette. Their second daughter, the Princess Anne, who was four years old, began to sicken with what—though they did not suspect it—must have been consumption. On the evening of the 8th she was told that it was time to say her prayers :

"I cannot say my long prayer," she said, "but I will say my short one—'Lighten my eyes, that they sleep not in death.'"

Almost immediately afterwards the little life flickered out.

It was Charles's habit to keep his feelings locked in his breast, and even the *Eikon Basilike* gives little indication of the agony of mind he must have been suffering at this time. But we know that he was a man of more than normal sensibility, and that the depression of his spirits had been evident long before the situation had become as patently desperate as it must now have appeared even in his eyes.

If Strafford had been the upholder of arbitrary government that his enemies made him out to be, it is possible that he would have counselled Charles to hold on, at all costs, to the vital prerogatives of his Crown. It might have been best, in the long run, to have defied Pym to do his worst, and saddle himself with odium in the shape of a Scottish occupation of London or an attack by the mob on Whitehall. It would, no doubt, have been putting his throne and even his life to the hazard—but it would have been extremely awkward, also, for Mr Pym, to have had his bluff called, and himself and his associates exposed to whatever penalties an aroused nation would eventually apportion to men who had surpassed all records in treason, by engineering the conquest of their own country or the murder of their own Sovereign. It is a sound principle in war to find out what move of yours is likely to prove most disconcerting to your enemy, and to make it. As for life and throne, they would not be saved, in the long run, by "calm, dishonourable, vile submission," to whatever terms an interested group of politicians chose to exact.

But Strafford, Parliament man to the last, was for a policy of acceptance and conciliation, and Charles, without Strafford, and perhaps even with him, would have had to change his nature to embark on one of naked defiance. Sooner or later, he may have thought, the appetite for change would be sated and reason prevail. And as for Strafford's own safety, it was almost inconceivable to one of Charles's temperament, that unreason could so far prevail as to secure his condemnation on a charge so impudently absurd as that of treason, especially as, in the last resort, the King's lawful right to cancel any sentence was beyond doubt—legally. That guilty men, with the ghastly penalties of treason in prospect, might contrive to make as short work of the law itself as of the prosecutor, does not seem to have suggested itself to him.

So the revolution was hurried forward without resistance at the utmost speed at which the machinery of Parliament could be made to function. The first thing was to intensify the terror by striking or threatening every one whose conduct or principles had rendered him obnoxious to the Parliamentary leaders. Anybody who had been concerned in the collection of money for the navy, was deemed to have committed a criminal offence ; "so that in a moment," says Clarendon, "all the lords of the Council, who had been deputy lieutenants or high sheriffs, during the late years, found themselves at the mercy of these grand inquisitors ... no wonder if men desired by all means to get their favour and protection." The unfortunate officials who had collected coat and conduct money for the troops, found themselves liable to be cast in damages by anyone who liked, or could be put up, to petition for redress against this newly-discovered illegality. Bishops who had made themselves especially unpopular were required to enter into huge recognizances to come up for judgment when called upon. Clergymen who were suspected of High Church tendencies were subject to a peculiarly ingenious form of inquisitorial persecution, by means of petitions—only two signatures being enough to get any helpless incumbent sent up to Westminster and kept hanging about indefinitely, bailed in large sums, and subjected to an endless series of examinations.*

But these measures were mild and reasonable compared with the open terrorization of the judicial bench, in a way that the most tyrannous Sovereign would never have dreamed of doing. Some wag had managed to write up, on the door of the Commons' House, "Remember the Judges." It was a wholly superfluous reminder. The majority of the twelve, who according to their consciences, had decided in favour of the prosecution in Hampden's case, now found themselves exposed to the full blast of the vengeance of the defendant and his backers. Even Sir John Bramston, who had found for Hampden on technical grounds but had ruled against him on the main issue, was impeached with the others. And Sir John Berkeley, one of the greatest legal luminaries of his time, was actually arrested when he was trying a case, and haled by Black Rod from the King's Bench to the Tower on a charge of high treason, "which," says the Roundhead Whitelocke, "struck a great terror in the rest of his brethren then sitting in Westminster Hall, and in all his profession."† And no wonder, since it was now apparent that a judge whose opinion might turn out to be obnoxious to the dominating faction, not only in the sitting, but in any future Parliament, would render himself liable to imprisonment and ruin, and in theory, to rope, knife, and quartering block ! A fine incitement to judicial impartiality !

It goes without saying that the persecution of Catholics, that had been suspended during the "tyranny," was now taken up with a holier zeal than ever. It was announced that the law against priests would be put into force with all its ghastly rigour. In January there was a tremendous outcry, when it became known that the King had intervened to save a priest from martyrdom—the City of London actually went so far as to withdraw the offer of a loan unless that mercy was revoked. This particular Father ultimately got off with nothing worse than imprisonment, and it was not till six months later that the Long Parliament tasted first Catholic blood, in the disembowelling, and the rest of it—happily after death—of a venerable Franciscan. There were more to follow.

* *John Pym*, by C. E. Wade, pp. 226-7.
† So indispensible were his services, that Parliament itself, in the ensuing Michaelmas term, while his own trial hung fire for lack of evidence, was forced to bid him resume the ermine. But that did not save him from disgrace and ruin in due course.

IO

REVOLUTION BY LAW

OF more permanent importance was the work to which Parlia-. ment set its hand, of breaking down the whole fabric of royal Prerogative, with the object of reducing the King to being the puppet and figurehead of whatever set of politicians happened to be in the Parliamentary ascendant. The first and key measure of the whole series differs from nearly all the other legislation of this Parliament, in bearing the impress of constructive states-manship. It provided for the calling of a Parliament at least once in every three years, and for the issue of writs of summons at the end of that time, with the King's will, or against it. It was the assertion of a great principle ; that henceforth Parliamentary government was no longer, as it had been hitherto, more or less of a chronic abnormality, an emergency meeting for the purpose —as the beautifully accurate prose of the Prayer-book has it— of "ordering and *settling*" whatever business had compelled its summons ; but the very heart-beat of the Constitution, without whose regular functioning its whole life would come to a stop. We who know what Parliament was, at the time, and into what a stronghold of class tyranny it was destined to develop during that and the ensuing century, may be tempted to say, "So much the worse for England !" But when we take a longer and perhaps a more penetrating view, and when we compare England with other countries whose soul has never absorbed the Parliamentary tradition, we shall have to give the Long Parliament credit for having ordered and settled this vital matter, at least, "upon the best and surest foundations."

Whether they realized what they were doing, any more than King John's Barons at Runnymede realized that they were laying the foundations of English liberty, is an entirely different matter. They were playing the correct and—one might almost say—the obvious opening in their revolutionary game. And we must remember that if the road on which they had put England was to lead her, after the windings of many generations, to a Commonwealth of free nations of which none of them could have had the faintest pre-vision, its first stage was broad and direct, through bloodshed and chicanery, to such an armed and lawless despotism as had never been dreamed of since England had acquired a national consciousness.

This Triennial Act, as it was called, would appear to be more worthy than the Petition of Right to rank with Magna Charta as one of the four or five high lights in the history of the Constitution. The transition from occasional to regular Parliaments was the essential change wrought by the English revolution of the seventeenth century—the full Parliamentary sovereignty of the eighteenth followed from it with something like the certainty of a logical conclusion. And never, except for one brief period in the reign of Charles II, was there any question of going back on the decision thus registered, though an Act at the Restoration contented itself with the mere assertion of the Triennial principle, while ceasing to put coercion on the King to implement it. Parliament, as a matter of fact, was to become not a triennial but an annual event.

It is, then, as a declaration of principle, like the Rights of Man in the French Revolution, that the Triennial Act is important ; for Parliament was not slow to follow it up with legislation that rendered it practically superfluous. All the resources that legal ingenuity could suggest had proved barely enough to enable the King to live of his own, with the most rigid economy, in time of peace, and wholly insufficient to finance even the briefest campaign. And now every one of these resources was to be cut off by successive acts of legislation, which the King would have no choice but meekly to sign, to the effect that not a penny could be raised for the navy, or collected by the customs officers, without the explicit sanction of Parliament, and all the minor ways in which the King had contrived to supplement his income by driblets would be legally barred. Except by feeding out of Parliament's hand, he must starve. A prisoner may dislike, above all men on earth, the jailor who brings him his daily meal, but there is no man on earth of whose presence he stands in such need, or whose wishes he can less afford to disregard.

It only remained to complete the dependence of the Crown, by cutting off from it not only its source of financial independence, but also from those reinforcements of its power that had enabled it to impose its own and the nation's will upon anarchs whose land or money put them above the ordinary law. The Court of Star Chamber, against which the bitter cry of the oppressor had swelled so loud and long, that even now the very name stinks in

ordinary nostrils, was swept away—doubtless to the delight of
such injured innocents as Lord Savile. With it went the rest
of the prerogative jurisdiction ; the Councils of the North and of
Wales, of Chester and of Leicester, by which the forces making for
order and civilization had been strengthened in backward districts.
Cut, too, were the claws of the Church ; its Court of High Commission was suppressed. Henceforward the glorious freedom of
the sons of Belial, in matters of morals, would—above a certain
level of income—never again be subject to prelatical or priestly
limitation.

With these measures, which were complete by the summer of
1641, the principle of the Triennial Act was given practical
application, and all that was destined to endure in the revolution
effected by the Long Parliament completed. For the sake of
clearness I have anticipated the course of the narrative by treating
all these things as organically one, like a sentence that makes
nonsense unless it is spoken to the end—one grand gesture of
dismissal to such a national monarchy as the Tudors had built
up above the ruins of feudal and Papal power in England.

But during these months other things had been done, and
other tendencies put in motion, to which we must now recur.
For the men in control of Parliament were not statesmen with a
programme of reform, but politicians playing their party game
to the bitter end. It was time and not they that determined that
this portion of their work, and no other, should be destined to
endure ; time, that so often raises its fairest flowers from soil
most saturated with the products of corruption.

I I

THE GREAT REFUSAL

No more in the seventeenth century than our own, could the
claims of abstract principle compete with those of human interest
upon the public attention. It was not upon the tremendous series
of measures that were altering its whole constitution, that the
attention of the country was focused, but on the fate of one man,
and on the greatest of all treason trials that was known to be
impending.

The towering eminence of Strafford's personality was never more manifest than in these dreary winter days when, stripped of all his honours, he was confined, sick and infirm, within three rooms of that same Tower, whose chill gloom had so recently been the death of that other invalid, Eliot. Not even his worst enemies—they less than anyone—doubted that in the tremendous struggle that was taking place between the old order and the new, the whole issue turned upon the fate of this lonely man. The question was, not whether he was guilty, but whether the head-hunters, who had driven him to bay, could make sure of their trophy. Mr Pym at least—and every one of his actions proves it—was under no illusions about justice ; what he wanted was to liquidate this embodied danger to himself and his party, and there were no means at which he was prepared to stick in pursuit of this end.

If behind Pym's heavy *bonhomie* there had lurked the least glimmering sense of humour, they might have relaxed in a chuckle at the thought of how neatly the tables had been turned. He knew, none better, of what treason Strafford had been on the point of arraigning him when his mouth had been shut—aiding and comforting the King's enemies, plotting to maintain a foreign army on English soil. And here was he, John Pym, standing forth, in the strength of that very treason, to accuse the most loyal subject in all England of the one crime of all others of which it was least thinkable that he should be guilty, a charge for which no man of Pym's intelligence could have imagined that there could be the remotest shadow of evidence of plausibility. And the best of the joke was that Pym, as he was quite capable of foreseeing, had only to manipulate his cards aright, to be reasonably certain of bringing it off. Only five days after Strafford's arrest, we find Sir John Coke writing to inform his father, an aged ex-minister, that "it is thought the Lieutenant (Strafford) and the Secretary (Windebank) are both lost men."* And Strafford had not, like Windebank, the option of becoming lost in another sense.

In all the records of judicial murder, it would be hard to find any prosecution so elaborately shameless as this, which was undertaken by the Commons of England, under the leadership of Mr Pym. It would take a clever lawyer indeed to suggest any possible unscrupulous or dirty expedient that was not exploited

* *Historical MSS. Commission*, XII, 2, 264.

to the uttermost. Pym and his associates—who well may have apprehended that Strafford, if left alive, would sooner or later call them to account for that little affair of the Scottish army— were not the men to do things by halves. The axe's head, once turned away from Black Tom, would point towards the Patriots —and that was sufficient justification for any deviation from the path of pedantic rectitude.

The first thing, of course, was to eliminate as many as possible of the witnesses for the defence. They had shut up or driven over-seas those of the prisoner's colleagues on the Council who were most capable of giving testimony in his favour. But the deadliest attack was intended to be delivered upon his Irish administration. For this it was all-important to muzzle Strafford's friend and principal witness, Sir George Radcliffe. It was delightfully simple—the unspeakable Clotworthy was put up to suggest a bogus charge of High Treason, and Radcliffe was safely clapped into the Gatehouse pending an impeachment never destined to materialize ; for Pym, to do him justice, was no hunter of unnecessary heads.

A similar procedure of elimination was applied to those others of Strafford's supporters in Ireland whose evidence might have told in his favour.

From the very first, the Commons, or rather the picked team of managers who under Pym's leadership conducted the prose-cution, dropped even the pretence of justice or the desire to see fair play. They were out to get their man, and they made no bones about it. They would have denied him, if they could, not only witnesses but counsel—and succeeded so far as to get their services restricted to points of law. Every effort was made to deny him time to prepare his defence when fresh charges were sprung upon him ; to restrict his opportunity of examining witnesses ; and to intimidate those who offered testimony in his favour.

Before the trial came on, Denzil Holles, who had been ap-pointed one of the managers, and who, though a brother of Strafford's second wife, was at the time among the most un-compromising of the extremists, had been unable to stomach the methods of the prosecution, and had washed his hands of it— unfortunately, as it turned out, for Strafford, as his place was taken by Hampden. More significant still is the fate of another of the managers, Geoffrey Palmer, who, though he pressed home the

particular charge allotted to him to the best of his forensic
ability, did so with such courtesy and respect for the prisoner
that he was never forgiven—his credit with the extremists was
gone.

The none too easy business of concocting some sort of an
indictment took a good two months, and after that the Peers
could not in decency refuse the prisoner a time—cruelly inadequate—to prepare his defence, though even this poor concession to fair play roused the Commons to a perfect frenzy of
indignation, and there was talk of their going on strike by refusing
to sit so long as the proceedings were delayed. It was not till the
22nd of March that the great trial was actually started.

Meanwhile events had been moving rapidly. The King was
evidently determined to do everything in his power to win the
hearts of his Commons, by accepting his defeat, and the revolutionary changes it involved, not grudgingly, but in a spirit of
cordial goodwill. When, on the 16th of February, he gave his
consent to the Triennial Act, the greatest defeat ever sustained by
the Crown since the sealing of Magna Charta, he accompanied it
with a plea for conciliation of moving earnestness :

"This," he said, "is the greatest expression of trust ; that
before you do anything for me, I do put such a confidence in you."

They replied by waiting on him with the most flowery expressions of thanks, which some of them may quite possibly have taken
seriously. They rewarded him with four subsidies over which he
had no control, but were ear-marked, principally, for the maintenance of the invading army on English soil. Mr Pym and his
associates gathered in the trick, and continued to play the game
with unabated rigour. The next point to be scored was the death
of Strafford.

Pym was playing the Scottish occupation for all it was worth.
It was a terribly expensive game for the country, and something
worse to the people of the two occupied counties ; but this was
hardly the sort of consideration to weigh with the Patriots :
though Pym had come out with a modest proposal—evidently a
little too strong to go down with a Parliament not a fortnight
old—to finance the invaders out of the estates of those who were
authors of the mischief ; in other words, by plundering his
political opponents.

Everything was done to reconcile the country to its strange
guests. The Scottish Commissioners were lionized ; Scottish

preachers drew vast audiences to their sermons—only those who got their seats hours beforehand had a chance of being regaled by that rare and refreshing fruit of Calvinist disquisition. But it was fruit of a different kind that the armies of the Lord demanded for their temporal refreshment. Business was business, and the £850 a day that was being extracted from the pockets of the English taxpayer, was merely by way of a modest refresher, over and above the bill of costs that, now their hosts were in such a favourable mood, it was safe for the Scots to present. This amounted to well over what was then the huge sum of half a million—though the creditors hinted that a certain reduction for cash might be considered. It was merely another sermon on the text, "It is more blessed to give than to receive."

But it was hardly calculated to sound sweetly in the ears of the nation-wide congregation who, having been compelled to come in, were also expected to empty their purses into the plate. Already, in a quarter of a year, the effect of the Long Parliament had been to surpass all records of taxation within living memory, and there seemed no end to the process, as long as England remained in the position of a conquered country being squeezed for ransom. No wonder that even devout Protestants were beginning to ask themselves when the Scots were ever going to depart. But Mr Pym could by no means afford to part with these expensive auxiliaries, until the yoke of the faction he represented had been so irremovably fixed upon the country, as to render foreign aid superfluous. And this could never be, so long as Strafford remained alive, and so long as it remained in the King's power to appeal from this revolutionary Parliament to the people it was supposed to represent—or even to that very limited sample of it constituted by the electorate. Until then the country must pay whatever blackmail its conquerors chose to exact, and it was Mr Pym's business to keep it paying cheerfully.

But there were developing signs of restiveness. Even the City financiers were beginning to make difficulties about further advances, and when it was proposed to give yet another turn to the screw by extracting two more subsidies from the unhappy country, by way of providing security for these usurers, murmurs began to be heard even within the walls of Parliament, and one member went so far as to voice the ominous demand that the Scots should be paid off once and for all. This must have commanded some pretty obvious sympathy, for Pym appears to have completely lost his head, and to have blurted out the proposal to make the loan compulsory, a form of plunder that, as another member pointed out, would merely have had the effect of driving everyone with capital "to convey away their monies into secret places where it shall never be found." Pym saw that he had gone too far, and the subsidies were duly voted—but he must have realized that this process of bleeding the country white for the benefit of the opposition was one that even the most cunning propaganda could not induce it to stand indefinitely. The essential work that had to be accomplished, before it would be safe to get rid of the Scots, could not be hurried on too fast. Mr Pym was himself again, and was going to make no more mistakes. In solving the difficult problem before him, in the limited time at his disposal, we see him at the height of his political genius. For it was not only a question now of doing Strafford to death, but in one and the same process of converting the Long Parliament into a sovereign oligarchy beyond the power of its constituents.

It was all-important now to kill these two birds, if possible, with one stone, because only the excitement of the great trial could be relied upon to keep the country's attention safely diverted from the growing inconveniences of the Scottish conquest.

There was another and simpler way that Pym might have taken, one that offered a happy escape from the bitterness and bloodshed of another Merciless Parliament pursuing its advantage to the bitter end. Let the King call upon the opposition to form a Government ; let him put Pym and his friends in control of the machinery of state, and give them a free hand. What more could any statesman want ?

And this was precisely what the King was prepared to offer. The result of the Terror had been to create vacancies in several of the key posts of government ; the holders of others were, under the circumstances, more than willing to retire from their Damoclean eminence. And the King—largely, it is said, at the unwontedly wise suggestion of Hamilton—was ready to fill these posts with opposition nominees. Early in the year he had taken the first step, by the appointment of St John as Solicitor-General. And he immediately followed up his great gesture of conciliation in passing the Triennial Act with one hardly less significant, in calling eight of the chief opposition peers—not excepting the forger Savile—to the Privy Council.

It is true that a seat on the Privy Council was, even in those days, more of honour than of power ; it was not by that larger body that the vital decisions were taken, but by a selected few who were acquiring the name of Cabinet. But this was only a beginning, and Charles was prepared to go the whole way. Negotiations had been taking place for some time of which we know tantalizingly little, but in which the Queen—surprisingly enough—seems to have played a part, very likely on the initiative of Hamilton. Mr Pym himself is believed to have been approached by her personally, with a view to offering him the post of Chancellor of the Exchequer, with his patron Bedford at the Treasury. Imagination boggles at the thought of the vivacious little Queen trying her most winning blandishments on the stolid, elderly politician, who was distinguished, even among Englishmen, by the nickname of the Ox.

In this new Bedford Government, Lord Saye was to have succeeded Cottington as Master of the Wards, and Holles to have been Secretary of State in succession to Windebank ; Hampden was to have been responsible for the upbringing, on sound Protestant and Parliamentary principles, of the future Charles II—another odd conjunction, if it had ever materialized. Places were to have been found for Essex, Kimbolton, and other opposition leaders. What more Charles could have offered, or an honest opposition demanded, it is difficult to conceive. He was ready to part with all those prerogative rights that had been the grievances of the last ten years ; to place himself wholly at the mercy of Parliament, and to commit his Sovereign rights in trust to its leaders. Nor is there the least reason to doubt his sincerity.

And yet we know that the whole design did, in the event, fall flat. The opposition were ready to make it impossible for anyone else to govern, but nothing would induce them to take over the business themselves. The reason for the great refusal can only be inferred, for the secret history of those negotiations will never be recovered. That Pym should have deliberately thrown away one of the greatest chances ever offered to a statesman may seem sheerly perverse. And yet whatever else Pym may have been, he was one of the most level-headed politicians that ever existed.

That he was a politician first and last, without the least capacity for constructive statesmanship, is probably true—but it is not an explanation. Few politicians are averse from trying their hands at statesmanship when they get the chance, and the treasurer of

the Providence Island Company was at least a competent financier. It is difficult to avoid the conclusion that it was *per viltate*
that the great refusal was made. Mr Pym was afraid. He did not
trust the King, not because the King had shown himself unworthy of trust, but because he, Pym, dared not.

"Even Christ could not forgive Judas," and there is a depth of
treason that no Sovereign can be expected to forgive, however
much he may seem to overlook it ; nor any nation, once the
scales are lifted from its eyes.

And it was not only, nor principally, of Charles that Pym was
afraid. It was understood on both sides that if Charles were to
surrender the reins of Government, he would stipulate but one
thing in return, that he should be allowed to honour his solemn
pledge to Strafford. The hunt for his head should be called off—
banished he might be from the King's counsels, and perhaps even
from his realm ; but in life, honour, and fortune, he should not
suffer.

But while Strafford's head was on, Pym could never feel his
own safe. He knew what charge Strafford had been preparing to
level at him when his mouth had been stopped by impeachment.
And he knew that such men cannot be permanently relegated to
obscurity. Some day he would surely return, and there would be
another treason trial, at which there would be no need to fake an
indictment.

I do not say that this was the sole reason for Pym's refusal—
and it was his choice that must needs determine the fate of the
scheme—but it was a necessary reason, and one that would have
been sufficient by itself to have kept him from any arrangement
that left Strafford alive.

12

TRIAL AND NO TRIAL

THE trial was staged with every intention of exploiting its possibilities as a sensation. Westminster Hall had been selected,
because the House of Lords was not large enough to hold it.
Galleries for the privileged spectators had been run up from
floor to roof, and whenever there was a pause in the proceedings,
judges, accusers and spectators mingled in a noisy babel, like

the interval at a low class entertainment. There was much public eating of meat, bread and sweet-stuffs ; bottles of wine and beer were passed from mouth to mouth ; and the impossibility of leaving the Hall led to even less refined, though not less public, answers to the call of necessity. The King himself, with the Queen and Prince of Wales, was in constant attendance—they had put up a grille in front of the royal box to prevent his presence from being felt ; but this was a little too much, and he tore the flimsy thing down. The royal couple were constant in their attendance, in the hope that their presence might put heart into the prisoner, and inspire him to put up a good fight ; but, as Henriette records, they never returned to the palace without grief in their hearts, and their eyes full of tears.

The tribunal, whose members showed so little decent sense of the gravity of the proceedings, was undisguisedly hostile. Strafford's proceedings had not been calculated to endear him to the overweening magnates with whose pretensions he had dealt so cavalierly. Presiding over the court was the Earl of Arundel, who, though he may not have particularly cared for functioning as commander-in-chief of the royal army, had been offended beyond forgiveness that, at Strafford's instigation, his valuable services had been dispensed with for a second campaign. But the Peers, and even Arundel himself, were not so lost to all sense of decency as to turn their court into one of Lynch law, as the Commons would have preferred. Biased they may have been, and ready to decide every doubtful point against the prisoner, but they were not, like the judges who were shortly to sit in the same building to try an even greater delinquent, inspired by the motives of a murder club.

It was no wonder that Pym and his friends had been a good two months in framing the indictment, which, when it appeared, turned out to be composed, for the most part, of straws of malicious tittle tattle sedulously muck-raked together, and degenerating into such palpable absurdity as to constitute a positive insult to their lordships' intelligence. The choicest item in the whole collection was constituted by the 28th and last article, in which Strafford was charged with having deliberately exposed the army to defeat at Newburn Ford, and prevented the fortification of Newcastle. No wonder the Earl was jubilant when the indictment was presented to him, for there was nothing in it that he was incapable of demolishing with the utmost ease.

But even assuming that it could be proved from beginning to end, there was nothing in it that could, before any fair tribunal, have put him in the remotest danger of a conviction. The charge was one of treason, and treason, in English law, was rigidly defined, and limited to certain specific acts or intentions, none of which, or anything approaching it, was so much as alleged against Strafford—unless it were that last item about betraying the army, which nobody was likely to take, or press, seriously. The fact was that nobody in his senses could have imagined that Strafford had ever dreamed of committing what in law, or in plain English, constituted treason.

This might have been enough to baffle any ordinary prosecution, but Mr Pym was equal to it. He boldly put forward what, when stripped of its rhetoric, amounted to a claim to make the law fit the charge, instead of framing the charge to conform with the law. In the lengthy and venomous speech with which he opened the prosecution, he did not even attempt to prove a breach of any other laws than "the law in every man's breast ... the light of common reason, the rules of common society," which of course might be anything that Pym chose to make them. A great deal of play was subsequently made with certain fundamental laws of the land which, unlike the Law of Treason, had never had any existence except in an accommodating imagination.

Even more startling was the doctrine, formulated by Pym, in characteristic anticipation of modern totalitarianism, that habits of mind were more important than acts, or in other words, that an unfavourable diagnosis of the prisoner's psychology could be a hanging matter. And finally it was again and again insinuated by the prosecution that even though such and such alleged actions might not in themselves be treasonable, yet an accumulation of them might—as if a man might be sentenced for stealing a horse, on the ground that he had taken a dozen peeps over the hedge. Treason was, in fact, whatever the leaders of the Commons chose to make it, for the purpose of doing to death anyone who stood in their path. To-day it was the most loyal of the King's subjects— to-morrow it would be the King himself.

It was not that they hated Strafford. Of Pym, at any rate, there is no reason to believe that he was impelled by any motive so human. But they were mortally afraid of him—and with good reason. He knew too much about them. Once set him free to proclaim that knowledge, in those tones of thunder that he could command, and they were all dead men. Now that they had him fast, they had got to finish him off, and they would stick at nothing to do it.

At nothing did they stick. There was not a crooked or a dirty device by which judgment is turned to wormwood, that they hesitated to employ against him. The aristocratic racketeers, on whose corrupt tyranny he had performed such priceless service to Ireland by putting a curb, were brought over to get their own back on him by perjury. It is characteristic of Pym's thoroughness that when one of his Irish witnesses turned up looking so obviously disreputable as to discredit his testimony in advance, he went to the length (no doubt out of the common purse of the ring) of providing the fellow with the wherewithal to buy a satin suit and cloak. One would like to think of Pym exchanging a wink with Hampden as they decided to add this item of service to the good cause—but such levity is quite out of character with either of them.

Even so, as the trial proceeded, it appeared less and less thinkable that there could be any question of a conviction. In spite of the frantic eagerness with which the managers of the impeachment, and the extremely able counsel they had briefed, fought every point, Strafford had not the least difficulty in turning their most venomous shafts, and counter-attacking with deadly effect. Never in the days of his power had his dominance been so unquestioned. Never losing his temper for a moment, and often with flashes of scornful humour, he dealt with the Anglo-Irish bosses who were the principal evidence for the prosecution—Cork, Mountnorris, and the rest of the gang ; and contrived to make their evidence the means of covering not himself, but them, with discredit. The Peers may have been prejudiced, but they were not quite inhuman, and it was evident that as one after another of the counts of the indictment broke down, or had to be abandoned, sympathy was rising in favour of the prisoner.

It was also evident by this time that the prosecution was on the verge of ending in a fiasco. There was nothing in the evidence that appeared to offer even a plausible excuse for a conviction. Strafford was easily and manifestly in control of the situation, and the fearful possibility of an acquittal must have loomed more and more ominously before Mr Pym. For whatever else may or may not have been treason, there was no doubt whatever about "aiding and comforting the King's enemies." And this was a charge that an acquitted Strafford could be relied upon, at his chosen moment, to drive home in the appropriate quarter.

Pym's dogged resourcefulness was never more *en évidence*. He had still one card to play, that he hoped might prove a winner. But for this to be possible, he had to effect one more revolutionary straining of the law. Hitherto the opinion expressed by the King's ministers in the privacy of the Council Board were, as they are to-day, and as they obviously must be in every decently run State, secret and confidential. But the prosecution demanded, and got that prejudiced tribunal to concede, that ministers could be called upon to reveal their own and their colleagues' most secret deliberations.

The reason for this—apart from the new and deadly blow it struck at the Crown—was to enable Pym to bring into play the evidence of his one practicable remaining witness, Sir Harry Vane. That worthy was known to be ready to go all lengths to revenge himself on the man who had forestalled him in his coveted Barony. And Strafford's friends on the Council, like his friends in Ireland, had been judiciously eliminated from the possibility of bearing witness.

Vane's titbit of evidence consisted in some words of Strafford's he professed to have heard at the Council Board on the 5th of May, immediately after the dissolution of the Short Parliament :

"You (the King) have an army in Ireland that you may employ to reduce this kingdom."

The explanation, if they were ever spoken at all—and neither Juxon, Cottington nor even Hamilton, who had been present, had ever heard them—was the simple and obvious one that "this Kingdom" referred to Scotland, and not, as the prosecution insinuated, to England. Vane's unsupported testimony, in any case, was not evidence on which a tribunal could convict—and Strafford was enabled to retort, in a burst of passionate eloquence, that "if words spoken to friends, in familiar discourse, spoken in one's chamber, spoken in one's sick bed, spoken perhaps, to gain better reason ... if these things be strained to take away life and honour, and all that is desirable, it will be a silent world ; a city will become an hermitage and sheep will be found among a crowd and press of people, and no man shall dare to impart his solitary thoughts, or opinion, to his friend or neighbours."

Pym had played his trump card, and it was Strafford who had taken the trick. It was evident by this time that the prosecution had hopelessly broken down, and that all that its utmost malice had succeeded in effecting was the triumphant vindication of the prisoner. He was now on the offensive, and on the morning of the 12th of April, had them outmanœuvred so hopelessly that the proceedings ended in a scene of wild confusion, the Commons bawling "Withdraw !" to their own managers, and the Lords "Adjourn !" to the President of the Court. As the whole mob of legislators stampeded tumultuously from the Hall, Strafford, looking up at the royal box, caught the King's eye, and the two friends laughed.

But Pym was never so dangerous as when he seemed beaten. He, as well as Strafford, was fighting for his life, and he had no sentimental notions of fighting fair. If the course of justice could not be perverted to Strafford's destruction, he was prepared to drop even the appearance of justice, and butcher him by Act of Parliament. Charles and Strafford might have laughed on the other side of their faces, if they could have seen what was in the pocket of one of the baffled Commons' members, a certain Sir Arthur Haselrigg, whom Clarendon, in one of his inimitable vignettes, describes as "brother-in-law to the Lord Brooke, and an absurd, bold man, brought up by Mr Pym, and so employed by that party to make any attempt." The paper was the draft of a Bill of Attainder to be passed by King, Lords and Commons, sentencing Strafford to the extreme penalty of the law for treason. This selfsame afternoon, a Saturday, the Bill was produced in the Commons and passed through its first reading. On the following Monday, if the hotheads could have had their way, it would have been rushed through its second—but Pym was not to be hurried out of his stride. There was a decency to be preserved in these matters, and a precipitate abandonment of the impeachment would have been a grave error in tactics. Holding the House well in hand, he accordingly slowed down the pace of the Attainder, while the now meaningless trial entered on what would have been its concluding phase, with Strafford's final speech in his own defence.

This, by universal admission, was a masterpiece of oratory. Whether or not the Earl realized that even an acquittal could not help him now, he was determined to do himself the justice that his enemies denied him. Conquering his bodily infirmity—for he had once collapsed during the trial—by a supreme effort of will, he dealt clause by clause with the already discredited indictment.

It was no longer a battle, but the annihilating pursuit that follows a victory. And then, in conclusion, he raised the whole issue to a more exalted level than that of one man's guilt or innocence, life or death :

"My lords," he pleaded, "do not through me, wound the interests of the Commonwealth ; for however these gentlemen at the Bar say they speak for the Commonwealth, and they believe so ; yet (under favour) in this believe I speak for the Commonwealth too."

And he spoke, with prophetic insight, of the miseries that would follow his condemnation ; no Minister of State daring to render faithful service to his King or country ; and no man, with this arbitrary law hanging over him, knowing what to do or what to say.

And now, at last, in conclusion, he permitted himself to strike a personal note. He apologized for having troubled them so long : "Were it not," he said, "for the interest of those pledges that a saint in heaven left me, I would be loth, my Lords——" and the strong voice faltered ; his tears stopped him :

"You will be pleased to pardon my infirmity, something I should have said, but I see I shall not be able, and therefore I will leave it."

In cold print there is something inexpressibly moving about this, and we can only imagine its effect on that crowded audience, whose feelings had been already worked up to a pitch of extreme tension. It would seem to have been not altogether without its effect even on the tough nerves of Pym, whose business it was, following the leading counsel for the prosecution, to do his utmost, by launching out into generalities, to cover up the effect of the breakdown of the particular charges, and to neutralize any effect that Strafford's eloquence might have produced. But at one point an almost incredible thing happened—Pym himself, quailing, perhaps, before the flashing indignation of Strafford's eye, broke down in hopeless confusion, pulled out a sheaf of notes, from which, after a long pause, he started to read, giving away that the whole effort was a memorized set piece, carefully thought out and prepared in advance of the speech to which it was supposed to be an answer.

Never had the collapse of a prosecution been more complete and sensational. Strafford had triumphed easily all along the line ; his vindication was as complete as any man's could be. Unless by the most shameless cynicism, it would be impossible for the Peers to convict. There was nothing for it now but for Pym to switch over all his forces to the alternative and more deadly line of attack, and while the trial still marked time, to hurry on the Bill of Attainder with all possible expedition. It was a thing that needed very delicate working, for the sudden ostentatious withdrawal of the prosecution from the original trial amounted to such obvious contempt of court as to bring the two Houses to a verge of a quarrel, that might easily have wrecked the Bill as well as the Impeachment. It was for Hampden to save the situation by one of those rare but decisive interventions of his, and with Pym's backing to persuade the House to keep up the insincere farce of sending its managers to listen to legal arguments in Westminster Hall.

The only new evidence that Pym could produce for the Attainder was in support of Vane's story about Strafford's advice on the Council, Vane's eldest son—one day to be the Sir Harry of Cromwell's Litany, and even now notorious for his fanatical Puritanism—was put up to relate how, in his father's absence, he had been poking about among his private papers, and had happened to light on and copy out his report of the meeting in question, with the damning sentence in it. He had confided his discovery to Mr Pym, who had most obligingly, on patriotic grounds, absolved him from the scruples that honourable men usually feel about the publication of confidential documents ; and a very pretty quarrel was then staged between the two Harrys as evidence of the father's entire lack of complicity in the transaction—with the Commons, headed by the Speaker, intervening, and begging them to be reconciled ; though they kept up, for some days, a certain stiffness in public. This overcame the difficulty of the single witness, since Pym had the face to argue that the young Harry made another, equally competent, to the truth of the story.

But the Bill did not pass the Commons without opposition from an unexpected quarter. Lord Bristol's eldest son, Lord Digby, a brilliant young man who had been one of the foremost promoters of the impeachment, and was still as convinced as ever that Strafford was the "grand apostate to the Commonwealth, who must not expect to be pardoned in the world till he be dispatched to the other," but who had been scandalized by the shameless methods employed to compass Strafford's destruction, now implored the House to consider whether this was justice or murder on which they were set. For his own part, he washed his hands of it :

"My vote," he said, "goes not to the taking of the Earl of Strafford's life."

But this courageous protest, though it might embarrass, was only calculated to harden still more the purpose of those implacable men who felt their own safety bound up with Strafford's destruction. Digby had offended beyond the possibility of forgiveness and, though he got off with no more direct consequences than a demand for explanations and, some time later, with the burning of his speech by the hangman, he was henceforth a marked man. His speech, however, would seem to have had some effect, for though there were only fifty-nine members who dared to vote against the Third Reading of the Attainder, not far short of half the members were significantly absent from what must have been the most critical division yet of that Parliament. It was the first sign—as Pym's acute eye can hardly have failed to notice—of a reverse swing of the pendulum.* The opposition chiefs must drive home their advantage now ; they must get Strafford dead, and not only the King, but the country, irrevocably under their yoke, before the reaction against them had time to gather strength. What Pym had to do he must do quickly.

The battle had entered upon its culminating and decisive phase. It was time for Pym to throw in his last reserves ; to call up every ally ; to employ every weapon at his disposal. No question now of justice or of compromise : it was all or nothing ; my life or yours.

13

PLOT AND PROPAGANDA

EVEN now, with the bill to murder Strafford safely through the Lower House, the King, though he realized the gravity, does not yet appear to have grasped the almost hopelessness of the situation. He was still thinking in terms of the law ; still simple enough to

---

* Sir J. Coke, jun., writes that "The Bill . . . passed not without more opposition than was expected, it seeming to divers men of good sense and understanding a very hard case that a man's life should be taken away by an Act of Parliament made for that purpose."—*Historical MSS. Commission*, XII, 2, 229.

imagine that his opponents, like himself, would be bound by the rules of the game. On this showing the Attainder was a shade better than the Impeachment, for an impeached man could be condemned to death at the sole discretion of the Peers, while in an Attainder, the King himself acted the part of final judge, and had to be a consenting party before it could pass into law. And this, in face of his pledged word to Strafford, he was prepared to die rather than become.

It was not yet a foregone conclusion that the Bill would ever get beyond the Lords. It was a desperately high-handed action that the Commons were taking, and though their Lordships had no love for Strafford, they had a keen enough sense of their own dignity and self-preservation. If they were to allow the scales of justice thus rudely to be snatched from their hands, and if they were meekly to surrender the Lord Lieutenant's life to this peremptory demand, they would be creating a precedent that might be used with deadly effect on any other Peer who might have incurred the Commons' displeasure. When, on Friday the 23rd of April, the Bill was introduced into the Lords, there was quite a scene ; Savile, of all people—and he was at least a fairly accurate weathercock—loudly declaring that their privileges were being violated.

What was more important, an influential group was beginning to work for a compromise that should be satisfied with Strafford's political, without his personal death. Bristol, still as loyal, though as independent as ever, was working hard for this end, and he was now joined by an even more important personage, in the shape of Bedford. The head of the Russells, though as alive to his own interests as any other titled plutocrat, had a not undeserved reputation for wisdom, of the worldly variety, and he had begun to have some inkling that a revolution, once it had gathered sufficient momentum, might get out of aristocratic control. He lamented, he told Hyde, "the misery that the Kingdom was likely to fall into, by their own violence and want of temper, in the prosecution of their own happiness."

And Bedford was to be the head of the opposition ministry that the King still hoped to form, and would already have formed, but for his one stipulation of preserving Strafford alive. This Bedford was at last prepared to concede, and the patron of Pym might reasonably be expected to bring him and the other extremists into line.

The King, for his part, was prepared to come more than half way to meet them. He was resigned now to losing the services of his ablest councillor and the greatest statesman in his realm. That same Friday that the Attainder came up to the Lords, Charles wrote to break to Strafford that he must lay by all thought of employing him henceforward in his affairs, but, he hastened to reassure him, "on the word of a King, you shall not suffer in life, honour or fortune. This," he added pathetically, "is but justice, and therefore a very mean reward from a master to so faithful and able a servant ... yet it is as much as I conceive the present times will permit ; though none shall hinder me from being your constant, faithful friend, Charles R."

It is hard to see how—short of sacrificing everything, including honour—Charles could have taken a more conciliatory line. He was ready to transform himself into a constitutional monarch in the modern sense, and to entrust his ancient prerogative of governing the country to the men who had hitherto been his bitterest opponents. What more could they want ?

The whole project was ripe to be put into effect, and the sooner, from the King's point of view, the better. Bedford was ready to take over.; the Exchequer was waiting for Pym. In the past few days that formidable personage had twice been admitted to interviews with His Majesty. Over these, as over all Pym's direct dealings with the Court, there hangs a veil of impenetrable mystery. We can be certain that he was profuse in expressions of loyalty ; we can be certain, also, that he remained doggedly, stolidly, impracticable. Bedford or no Bedford, Strafford's death was Pym's, as Strafford's life was the King's, irreducible minimum. And Pym had other ends, as yet undisclosed, to compass.

For now, with a majority of the Commons at his back, he was beyond the control even of a patron. No sweets of office could tempt him to draw back. He was too deeply committed. Unless the royal power were wholly taken away, and that of the Broughton Camarilla established on a rock of perpetuity, there could be no more ease for him on his ministerial seat, than for Damocles in his bed.

The extremist pack, hunted by Pym, had run its quarry into view, and were too mad for blood to be called off by a few tentative toots of a noble Master's horn. Bedford must have realized something of what he was up against, when he employed Hyde and the newly-created Marquis of Hertford to persuade the

Earl of Essex, who since the loss of his command had gone more than ever over to the opposition, to some compromise by which Strafford's life should be spared. All they could get out of that depressing personage was a portentous shake of the head, and the brutal remark,

"Stone dead hath no fellow,"

which, if not borrowed from Mr Pym, exactly expressed his sentiments.

Any chance that might have remained of the Bedford-Bristol combination being strong enough to put a brake on Pym's intransigence, was to be dissipated by another of those extra-ordinary strokes of ill-luck, of which Charles's career was so prolific. Bedford, on whom everything now depended, began to sicken for smallpox. In little more than a fortnight, and three days before Strafford, he was dead. The field was clear for the extremists.

It was time now for Pym to bring forces into play that would make it impossible either for the Peers to hold up, or the King to veto the Attainder. It was not enough to rely on the mere threat from beyond the Tees—pressure must be direct and continuous. And that could only be applied by the second of Pym's two great allies, the London mob.

Now it is the mark of Pym's genius as a politician, that he, in advance of his time, had discovered the scientific use of mob action. He was no demagogue in the ordinary sense ; apart from his one election campaign, he kept his eloquence for the Commons. But he was a master in the art of working by suggestion on the mass consciousness—and most especially of exploiting the master passion of fear. Only panic the mob sufficiently, and you might get it to charge in any direction like a herd of maddened buffaloes, trampling down everything in its path.

Pym's technique comprehended the use of two main gener-ators of panic ; the fear of Popery, and the fear of military violence.

He knew, though he had kept his counsel till the time was ripe, that fortune had put into his hands a priceless gift, in the shape of a military plot that, unlike the one he had been trying to father on Strafford, had some foundation in fact.

This affair was the direct and almost inevitable result of

Parliament's action, or lack of it—though it would perhaps be rating Pym's genius too high to credit him with foreseeing that. The Long Parliament was to acquire an evil reputation in later days, and work its own ruin, by bilking the soldiers who had fought for it of their lawful pay. But what is less notorious, is that it had started this unpleasant practice in the very first months of its existence.

For with Leslie on the Tees, reinforced, as he was, and fortifying Darlington, it was impossible to disband the English army, Strafford's former command, that faced it in Yorkshire ; nor even, perhaps, desirable, since it had proved itself quite incapable of stopping the Scots, and constituted an additional drain on the royal exchequer. The small but disciplined force that the King held ready in Ireland to come to its assistance was on a different footing—that was a grievance, because Irishmen, unlike Scotsmen, were outside the religious pale.

The record of the English army had been poor enough in the previous summer, but no force that has remained under arms for months on end can fail to acquire some measure of discipline and *esprit de corps*. The Scots, whatever the Members at Westminster may have thought about them, were the enemy to the troops in Yorkshire, who were straining at the leash to get at them and avenge the shame of Newburn. When, under the specious plea of food shortage, they started encroaching still further southward, the English commanders on the spot begged Parliament for permission to drive them back, in order, as they put it, "to escape shame or save England from further harm." This was the last consideration likely to weigh with the Patriots, and peremptory orders came back that the troops were on no account to leave their winter quarters.*

It was not hard to deduce that the politicians at Westminster had a very good understanding with the enemy. This was bad enough, but it was worse still when the suspicion was confirmed in terms of hard cash. In spite of the unprecedented taxation, both officers and men were disgracefully in arrears with their pay, while the enemy, with his £850 a day, was notoriously doing very well indeed. The culminating outrage was when a consignment of arrears was at last sent up North to the extent of £10,000. Those who best know the British soldier, can imagine his feelings, and his language, when, on the eve of disbursement, orders arrived

* S.P., Ven., the 19th of April, 1841.

from Parliament countermanding payment, and directing that every penny be sent on to the Scots. It is said that "grammercy good Scot" was a popular catch among the propaganda-drunken citizens of London. But it is something more than doubtful whether this was precisely the slogan of the York garrison, as they saw the long-awaited convoy lumbering on in the direction of the enemy lines. How it failed to be rushed, then and there, must remain one of the unsolved problems of military history.

It is small wonder, after this, that a mutinous spirit should have been rife in the army, and particularly among the commissioned ranks. The gilt was off the Parliamentary gingerbread with a vengeance, and it was only to be expected that high-spirited young gentlemen, kept hanging about in humiliating inaction, and running into debt for want of pay, should have turned to even more dangerous solaces than drinking and dicing.

There was no deep-laid conjuration. What happened was as spontaneous as it was human, and piecing it together, would seem to have originated less in some conspiratorial cellar, than over the cups of a few amiably irresponsible bloods, two of them poets—Suckling, the typical laughing cavalier, and D'Avenant, who may just conceivably have been a son of Shakespeare. There was Henry Wilmot, the young cavalry officer who had led the charge at Newburn, and been taken prisoner there ; and as no conspiracy would have been complete without a Percy, there was one to hand in the shape of Northumberland's, and Lucy Carlisle's brother, Henry.

It does not appear that the "conspiracy," in its opening stages, consisted in more than the letting off of a little harmless steam, or that any more desperate design was afoot than that of getting up a petition, setting forth the army's undoubted grievances. But in such company, there is always one member who will be ready to go farther than the rest—in talk ; and sooner or later some really dangerous character will get drawn in. Both these things happened.

Suckling, whose reputation among his brother officers was that of an extravagant ass, and who, in the Border campaign, had equipped and clothed at his own expense a squadron whose gorgeous fancy dress had made it the laughing stock of the whole army, was struck with the bright idea of bringing up the now thoroughly disgruntled troops to London, to enforce some reasonable settlement of the political crisis. This sage counsellor, who had just written a topical play called *The Discontented Colonel*, now actually had the assurance to draw up a paper of advice to His Majesty, to the effect that it was "not only the opinion but the expectation of the wise" that "it is fit for the King to do something extraordinary."

Charles was the last person to be impressed, or even amused, by stuff of this kind, though its reproduction in the form of a printed pamphlet was providing Pym with just the sort of propaganda he wanted. But the idea of "doing something extraordinary" had caught on with one or two others of "the wise," and a scheme was mooted in which a complaisant commander-in-chief should be appointed, with a second-in-command who should be the real head of the plot. Who these should be and what exactly they should do was not generally agreed—the more cautious section were even for making the best of both worlds, by selecting opposition chiefs like Essex and Holland ! But the thrusters were for the Earl of Newcastle as figure-head, and, for the real leader, George Goring, one of the regimental commanders, who had recently received the Governorship of Portsmouth.

Now Goring was a boon companion of Suckling's, and a person, by all accounts, of much the same kidney, except for the fact that he was a soldier of proved merit. He had the reputation of being the best fellow in the army, a swashing, careless *beau sabreur*, and a mighty lover of wine and women. Even Strafford had been charmed by "his frank, sweet, and generous disposition," and had predicted a brilliant future for him. As a matter of fact, Goring, beneath his jolly exterior, was one of the most thorough-paced rogues that have ever walked, his peculiar speciality being in the art of lying, which he practised with a skill that would have rendered him the delight of Machiavelli or Oscar Wilde.

When the idea was put to him, he received it with acclamation. Whatever else he may have been, he was no coward, and his ambition fell not far short of megalomania. Visions flashed before his eyes of himself as the man who, with the army at his back, would hold the fate of the kingdom in his hands—all that was necessary being to act with boldness and stick at nothing. He would march the army on London ; he would seize the Tower ; he would put back the King in enjoyment of his own—with himself, no doubt, as the all-powerful dictator. There was one flaw, that does not seem to have occurred to him, in this promising scheme : even could he persuade the army to follow him to

London, Leslie would beyond a doubt arrive at his heels, and the result would be a catastrophe in which not only the conspiracy, but probably the Throne itself, would be overwhelmed for good and all.

It was towards the end of March that the plot, or plots—for there was no sort of unity among the malcontents—threatened to come to a head. There were meetings in London, for some of the officers had seats in Parliament. There was an oath of secrecy, taken in Percy's lodgings. And, as was only to be expected, there were attempts to enlist royal support for the venture.

The King was no more inclined to do something desperate with Goring, than he was to do something extraordinary with Suckling ; but with the Queen it was different. Henriette had rather less than the average woman's taste for politics ; but as the net began to close round the faithful servant, whom every consideration of honour and gratitude bound her husband to save, and whose death was but a calculated preliminary to the downfall of monarchy in England, she felt that it was time to bestir herself. It is easy to use glib phrases about an intriguing woman, but Henriette would be a less attractive figure than she is, had she been so very sensible as to sit by with hands folded while Strafford was butchered in cold blood for the crime of loyalty.

It is hard to blame her for doing everything she could to bring her personal influence to bear upon the most uncompromising, or, as she herself put it—"*méchants*"—of the opposition leaders, and to endeavour to find some basis of conciliation. Night after night one or other of these redoubtable bosses would be conducted by a private staircase to the room of a maid of honour, who happened to be away in the country, and there, by the light of a solitary torch, that she herself carried, the Queen of England would interview him—imploring, offering every imaginable concession. Poor woman ! She little realized the nature of the men with whom she was dealing ; or that the only consideration likely to have prompted them in accepting her invitation, was the chance of entrapping or pumping her into some useful admission.

When the first contact was made between the Court and the discontented officers, it was too much to expect that she should have refused them what she granted even to Pym—the courtesy of a hearing. It is easy enough for us to see that this would have been the wisest course. But it was much to ask of her, in the desperate straits to which she was driven, that she should concede to

Mr Pym and his friends a monopoly of plotting, and coldly snub these gallant gentlemen who, when all the world was forsaking her, were ready to put their swords at her service. The go-between was her Master of the Horse, Sir Henry Jermyn, one of those perfect courtiers whose key to success in life is a cultivated charm, and a faculty of rendering themselves indispensable to the right people. Jermyn had already become, what he was to remain through good and evil fortune, indispensable to the Queen as her confidential assistant, adviser, and companion. There were even those who, after the King's death, credited him with being her consort in secret. That is almost certainly nonsense—the relationship, which was cordially encouraged by Charles, was not of that sort, though no doubt Jermyn, who had earned for himself something of the reputation of a Don Juan, was hardly capable of addressing a woman without some subtly flattering implication of tenderness. But that was, after all, part of the technique of indispensability.

Jermyn was naturally *au fait* with the gay set to which Goring and Suckling belonged, and being genuinely loyal, was ready to go to any lengths with them. The Queen, as a matter of fact, seems to have been more sensible than her husband of the danger of letting Jermyn get mixed up with the affair ; for Charles, without committing himself, was characteristically anxious to explore every possible avenue to Strafford's deliverance. He thought, the Queen records, that all ought to be risked for so great a good. But it did not take long to convince him that the project was a blind alley—particularly when it became a question of military counter-revolution : "All these ways are vain and foolish, I will think of them no more," was his last word on the subject.

It would have been more prudent had it been his first. For these roysterers were not of the Guy Fawkes breed. Most of them were playing their own individual hands, and few were seriously prepared to stake life and fortune on a throw. Least of all were they game for a march on London under the leadership of Goring. A Goring dictatorship was, in fact, a prospect whose attractions were apparent to nobody except Goring himself. Percy and the more moderate section were neither willing to accept him as Lieutenant-General, nor yet to commit themselves to a breach with the Commons. Wilmot would have gone as far as Goring— with himself as leader. Any attempt to proceed from talk to deed was bound, under these circumstances, to end in hopeless disagreement.

It was soon apparent to Goring that the daring and desperate venture he advocated was not practicable, and that the supreme control for which he had bargained was not in the least likely to be conceded to him. This not only seriously piqued him, but placed him in a very awkward dilemma, for if he were merely to wash his hands of the conspiracy, sooner or later the part he had proposed to play would only too probably come to one of Pym's many ears, and then ... there was only one way out of it. Goring would put himself on the winning side by quietly betraying the whole plot, and making out that his own part, from the first, had been that of an honest detective ; he even had the superb audacity to assert that he had "propounded impossibilities to divert them from their thoughts." All this was imparted to the opposition chiefs in the strictest secrecy, and when Goring went down to take his command at Portsmouth, the Queen was assured that if the worst came to the worst, here at least she was sure of a refuge under the protection of this simple and loyal soldier.

Whatever Pym's private opinion may have been about Goring's story and character, it was obviously his cue to welcome the newcomer into the fold in no doubting spirit. But with masterly restraint he kept his knowledge to himself, until the time came when he could make the deadliest use of it. A military plot ! That was a godsend indeed—the very scare he needed to make sure of Strafford's head, and of consummating the revolution to which its taking off would open the way.

14

SUPREME ACCEPTANCE

It was on Saturday, the 24th of April, the day following the King's renewal of his pledge to Strafford, that the first blow was struck in the new and deadly offensive that was to force him from his last, and seemingly impregnable, line of defence. Among the many means of opposition propaganda, none had been more effective than the manufacture of petitions, which had already been forthcoming in great numbers, bristling with grievances, to force the pace of revolutionary legislation in the Long Parliament, and to strengthen the hands of Pym and his confederates.

Now, at the exactly appropriate moment, came a petition from London itself, purporting to be signed by 20,000 of its citizens, anticipating the result of Trial and Attainder, and demanding Strafford's blood, on the very practical ground that it would be good for trade to have him put out of the way. This was obviously intended as something more than a hint for the Lords, whose business during the next week would be with the Attainder, and whose mood appeared to be stiffening against being rushed by the Lower House, into what was becoming more and more openly the barefaced murder of one of their number.

Another object of the London Petition—and we can see with what scientific forethought, the plain mark of a directing genius, the whole thing was being engineered—was to stoke up the Popery scare, by demanding that Catholics should be disarmed and persecuted to the full extent of the law, and also that Charles's Irish army should be disbanded. The Commons were at once made to take this up and, after a conference of both Houses, pass on the request to the King. On Wednesday, accordingly, he summoned them to his presence, and after a conciliatory assurance about disarming Catholics, proceeded to do what was a fatally undiplomatic thing, by answering them with what must have been maddening, because unanswerable reasonableness, pointing out that such a unilateral disarmament would present some difficulty in practice, and begging them to advise him how it could be done.

"I conjure you," he said, "as you will answer the same to God and to the country, to join with me heartily and speedily in disbanding the two armies in England ; to which end there are two things requisite ; money and the conclusion of the Scots treaty."

To his simple mind it must have appeared sheerly inconceivable that any responsible Englishman could have seriously expected him to disarm the loyal forces, while the enemy lay encamped on English soil, still less that the last thing the Patriots were likely to do was to throw in their political hand by getting rid of this incubus.

Pym had scored the exact point that he must have foreseen ; the King had refused to redress a grievance, and another nail had been knocked into Strafford's coffin.

The day before, the Attainder had entered on its Second Reading in the Lords. On Thursday, the House listened to a long legal argument, on behalf of the Commons, from the Solicitor-General, St John, a three hours' catalogue of precedents, raked up from the law books of the past few centuries—a recital that only threw into more brazen relief the one or two sentences towards the end, in which the learned advocate came to the real point, namely, that in Strafford's case they might, with a clear conscience, dispense with the law altogether, because, in St John's own, almost unbelievable words :

"It was never accounted either cruelty or foul play, to knock foxes and wolves on the head, as they can be found, because these be beasts of prey."

It was no wonder that Strafford, listening in silence, should have raised hands and eyes to heaven in horrified appeal.

On that same day another significant thing happened. The London mob started rioting in the streets—the first fruits of the No Popery drive. It was their first blind instinct to pull down the Spanish embassy and kill the ambassador—it needed the personal intervention of the Lord Mayor to stop them. Mr Pym must have smiled when he heard of it : the last ally had taken the field, and all was going according to plan.

Charles himself was beginning to have some inkling of the danger ; for the first time, it would seem, he had become seriously alarmed for Strafford's life. The game had arrived at that supremely critical phase when a single false move would tilt the balance irrevocably. And in nine such cases out of ten, that move may be expected to come from him whose heart is most warmly concerned with the issue. Pym was making no mistakes ; move had followed move with calculated accuracy. Charles had even yet hardly begun to realize what game his opponent was playing.

His salvation now, as Strafford at least realized, was in a masterly inaction. The one chance of the Lords throwing out the Attainder was in the unwillingness of every Englishman, Peer or Commoner, to be driven, and the Commons were driving the Lords dangerously hard. They might be driven even harder, in the next few days—till they turned and would go no further. For this reason it was of the first importance for the Crown to refrain from the least appearance of trying to influence them in the contrary direction.

Had Charles been a Prince in the Machiavellian tradition, no doubt he would have left the running to Pym, and kept himself discreetly in the background. But he was desperately, and honourably, eager to do something—anything—to save his friend, and to redeem his pledge. And there was scarcely any reliable counsellor left him in this extremity. The accounts are conflicting, but if we may trust that of Clarendon, which seems most perfectly to fit in with the rest of the story, it would appear that the King allowed himself to be advised by—of all people— the new Privy Councillor, Lord Saye ; and by whom Saye was likely to have been primed we can guess. It would certainly have been Pym's master-stroke, could he have furnished his adversary with instructions to play into his hands.

That, at any rate, was what Charles did, and in the most fatally plausible way. He again, on the last day of the week, summoned both Houses into his presence. He begged them to believe that there had never been the least question of bringing, an Irish army to England, or of altering the laws—"I think nobody," he said, "durst ever be so impudent as to move me to it." He was willing to allow Strafford to be debarred henceforth from occupying any position of trust, even if it were that of constable ; but he could not, in his conscience, convict him of anything worse than misdemeanour.

"My Lords," he pleaded, "I hope you know what a tender thing conscience is ; yet I must declare unto you that to satisfy my people I would do great matters ; but this of conscience, no fear, no respect whatever, shall ever make me go against it. Certainly I have not so ill deserved of the Parliament at this time, that they should press me in this tender point ; and therefore I cannot expect that you will go about it."

It is difficult to read this appeal, so heartrending in its transparent sincerity, and understand how it was that in this audience of subjects, who had so often overwhelmed their King with professions of their love and loyalty, it could have fallen upon deaf, and worse than deaf, ears. But that the King should have intimated, however humbly, his refusal to violate his conscience by conniving at an innocent's man's death, was twisted into an intolerable defiance. Worse still, it was discovered that in admitting to as much knowledge of a Bill still under discussion as was in fact possessed by the whole of London, His Majesty had violated the sacred privileges of Parliament.

The tilt had been given to the delicate balance. From this point we can say, with something approaching certainty, that nothing but some false move on Pym's part, that he was not likely to make, could have saved Strafford.

Next day was Easter Sunday, and a great day at the Court, for the first royal wedding, since that one at Canterbury sixteen years ago, was to take place. Prince William of Orange, a boy of fifteen, had come over to marry the little Princess Mary, who was only nine. It was a marriage that the King and Queen of England would have thought terribly beneath their dignity only a short time ago, but now they had come down in the world enough for Charles at least to grasp at it with eagerness, especially as it might be hoped that this alliance with Calvinist Holland would do something to conciliate Parliament. As a matter of fact, it only produced a fresh crop of rumours about his dark designs of using Dutch troops and guilders to overawe Parliament—for the last thing that the opposition wanted was that the King should, under any circumstances, have the credit for doing anything right.

The age of this extremely young couple was typical of the dreadful unreality that invested the splendour and pageantry of the proceedings, and culminated in bride and bridegroom, by way of formal consummation, being made to get together into one big bed, and there to remain for two hours with curtains undrawn, in presence of the whole Court, after which the King took off young William, of whom he was very fond, to sleep in his own bedchamber. One of the guests was, or ought to have been, the Elector Palatine, who chose to go off and sulk by himself, on the ground that poor little Mary's immature charms should, by right, have been his.

What dark fears or suppressed agony lurked in the bosoms of the bride's parents, or of the poor old grandmother, Marie de Medici, who was on the point of being driven back into her poverty-stricken exile from a kingdom where her life was no longer safe, we can but dimly imagine. Before Charles's eyes must certainly have floated the vision of a solitary man, sitting in his stone-walled room ... and, less certainly, of another man, in his lodgings close by, putting the last touches to certain arrangements.

That very morning an event had occurred the news of which must have struck like a note of doom on his heart. He had ordered

Captain Billingsley, with a company of infantry, to reinforce the Tower garrison. The Governor was Sir William Balfour, a trusted officer, who had held the appointment for the last eleven years. Balfour was a Puritan Scot of the sternest persuasion—he had once thrashed a priest whom he had found trying to convert his wife—and was, according to his lights, an upright man. He had some reason for being suspicious, for there were stories of plots afoot to get Strafford away, of a mysterious ship lying in the Thames. He was determined to take no risks, and flatly refused to admit the new-comers. It was an act of open defiance and mutiny by the commander of the first fortress in the Kingdom ; the real beginning of the civil war. And Charles was helpless to resent it.

Next day the storm that Pym had been sedulously brewing, broke with full violence. The Lords were slowing up the Attainder in a way that quite exhausted the patience of those simple souls who had been taught to believe that some frightful and imminent catastrophe could only be averted by the sacrifice of Black Tom. It is almost impossible for us to imagine the susceptibility to panic, about anything or nothing, that intensive propaganda, by pamphlet, sermon, and rumour, had engendered in the London crowd. The Roman mob staged by Shakespeare was wise and temperate by comparison. There was no story too extravagant to be believed, particularly if it could be fastened on to the Papists, who, if not capable of setting the Thames on fire, were credited, according to one story, with undermining it, in order to blow it up, and thus flood the whole city !

On Monday morning, before the sitting had begun, the entrance to the House of Lords was beseiged by a howling mob, several thousands strong, consisting partly of "porters, carmen, and other dissolute and rude fellows," but also, it would seem, containing a fair proportion of substantial citizens. Every lord who came out or in had to run the gauntlet, while they swarmed round him bellowing "in a loud hideous voice"* their slogan of "justice and execution."

Arundel, who, as Lord Steward, naturally came in for special attention, tried to put them off with a promise of justice, but they refused to let him go till they had extracted one for execution into the bargain, and even then he only got away from them with difficulty, amid growls of, "we will take your word for once."

As for Bristol, who was known to be working for a compromise,

* Baillie, *Letters*, I, 351.

he was denounced as an apostate to the cause of Christ, and threatened, along with his "false son Lord Digby," with the same fate as Strafford. One voice was even heard to cry,

"If we have not the Lieutenant's life, we will have the King's !"

Terror was abroad with a vengeance, and it was not only the Peers to whom it was applied. That day a paper was posted up at the corner of Sir William Brunkhard's house, in Old Palace Yard, as well as in various places in the City, in which the names of fifty-six Members of the Lower House, substantially identical with those who had voted against the Attainder, were listed under the caption, "These are Straffordians, Betrayers of their Country," and followed by the open threat, "This and more shall be done to the enemies of justice before written." Never since Parliament began, had there been so monstrous a breach of Privilege, and it was evident that this strikingly accurate list must have been supplied from inside knowledge. And yet neither Pym, nor Hampden, nor any of the great champions of Parliamentary liberties, raised a finger or spoke a word in protest.

Pym had quite other work on hand. Victory was in sight, and it was time to strike as hard and as often as possible. The Scottish Revolution had started with a No-Popery Covenant; what could be more appropriate than to come out with an English equivalent ? The ground was skilfully prepared by Pym, who, without even yet disclosing his full hand, made their flesh creep with information he professed to have received of desperate designs, oaths of secrecy, endeavours to disaffect the army, a plot to seize the Tower, and a wholly imaginary French army that was supposed to be approaching the Picard coast with the object of taking ship for Portsmouth. In the debate that followed, a certain Sir John Wray did the expected thing, by exhorting the Members to become holy pilgrims and loyal Covenanters, and take a national oath, and "not a Straffordian or prelatical one"—as he was careful to add.

No sooner said than done. The Oath or Protestation in question was ready drafted, and in the excited temper of the House there was no doubt about its being signed. It was deliberately intended as a test, whereby anybody refusing to sign might be marked down as a public enemy. Next day it was to be presented to the Lords, and after that, like the Covenant, to the whole nation.

The events of that day had sufficed to convince one observer, at least, that Pym's immediate objective was now in his grasp.

Calmly surveying the situation from his solitary room, Strafford came to the conclusion that nothing now could stop the Attainder going through the Lords. In a day or two, at the most, all that would stand between him and death would be the solitary figure of the King, armed with nothing but his veto, and exposed to the full fury of a populace worked up to the madness of panic. That Charles would honour his pledge, even to death, Strafford had not it in him to doubt. But the odds, as he must have reckoned them up, were overwhelming.

Loyalty had been the master passion of Strafford's soul. The supreme test had now come, and not for a moment did he hesitate. Summoning to his aid all his powers of tact and persuasiveness, he took up his pen to perform what he must have felt to be the well-nigh hopeless task of persuading Charles to accept release from his pledge of kingly honour.

He recalled how the constant burden of his advice had been to procure a happy understanding between King and people, and to persuade His Majesty to cast himself entirely on the loyalty and affection of his English subjects. Now, however, he found himself branded as a sower of dissension between them, and "under a heavier censure than this," wrote Black Tom the Tyrant, "I am persuaded no gentleman can suffer."

And so he was brought into a very great strait. Before him on the one hand was the ruin of his children, and a family whose honour had never yet been touched by any aspersion of crime ; on the other, the ills that must result to the King and the whole kingdom from a breach between Crown and Parliament. "Here are before me the things most valued, most feared, by mortal men, life or death."

"To say, Sir," he went on, "that there hath not been a strife in me, were to make me less man than, God knoweth, my infirmities make me ; and to call a destruction upon myself and young children (where the intentions of my heart, at least, have been innocent of this great offence) may be believed, will find no easy consent from flesh and blood."

To pronounce his own death sentence is easy for no man, and least of all for one in whom the creative energy, which is life, is so strong. But in such a mind as Strafford's there could be no real doubt. It best became him, he decided, to regard the welfare of the King's sacred Person and the Commonwealth as things infinitely before any man's private interest. It was on these grounds that he now not only released Charles from his promise, but implored him, in the public interest, to consummate the act of murderous injustice that should send him to the scaffold.

"Sir, my consent shall more herein acquit you to God than all the world can do besides ; to a willing man there is no injury done : and as, by God's grace, I forgive all the world, with a calmness and meekness of infinite contentment to my dislodging soul ; so, Sir, to you I can give the life of this world with all the cheerfulness imaginable, in just acknowledgment of your exceeding favours. ... God long preserve Your Majesty !"

Thus, through greatness of soul, had Lord Strafford made the supreme acceptance. Never had he put forth his energy and skill with less stint than in this task of compassing his own destruction. But when all was done ; when the letter was signed and sealed and on its way to Whitehall—did he in his heart of hearts believe that he had been successful ? He must have known what he himself would have done with such a permission.

15

PYM'S MASTERSTROKE

WHAT was apparent to Strafford cannot have passed unperceived by the equally penetrating eye of his great adversary. The defence was crumbling ; the pressure had only to be kept up, and still further intensified, for the whole line to give way in hopeless rout. Pym had two vital points of resistance still to overcome. The first of these, the Upper Chamber, had become untenable by its now thoroughly demoralized garrison, and when that fell—as it might at any moment—the pressure on the Crown would become overwhelming.

But not even Strafford can have grasped the full scope and subtlety of Pym's plan. It is evident, from his letter, that he fondly imagined that his own death would satisfy the demands of the opposition, and open the way to future co-operation between the King and his Commons. But with Pym, the elimination of Strafford was but a means to an end. He had in contemplation a *coup* the most audacious and revolutionary on English record, the effect of which would be to cut not only the power of the King, but also that of the people, out of the Constitution, and to substitute an oligarchy under the control—if all worked out to plan—of King Pym and his associates.

The beauty of the plan was this—that Pym had calculated upon foisting this tremendous change on the country without anybody noticing it or realizing what had happened. This he designed to effect, by rushing through, along with the Attainder, another short Act making the present Parliament perpetual, except in the highly improbable and—if he knew anything about it—impossible, eventuality of its committing *hara-kiri* by dissolving itself. When that had become law, then perhaps the opposition chiefs would be able to sleep quietly in their beds. For never again were they likely to see a Parliament so ideally constituted from their own point of view. The election had been a landslide in their favour ; and as if this had not been enough, the triumphant majority did not hesitate to doctor the composition of the House by keeping a sharp eye on doubtful Members, and then, if any possible excuse could be found for disputing their elections, of voting them out of their seats. Even so, signs had not been wanting of a certain restiveness even among the well-disciplined ranks of the Commons, the first symptoms—it might be—of a moderate or counter-revolutionary reaction. But this Pym might count on keeping under reasonable control in such an assembly of picked extremists. What he dared not face was the weapon that the Constitution had put into the King's hands, of dissolving Parliament at his chosen moment—which would be when the reaction had gathered sufficient strength—and appealing to an electorate that might quite conceivably return him a royalist majority. And then, it might well be that Strafford's vacated lodging in the Tower would put up another traveller by the same road. Pym would prevent this, even at the cost of ending, or indefinitely suspending, the Constitution.

The Bill that was drafted, forbidding the King to dissolve or even adjourn Parliament without its own consent, was as short and unpretentious as it could be made, and bore an innocent looking preamble, to the effect that it had become necessary to afford additional security to those to whom the House applied for loans.

To smuggle this through, without its significance being appreciated, it was necessary to work up popular excitement to a climax.

On Tuesday, the day that Strafford had written to the King, the mob was out again, noticeably rougher and tougher than the day before, and succeeded in presenting a petition demanding Strafford's instant execution, to avert the sudden destruction of King and kingdom. London was, in fact, mad with panic, and no rumour was too dreadful to find credit. As if the opposition propaganda agencies were not enough, the egregious Suckling had made his contribution by collecting, on Sunday, sixty armed and probably thirsty individuals, in the appropriate location of a tavern.

The ground was fully prepared, now, for Pym to tell the world all, and considerably more than all, that he had found out about the terrible army plot that Goring had revealed to him. The myth of the French invasion and seizure of Portsmouth was, of course, exploited for all it was worth. It was more than ever valuable for Pym's purposes, because it was possible to involve the Queen in it. For in this London, given over to panic-stricken blood lust, it was evident that the lives of the Royal Family could no longer be considered safe, and least of all that of the Catholic Queen, who was the target of every sort of calumny. There had been talk of flight ; the King would go to York and throw himself on the loyalty of his army, and Henriette would seek shelter in Portsmouth, under the protection of him whom she still thought of as the devoted and chivalrous Goring. Nothing that was whispered in the palace failed to get to Pym's ears, and it was at once put about that this terrible woman was going down to Portsmouth in order to hand it over to the army of her countrymen she had invited over to conquer England.

By this time the Commons had been worked up to as acute a climax of hysteria as the mob itself. A certain Sir Walter Earle was helping on the good work by informing them of a conspiracy, that he had just discovered, to blow them all sky high, in the good old Guy Fawkes way. This news worked so much upon the feelings of two very portly Members sitting in the gallery, that they leapt to their feet, causing a board beneath them to give an audible crack. The ominous sound seemed to the House the confirmation of their direst fears, and Sir John Wray, who had so recently exhorted them to be holy pilgrims, now jumped up with the announcement that he smelt gunpowder. At this there was a stampede of fear-stricken legislators out of the House and the galleries, through the lobby, and thence into the hall, shouting that the Parliament House was fallen and the members slain. In vain did one valiant soul, Sir Robert Mansel, with drawn sword strive to rally the flying rout. They rushed past him, some into the street, and some to any boats there were available to row them from the scene of danger. These latter carried the alarm to the City, and excited citizens were crowding tumultuously to Westminster to save their representatives from they knew not what. In the midst of the hubbub were heard the drums and tramp of a regiment of Trained Bands, whom their Colonel had, with great presence of mind, mobilized, and marched upon Covent Garden, whence, finding no enemy worthy of his steel, he brought them safely home again.

Meanwhile the Commons, or such of them as had dared to remain in their gunpowder-scented House, were dealing with the situation as if the French armada had already been sighted. Peremptory orders were dispatched to close the ports ; to call out the Wiltshire and Berkshire militia for the defence of Portsmouth ; to take measures for the security of Kent and the Channel Islands ; to press additional sailors into the navy. The Queen was humbly entreated not to go to Portsmouth, since none knew what danger she might incur ; which was the polite way of saying that whatever danger she might incur by staying in London, stay she must. She embraced the necessity without flinching.

Finally, the arrest was ordered of those foolish young officers whom Goring had vainly endeavoured to enlist for a military *coup d'état*, and whom he had subsequently denounced as heads of a military plot.

They did not wait to be seized, but made off at the first warning overseas. All got away, except D'Avenant, though Jermyn had a narrow escape, since, by a natural instinct, he had fled to join his friend Goring at Portsmouth. But there were depths of treachery to which even Goring could not descend, and though he had actually received instructions for Jermyn's arrest, he hurried him on board ship, and then lied with his usual blandness to Parliament that their orders had unfortunately arrived just too late. It was with no humorous intention that the Commons voted that Colonel Goring had done nothing contrary to justice and honour.

Amid all this panic and preparation to die in the last ditch against non-existent enemies, nobody noticed that something had been quietly accomplished, that was fraught with deadlier peril to the country than the Spanish Armada itself had been. For in the excitement, that Act of revolution, making the existing Parliament a perpetual oligarchy, was rushed through all its stages in the Commons practically without opposition. On Friday it was introduced into the Lords, who did at least make a feeble suggestion that its operation should be limited to two years. But Pym was having no nonsense of that sort, and their Lordships quickly dropped the point.

The end was now at hand. After the lesson they had had during the week, it was common knowledge that the Upper House would come to heel at the crack of Pym's whip. No consideration of right or justice any longer swayed its decisions. Even Bristol had retired from the fight in hopeless despair. It is practically certain that on a free vote, in a full House, Strafford would never have been condemned. Only thirty-seven Peers could be whipped up, on Saturday morning, to vote for his final condemnation. But only eleven noblemen could be found with enough of nobility in them to risk their skins for their consciences. The rest contrived to stop away.

That same fraction of the House completed its allotted task by passing the No-Dissolution Bill.

Whatever else the House of Lords had done that morning, it had utterly shattered its hitherto considerable power and prestige. For the next few years it contrived to drag on an ignominious existence, until, having ceased to be either useful or respected, it was ignominiously closed down pending the restoration of the monarchy that its own nobility had so signally betrayed.

16

BILLS FOR SIGNATURE

NOT a moment was lost in sending the two Bills across to Whitehall for the final act of surrender. The supreme crisis of King Charles's life had now arrived. The demand, which his nobles had conceded, to their shame and undoing, was passed on to him. It was that he should yield to overwhelming force, and sanction what he

knew to be, in itself, an act of murderous injustice ; and incidentally—though this he may not have realized—the virtual abolition
of representative government in England. He had to choose
whether he should honour his kingly word, and obey the dictates
of his conscience, regardless of all practical considerations ;
whether, in the last resort, he was ready to immolate his throne
and family on an altar of abstract principle, without even the
prospect of averting Strafford's doom.

To some rare and heroic spirits there would have been no choice
in the matter. Without thinking of the consequences, they would
have answered, out of the depths of their moral being, and in the
most literal sense of the words,

"Sign ? I'll be damned if I do."

That, or its equivalent, would have been the unhesitating
answer of a Strafford. It would also have been the answer of that
equally gallant gentleman, Don Quixote de la Mancha.

It appears to have been the first impulse of Charles himself.
To the deputation of Peers that waited upon him for his signature,
he returned a blank negative. But so plain and brutal a refusal was
repugnant to his nature, nor could anything have been more
impolitic than the appearance of riding roughshod over the will
of Parliament. No blame can therefore attach to him, that at the
second time of asking, he consented to receive both Houses in the
afternoon, and give them his answer in person. It was presumably
his intention both to give and to justify his refusal in the most
conciliatory manner possible.

But by the afternoon the situation had already got out of control.
The invisible grip of Mr Pym was on the King's throat, tightening
every moment. His genius for mass-suggestion was now put to
the supreme test. After the state of wild hysteria in which the
mob had been maintained all through the week, it must have
seemed an almost superhuman task not only to hold off
the inevitable reaction of overstrained nerves, but actually to
work up the fury and panic to the required climax of insane
strength during this all-important week-end. But Pym was equal
to a task that might have overtaxed the resources of a Hearst or
a Goebbels.

The closing of the ports, like so many of Pym's moves, compassed not only a direct, but an indirect and more important
objective. Even three days of stagnation on the Thames were
enough to prevent a good many ships from putting to sea ; and

to turn loose their crews, without work or pay, to employ themselves in looting or rioting, was to form just the same sort of spearhead as the Marseillese were to prove for the Paris mob that stormed the palace of Louis XVI. The mob, therefore, employed to terrorize the Crown, was an even more dangerous monster than that which had already put the fear of Pym into the hearts of the Lords.

The propaganda barrage was quickened up to drumfire intensity. Every sort of rumour ran riot. The wholly imaginary French war had opened with a blood-curdling disaster—the enemy fleet was reported to have seized the Channel Islands. The Papists were ready to rise ; the Northern army to march on London ; at this very moment the armies of Louis XIII might be disembarking at Portsmouth, whose fall, if it had not occurred already, was hourly expected : to old men it must have seemed as if the Armada days had come again, with the trifling difference of there being no Armada on the horizon. But for panicking the mob a phantom Armada was every bit as good as a real one, if not better. Only by the magic act of removing Black Tom's head, would it be possible to save the country from the most horrible horror of horrors that it was possible to imagine.

Before the Houses had arrived at Whitehall, the appalling news had come through to the Court of Goring's treason. The secure refuge to which Charles had still counted on getting his wife, in case of emergency, had been handed over to Pym's emissaries. He must have felt that they were caught, like rats in a trap, in this mad London.

When the Lords and Commons arrived at Whitehall, the mob arrived with them, only too plainly bent on storming the palace if the King's answer took the form of a refusal. He was utterly without the force to resist them. To have answered as he had intended, would have been to precipitate a catastrophe in which the Queen, on whom the bitterest hatred of the populace was focused, would only too probably have been torn limb from limb. With melancholy eyes Charles took stock of these subjects of his who had forgone their allegiance. For the second time that day, he decided to temporize. He therefore dismissed the Lords and Commons, promising them that they should have his final answer on Monday. Again, it is difficult to see what other sane choice was left to him.

Even as it was, it was touch and go whether the mob would not have proceeded to extremities there and then. They were not in a mood to wait over the week-end for the surrender they had come to exact. But while they were still in that state of leaderless suspense in which any chance impulse might have sent them surging forward, an ecclesiastic—and from subsequent events it is not difficult to guess who—took upon himself to appear at a window, and promise them a favourable answer, in other words Strafford's death sentence, on Monday. By thus compromising the King, he at least gained time, if only a matter of hours.

II

Double Surrender

I

LONDON COMES TO WHITEHALL

IT was Sunday, the second after Easter, in the year 1641. The date was the 9th of May, though by our modern reckoning it would correspond to the 22nd or the 23rd, and the hawthorns in what was even then known as St James's Park must have been foaming over with blossom ; for that comparatively recently reclaimed marshland had not yet been formalized, as it was to be in the next reign, by the amalgamation of its various pools into one ornamental canal, flanked by avenues of unswerving correctitude, and with the massive fabric of what is now Buckingham Palace for a background. That site, at the time of which we are speaking, was occupied by a royal mulberry garden, and the only avenue was one of trees that followed the line of the present Mall, and connected the subsidiary palace of St James, on the North side, with that of Whitehall—a walk of some ten minutes or, to so brisk a walker as the then owner of the two palaces, perhaps not so many.

Unlike St James's, Whitehall did not give directly on to the Park. It was masked by the line of its own outbuildings—tennis court, cockpit, and so forth ; though high over all their roofs must have towered the facade of the new Banqueting Hall, the masterpiece of a still living architectural genius, the Welsh Inigo Jones, and by him intended to be first constituent of a vast design, covering 24 acres, that would make every palace in Europe seem puny by comparison. But though the spirit was willing—for no monarch had ever been more capable than King Charles of appreciating noble architecture—the resources were lacking, and His Majesty had wisely resolved to devote what little he could scrape together, to the comparatively inexpensive hobby of collecting pictures. He had, therefore, made do with the untidy complex of buildings that had originally housed the more than regal magnificence of Cardinal Wolsey, and which, since its inevitable appropriation by Wolsey's master, Henry VIII, had

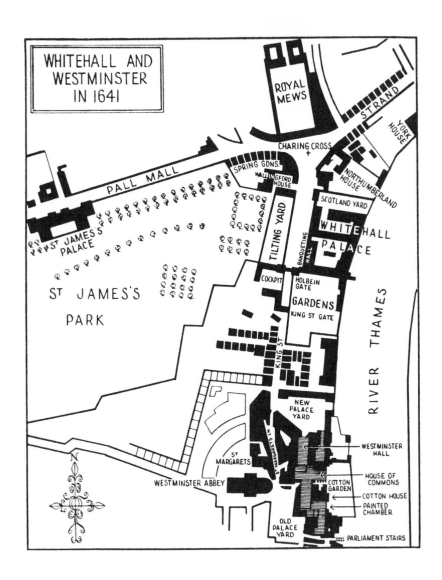

been added to piecemeal by him and his successors, until the best that could be said of it was that it was "a good hypocrite, promising less than it performeth, and more convenient within than comely without".

These Tudor buildings, so painfully out of proportion and harmony with the severely classical style of the Banqueting Hall, lay on the north or Charing Cross side of it. In front was not a street, as now, but a spacious enclosure, a *cul de sac* open at the north end and broad enough, with the addition of the Royal Tilting Ground, that included most of what is now the Horse Guards, to accommodate as big a crowd as even London was capable of disgorging. In the sack's mouth, almost on what is now the site of King Charles's own statue, stood the lovely Eleanor Cross of Charing—though it would not be suffered to stand for long. At the otherwise closed South end, access was given to Westminster through a turreted and battlemented gateway built to the design of no less an architect than the painter Holbein. Beyond this, and another gateway whose turrets had domed instead of embattled tops, rose what had been a royal palace long before the days of Whitehall, but which now accommodated the two Houses of Parliament. Most conspicuous among its cluster of buildings was Westminster Hall, said to be the work of William Rufus. Behind loomed the sombre mass of Westminster Abbey, where so many Kings and Queens lay sleeping, among them the father of the reigning monarch, and his tragic grandmother who had perished in the Hall at Fotheringay by the executioner's axe.

It was such a day, and, from the upper windows of the palace, such a prospect, as were most calculated to rejoice the heart, in an England that still retained the style of merry, and so many of whose songs rang changes on the theme of

O the month of May, the merry month of May,
So frolic and so gay, and so green, so green, so green !

But it is unlikely that any eyes in the palace, except perhaps those of the little princes and princesses, can have had a glance to spare even for the loveliest of prospects, or that in any heart there can have stirred the faintest chord of merriment. Grimmer business was on hand than that of Maying. In passages and on stairways gentlemen, in their incongruously gay court attire, were making hasty preparations for defence. Out of sight, in the Queen's apartments, other gentlemen and ladies, of a proscribed faith, were making what might be their dying confessions to Capuchin fathers, who themselves expected nothing better than martyrdom in the event that no one would have dreamed possible before yesterday, but which had now become one of imminent probability—the storming of the King's palace by his own subjects.

How probable, any one could have judged for himself who looked out of one of the palace windows. For the enclosed space on the Park side was swarming with "a rabble", as one observer described it, "of many thousand people",* excited and vociferous, the London mob in its ugliest mood, working itself up, in the way mobs do, towards the detonating pitch of concerted violence. That mob had come swarming up the road from the City to Westminster with diurnal regularity during the past week. On its first appearance, on Monday, it had been reckoned at about six thousand, "with swords, cudgels and staves" ; since then passion and panic must have swollen its numbers progressively, and it had received a formidable reinforcement from the crews of the ships that were lying idle in the Thames owing to a cunningly timed war scare. But it was only on Saturday afternoon that it had made its first appearance in front of the palace. Previously to that it had been crowding the approaches to Parliament, putting fear into the hearts of such Peers and Commoners as were reputed to be opposed to the will of the people, a will that conformed with weathercock accuracy to that of the junta of plutocratic bosses, or, to give them their more familiar Victorian title, Patriots, who dominated the majority of the Commons. To-day the climax had come, and it was the turn of monarchy to experience this form of democratic persuasion.

That it *was* the climax must have been obvious to every one, both within and outside the palace. The fact of its being Sunday must alone have set free vast numbers who, during the week, would have been tied to their counters and benches ; including the full force of London's apprentices, hefty young fellows largely sprung from prosperous middle and even upper class families, as politically conscious as Continental students nowadays, and at this time militantly Protestant and Parliamentarian. To watchers from the windows it must have been apparent that far

---

* Whitelock's *Memorials*, p. 43.

from the crowd showing any tendency to disperse, it was being reinforced, at uncertain intervals, by a sudden jet or spurt of humanity, indicating the arrival of some belated congregation whose passions had been fomented for anything up to a couple of hours on end by some pulpit-thumping gospeller, who was now bringing them, primed for the Lord's work, up to the scene of necessary action.

The spectacle from the palace windows must have been calculated to daunt the stoutest heart. London had come up to Whitehall—not for the last time. "A rabble of many thousand people besieged that place, crying out *Justice, justice ; that they would have justice* ; not without great threats and expressions what they would do if it were not speedily granted." And as any one can tell who has consulted the immemorial dictionary of mob language, by justice was signified its exact opposite. This mob was out for blood. The hunt was up, and it was a head hunt. The pack, which had been hallooed on to its human quarry all the week, was now in sight of a kill. It would be dangerous, not to say fatal, to oppose it by any other argument than that of overmastering force. And such force was not to be found at Whitehall—not yet ! There had never been a time during a century and a half of Tudor power or Stuart "tyranny", when the Sovereign of England had not been utterly at the mercy of his people, or, when in residence, of the citizens of his own capital. A regular army worth speaking of was a Continental luxury such as no King of England could have afforded, even if he had wanted to. And none of them had.

But then at no time since the dawn of the modern age had the will been present to the people of England—or, within living memory, to any substantial part of them—to use the power that they had always possessed of proceeding against their Sovereign by violence. That would have been treason, the most abhorred of all crimes, and the one for which there was the least mercy or popular sympathy. For to strike at the King's power was to strike at his peace, and the King's peace was the guarantee against the return of those bad old days of anarchy and civil war the fear of which, ever since pre-Tudor days, had constituted an obsessive fixation.

But here were the people of London besieging the approaches to the royal palace, and threatening with a myriad tongues to storm it out of hand, unless he, for his part, would consent to deliver over to the hands of the executioner a man whose alleged guilt, by a ghastly irony, was of this very crime of treason.

Which treason notoriously consisted in a too uncompromising loyalty to this Sovereign of whom his blood was required.

2

THE BELEAGUERED PALACE

THRONGING the halls and antechambers of the vast, rambling palace was another mob in a state of equal agitation, but united by no common purpose such as terror and propaganda had instilled into the crowd outside. Here loyal courtiers who, whatever their political opinions, were prepared to die in defence of their Sovereign, rubbed shoulders with titled magnates who were shortly destined to take the field against him ; here were friends of Black Tom, like his secretary, Sir George Radcliffe, to whom he was not a tyrant but an idolized hero, and who were distractedly canvassing any ways and means that might yet be available for delivering him from the trap in which he was held fast, before its teeth had crushed the life out of him ; there were officers on leave from the army in Yorkshire, muttering unadvised things about the Patriot politicians who were bilking them of their pay in order to provide blackmail for the invading army from across the Border, whose peaceful possession of English soil the said Patriots, for reasons of their own, would not suffer to be disturbed —things doubly dangerous because the chief Patriot had eyes and ears everywhere ; there were the ambassadors and agents of foreign Powers, eagerly noting every fresh development of this crisis that had reduced England to a European cipher ; and there were, we may be quite sure, a large proportion of both sexes who even at such a time were only concerned to enjoy each successive thrill of a supremely dramatic situation.

There was enough to satisfy their appetite, even apart from the spectacle without. For there was continual coming and going along the great gallery of Henry VIII, from whose walls now glowed the Titians and blazed the Rubenses added to it by the first connoisseur in Europe. There had been His Majesty's ministers and privy counsellors, there had been the bishops, there had been the judges ; then, after a longer interval, it had been the bishops again. With pre-occupied aspect each new arrival had passed down the long vista, followed by a buzz and murmur of the throng on either hand, to the Horn Chamber, and beyond to where the yeoman halberdiers, in their scarlet, stood on either side of the entrance to the Cabinet Chamber. The doors had opened to receive him and closed behind, and nothing had been heard but the cries without of "Justice ! Justice !", mingled perhaps with others of even more ominous import, amid which *Her* Majesty's name had begun to be distinguishable. And then the doors had been opened and necks craned forward and there was a ripple of excited questioning. Surely this time ? How much longer would *He* take to make up his mind and reconcile his conscience to what every one knew to be inevitable ? When at any moment a word or a cry might give the impulse to these overwrought demonstrators that would unite them in a common purpose of rushing the main entrance. And then it would be too late to decide anything.

3

LODGINGS AT WESTMINSTER

IF there were heavy hearts and racked nerves in Whitehall, there must have been equal anxiety in a little court, hardly a stone's throw away, behind Westminster Hall, that contained the lodgings in which those two redoubtable chiefs of the ruling faction in the Commons, Mr John Pym and Mr John Hampden, found it convenient to reside when the House was in session ; and where the inner ring of plutocratic revolutionaries to which they belonged was in the habit of foregathering, not only to transact its secret business, but also, by common subscription, to keep open table for those "of whose conversion", as Lord Clarendon puts it, "they had any hope".

Mr Pym was not the man to advertise his whereabouts at such a time, but I do not think we shall go far wrong in assuming that he and Hampden were at these headquarters of theirs, keeping in constant touch with a situation that had got beyond even their power to control. It is true that the great gates, with their flanking houses, shut out the view of what was happening in front of the palace ; but the crowd, though invisible, cannot have been inaudible at so short a distance ; and in any case there could have been no mistake about the sound they must have been dreading to hear at any moment, the hoarse roar that would signify that the last bonds of restraint had snapped, and that the assault on the palace had begun.

Though assuredly this formed no part of their programme ! So catastrophic an event as the storming of the King's own palace, with its only too probable accompaniment of the lynching of his Consort, would have raised a storm of revulsion in the country by which they themselves would have been the first to be swept away. It is the supreme proof of Pym's genius, that three centuries before the writing of *Mein Kampf* he had discovered the technique of conditioning mobs, and producing them like aces from his capacious sleeve to over-play the King. But there was a risk attached to the use of such live cards ; for though there is a black art, known to its masters, of raising the devil in masses of men, the wizard has yet to be born capable of laying that devil, except by a whiff of grapeshot or its equivalent, once it has taken uncontrolled possession.

Pym had hitherto played his difficult game, move by move, with a combination, seldom equalled, of daring and calculation. And now that he had both his Sovereign and his rival in his grip, and was on the verge of bringing off the greatest coup in English political history, there was this unpredictable hitch putting everything in jeopardy.

Who could have thought it of a King, who had up to now meekly conceded every demand that even this Parliament—which was as good as to say Pym himself—had made upon him, that he would sit balancing and deliberating in face of the overwhelming concentration of forces, partly of terror and partly of persuasion, that had been brought to bear on him for this last push over the edge ? Were it not at least better to surrender at discretion and be maintained in such dignity as it might be judged safe to concede to a crowned puppet and mouthpiece, than to immolate himself, his throne, and everybody dear to him, for the sake of presenting his vanquishers with a posthumous tit for tat ?

But the die was cast and there was nothing to do now but to stand the hazard. No one can have been better aware than such hardbitten players for sovereignty as the Patriot chiefs, that the greater the stakes in the game, the greater the risks. And the stakes for which they were playing were as high as any on political record. It was not only Lord Strafford's head that they looked to sweep into their winnings ; the taking off of that was an essential preliminary—for while it was on they could never feel their own secure upon their shoulders—but still only a preliminary to the dazzling prize now almost within their grasp.

For though Mr Pym had slipped his card so skilfully that to this day the sleight has almost escaped the attention of historians, and even, in at least one instance, that of his own biographers, what His Majesty had lying on his table for signature was not one Bill but two : the first of these providing for the liquidation of Lord Strafford ; the second for the conversion of the existing House of Commons, which Mr Pym could now fairly count upon keeping obediently responsive to his own control, into a close corporation or oligarchy, incapable of being dissolved except in the wildly improbable event of its performing that happy dispatch upon itself, and cut off entirely from its constituents, except at occasional by-elections, the results of which could at the worst be easily reversed in the interest of the reigning majority. In short a Bill for the suspension until the Greek Kalends of all that had ever been, or was yet to be, identified with the English notion of Parliamentary government.

That and nothing less was the plain meaning and intention of the short Act that lay on the King's table beside that for the butchering of Strafford, and only needed his assent to make it the law of the land.

The great political artist whose master-stroke it was, would have been more than human if he had not betrayed a certain anxiety to his colleague as the minutes lengthened to hours, and still there was no slackening of the tension within or without the palace, and still the long overdue message failed to arrive, signifying that the irrevocable step had been taken and the way was now open for the unfettered dominance over monarchy, Parliament, and people, of the powerful landed and financial interests combined under the leadership of him who was shortly to be dubbed by the informal, but too modest, title of King— King Pym.

4

THE MAN AT THE COUNCIL BOARD

THE Cabinet Chamber did not look out upon the front of White-hall, but on to the Privy Garden on the River side and the sounds of turmoil can only have penetrated faintly through its closed windows. Could we be transported thither through time, and clothed with invisibility, none of us, even if quite unprepared for the experience, would fail to recognize who it was that occupied the carved and gilded chair at the head of the Council Board. Even so scarcely imaginable a visitor as never to have heard of King Charles, would assuredly know himself at first glance to be in the presence of the King.

Not however by any conscious ostentation of royalty. The man on the chair was richly, but not conspicuously, attired—he favoured sombre rather than gaudy colours. It was only after you had had time to let the impression sink in, that you would have realized why it was that he had struck you as well dressed, in so royally different a sense from flaming dandies about Court like the Earl of Holland : the sense, that Beau Brummell afterwards imparted to the phrase, of an exquisite appropriateness. But unlike that of the Beau, you would have felt that this man's dress was as essentially part of himself in real life, as of his portrait on one of Van Dyck's canvases.

I do not mean to imply that there was about it, or him, any-thing that would have struck you as quite spontaneous or unstudied. Every minutest detail bore the marks of meticulous forethought ; and in that rather slapdash and, to our notions, unhygienic time, what I think would have most struck the modern observer would have been the exquisite neatness and propriety in every detail ; not a ribbon out of place, not a speck on the purity of lace or linen ; the long, essenced curls, the pointed beard, coiffured to the last hair, not foppishly, but exactly—hypercriticism might have said, too exactly. There was a certain Parson Herrick whom his Majesty had presented to a living in remote Devonshire, who might have had something to plead for the advantages of a certain disorder, but luckily for that singu-larly unclerical divine, nothing of his life or works was known to his royal patron.

If you had waited to hear the King speak—and you would not have had to wait long, since for many weary hours he had been in one consultation after another—you would have felt that his speech was as much the expression of his personality as his doublet, and all the more so from being as meticulously studied in every detail as some masterpiece of the goldsmith's art. But when you had listened for a little time you might have begun to feel that a more emphatic word was needed ; this audible attire was not only meticulously, but painfully studied. There was something wrong about it—something not easy, at first, to specify. Not a stammer—but what might, if attention or control had been relaxed for an instant, have developed into a stammer.

But not for the fraction of a second was that attention off the stretch. Charles had not been able to speak at all for his first five years, and he had had to conquer the art as he might some hostile territory, that even when occupied requires to be policed with unremitting vigilance.

Of this vigilance there can—or we should certainly have heard of it—have been no relaxation at this supreme crisis. Even though every minute's postponement of a decision was fraught with mortal peril, we should have perceived no sign of hurry in his speech to these agitated relays of councillors. His words came slowly, and he chose them as carefully as if they had been pictures for his collection. Any attempt to quicken the pace of the discourse, or to hustle him out of his stride, would have been checked by a courteous "By your favour, Sir, I think. ..." and no repetition of the hint would have been called for. For not even those who rebelled and plotted against King Charles ventured on liberties to his face.

As far as the phrase can be used of any Sovereign, there was a divinity that hedged him, a dignity all the more impressive from being wedded to the humility of a Christian gentleman. That hedge was not only a defence but a barrier ; a necessary barrier, but a barrier all the same. In personal interchanges, especially at such a time as this, he was at a chronic disadvantage. The other party had only to think of what he wanted to say, not of how he was going to shape it into words. The meaning, like a torrent, could force its own channel. But King Charles could never give his undivided attention to what he had in mind to say. He had all the time to be thinking of two things at once ; every word and syllable had to be consciously chosen and formed, and perhaps with one of his temperament could be called a minute work of art. That was what was wrong—not that he stammered, but that he had conquered the stammer and had to conquer it anew with every word he spoke.

That was no necessary part of the burden imposed on him by fate. There have been stammerers, like Charles Lamb, who by accepting their weakness have turned it from a liability to an asset. A bell-voiced Elia would lose half his charm for posterity. And more than with lesser folk, the little human foibles of Royalty are a means of endearing them to the common man. Farmer George's "Eh, what ! what ! what !", Sailor George's reputed lapses into nautical language, were no small element of their popularity with their subjects.

It is conceivable that if King Charles had been content to go through life stammering, there would have been no Civil War and no Charles the Martyr. Though whether he or we would have been gainers by that on an ultimate reckoning is more than any of us have the means of finding out on this side of the grave.

We shall be wise, then, to defer the consideration of what might have been, and try to understand what had to be. For if we can talk of any one key to the understanding of King Charles, it is surely this suppressed impediment of his speech.

Not that its total effect is necessarily to be reckoned for loss. If it be held accountable for the long tragedy of his life, it may also have been the means of qualifying him for the hero's part. For those who have most profoundly studied the art of practical psychology are agreed in regarding it as essentially a training in concentration. Now the chafing of King Charles's thorn in the flesh forced him to keep his attention on the stretch without intermission, except when he was alone and without the necessity of speaking. It was thus an education in self-control rarely to be paralleled in the records even of monarchy, where it is needed more emphatically than in any other calling of life.

King Charles was to give proofs of this quality to a degree passing the normal of human capacity. But the most impressive of all had been twelve years previously when he had received, during Mattins, the most agonizing shock that can come to any man, in the news of the murder of the friend to whom he had given, however unworthily, his whole heart, and from whom he had parted only a few hours previously—the Duke of Buckingham ; and when he had remained on his knees, without giving a sign, till service was over and he could retire to his own chamber to ease his heart in weeping. Only such a discipline could have qualified him to enact a victor's part on the tragic scaffold of his own martyrdom.

But there is loss, and that of the most grievous kind, to be taken into the reckoning. For the man who is unable, without taking thought, to articulate a syllable, finds an invisible gulf fixed between himself and the rest of mankind. It is only with difficulty, and by dint of long association, that he is able to establish human contacts ; for where there is no free flow of speech, there is no medium through which such contact can be made ; no common measure, so to speak, of understanding. And thus it is less to be wondered at not only that King Charles should be among the most persistently misunderstood characters in history, but also that he himself should have suffered from a certain slowness in the human uptake. He was both too tardy, and too simple, in his judgments of men. He did not realize, till too late, what he had got in Strafford ; and never at all what he was up against in Pym. The most fatal mistake in his life was to have taken the stage hero in Buckingham for the real thing ; and some might argue that his most fatal lost opportunity was that of exploiting the possibility of human contact with Cromwell. Again and again, in his dealings with men, whether as servants, or counsellors, or enemies, we find him guessing at what, with the gift of free speech, he would have divined intuitively about their characters—and guessing wrong, or what is sometimes worse, mistaking part of the truth for the whole.

The habit of keeping the conscious attention perpetually on the *qui vive* has another effect on the personality that, though it may be counted for gain in the long run, may also be a crippling handicap in the ordinary run of human affairs. King Charles was one of those people who are seldom capable of taking any decision until they have considered it in every aspect, and satisfied themselves that the line proposed is ideally best. Best not only as a means to an end, but still more, as a means to the best end—the end most in conformity with God's Will. For, as I hope the present record will make clear, Charles was a man of sensitive honour and unswerving principle, conscientious, if such a thing be possible, to a fault ; one who, so far as it can be said of any human being, tried to rule his life in the spirit that a divine of the ensuing generation was to crystallize in the lines :

> Let all thy converse be sincere,
> Thy conscience as the noonday clear ;
> Think how all-seeing God thy ways
> And all thy secret thoughts surveys,

of which the latter couplet * might have appealed equally to Oliver Cromwell, though in every other respect these two tragic protagonists were at opposite poles of temperament.

For Cromwell, in one of his flashes of demonic intuition, revealed the heart of *his* secret when he said that a man never rises so high as when he does not know where he is going. And indeed Cromwell made a point of always starting down whatever path lay before him, crashing his way through all opposition to some blind end that he would not have dared to envisage. Charles, on the other hand, was apt to spend so long in pondering over his plans and his principles that, when he had finally satisfied himself that the end was right and the means effective, he might only too easily find, in the words of a later statesman, that he had missed his bus. There are some who will say that it is better, even so, to risk being stranded than violently to board the first bus that comes looming through the fog and trust to the Lord for its destination.

It is significant that Cromwell, when he got into difficulties with his speech, did so not through inhibition, but explosive incoherence.

There is one thing more that needs to be said about this fateful impediment of King Charles's speech. It was not the same always or under all circumstances. There were times, it would seem, when it was less noticeable ; times when he was able to put off his royal dignity, with its accompanying inhibitions, and enter that world of creative art in which it was an honour for the King himself, an honour unique in the annals of English monarchy, to be admitted to converse on a footing of equality with a master ; which he did whenever he could snatch an hour from the weary routine of State business to drop down the Thames in his barge to visit the studio of the friend whom he had dubbed Sir Anthony Van Dyck, and with whom he could converse as freely and

---

* Though hardly the first line, if it be truly alleged that he held it "lawful to play the knave with a knave."

knowledgeably on the fine points of connoisseurship, as Rubens himself might have done in the old days of his association with Van Dyck at Antwerp.

And it must be remembered that such a tendency to stammer was almost certainly due not to any physical cause, but to a habit of repression formed in infancy, and with roots so deep below the control of conscious will that neither effort nor skill could avail to cure it. But it might be that some volcanic uprush from these depths might sweep aside all obstacles to its expression in speech. It had been observed that during the trial of Lord Strafford His Majesty had seemed to talk without his usual difficulty. It would be observed even more indubitably at a later trial.

5

THE CONSCIENCE OF THE KING

Of a man so handicapped, it is nothing remarkable that at the supreme crisis of his fate he should have spun out hours, when every minute's delay was fraught with mortal peril, in agonizing indecision. And no doubt King Charles's temperament contributed to prolong the agony. But it must not be forgotten that few even of the most uncompromising men of action have been exempt on occasion from a like suspension of will power. Even Cromwell confessed to having "sought the Lord night and day"—which is the elect way of making up one's mind—before committing himself to one of his catastrophic leaps into the dark.

King Charles had at least as much excuse for taking time to explore every avenue and avail himself of whatever counsel he could obtain from God or man, before deciding either to make, or to refuse, the supreme surrender demanded of him. For indeed, as much as it can be said of anything human, he had been manœuvred into a situation from which there was no escape except by surrender. He might be compared to a chess-player who realizes not only that he is unable to prevent the loss of an essential piece, but that any further hesitation to accept the sacrifice will involve him in even graver loss—perhaps of his Queen.

Even so, our analogy tends to simplify the case unduly. For the chess-player, however intricate his calculations, has only one end

in view, and his choice of means is unbiased by moral considerations.

But with King Charles it was the moral aspect that obsessed
him, almost to the exclusion of the practical. Should he for any
consideration whatever of prudence or statesmanship make himself a party to the cold-blooded murder—for it was nothing less—
of the faithful minister to whose safety he had pledged and, but
a few days ago, solemnly confirmed his royal word ? It was thus
that the question shaped itself in his mind during these hours of
indecision. It was in that form that after his decision it would
continue to haunt him till his dying hour. And that it should have
been so, arose not so much out of the nature of the case itself, as
out of his own.

For to almost any of the strong and successful English
monarchs who had gone before him, or to the son who succeeded
him, it would have presented itself as a question of pure political
expediency. At times when popular discontent had been inflamed
to revolutionary pitch, it had been the recognized move for the
Sovereign to make a scapegoat of an unpopular minister, and it
would have been no more than the common form of English, or
any other royalty, had King Charles resolved to make the best
of a bad business, and do what he could to appease the Parliamentary leaders by a great show of alacrity in meeting their
demands in this matter of Strafford. And indeed it was precisely
this course that was being urged upon him by all but one of the
counsellors whom he had summoned to his presence and by none
more strongly and plausibly than by the Machiavellian churchman, formerly Keeper of the Great Seal and now Bishop of
Lincoln, who bore (as Oliver Cromwell would likewise have done
unless his forebears had elected to change it) the typical Welsh
name of Williams.

This rather slippery Shepherd of Souls harboured beneath his
mitre no scruples about morality ; but he was loyal according to
his lights, and so confident was he of his ability to rescue his
Sovereign, even in his own despite, in that he had already done
what he could to decide the issue in advance. For it was almost
certainly he who when, the previous afternoon, the bill for
Strafford's execution had arrived from Parliament, accompanied
by the mob, had parleyed with them from one of the palace
windows, and intimated that if they would only have patience
over the week-end, they would obtain full satisfaction of their

desires. By this wholly unauthorized blood pledge he could at least flatter himself that he had procured for his Sovereign thirty-six hours' respite ; and I cannot help thinking that the confident expectation of its fulfilment accounts for the otherwise inexplicable failure of the mob to proceed to extremities during all those long hours of unsatisfied agitation, on Sunday, outside the palace.

Now all that remained for the good Bishop to do was to provide his Sovereign with a formula calculated to eliminate the moral bias, and reconcile his conscience, in the brief interval thus secured, to the acceptance of the inevitable. And who was so well qualified to do this as one of the revered hierarchs of his own Church ? Or what argument could be better adapted to the purpose than that which His Grace of Lincoln actually advanced : "that there was a private and a public conscience ; that his public conscience as a King might not only dispense with, but oblige him to do, that which was against his private conscience as a man : and that the question was not, whether he should save the Earl of Strafford, but whether he should perish with him : that the conscience of a King to preserve his kingdom, the conscience of a husband to preserve his wife, the conscience of a father to preserve his children (all of which were now in danger) weighed down abundantly all the considerations the conscience of a master or friend could suggest to him, for the preservation of a friend or servant."

With such "unprelatical ignominious arguments", as Lord Clarendon describes them, did this spiritual consultant ply his royal client in order to convince him that it had now become the dictate not only of expediency, but actually of conscience, to implement with his signature the Act for the taking away of his minister's life.

Unprelatical and ignominious ! It was natural for Clarendon, who knew what had come to King Charles as the result of yielding to such counsel, thus to characterize it ; easier still for us, brought up to accept propagandist myth for good history, to cry shame on the sanctified sophist who could give, and scorn on the false King who could yield to, such advice.

But if it were possible for us to be transported through time to that Cabinet Chamber at Whitehall, with the sound of the mob borne fitfully to our ears, and no more knowledge of the facts and the future than was possessed by the men on the spot, we might have taken a somewhat more charitable view, even to the extent

of conceding that the Bishop's advice was the soundest possible
under the circumstances, and that the King would have been mad
to refuse it.

For self immolation—let alone that of wife and family—on a
point of abstract principle, is even less fashionable in the twentieth
than it was in the seventeenth century. And no determination of
the King to sacrifice himself could by any possibility have saved
Strafford.

It had come to this. Humanly speaking the Earl was a dead
man already ; and nobody knew better than himself, as he sat
poring over his Bible in his room in the Tower, that he would
never see another Sunday. These men who had stuck at nothing
to compass his destruction were not going to miss the opportunity
they now had of consummating it. They were too much afraid of
him—and well he knew it—to risk his survival.

Mr Pym and Mr Hampden may not have been quite all that
current mythology has depicted them, but Strafford himself
would never have called them fools ! And even their depressing
associate, the Earl of Essex, had enough wit to comprehend that
for men who had such excellent reason for loving darkness rather
than light, there was only one way with him who of all others was
capable of unmasking their proceedings :

"Stone dead", he had said, "hath no fellow."

It was his life or theirs ; and now that they had got him, they
would have been fools not to finish him.

They had got his master too ; held as fast in his own palace as
his minister in the Tower, and as powerless to aid him as Lazarus
to bring comfort to Dives. In the ancient fortress of the Kings of
England, the King's authority was no longer regarded. Even the
rumour that he intended to garrison it with soldiers he could trust,
instead of the Tower Hamlets militia whom the Patriots could
trust only too well, was brayed through all the megaphones of
Pym's propaganda as an "army plot". Moreover, in his frantic
efforts to conciliate them, he had appointed as Constable the
Earl of Newport, who, before he had veered over to the winning
side, had accumulated a respectable fortune in the King's service
by systematic graft. This worthy Patriot had obligingly undertaken, in case His Majesty should prove difficult about making
Strafford's murder legal, to make it actual on his own responsibility, law or no law, in the well-founded confidence that they,
for their part, would be no less able than willing to shield him

from any unpleasant consequences that might otherwise have ensued. So that it came to this : the utmost that the King could now do for Strafford would be to have him stabbed or smothered quietly in his cell, instead of subjecting him to the pompous formality of a public execution. Which method the Earl would have preferred we have no means of ascertaining.

What we do know is that he had taken calm stock of the situation, and decided that all that was now left for him to do was to resign himself to the inevitable, and concentrate only on preventing his own fate from involving that of his master. His letter formally releasing his master from a promise that it was now out of his power to fulfil, must have been lying on the King's table through those hours of agony. Certainly it could not fail to influence his decision. But to what end? Could he in honour accept the sacrifice? For between men of honour, loyalty is mutual, and competitive.

But what else could he do? Strafford would not have qualified for the name of hero unless he had also been a realist. He had taken stock of the King's situation, and with a noble common sense counselled him to salvage what was yet to be retrieved from the shipwreck of constitutional Monarchy in England. That did not include the minister whose creative genius had conceived the idea of breathing new life into that ancient polity, and putting it to work with a power and beneficence such as it had never possessed even in the palmiest days of the Tudors. The wreckers had made sure of him ; to try to save him now would be to pre-cipitate the loss of everything. But for the King, the Royal Family, and the Monarchy itself, all in imminent and deadly peril, there might still be a chance. Let the King write his servant's life off the account and concentrate on saving them. Such was the gist of Black Tom's advice. As it was, indeed, of all the advice, with the exception that I have yet to tell, that the King sought and received. "Sign !" had been the unanimous voice of his Privy Councillors ; the judges had devised a formula by which the most loyal subject in the realm could be roped in technically on a charge of treason ; all but one of the Bishops were in agreement with Williams that it would be madness under the circumstances for God's Anointed to bind his conscience to the fulfilment of a pledge that he had no power to implement, and that he could only immolate himself in attempting to fulfil.

6

THE LAST TURN OF THE SCREW

SUCH a reign of terror now prevailed that it was almost impossible for the King to get any advice at all that was not tainted either by fear or covert treason. As in Totalitarian countries to-day, it was well known that any man who set himself against the dominant faction would, however high his position in the State, be marked down for vengeance. The very judges found that impeachment was the penalty for any word spoken in the execution of their office calculated to offend Patriot susceptibilities, or lighten Patriot pockets. With judicial impartiality thus equated with treason, is it any wonder that His Majesty's judges, being human, should have played for safety? There have been heroic judges as there have been saintly bishops, but human nature being what it is, the desire for a safe life must be expected to be more potent in the average, than the courage that breaks rather than bends on a point of principle, when it really is a choice of bend or be broken. We must not blame these old gentlemen too much if they put their legal ingenuity to work to find a way for themselves and their Sovereign which, if a shade devious, at least did not lead both straight to the precipice.

Such was all the support that the King could get from these cowed "lions under the throne". But when he turned from the judges to his ministerial counsellors for their advice, he might account himself lucky to get it from terrified men playing for safety, and not from traitors covertly bent on his destruction. For in his desperate efforts to secure the goodwill of the Parliament and its leaders, he had allowed ministerial posts to be filled by men like Oliver St John, the saturnine, sardonic lawyer, whom he had appointed Solicitor General, who had been Hampden's leading counsel in the ship-money case, and was now one of the innermost ring of the conspiracy for wresting the controls of the State out of the hands of its lawful Sovereign. We, who have had only too much experience of the way such things are done, know that it is a first principle of those who wish to wreck an administration to plant a creature of their own on it. There is little in *Mein Kampf* of which Mr Pym's genius had not apprised him three centuries in advance.

A second principle is to strike down every minister capable of giving service both loyal and competent. This also had been fully honoured. The great royal administration that had made England a haven of peaceful prosperity when Europe had been distracted by the most devastating of all its ideological wars, had been hopelessly broken up ; some of its members had fled overseas for their lives, others were rotting in prison ; those who were left knew that every word and every action of theirs was marked, and that there would be no mercy and no escape for suspected traitors to King Pym. What counsel could the ostensible King have expected, but that which he got, namely to sign the Bill for eliminating Strafford in the way most convenient to those who had put him—as we should say nowadays—on the spot ?

For we must realize, if we are to appreciate the nature of the choice that lay before the King, that not only within, but without the palace, reigned a terror of a kind that had never been seen before, and has hardly since in England, unless we are to count as its equal that engendered in the next reign by the scare of the Popish Plot. The very mob was even more terrified than terrible, such was the skill with which its fears had been wrought upon.

It was terror, but terror applied with superb psychological insight and consummate timing. And now it had come to what Pym himself must have realized to be the hardest and most perilous task of all, that demanding the supreme concentration of all the forces of terror on the Sovereign himself. For Mr Pym would never have arrived thus far if he had been as prone as some of his posthumous *claque*, to imagine that Charles was a reed shaken with the wind, and not a man of unswerving honour and all but invincible determination not to budge from what reason and conscience had apprised him to be the *ne plus ultra* of concession. This was no time-serving Peer or panicky Commoner, but an opponent worthy of even Pym's steel. That he realized this is, I think, proved by the fact that the masterpieces of his political strategy, both for subtlety of conception and calculated daring of execution, were those which were evoked by the direct struggle with his Sovereign, for that Sovereign's political if not necessarily his physical annihilation.

As with all great strategists, Mr Pym's mastering conceptions were simple. It was always his first care to find the psychological key to his opponent's defences. In dealing with Charles, this was constituted by his affection for the Queen. Let her safety be threatened, and there was hardly anything that he would not do or concede to save her. He loved her with all the concentrated strength of a reserved man's affection. And her safety was only too easily threatened. She might be a charming and an accomplished woman, a faithful wife and a devoted mother ; but in an England fermenting with Calvinist ideology, all this counted for nothing in comparison with her being not only a foreigner, but also a Catholic, and as such, believed capable of any devilry. Her marriage, though part of a foreign policy aimed at a peaceful *entente* with France, had put far too great a strain on public opinion in England. Henriette was not by nature a devout, any more than she was a politically conscious woman, but she had a proud and gay loyalty to any cause and person to whom her heart was once committed ; and though she may not have been a very strict practising Catholic, she would no more have dreamed of playing false to the faith of her childhood, in which she had been instructed by that saintly mystic, Cardinal Bérulle, than of betraying her husband. In such matters she was completely without fear and, as is common with fearless people, inclined to be lacking in prudence.

Thus though her interests were almost entirely centred on her husband, her children, and the masques and innocent gaieties of court life, the mere fact that she never would stoop to the least dissimulation about being what she was, rendered it easy, for those who had an interest in doing so, to present her to the popular imagination as a kind of female Guy Fawkes, a desperate intriguer plotting the enslavement of the nation, the rekindling of the fires of Smithfield, and heaven knows what beside. The mob, that still imagined itself loyal to the King, had been worked up into almost as great a terror of this delicate little creature as of Black Tom himself ; and a terrified mob is the most implacable monster on earth. If this mob were to storm the palace they would go straight for the Queen, and the King knew it, and Mr Pym knew that he knew it. That was his strangle hold, and that was why it had been so deadly and essential a move in his game to fix her at Whitehall at this hour of decision.

The wife whom King Charles still, after sixteen years of married life, adored as passionately as when he had caught her up, a laughing-eyed slip of a bride of fifteen, in his arms at their first meeting in Dover Castle ; his children, whom he cherished with a deeper affection than ever, since the grave had just closed over the head of one poor little princess : these it was in his power to save. To save Strafford in the Tower was beyond any power on earth. That was the inexorable truth that stared him in the face.

It is the fashion, even in the most recent biographies, to assert that the Queen herself, by dint of tears and entreaties, played a major part in inducing her husband to surrender. We read of her shivering in her apartments, losing her nerve, blubbering and nagging at her husband to save her by betraying Strafford.

It would be interesting to know on what evidence these confident assertions, so contrary to all that we know of her character, are founded. Certainly all this is very different from her own account of the matter,* and there is no other even alleged witness of what, if anything, may have passed between the two during these agonizing hours. What we do know of her is that when Charles had been informed only three days before, that her escape was vetoed by his faithful Commons, she had rallied his drooping spirits by exclaiming :

"I am my father's daughter"—and that father Henry of Navarre and Ivry—"and he never knew how to fly. I am not going to learn now."

So that in default of evidence to the contrary, it is common decency to assume that on this, as on every other known occasion, she was her own queenly self, and that the daughter of the White Plume did not now show the white feather.

But for King Charles the dilemma was the most terrible one on which a loyal and a loving soul can be impaled. And it will suffice to quote the words of one of the most consistently prejudiced of all his detractors, the historian Gardiner, who despite his family connection with Cromwell, and a mind saturated in the most orthodox Whig mythology, did nevertheless strive to be as fair as he knew how :

"Let him who has seen wife and child, and all that he holds dear, exposed to imminent peril, and has refused to save them by an act of baseness, cast the first stone at Charles."

Some husbands and fathers might even be inclined to wonder whether "act of baseness" is not, under the circumstances, a contradiction in terms. Let every one who reads these words ask himself whether, so circumstanced, he would not have deemed it

* To Mme. de Motteville she put the blame on the bishops and adds : "Le Roi . . . en signant l'arrêt de son ministre . . . signa aussi celui qui peu de temps après fut prononcé contre lui." Is it conceivable that she could have borne to say this if she herself had been the person who had made him sign ?

baseness amounting to criminal lunacy, to abandon his loved ones to the tender mercies of an enraged rabble, for the sake of formally honouring a promise that, through circumstances utterly unforeseeable at the time he had made it, it was no longer in his power to fulfil.

Unforeseeable because, by all the rules of the game, as it had been played from time immemorial, he had had every right to assume that it was actually, as it was legally and constitutionally, well within his power to guarantee Strafford's safety.

That amazing week of deliberately engendered terror and mob law, in which stroke had followed stroke, with deadly precision, had altered the whole face of the situation.

Judgment of men may not have been King Charles's strongest suit, but it is hard to blame him for having failed to divine the unique quality of a genius and technique that camouflaged itself so successfully that Mr Pym's biographers are to this day capable of exhibiting him as an exemplary but rather dull Patriot *ingénu*, instead of the most finished exponent, before the Totalitarian masters of our times, of the technique of achieving power by fretting and playing upon the passions of men in the mass.

It will be time to blame King Charles for not having penetrated the secret of his opponent's strategy and anticipated it by the appropriate counter-measures, when we ourselves, after three centuries of research and exposition, have begun to get some inkling of its real methods and object.

7

DIVINE IMPERATIVE, HUMAN VETO

In such a case of mortal urgency, the only wonder is that the King could have hesitated for so long to resign himself to what his legal, political, and spiritual advisers concurred in urging upon him, and what, judged by all worldly standards, was the only course open to him.

And here it was that the counsel of the subtle Williams offered the best chance, if not of checkmating Pym, at least of robbing him of that irreversible triumph at which he was aiming. The

Bishop of Lincoln was about as much of a saint as the Patriots were patriotic, but for that very reason he was qualified to meet them on their own level ; and he alone, amid all the agitation and agony of the crisis, kept the head and nerve to perceive that the personal issue was not the only one, and that though the removal of Strafford was a necessary preliminary to Pym's campaign, it was not his ultimate or even his main immediate objective. Pym was aiming at an even higher target :

> To pluck the precious diadem from the shelf
> And put it in his pocket,

in other words, to overthrow the Constitution, and shatter that whole fabric of Parliamentary government in England, of which, with consummate assurance, he was posing then, as he has succeeded in passing himself off ever since, as the most fanatical champion.

That this is the language of sober truth will be evident from the perusal of that little Bill, slipped through the Houses under a smoke screen of panic, to cut off Parliament from its constituents and the King from all possibility of appealing to his people ; a Bill the effect of which was to set the second Parliament of 1640, then at the height of its prestige and power, on the long, slippery downward way that was to lead it through the utmost extremes of contempt and infamy, to the point at which its ignominious remnant, or Rump, was booted into the street by one of its own members, and "not a dog barked at their going".

Williams alone, as far as our knowledge goes, saw that it was more important, as a matter of political strategy, and of that public conscience that he urged the King, as King, to set above his conscience as a man, to guard the fabric of the Constitution from this mortal blow, than to save the life of any individual whatever. It is better that even the greatest of statesmen and the most loyal of subjects should perish, than the *Res Publica*. It is expedient, as a former ecclesiastical dignitary had put it, that one man should die for the people.

For Williams' advice was simple : sign the Attainder, and veto the Perpetual Parliament Bill. That would have been a counter for which even Pym would have been taxed to find a reply. For this mob had been worked up for a head hunt, and nothing else.

All would be merry in England once Black Tom's head was off. They had been told nothing, and would not have enthused if they had known, about Mr Pym's little plan for cutting off such of them as had votes from the possibility of using them. Unlike Black Tom's head, this item was not advertised ; in fact it had been the whole point of Mr Pym's strategy to slip it through as unobtrusively as possible. They were not going to storm Whitehall for that ; whatever, once they had tumbled to its purport, they might have done to certain lodgings behind Westminster Hall. The King's refusal would have brought Mr Pym into the open, and this particular Bill into the forefront of public interest—which was the last thing Mr Pym wanted. At the best, he would have saved himself by as unobtrusive a climb-down as possible, and sought to divert attention by starting some other hare.

The argument was specious, and we may be sure that Williams pressed it home with all the subtle persuasiveness at his command. Nor was so keen an intelligence as that of King Charles incapable of taking the point. But there was another counsellor at hand who, though also one of that now rare class of churchmen who had been employed in secular politics, was the exact opposite of Williams in being a man of God engaged in the service of Caesar.

This was William Juxon, Bishop of London since the great little William Laud whose right hand man he was, had been promoted from that See to the Archbishopric of Canterbury. Up to a fortnight ago, he had with conspicuous ability discharged the thankless office of Lord Treasurer for a Government perpetually starved of funds ; but by sheer honesty and businesslike method he had managed to provide out of next to nothing not only for the efficient functioning of the departments, but also for the necessary expenses of a court that combined in the highest degree those two generally incompatible qualities of moral purity and æsthetic distinction.

In a time that was certainly the golden age of the Church of England, a time gloriously prolific of brilliant and saintly personalities, Juxon was undoubtedly the man of all others—with the possible exception of George Herbert—to whom the word "lovable" is most conspicuously appropriate. It would have been literally true to say of him that he never had an enemy in the world, and this though he had filled more than one position in which any other man would automatically have become the object of the most venomous and holy hatred. "Neither as Bishop or Treasurer", says his former Secretary, Sir Philip Warwick, "came there any one accusation against him in that last Parliament of 1640, whose ears were opened, nay itching, after such complaints. Nay, even after the King's being driven from London he remained in his house belonging to his Bishopric, in Fulham ... and found respect from all, and yet walked steadily in his old paths."

As for King Charles, there was no man for whom he had more affectionate regard than for Juxon, and "this", he once said, "I will say of him : I never got his opinion freely in my life, but when I had it, I was ever the better for it."

We can imagine how eagerly after listening to the advice of so many terrified or cunning counsellors, all to the same effect, of sacrificing principle on the altar of necessity or policy, he must have waited for that of the gentle Juxon.

There is no record of that interview, but we know what was the effect of the Bishop's advice. It was for the King to do God's Will and trust God for the consequences ; to refuse on any plea whatever, of necessity or policy, or even the preservation of those whose lives he valued more than his own, to put his royal signature to what his conscience must have told him was a plain violation not only of his promise to Strafford, but of his coronation oath to do justice and to stop the growth of iniquity. For what fouler injustice could there be than the slaughter of an innocent man ? and what blacker iniquity than the traitor's block for the good and faithful servant who was pleading to lay down his life for him ?

It may well be that he reminded Charles of the verdict passed by posterity on another ruler, who when he saw that he could prevail nothing, but rather that a tumult was made, took water and washed his hands, saying :

"I am innocent of the blood of this just person. See ye to it."

How much more was that way of escape barred to a King of England, and a Christian gentleman !

Such was the counsel of a saint, though of a saint who had also shown himself to be a highly competent statesman. And as such, it enjoined willingness to fly in the face of all worldly calculations, and to embrace martyrdom rather than yield an inch on a point of vital principle. That Charles was capable of accepting martyrdom, he himself was destined to prove. But now something more was demanded of him, a sacrifice from which the best and bravest man might shrink. And though the Bishop may perhaps have reminded him of the uncompromising austerity with which the gospel commands a man to sacrifice even his dearest affections on the altar of God's Will, to such a husband and father as Charles, the saying was hard indeed.

8

ROYAL DEATH-WARRANT

AND so the afternoon wore on to evening ; the King continued to seek for some avenue of escape from his terrible position, and the mob to surge and roar like an angry sea against the walls of the palace. The anxiety within was sharpened by the fact that they were threatening also to storm the neighbouring palace of St James, which had been assigned by her son-in-law as the residence of Marie de Medici, who, for all her faults, was a defenceless, ageing woman, and an impoverished refugee, but to Mr Pym, just one more useful hate stimulus, and to the honest Londoners, as diabolically inspired as any of her humbler sisters who formed the quarry for the good, Puritan sport of witch baiting.

But in the knowledge, as we are almost bound to believe, of Bishop Williams' unauthorized promise of a death sentence over the week-end, the mob refrained from anything more harmful than noise, and as the darkness began to fall on the unlit streets, its members gradually dispersed and drifted off city-wards. But it must have stood beyond any doubt whatever that they would be back to-morrow, and back for a kill. Of whom, and of how many, rested with His Majesty.

Meanwhile the issue had defined itself with ruthless clarity. On the one side was the opinion of all the judges, all the lay ministers, and all but one of the bishops, based on the patent fact of the situation, that to hold out longer would be to throw good and precious lives, and not improbably the Monarchy itself, after a life already lost ; on the other there was the voice of the good Juxon, which must have seemed like that of conscience itself, pleading for unconditional surrender, not to man, but to God.

It is significant that after having gone through the whole series

of counsellors, the King, as a last resort, should have summoned
the Bishops again. That was only what was to have been expected
from the most devoted royal son of the Church of England, and
as devoted a son, without any qualification, as that Church has
ever had. He must have felt how little reliance was to be placed on
those too worldly-wise, secular counsellors ; but surely these
reverend Fathers in God were a rock on whose integrity he could
rely, when all else was crumbling beneath him. For those, if any,
who have studied the words and acts, rather than the myth of
King Charles, will realize that his was a nature trusting to a
fault, and that once he had given his confidence, there was hardly
anything that could make him withdraw it.

Of this final interview we have again no record ; but we may
be sure that it resolved itself into a contest of pleading between
these two advocates, respectively, of worldly and heavenly
wisdom, the Bishops of Lincoln and of London. Only on this
occasion Juxon found a new ally in another hardly less eminent
churchman, Archbishop Ussher, of Armagh, a scholar of fabulous
erudition who is still remembered as the author of what, up to
recent times, was the accepted system of Scriptural chronology.
Ussher, like Juxon, was of a gentle and lovable disposition,
though underlying it was a vein of austerity that rendered him
both incapable and intolerant of compromise on any plain issue
of right and wrong.

Ussher had little enough reason to love Strafford. Though the
evidence is a little obscure, it does not appear that the two had
seen eye to eye during Wentworth's—as he was then—masterful
tenure of the Lord Deputyship of Ireland. But to a man of
Ussher's calibre, personal feeling, either his own or the King's,
could not enter into the reckoning. Strafford was innocent :
Charles was the Lord's anointed. There could be no evasion,
before God, of the blood guiltiness of his consent to an innocent
man's death.

That much we can state, with confidence, about Ussher's part
in the interview ; for such a man could not fail to be true to form,
and Ussher imparted the meticulous exactness of the chronologist
even to his moral judgments. It is not difficult to imagine how
Williams, with his two or three colleagues murmuring assent,
would have pitted his bland eloquence against the moral intransigence of Ussher and the gentle remonstrances of Juxon, and with
what deadly effect he would have worked upon the feelings of

the weary man in the chair, who must have felt himself now almost at the point of collapse from sheer exhaustion and hopelessness.

And meanwhile the fresh stillness of a May night had descended upon Whitehall. The ominous sounds had died away, and the enclosed space in front of the palace was empty. It was about nine o'clock when the tension was at long last snapped, and King Charles, with the tears streaming down his cheeks, signified, in broken accents, that he could hold out no longer :

"If my own person only were in danger, I would gladly venture it to save Lord Strafford's life ; but seeing my wife, children, and all my Kingdom are concerned in it, I am forced to give way unto it."

Words of more agonizing poignancy have never been wrung from any human heart. His surrender was unconditional. He had, in spite of the warnings and persuasions of Williams, decided to pass both Bills, the one for suspending the Constitution of his realm, as well as that for butchering the greatest man in it. Why, we may ask, with his eyes thus opened, should he have conceded this utterly unnecessary and fatal advantage to his enemies ? Why indeed ?

In the light of all that we know, and that I shall have to tell in the ensuing pages, of King Charles, I can think of only one possible explanation. Such horror of black shame and despair had come upon him, as can only be understood by those to whom their honour has been more than their life, and who, on any plea whatever, have allowed that honour to suffer stain. To such betrayal of himself had King Charles been driven. It is true that he had yielded to arguments that to the overwhelming majority of workaday human beings would have seemed imperatively convincing. But he had listened to the tearful reproaches of Archbishop Ussher after his surrender ; he had seen the grief in the eyes of Juxon. These were the men whose judgment he respected and endorsed.

Never, never, would he forgive himself. Even in the hour of his own martyrdom the thought of that sin haunted him ; he could not lay his head upon the block before easing his heart of it in words of burning repentance and humiliation.

If he must needs do this dreadful thing, he would at least not stoop to the ultimate degradation of profiting by it. Never should it be said of him that he had sacrificed Strafford as a piece in a political gambit ; as it would have been said, had he followed Williams's advice, and passed the Attainder in order to reject that other Bill the effect of which was to cut him off from the possibility of appealing to his own people. At least, if there were no other way to save his Queen and children than to sacrifice his minister, he himself should be the greater sacrifice. For in his agony of defeat—such agony as can only be felt by a man of sensitive honour who knows himself to have betrayed his ideal— he was oblivious to every other consideration. He had no ears for Williams' prudent advice. If the Act suspending the Constitution had been his own death-warrant—and that, in the long run, was what it proved to be—he might have signed it with equal indifference. The most daring, and cruel, of Pym's calculations had proved correct.

Then he retired to far other than those untroubled slumbers that were to visit him on the night before his execution. Next morning he had that to perform, of which he would not dare to look Juxon in the face and say,

"I have a good cause and a merciful God on my side."

The words that did actually burst from his heart, as he implemented, with his royal signature, the act of Strafford's murder, were,

"My Lord of Strafford's condition is more happy than mine."

9

"LIKE A GENTLEMAN AND A CHRISTIAN"

THAT night the Earl of Dorset, one of the King's few thoroughly loyal nobles, took leave of him with these words :

"Good night, sir. I may live to do you kindness, but you can do me none."

There was but one hope left to him now. It might be that these stern men, who had broken his royal authority, would have some spark of pity in their breasts—and what could be more calculated to excite pity, than the spectacle of their Sovereign appealing to them out of the depth of his humiliation, no longer a master but a suppliant ?

On the day following his surrender—the eve of that appointed for Strafford's execution—he penned a distracted, heart-broken letter to the House of Lords ; he had satisfied the demands of justice, but now, "Mercy being as inherent and inseparable to a King as justice, I desire ... to show that likewise, by suffering that unfortunate man to fulfil the natural course of his life in a close imprisonment." He was ready to concede any terms, to agree to the sternest conditions, if they would only spare him the guiltiness of a friend's blood. But in his heart of hearts he seems to have realized what the success of his appeal was likely to be, for after his signature comes the most piteous sentence of all, "If he must die, it were charity to reprieve him till Sunday."

This he dispatched by the young Prince of Wales, the future Charles II, in the hope that the boy's urgent plea, added to his own, would do something to soften those hard hearts. But the Lower Chamber, so the Venetian envoy records, dismissed the Prince with scant civility and refused, in spite of His Majesty's request, to read either the letter or the cover. Well might Charles have echoed the dying cry of the first Henry Plantagenet :

"Shame ! Shame upon a conquered King !"

The story that Strafford, on hearing that Charles had yielded to his own urgent plea, rounded on his King and himself, by rising to his feet and saying "Put not your trust in Princes," rests on no reliable evidence. Strafford was not that sort of imbecile—or that sort of cad.

"I dare," he said to Balfour, when the time came, "look death in the face." It was no idle boast.

"He died," in the words of his friend, George Radcliffe, "like a gentleman and a Christian." This noblest of all tributes might with equal justice have been accorded to his friend Laud, and his master Charles, when their turn came. But something more is needed to express the distinctive quality of each of their ends. Laud, it might be said, died in that beauty of holiness that he had sought and ensued ; Charles was the intuitive artist, enacting the mystery of his own victorious resurrection as Royal Martyr ; of Strafford it is supremely appropriate to describe his death as that of a hero.

He went to the scaffold on Tower Hill as Shakespeare's Coriolanus would have gone, marching with head erect and flashing eye, as if—so it was remarked—he had been at the head of an army breathing out victory. Never, in the days of his power, had his been so unquestionably the dominating personality. It was estimated that a crowd of no less than 200,000 had come to see the end of this man whom they had been taught to regard as some embodied spirit of evil, the tyrant whose fall would be his country's salvation. Balfour had feared that all his men of the Tower guard would be unable to prevent them from tearing his prisoner to pieces. He need not have feared. When the proud figure appeared, bowing as he passed to right and left, not a man stirred ; the silence was profound.

It was only when the head was held up by the hair, and the headsman shouted those words of ironically tragic import, "God save the King !"—-for it seemed as if nothing human could save him after this—that the spell was broken, and they went mad with ghoulish ecstasy :

"His head is off ! His head is off !"

Far into the countryside galloping horsemen carried the news, and everywhere there was rejoicing, ringing of bells and lighting of fires.

III

Check to King Pym

I

STRANGLEHOLD

AFTER the stress and tumult of that terrible Sunday, tranquillity returned to Whitehall. In the open space in front of the palace there was no more than the normal coming and going. The mob showed no signs of putting in a fresh appearance on Monday morning, the centre of interest having shifted for the nonce to Tower Hill, where carpenters were hard at work rushing up stands, with tier upon tier of flimsy seats, for the monster entertainment that it was now known, for certain, would take place at 10 o'clock of Wednesday forenoon, and for which the whole of London was expected to turn out.

And meanwhile, within, the normal routine went on as it had every morning of royal residence during the sixteen years of the reign. Not a jot was abated of the ceremonial and respect with which their Majesties were hedged. From no officially recognized quarter had there been the least hint of open disloyalty. His Majesty's devoted Peerage and faithful Commons, who had been so active of late in devising measures for enhancing the glory of his throne and establishing it on the love of his people, had, with his gracious consent and co-operation decreed stern justice on the great subject who had devised treason against him. What could be more proper ? Or more satisfactory ?

And meanwhile, there was the day's work to be got through. The King's government, such as it was now, must be carried on ; the business of the nation could not be allowed to stand still. Though it was too much of a matter of course to be one of record, we can say for certain that from an early hour the manager of that business was in his accustomed place, as immaculately coiffeured and turned out as ever, listening with his accustomed patience to the reports of secretaries and carefully going through the papers they presented to him ; occasionally putting a C.R. traced with as exquisite a finish as he gave to every one of his actions, at the foot. And we may be sure that he went through these tasks with his accustomed patience, and a courtesy that differed in no outward respect from that of any other day. But those who knew him well cannot have failed to remark a pallor of his cheek and heaviness of eye as of one who had watched out two nights now, as the Venetian Ambassador records, "in great agony".

And no wonder ! For even if we leave out of account what, to a man of honour and principle who has been forced to compromise with both, is agony stronger than death, his real situation—apart from those ironical forms and trappings of majesty—was about as desperate as it would be possible to conceive. For by any rational calculation, it must have seemed that from the signing of Strafford's death warrant Charles was a beaten man, without hope and doomed. As fast as his friend in the Tower was he held in the net spun by that bloated spider, John Pym. It is true that he had procured for himself and those dear to him some precarious respite while the first victim was being digested. But the spider had got him fixed where he wanted, and it was only a question of time when he would be ready for the next meal. For the liquidation of Strafford, however necessary it may have been to Pym as a measure of self-preservation, was also an essential, and decisive, part of his campaign against the Crown.

No doubt, when he had recovered enough from the blackness of his first despair to take stock of his own situation, His Majesty began to realize how fatally he had barred his last avenue of possible deliverance, by refusing to take the advice of Bishop Williams, and interpose his royal veto against Pym's Perpetual Parliament Bill. For now that he had been deprived, by death, imprisonment, or flight, of the pick of his ministerial team, and had become utterly dependent for the means of governing at all on continual doles from a Parliament that would only grant them on condition of his abject subservience, a Parliament swept to Westminster in a mood of inflamed passion worked up by Pym himself in the election campaign, his one hope lay in an eventual appeal to his people, no longer drunk with propaganda but sobered by bitter experience. For the time would surely come when experience of King Pym's rule would induce them to revise their estimate of its superior attractions over that of King Charles. And then would be the time for a government that was still after all the King's government, to appeal to the country.

The most consummate of all political strategists must have had this possibility continually before his eyes. For Pym, like most highly suspicious men, had a well-developed sense of self-preservation. He knew—no one better—how desperate was the game that he was playing, and how, having committed himself so far, it would be ruin for him to abate a jot of its rigour until he had cleared the whole board. He had destroyed Strafford just in time to cover up his own traces, but not until he had piled treason on treason, in the old-fashioned sense of the word ; for besides having been the prime agent in inciting a foreign army to invade England and occupy part of it, he had stirred up the King's subjects, by propaganda and panic-mongering, to besiege him in his own palace and force him, at the peril of his life and that of his Consort, to connive at what in his heart and conscience he believed to be an outrage on justice.

It may be argued with more or less of plausibility that, in doing all this, Pym, and the junta of wealthy politicians of which he had come to be the moving spirit, were inspired by motives of pure, disinterested patriotism. But no one knew better than Pym himself how little such arguments would have weighed at the trial that, once his stranglehold on the Monarchy was relaxed, he would have to face before the King's judges on a plain issue of treason under the law of Edward III. A swing back of popular opinion to its traditional loyalty would have given the King the opportunity that Pym at least would have credited him with seeking, of turning the tables on his persecutors.

There was only one answer to this : *a stranglehold must be put on the people as well as the King.* He must be prevented from appealing to them, and they from coming to his aid. The pendulum must be tied. If the will of the electorate showed signs of veering back to its traditional allegiance, Parliament must at all costs be prevented from registering it. It must in fact cease to be a representative body in any other sense than that of the Totalitarian assemblies with which we have been, and have not ceased to be, familiar—that of a collective rubber stamp, for endorsing the ukases of a permanently ruling faction and its chief. That is what this Parliament had in effect been, thanks to Pym's consummate management, during this first half-year of continuous session. And that is what—provided only that Pym could keep it fixed in this habit of responsiveness—his Perpetual Parliament Act guaranteed that it should remain until the Greek Kalends.

2

WHOSE END IS DESTRUCTION

So far, so good. Pym might congratulate himself on having achieved a victory complete beyond example. Every item of the ambitious programme he had set before himself had been punctually achieved. He had reduced the Sovereignty of the Crown to a mockery and a shadow. He had cut off the King from his people, and Parliament from its constituents. And at about noon on Wednesday sounds must have reached his lodging at Westminster of clattering hooves and the voices of excited horsemen, bound for the country, bawling out the expected tidings, "His head is off ! His head is off !"—the one head in the country with brains capable of fathoming and outwitting even Pym's combinations.

We can only imagine what was passing in his mind, for we have no record of what he was doing or thinking at this supreme crisis of his career. Modern historians of this time proceed so glibly by the road of assertion, that no one would imagine how flimsy and fragmentary is the evidence on which—even when every document has been unearthed and examined—the most pregnant of such assertions have to be based ; how much that is stated for fact is, in fact, more or less biased inference or intelligent guesswork. If only Pym, or any of those in intimate association with him, had committed to paper a record of their thoughts, or even their outward movements !

And yet, if we could fathom his mind at this moment, we should have the clue to the whole course of the subsequent tragedy. Now that he had eliminated Strafford, and overthrown the constitutional balance of sovereignty between Crown and Parliament, had he the will, or capacity, for switching over from the engineering of destruction to the architecture of constructive statesmanship ?

For that, after all, is the test by which Pym or any other wrecker of established institutions must abide. Government has to be carried on somehow, and by its fruits it will be judged. Are the fruits of the new way better than those of the old, and—most people to-day would agree to add—better for the whole people and not merely for some privileged section or class of people ?

Now the personal government of King Charles, of which Strafford and Archbishop Laud had been the main pillars, and which Pym and his associates had gone to such desperate lengths to subvert, might or might not have justified their epithet of tyranny, but it had at least given England a peaceful prosperity such as she had seldom enjoyed, and had pursued a constructive and brilliantly successful policy in every main field of national activity. Such being the fruits of the corrupt tree of tyranny, and that tree having been hewn down by the axes of Pym and his fellow Patriots, the question would surely be asked of them— what fruits they proposed to garner, for the benefit of the common Englishman, from the good tree of constitutional liberty that they were planting in its place.

Tyrants or not, Black Tom and Little Laud had had a constructive policy, or as we should call it nowadays, a Plan. That plan Mr Pym had patriotically wrecked, even though he had had to plant an invading army on the North and create a reign of terror in the South in order to do so. But had Mr Pym a plan of his own, that differed in any essential respect from that of the bull buffalo, who after he has charged down his victim, goes on savaging and goring whatever is left of him? To strip the Crown of every vestige of its sovereignty and transfer it to the ring of bosses or Patriots who dominated the Perpetual Parliament, was certainly a plan of a sort—though a negative sort. But can we find in any of the recorded utterances or actions of Pym himself or any one of his associates, the faintest glimmering of a positive notion of what they intended to do with the sovereignty when they had got it? Were they even capable of forming a government? The King had already implored them to do so ; but Pym had suddenly drawn back and wrecked the whole project—not for the last time. It is assumed by his apologists that Pym did not feel that he could trust the King, and it certainly would have been a little rash to have trusted the King to trust Pym on Pym's past record. But a Great Commoner, in control both of the ministry and the House of Commons, and with the King utterly at his mercy, could have gone ahead with his policy till the trust had been fairly earned.

But whatever his motives, the policy he did in fact pursue was to make it impossible for the King to govern the country on any terms or through any ministers whatever. He was the leader of a wrecking opposition that would neither formulate an alternative

policy, nor form an alternative government. And it is an only too
plausible inference that they would not, because they could not.
Strafford, the one man among them with the instincts of a
statesman and the willingness to shoulder responsibility, had
parted company with them a dozen years before and now—
his head was off.

His head was off, and though we have no record of Mr Pym's
reaction to the news, we may be sure it did not take anything
resembling the form dramatized by Robert Browning, in high-
falutin' blank verse, about a renewal of their friendship in the
Elysian fields, a friendship sacrificed on the altar of patriotism.
This man who was called the Ox was not of the stuff of which
romantic idealists are made. I can rather imagine him, as the
sense of those four expected words penetrated his brain, stroking
his beard, and muttering—

"Yes—but ..."

*   *   *   *   *   *   *

For perhaps even now Mr Pym did not feel his own head quite
so secure on his shoulders as he would have preferred. The
minister's head was off, but the crown was still on that of the
Sovereign whom King Pym had so mortally and cruelly injured.
And though intensively worked up propaganda about tyranny,
Popery, army plots, French invasions, and this, that and the
other bogey, might have panicked the citizens of the capital into
a mood of revolutionary hysteria, it is safe to assume that the
man who had employed this new technique of mass suggestion
with a mastery so far in advance of his age, would have been the
first to realize how unstable such artificially worked up passions
must of their very nature be ; and how, unless they can be continually kept up by new and progressively stronger injections of
the same dope, they are bound to be followed by a proportionate
reaction against their begetters. Hence the fatal compulsion that
has driven such practitioners, in our own time, as Hitler and
Mussolini, from outrage to outrage and violence to violence in a
panic-stricken flight from the nemesis of their own success.

Had Pym possessed the constructive urge even of a Mussolini,
he might at least have hoped to prove an exception to an almost
universal rule, by laying the devils he had raised, and turning
from conspirator to statesman. But there is nothing in his record
to suggest that he was even capable of forming such a notion.

With his deliberate, ox-like gait, he had out-distanced all his more showy competitors, the temperamental Eliot, the saturnine St John, the sleek Hampden, the learned Selden, on the long, steady ascent towards supreme power. But throughout it had been by unrelenting concentration on a gradually unfolding purpose of pure destruction, pursued with infinite caution and self restraint, never taking an avoidable risk or envisaging a premature objective.

To what lengths of destruction he, and those in his innermost councils, intended ultimately to go, we have no clue, except what we can infer from their subsequent proceedings. It would be more to the point to ask where, having gone so far, they would have dared to stop. For there must have been ever present to them the danger of a popular rally to the King's support. They had cut him off by law from appealing to such of his subjects as had votes, but there is no law that can bind the heart. They might strip him of his prerogatives, but so long as the crown was on his head, or even his head on his shoulders, he was still, in the eyes of his people, their lawful Sovereign, the Lord's Anointed, representative of them in a way that King Pym, who derived his mandate from a few score burgesses of Tavistock—and that only by grace of his and its patron, the Earl of Bedford—could never be. Pym had cast his spell on the London mob, and so long as he could keep its passions on the boil, he held his Sovereign in the hollow of his hand. But once give those passions time to cool, and he would be in danger of an alliance of Sovereign and people, against which even his control of an irremovable Parliament might not avail him. And might not even that control turn out to be a wasting asset? For six months the members had plunged forward, blindly responsive to the crack of his whip, to lengths that few of them could have foreseen. But the pace showed no signs of slackening and there were revolutionary extremes at which some of them at least might be minded to draw the line. Substantial English gentlemen are ill conditioned for the rôle of party stooges, and the month of May was not out before the first stirrings had become perceptible of a Parliamentary opposition, not to King Charles, but to King Pym.

Under these circumstances Pym must have felt it imperative upon him to drive home his advantage over the King with the same ruthless energy with which he had pressed his offensive against Strafford. If not physically, at least as a sovereign power in the State, Charles must be finally eliminated. He must never, so far as it was possible to safeguard against it, be in a position to come back on a wave of popular reaction, and revive, with heavy additional counts, that indictment which Strafford had been only just forestalled from presenting. It was not that the King had ever, even in private, expressed the least vindictive intention, but that monarchs are notoriously prejudiced on the subject of treason. "Even Christ", as King Alfred had put it, "could not forgive Judas."

Even if Mr Pym had been capable of conceiving of principles rather different from his own, by which a Christian monarch might be actuated, so hard-bitten a political campaigner would hardly have deemed it safe to count on them. For the initiates of this world's wisdom the principle has ever held good, "Do unto the other man as he (or a man precisely similar to yourself in his shoes) would like to do unto you, *and do it first !*"

3

A LITTLE CLOUD

NEVER, since the *Oedipus Rex* has a tragedy run so straight and inevitable a course, as this of King Charles. The surrender of Whitehall may be likened to the fissure in the wall of a reservoir, high up in the hills. For a brief space there is no more than an increasing leakage, but any knowledgeable observer will realize that the situation is now irremediably out of hand ; the water will soon force its way in a resistless flood, and then no human contrivance can prevent those fat and smiling pastures, those peaceful farms and cottages far down in the reclaimed valley, from being utterly submerged.

Of the tragedy of King Charles I believe it would be true to say that the starting point we have chosen, that of his surrender to Pym's mob-backed ultimatum, is that from which—given the man Charles was, and the men his enemies were—it begins to gather irresistible momentum towards the final catastrophe. It passes from the province of Can-be to that of Must-be. And that, not because of his passing Strafford's Attainder, but because, in his blind agony of conscience, he had allowed Pym's Perpetual Parliament Bill to pass at the same time. Had it not been for that

fatal blunder, from which Bishop Williams had in vain endeavoured to dissuade him, he would only have had to bide his
time for a very little longer, to have rallied all the moderate
opinion in the country to his support, and if not to have recovered
his old power in the Constitution, at least to have achieved one
of those illogical compromises so dear to the English heart, between
the right of the King to govern the country and of Parliament to
govern the government, that, like so many theoretical impossibilities on English record, might have come off in practice.

For Pym was bound to overplay his hand, if indeed he had not
overplayed it already. In the very completeness of his success
lay the danger of its reversal. For two years now he and his fellow
Patriots had pursued a remorseless offensive against an almost
unresisting Sovereign. They had loaded him with defeat on
defeat, and humiliation on humiliation ; and now that they had
him down and helpless, they were plainly determined to finish
him off. But neither the bully nor the extremist has ever been a
popular character with the English people, which was, besides,
beginning to make on its own behalf a similar discovery to that of
the frogs in the fable who called in King Stork to deliver them from
the tyranny of King Log.

King Pym had indeed gorged them with propaganda ; but
this, though an exhilarating, is hardly a sustaining diet. And now
that they were beginning to sweat it out of their systems, they were
gradually awakening to the fact that their pockets were being run
through to a greater extent in a few months, by their new masters
—largely to pay for the luxury of a Scottish occupation—than in
the whole eleven years of the "Tyranny" ; that a reign of terror
had been set up such as put all the worst excesses even alleged
against the Monarchy and the Star Chamber far into the shade ;
that a campaign of fanatical destruction was on foot against all
that was most sanctified by tradition in the heart of the common
Englishman, all that might be lovely to his eye or pleasant to his
senses : in short, that the little finger of King Pym was thicker
than King Charles's loins.

This was driving the mob—it might even be driving Parliament
—too hard to be endured indefinitely. And yet so far from even
the removal of Black Tom bringing any lightening of the burden,
it seemed as if Pym were determined to pile it on more mercilessly
than ever. Six subsidies, an unprecedented amount even in time of
war, had been screwed in a single session out of the unhappy

taxpayer, who had almost forgotten, during the "Tyranny", what the word "subsidy" meant ; but now on the top of all this his burden was to be doubled by the imposition of a poll tax—a name that had stunk in English nostrils since the days of Wat Tyler ; and this new net was drawn with so fine a mesh as to catch those lucky or cunning enough to slip through the many gaps in the old. A total demand up to date equivalent to twelve solid subsidies, with heaven knew how many more to follow ! Something worse than what would, but recently, have been the taxpayer's worst nightmare.

And yet there was nothing surprising about it when you consider that for the first time, since the far distant days of the Danegeld, England had got to comb herself out for the where-withal of a war indemnity. This was the price she had to pay for the success of the Patriots in planting an invading army on English soil as a clinching move in their own political game. The Scots, only too delighted to cash in on the differences of their neighbours, and secure in the circumstance that such English forces as remained mobilized were under strict orders not to disturb them, had spread themselves out comfortably enough over the Northern counties, and, as occupying armies go, had behaved reasonably well, in consideration of the willingness of their collaborators at Westminster to apply, on their behalf, to the whole of England, the good old Border custom of levying blackmail. And now that they themselves were no longer required to serve the purpose of a blackmailing counter, they were demanding, over and above all that they had extracted up to date by monthly instalments, a lump sum of £300,000 (a swingeing total in those days), for the favour of going quietly home. Nor were the Patriots in any condition to refuse them.

Poor old England, indeed, had come to a pass in which she might count herself lucky to get off with nothing worse than a fine. For the Scots had been audacious enough to press for her to bow her neck to the yoke of a Presbyterian Kirk on the authentic Scottish model. This was a little too much for even the Patriots to swallow at one gulp, especially when it was coupled with renewed demands for a customs union : and it was this selfsame customs union that the mercantile interests of the City had wrecked the late King James's project of a united Great Britain rather than concede. So within a week of Lord Strafford's death Parliament was directed to return a temporizing answer, in terms so propitiatory as to be almost abject. But this time even the crack of Pym's whip failed to produce the automatic unanimity of response to which he had been at such pains to condition that pliable assembly. Voices were actually raised in opposition. Mr Edward Hyde, the pink-cheeked, blond, and rather eupeptic young man, who, having built up for himself one of the most lucrative practices at the Bar, was now, both as a debater and a chairman of committees, beginning to be talked of as one of the coming men in the Commons, rose in his place to put in a modest demurrer on behalf of the Church of England, whose sacrifice the Patriots appeared to be contemplating, over and above the indemnity, as part of the peace terms. The House must have pricked up its ears at intervention from such a quarter. For Mr Hyde had hitherto displayed the most conformable zeal of advocacy for the Patriot brief.

We have not the report of his speech, and no doubt it was framed in much more guarded terms than he felt free to employ in after years, when penning his monumental history :

"Without doubt, when posterity shall recover the courage and conscience, and the old honour of the English nation, it will not with more indignation and blushes contemplate any action of this seditious and rebellious age, than that the nobility and gentry of England, who were not guilty of the treason, should recompense invasion from a foreign, contemned nation, with whatever establishments they proposed in their own kingdom, and with a donative of three hundred thousand pounds, over and above all charges, out of the bowels of England ..."

But however adroitly the pill may have been sugared, Mr Pym must have stroked his beard rather more thoughtfully than usual at this gesture of opposition from—of all unlikely people—the urbane Mr Hyde, Ned Hyde as he was to all that comprehensive range of acquaintances, from Archbishop Laud to the most intransigent of the revolutionaries, into whose confidence he had had the knack of insinuating himself, and in all the diverse circles, political and literary, into which he had contrived to fit so agreeably. Mr Pym would not have got where he was unless he had been an adept in reading the first signs of a political change of weather ; and he would not have been what he was, had he not attributed the like faculty to the successful barrister politician.

What could Ned Hyde be banking on ?

4

AN OPPOSITION IN BEING

THIS much at least Pym could have inferred, even if he had not
been, as he was, apprised of it already : it was no lone hand that
Hyde was playing. An even more unexpected voice was to be
joined to his in this nascent opposition, that of the most brilliant
young man in the country, Viscount Falkland, whose mansion at
Great Tew, near Oxford, was the nearest English equivalent to
the Hotel de Rambouillet and other aristocratic *salons* that were
beginning to exercise so profound an influence on French culture.
He himself was a classic and theological scholar of an erudition of
which that age was uniquely prolific, and he could turn his pen
with equal accomplishment to either prose or verse. But for his
insignificant presence, clumsy movements and scrannel voice,
and still more, his entire lack of creative originality, he might
have become what Sir Philip Sidney had been to the Elizabethan
age. But Sidney himself had not diffused the fragrance, nor
bequeathed the memory, of a more endearing personality ; one
that more harmoniously combined the magnanimity of the Greek,
with the sweet courtesy and charity of the Christian ideal of a
gentleman.

Mr Pym must have been even more surprised, though he may
have been less concerned, at Falkland's defection than Hyde's.
No Patriot had thrown himself with such unbridled enthusiasm
into the Parliamentary cause, or had flaunted so austere a
determination to be free from the least suspicion of courtly
sycophancy as this youthful Mæcenas. But then the workings of a
mind like Falkland's were beyond the computation of so practical
an intelligence as Pym's, even if he had thought them worth the
trouble. For there was a strange lack of effectiveness about all
that Falkland undertook, as if God, in endowing him with all the
talents and all the virtues, had added a certain fastidiousness
that had prevented him from ever marring their perfect bloom by
harnessing them to the rough work of life.

A person of very different calibre had intended to add his
protest to those of the other two. This was an impecunious
Kentish squire, Sir John Colepeper of Hollingbourne, who had
seen service on the battlefields of Germany and had, in the course

of it, acquired a certain notoriety as a duellist ; a rough, likeable sort of fellow, without much delicacy of sentiment or scruple, but with a fund of natural shrewdness and a true duellist's *flair* for the cut and thrust of debate. He was the member of the trio whom Mr Pym selected for the compliment of muzzling, by the simple expedient of voting him into the chair.

The motion was of course carried ; but the significant thing was that any opposition, however tentative, should have been allowed to raise its head ; and that none of the appropriate penalties for criticism, such as committal to the Tower or expulsion from the House, should have been visited on the recalcitrant Members. For we should be very wide of the mark were we to imagine that the notion of tolerance was one that would have been even intelligible to a mind like Pym's, or that privilege of speech in the Long Parliament included the right of individual members to assert themselves against the sense of the House, which for practical purposes meant the will of its ruling clique.

For the idea of important issues of policy being freely debated across the floor of a representative assembly was no more reconcilable with the intentions of Pym and his Patriots in the seventeenth, than with those of the Führer and *his* Patriots in the twentieth century. One could cite repeated instances of the inquisitorial promptitude with which the least symptoms of incipient heresy were pounced on and suppressed, nor could any modern Dictator have defined the standpoint with more total lucidity than Speaker Lenthall in the December of this same year, in the case of the famous Protestant divine, William Chillingworth, who had let fall some unguarded reference, in private conversation, to "the other side", which had been duly reported by Mr Pym's excellent intelligence service, with the following result :

"The said Mr Chillingworth being brought in again to the bar and kneeling all the time ; the Speaker laid open to him the greatness of his offences, in reporting that we had sides and parts in the House that was but one body and so to set division among us ... and that therefore the judgment of this House was ... that he should go to the Tower." And to the Tower Mr Chillingworth went.

So that we can infer with something approaching certainty that Mr Pym's failure to take any steps to make an example of Mr Hyde, Sir John Colepeper, and Lord Falkland, for this incipient attempt to constitute themselves "a side or part in the House", could have been due to one reason alone : that with his incomparable self-restraint and *flair* for political strategy, he judged that this threat to the very key of his security—his control of the Commons—was of too formidable a character to be amenable to tactics of direct suppression.

But for the moment at any rate it could be contained, with perhaps a fair hope of its very incongruous elements falling apart. But let it strike root, and on such a rank soil of popular discontent who could set limits to its expansion or the support it would get in the country, if it could avail itself of the still potentially inexhaustible reserves of loyalty to the Crown?

Could *that* be what Mr Hyde had been banking on ... ?

If so there was plainly not a moment to be lost. So long as Pym could be sure of even a working majority in the Commons, the opposition group was powerless to stretch out effective hands to the King on the right or the people on the left. Short of open rebellion, popular discontent could find no means of making itself effective. For between the King and his people the Perpetual Parliament Act had fixed a gulf that only a Parliamentary majority could bridge.

What, to an intelligence so acute as Pym's, must have followed from these considerations? Exactly what did follow in practice. His control of Parliament, held now on so uncertain a tenure, must be exploited to the grim limit while it lasted. The King must not be given a moment to recover himself, and above all must be prevented from making any fresh contact whatsoever with his people. The offensive against the Crown must be pushed on with unrelenting expedition and by all available means. And then if, and when, a royalist reaction did gather to a head, it would be too late.

For then it would be King Pym in the saddle, and Charles Stuart—where?

To that question perhaps not even Mr Pym himself could have returned a definite answer—as yet.

5

PARALYSIS OF SOVEREIGNTY

THERE is a kind of nightmare in which the sleeper knows himself to be in bed, with the familiar objects all round him, and yet feels something impalpable and malignant closing in upon him, with unseen tentacles, as he lies there unable to move a muscle trying to convince himself that it is, after all, only a dream, and that he has only to wake up for the life of that safe and familiar environment to resume its workaday course.

But with King Charles and Queen Henriette it was the visible life that was phantasmal, and the nightmare that was real, the thing that had them in its grip, and whose grip they felt to be deliberately, remorselessly, closing in upon them. For by this time they must have realized that the forces that had destroyed Strafford were implacably concentrated on *their* elimination. And yet they had no weapon with which to strike back, nor even power to flee. They could only go on enacting, with the competence of trained actors, day in and day out, the parts for which they were billed, of King and Queen in a national pageant play. There was the pomp and ceremonial of the Court to be kept up, even though the Court was honeycombed with Mr Pym's spies and there was hardly a face which might not be a mask for treason. Not even where their confidence was most unquestioningly reposed could they be quite sure of its firm ground not proving a quicksand.

There was Lucy, now Dowager Countess of Carlisle, the intimate, almost passionate friend of Strafford in his last days, and the trusted confidante into whose sympathetic ear the Queen could get some relief by pouring her anxieties—little dreaming that Lucy in her turn was in the habit of pouring confidences into the ear of the elderly Mr Pym, whose Puritanism, according to some blasphemous tittle-tattle, was susceptible of a certain relaxation in private life. But gossip, and even Lucy herself, were woefully out in their estimate of Mr Pym, if they imagined that even her Ladyship's rather mellowing charms could have moved him with the desire to embrace anything but the opportunity of tapping so priceless a source of information. Though from what, if any, means to so desirable an end Mr Pym's Puritan soul would, at a pinch, have debarred him, is another question that every student of his character is at liberty to answer for himself.

Not only the business of the court, but that of the nation had to be transacted somehow ; though how it was ever got through by the scratch collection of ministers, some of them more concerned to wreck the King's government than to carry it on, must remain a mystery. The immediate sequel to the death of Strafford was the resignation from the treasurership of the upright and competent Juxon, whose continuance in office, in view of the violent agitation that was being worked up against the Bishops, had plainly become impossible ; though so hopeless was it to look for anyone capable of taking his place, that the office had to be put, into commission. The last of the key men of the great government of the "Tyranny" was thus removed, and the ship of state was left to drift, like a derelict hulk, without course or control. Providentially the Powers of the Continent were too busily engaged in bleeding each other to death to have any attention left over for England.

Such a state of administrative paralysis was, even apart from its rendering the country helpless and defenceless internationally, utterly disastrous within her own confines, since the anarchic forces that had been so recklessly unleashed in the offensive against the Crown, were in danger of getting completely out of hand. And, let it not be forgotten, that the worst danger of anarchy was not that from below, formidable though it was when God-drunken sects and sectarians were goading on the mob to wilder and wilder extravagances of destructive hysteria ; but that which for centuries had never failed to result from any paralysis of the royal sovereignty—the anarchy from above, the unrestrained licence of the rich and powerful to constitute themselves a law unto themselves, and to tyrannize over their humbler neighbours in a way that no monarch, with the worst will in the world, could have dreamed of doing.

That was the danger which for centuries the occupant of that *siege perilous*, the throne of England, had been there to guard against ; and it was a task that only the strongest of monarchs, acting in the closest alliance with his people, could face with any chance of success or even of survival. In the days of the Plantagenets it had been the great feudal estate owners who had been in chronic conspiracy to dissolve the King's peace into a chaos of petty tyrannies. But the great Sovereigns of the Tudor dynasty, with the enthusiastic backing of their Parliaments and to the infinite relief of the country, had put an end once and for all to any question of even the most powerful subject setting himself openly above the authority of the State. The handsome head of Elizabeth's Earl of Essex had been the last that would ever need to roll in the sawdust to prove, to the satisfaction of all concerned, that the day of the baronial *putsch* was gone for ever.

But this sharp remedy had not killed the menace but only driven it below the surface, to revive and to confront the House of Stuart in an even deadlier form. For now the danger was no longer of individual anarchs playing for their own hands or fortuitously linked in *ad hoc* conjurations, but of a class or interest in the community seeking to impose its sway on the whole ; the danger no longer of a feudal revolt but—though the adjective had not yet been coined—of a capitalist revolution.

But any such attempt of one part of the nation to dominate the whole, the King, by the very nature of his office, was bound to oppose. That, at any rate, was the view that King Charles took, and for which he stood with unwavering consistency until he sealed his faith with his blood.

"I am entrusted," he said, when he came to look his murderers in the face, "with the liberties of my people. ... I have sworn to maintain the peace by the duty I owe to God and to my country and I will do it to the last breath of my body ... otherwise I betray my trust."

The King's peace, the liberties of his people, the way of lawful authority, as defined by the terms of the coronation oath, "to do justice, stop the growth of iniquity, protect the holy Church of God, help and defend widows and orphans ... punish and reform what is amiss"—such were the things for which Charles, with that obstinacy that has so often and so truly been remarked upon by his critics, conceived that it was his duty to stand against any argument whatever of superior force. He had yielded to that argument once when he had allowed what he himself would have defined as the "arbitrary way" to take its course in the matter of Strafford ; but the consciousness of that sin had burned deep into his soul, and produced the fixed resolve that come what might, it should be the last time. And come what might, and come what did, it *was* the last time.

But it was this very fact that rendered his sovereignty and ultimately his very existence, so uncompromising a stumbling block to that able and determined group of men who under the forms of constitutional liberty were determined to make their own arbitrary way prevail.

6

UNDERMINING THE THRONE

No more hopeless a situation could be imagined than that in which the King now found himself. For neither would the Parliamentary bosses suffer him to carry on his own government, nor consent to form a government themselves. The fact that he had freely conceded all their demands had only had the effect of sharpening their persecution of him. Their propaganda campaign was pushed to more outrageous lengths than ever before ; nothing was omitted that could blacken his reputation and still more, that of his Consort, in the eyes of his people.

"The King," reports that most competent observer, the Venetian Ambassador, "is deprived of his authority with the hatred of his people, which is even stronger against the Queen, who has been the subject of disgraceful pasquinades"—disgraceful indeed, when they did not stop short of imputing adultery with her own Master of the Horse, Sir Thomas Jermyn.*

This on the 28th of May : three days later we find His Excellency again writing in cipher to inform the Doge and Senate how every effort is still being made to saddle their Majesties with the guilt of conspiring to introduce a French Army—that masterpiece of Mr Pym's genius for fiction—into England. "These reports," he observes, "do not find general credit, as it is thought that they are spread to stir up the people still further against the late government and to keep them fast in their present licence."

"No one," he adds, "would venture to predict the end of these efforts. Every one fears that they are the fruit of secret intentions to lead these princes to the last calamity."†

No possible humiliation was spared them. Even the Queen's private correspondence was intercepted and pried into with the object of finding some unguarded sentence that could be quoted against her, and the poor lady had actually had to resort to the expedient of begging this same Ambassador, Giustinian, for the favour of smuggling through a confidential letter to her brother, Louis XIII, by entrusting it to his own embassy courier, whose dispatch case was diplomatically taboo.

* S.P. Ven., no. 191.   † Ibid., no. 192.

On the principle, it may be presumed, that every little helps, Marie de Medici, the Queen's mother, was now driven forth from the refuge with which her son-in-law had provided her, to tread once more the hard paths of impoverished exile on the Continent, where the implacable enmity of Cardinal Richelieu left her hardly a state whose Sovereign would be willing to receive her ; so that like a hunted vixen, she was forced to drag her weary bones from one stopped earth to another. She was a far from deserving old lady, but in England she had been quite harmless, nor had Mr Pym and his friends any special animus against her—they were even ready to dole out to the King a modest present to speed her on her way. But it was an essential part of the game they were playing—and that had in fact been Mr Pym's speciality throughout his career—of running the Catholic bogey for all it was worth against the Crown. And now Mr Pym's strategic eye had perceived that the most vulnerable point in the royal position was constituted by the Queen, and that any blow struck at her mother would be another nail driven into *her* coffin. Even in living chess, Mr Pym's judgment of the correct move was not likely to be deflected by sentimental considerations.

There was another and, for the Crown, highly ominous turn that was now being given to the screw. It is to be noted that while the revolutionary party leaders turned down every request of the King that they should form a ministry of their own choosing to take over the responsibilities of government, they were beginning to assert the claim to control the King's appointments piecemeal, or rather to wait till he made an appointment to some vacant office, and then insist on replacing his nominee by one of their own choosing. A way more certainly calculated to produce administrative chaos it would be hard to imagine. And this was only leading up to a claim to take the power of appointing to any office whatsoever out of the King's hands, except with the consent of Parliament—the Perpetual Parliament that they themselves looked to control : so that the royal authority would become a crowned seal to their own ukases. Whether, if and when the King's sovereignty had thus been formally abolished in all but name, they would have overcome their coyness about forming a ministry, or how else they imagined that the government of the country was going to be provided for, no man can do more than conjecture.

On the day after the killing of Strafford, His Majesty had to provide for the vacant Mastership of the Wards, and he named Sir Robert Heath, a judge of the King's Bench, and one of the soundest lawyers of the time. But this did not suit the book of the new masters of the State, who wanted the office for Lord Saye and Sele, in whose castle, at Broughton—it will be remembered— they had had their secret headquarters while their conspiracy was hatching. The King meekly submitted to the ignominy of dismissing Sir Robert within a day or two of his name being enrolled, to make room for this nominee of King Pym.

An even more significant appointment was to follow. The death of Strafford had left vacant the Lord Lieutenancy of Yorkshire. For this, His Majesty named Lord Savile, who, whatever his other deficiencies, might at least have been thought a *persona grata* to the Patriots, since he had done them yeoman service, at a critical moment, by placing his talent for forgery at their disposal. It can hardly be described as one of Charles's happiest appointments, though Savile's great position in the county and his own desire to go to all lengths to conciliate his opponents, may have made it seem the only thing to be done under the circumstances.

But the mere fact that the King should, without prompting, have elected to promote even so staunch an adherent of their own cause, was enough reason for raising doubts in a mind so honeycombed with suspicion as that of Pym. Savile, for all his patriotism, was hardly, to put it frankly, proof against being got at. And could it be that the King ...? Mr Pym was not the man to take chances. And besides, he may have reflected, it was all to the good that the man who still called himself King should be made "to acknowledge", as the Whig-Liberal historian Gardiner puts it, "practically, that he had found his masters". Such a lesson could not be rubbed in with too much emphasis.

Savile, accordingly, was somewhat incongruously made to share the fate of the blameless Sir Robert. The Patriots had got an even more significant candidate for the post, and, on the face of it, more respectable, in Robert Devereux, Earl of Essex. King Charles must have been lacking indeed in imagination, if the sound of this name did not strike on his ears like the knocking of fate on his door.

Not that anybody, at first glance, would have been inclined to associate this particular Essex with a part in high tragedy. If ever there was such a thing as a conspicuously commonplace person, it was this solid and stolid nobleman of fifty. Had he been born in our time, he would have been one of those public characters who are the despair of caricaturists and publicity agents, for neither in his appearance nor his character was there anything for the imagination to get a grip on—not even any salient foible, unless it was a certain hereditary itch for exploiting the popular line. But he was none the less the sort of man who comes to be thought of as indispensable for a leading, though never quite the supreme part, on the political stage.

But if the face that he presented to the world was commonplace, the memories that he bore in the depths of his soul, and about which he may well have forborne to discourse even to himself, were such as are wont to determine, for good or ill, that character which is a man's fate. It was when he was at the impressionable age of ten that his father—just the sort of parent whom a normal boy would have adored to distraction—had launched his suicidal attempt at a *coup d'état* against a royal mistress who was no more to be swayed by sentiment in matters of politics than Pym himself. The bereaved Robert had known what it was to lie attainted in blood and honour under the cloud of the terrible Queen's displeasure, and it had only been by grace of her successor, King James, that the ban had been lifted. Happy would it have been for him if the new King could have stopped here and not attempted to crown his favours by presenting the lad of sixteen with a girl bride from the great House of Howard ! Is it any wonder that when, after two years spent in completing his education on the Continent, he returned to consummate the union, he should have discovered that his sprightly Frances had no use for her repressed and heavy-going young consort in any capacity whatever ? But it was not Frances's way to stop short at a merely negative gesture ; she was not long in adorning her unhappy Robert with the most conspicuous pair of antlers in all England, on account of another Robert, whom an equally adoring Sovereign had created Earl of Somerset. The cup of poor Essex's humiliation was filled to the brim when King James caused a nullity suit to go through, on the novel ground that though the respondent was not incapable of marriage in general, he did happen to be with this particular lady ! That in the course of these proceedings Frances had found it necessary to remove, by poison, a too candid friend of the second Robert, only came out later, and forms no part of Essex's story.

On him, what other effect could such experiences have been expected to produce than to cause him to encase himself more and more with a protective shell of reserve behind which festered a lifelong distrust and resentment towards the occupant of the throne ?

Essex's career had for the next thirty years been characteristically solid and undistinguished. He had trailed for a while behind the front in Germany ; he had been one of the commanders of a naval expedition that had staged an ignominious fiasco on the scene of his father's triumph at Cadiz. And he had even tried his luck with a second wife, who presented him with a stillborn child and, as the world believed (though the lady denied it), with a similar adornment to that which he had received from Frances ; though this second matrimonial venture was at least so far an improvement on the last as is represented by the difference between annulment and separation.

But England is a country in which even so bovine a ponderosity as that of the last Victorian Duke of Devonshire is, if weighted by an ancient name and great possessions, capable of procuring for its owner the same sort of veneration as, in a more frankly superstitious environment, may have invested the shrine of some always about-to-be articulate, dumb oracle. The popular enthusiasm excited by the brilliance of the former Essex was mere froth on the surface, compared with the deep respect that had come to invest so impressive an inertia as that of his son. Mr Pym's judgment of men was never more vindicated than in his perception that the time had come, in his game against the Crown, to play this weighty piece for all it was worth. The revolution needed ballast—Essex was ideal ballast.

But Essex was after all only one of those great heads of noble houses who had inherited an immemorial tradition of disloyalty, and who, even when they did not condescend to active conspiracy against the throne, were so lukewarm in their allegiance as to contribute hardly less powerfully to the forces making for its ruin.

There is an incident recorded by Clarendon which shows just the sort of thing that made the King's task so hopeless in dealing with men of this stamp. After the first futile campaign that he had been forced to conduct on the Border, Essex, who had at least performed his part with his usual stolid correctness, was, on the general disbandment of the so-called army :

"Discharged with the crowd, without ordinary ceremony, and an accident happening ... whereby the forest of Needwood fell at the King's disposal, which lay at the very door of his estate, and would infinitely have gratified him, was denied to him and bestowed upon another : all of which wrought very much upon his rough, proud nature, and made him susceptible of some impressions afterwards, which otherwise would not have found such easy admission."

In other words, the refusal of the King to prostitute his royal power to the purpose of enabling this wealthy nobleman to swell the account of his already great possessions, at the expense of the probably superior claim of some humbler neighbour, is the decisive factor in turning the tepid loyalty of Lord Essex into a settled and, as far as the word can be applied to any conduct of his, active hostility to his Sovereign.

So, to revert to the account of our impartial observer from Venice :

"The King selected Lord Clavel [which was the nearest His Venetian Excellency could get to Savile] for Governor of the important county of York, and gave him patents for the office : but Parliament would not even let the King enjoy the use of appointment, which is his sole prerogative, and has [at this point the letter ceases to be *en clair* and proceeds in cipher] conferred the governorship on the Earl of Essex, the author of seditious designs, and a leader of the Puritans."

This is only a beginning. In July we find Essex invested with the white staff of the Lord Chamberlain, and, more significantly still, made commander of all the King's forces South of the Trent. In what spirit he would interpret that trust the ensuing months would reveal.

7

TERROR BY LEGISLATION

ONE part of Pym's programme was, to him at any rate, obvious. He must drive home the Parliamentary offensive against the Crown with furious expedition. So long as he could keep his faithful Commons responsive to the crack of his whip, he meant to drive them to the limit. The life of an M.P. cannot have been happy in that summer of 1641. The weather was oppressive and thundery, and as the days drew to their longest, the dreaded and chronic menace of a plague epidemic made its appearance in the London wards. The controllers of the Perpetual Parliament cast anxious eyes over the thinning benches and shrinking numbers in the division lobbies. It had never been feasible even for such a martinet as Pym to provide against any individual follower absenting himself without leave on unavoidable private business, but now so many individuals appeared to be doing the same thing at the same time, that there began to be some prospect of the House, if not actually dissolving itself by driblets, at least shrinking to such incalculable proportions as to give a well organized minority just the chance it needed of cutting in on a snap vote.

Under these circumstances, it had become urgently imperative to get the Houses adjourned at the earliest possible moment, for the recess that they had so well earned.

But Pym, had his prosaic soul been capable of such expression, might have anticipated the words of young Andrew Marvell,

> "At my back I always hear
> Time's winged chariot hurrying near."

For Pym, for all his ox-like deliberateness of progression, was too consummate a strategist not to be fully imbued with the import-ance of the time factor, and he must have realized that this factor was beginning to work against him with a steadily gathering momentum. Look in what direction he would, he must have been reminded of the words that a year ago had been spoken, with malign satisfaction, by the saturnine St John : "Things will be worse before they are better." Only then, "worse" had then signified worse for King Charles—but now ...

The country was getting restive, Parliament was slipping out of control, the army was no longer to be relied on, even the Scots were evincing something of the umbrageousness of the black-mailer whose demands have for the first time been whittled down ; and in these troubled waters what fishing might there not be for that other King ?

For King Pym was too shrewd a judge of human nature to make the mistake of his posthumous *claque* in under-rating Charles as an opponent, though I fancy that like all such masters of the political skin game, he was incapable of understanding that his opponent might not have been playing a game at all, but was simply holding a straight course by the compass of principle. Which may have rendered him a more formidable opponent than ever.

Pym therefore, in spite of the fact that he was straining the patience of his waning majority to danger point, dared not let them off till he had made his position as sure at all vital points as it fairly could be. Above all, he must carry through the great revolutionary programme of legislation, the most tremendous ever undertaken in one session of Parliament, on which he had embarked the previous December, and which was designed to smash the Sovereignty of the Crown beyond any possible hope of recovery. This had been inevitably held up by the all-absorbing business of liquidating Strafford, but now that he was out of the way, no time was lost in rushing through the essential Bills.

Upon one thing all the landed and financial magnates, even those of them who were destined to come over to the King's side, were enthusiastically agreed, and that was in sweeping away the so-called prerogative courts, that had been set up by the Tudors to supplement those of the Common Law, and of which the most prominent was the Court of Star Chamber.

Now these courts were abolished for ever by Act of Parliament. King Pym had no need to fear opposition to that part of his programme, in a House of Commons whose plutocratic membership could hardly, by the wildest stretch of imagination, have claimed to be representative of the bottom dog. The pauper Bests and Grace Tubbys, cut off from the fountain of royal justice, would henceforth be so entirely at the mercy of the Lord Saviles and Sir Thomas Jenkinsons,* that for generations to come they, and their grievances, would be as little accounted of as the vast slave majority of the Athenian population, by those who wax most lyrical about that

"Dear city of men without master or lord."

But it may be said, and said truly, that these courts administered a law that was not the English Common Law, and as such must sooner or later have been shed in the course of a healthy constitutional evolution. But it must be remembered that the prerogative courts had been called into existence to deal with a type of offender who was capable of setting the Common Law at defiance. Prerogative law may not have been ideal; but it was a great

---

* See *Charles, King of England*, pp. 277–288.

deal better than no law at all but that of the strongest arm and longest purse, and so long as the conditions lasted that had called them into being, the disappearance of these emergency courts—which was what they really were—though a godsend to the class in whose interests Mr Pym was acting, was a disaster of the first magnitude to that dumb majority who, if they could not look for justice to its fountain, might look for it elsewhere in vain.

It was not as if Mr Pym and his associates were fired by a disinterested hope of strengthening the hands of the Common Law judges to administer that justice which was no longer to be obtained by Star Chamber methods. The man who had plotted to convert the House of Commons into a permanent puppet show of his own legislative marionettes, was not likely to show greater respect for the law. Nor did he. For it was an even more essential part of his programme to create such a reign of terror in the courts, that no judge, who did not wish to be instantly ruined, would dare pronounce a judgment, or indeed utter a single sentence on the bench, adverse to the persons or interests of the faction in power. The savage example made of the judges in *Rex* v. *Hampden* was enough to strike the fear of the country's new masters even into the great lawyers' guild, which in some ways was a tougher nut to crack than Parliament itself.

This was a distinct improvement on the crude methods employed by Pre-Tudor baronial magnates, of intimidating jurymen, corrupting witnesses, and so forth. It was an ordered and scientific terror, whose effect was less to ride roughshod over the law in the interest of individuals, than to take over the law and run it in the interest of an oligarchy.

The voice of the law was still the voice of King Charles, but the will was the will of King Pym.

Having saddled the King with an indissoluble, and therefore unrepresentative, Parliament, Pym's next step was to compel him to feed out of its hand, or rather out of that of its masters, by keeping him chronically on the edge of bankruptcy. Every source of revenue was cut off from him, including, by specific enactment, his last lifeline of the customs duties. Nor was there any question of reviving the admittedly immemorial practice of granting them for life. They were to be doled out for the shortest possible periods, a month or two at a time, so that King Charles would constantly have to come hat in hand to King Pym to beg for a renewal of his favours, on such terms as King Pym might be graciously pleased to concede him, or see the whole machinery of government brought to an abrupt stop and the realm plunged into chaos.

King Pym meant there to be no mistake about this and he applied his customary technique of terror with even more than his customary thoroughness, by an act of vindictive tyranny which, if it had been perpetrated by any other king in our annals, would be spoken of to this day with bated breath. The collection of the customs, which had proceeded without a break from the remote middle ages, and whose sudden discontinuance would have thrown the whole elaborate system of trade regulation violently out of gear, had been a bone of contention from the beginning of the reign, owing to the determination of the Parliamentary bosses from the first, to blackmail the Crown by starving it of the bare necessities of government. So now Pym turned on the unfortunate customs officers, who had nothing to do with the quarrel but had merely carried out their immemorial duties according to the orders they had received, by first voting them all under Parliamentary ban as delinquents, and then, on the following day, mercifully allowing them to compound for their offence by the ruinous fine of £150,000—considerably more than the proceeds of a complete subsidy from the whole country ! Even the faithful Gardiner finds it a little hard to stomach this "precedent ... which did something to accustom the Commons to that chase after wealth which [the reference presumably being to the fines inflicted on overweening anarchs like Sir Thomas Jenkinson] had been one of the worst features of the Star Chamber."*

There was nothing that the King could do to protect his unhappy servants from this outrage, but he could, and did, resign himself to his own loss—by far the most crippling blow that had ever been inflicted on the Crown—in words of pathetic graciousness :

"I hope you do know that I do freely and frankly give over the right that my predecessors have ever challenged to them ... as a mark of my confidence to put myself wholly upon the love and affection of my people for my substance."

Such language, whatever effect it might have had on the people, was not calculated to mollify Pym. That Charles Stuart should seek to compass the love and affections of his people was in itself constructive *lèse majesté* to the *de facto* Sovereign.

* *History of England* IX, p. 379.

8

THE ATTACK ON THE CHURCH

BESIDES the Crown, the Parliament, and the law, there was a fourth objective that it was essential for Pym to dispose of before he could feel himself safe enough to call a pause in his revolutionary drive. This was constituted by the Church. For no one knew better than this great master of demagogic technique, that the populace is never more amenable to control than when it has been worked up out of its sober senses into a fever of ideological— or as it would then have been called—religious fanaticism.

Pym's quarrel with the Church had little enough to do with Christianity. There is not the least reason so suppose that either he, or any of the Patriot chiefs, were men of specially marked religious feeling. It is true that he had built up his Parliamentary reputation for the best part of a dozen years by concentrating almost exclusively on the task of keeping alive the bitterest extreme of persecuting phobia against the Catholics, since the no-Popery bogey served his purpose in as obvious a way as that of anti-Semitism was to serve Hitler's ; and when the time came for him to develop his attack on the Church and Crown, it was only to be expected that he should represent the one as being honeycombed by, and the other as engaged (through the Queen) in, a sinister conspiracy to bring back the country beneath the Roman yoke and relight the fires of Smithfield.

But that was all part of the game, a game whose nature the cunning Hampden indicated sufficiently by his admission that without constantly working up religious scares they could never keep the people on their side. What constituted from the Patriot standpoint, the trouble with the Church, was not only her loyalty to the Crown, but still more her championship of the people. Under Archbishop Laud the Church, like the Star Chamber, had fearlessly stood up for the rights of the bottom dog against his rich and genteel oppressors. Admittedly tact was not Laud's strong point, but where he gave most offence was in setting the example to his clergy of treating the squire and his relations as if they were of no different clay, in the eyes of God and the Church, from that of the humblest labourer. The scandals of the hall were no more exempt from rebuke than those of the cottage ; and to crown all his offences, this mitred busybody took upon him, on every possible occasion, to interpose the Church's authority against the now frequent attempts of the great ones of the land to enclose or otherwise gobble up the land of the little men. And what made it worse was that he, William Laud, was himself a fellow of the commonest clay, son of a Reading tradesman, who but for the Church would never have been in a position to come it over his betters.

> Remember now from whence you came,
> And that your grandsires of your name
> Were dressers of old cloth !

is what one of the many contemporary ballads that were being circulated against the Archbishop, puts in the forefront of the indictment against him. And indeed the real attitude of the party which is often spoken of as democratic, may be judged from the way in which one of its aristocratic leaders, Lord Brooke, in a book attacking the Bishops, is careful to emphasize that they are, in respect of their parentage, *de faece populi*—from the dung of the people.* For to his Lordship and his kind—as this passage only too plainly lets out of the bag—the common people are just dung !

It was inevitable therefore, that the attack on the Crown should broaden out into one on the Church ; though it had been no part of Pym's ostensible programme, at first, to interfere with her Prayer Book or her constitution. With his natural caution, and his dislike of taking on more than one task at a time, he would probably have been glad to finish with the Crown and leave the settlement with the Church till another day. But he could not help himself. The forces of fanaticism that he had set in motion against the Crown had gathered their own momentum ; not only were his allies, the Scots, clamouring for the complete Presbyterianizing of the Church of England, but their enormous demands for blackmail were causing more and more of Pym's supporters in Parliament to favour the notion of taking off some of the English taxpayer's burden, by a second Protestant plunder of Church property on a grand scale. And it was becoming a matter of urgency to get rid of the formidable obstacle constituted by the solid vote of the Episcopal Bench in an Upper House that, though it had been cowed and humiliated as never before in its history,

* *The Appeal of Injured Innocence*, p. 615.

had not entirely lost its spirit, and was evincing signs of rest-lessness.

In spite of all the ceaseless, and partially successful propaganda directed against Laud and the Bishops, the Church, if only through the incomparable beauty of her Bible and Prayer Book, had struck very deep roots in the affections of the country. Neither House of Parliament was prepared to be stampeded into a course of revolutionary destruction against her. The Lords, taking umbrage at a barefaced attempt of the other House to dictate the composition of theirs, threw out a comparatively modest bill for depriving the Bishops of their votes. Whereupon the extremist faction in the Commons tried to double the stakes by pushing forward what was aptly described as a Root and Branch Bill, for sweeping away the whole hierarchic constitution of the Church ; turning it in effect into an English version of the Kirk. And this bill, in spite of the fact that Pym and Hampden— probably after a good deal of anxious deliberation—lent it the whole weight of their authority, only scraped through its second reading by a beggarly majority of 27 over the new opposition that had sprung up under the leadership of Hyde, Falkland and Colepeper. Such a portent might well have been regarded, in the modern Parliamentary jargon, as the writing on the wall.

That it was so regarded, in the most significant quarter of all, is evinced by the fact that King Charles, watching the peril of his Church with an anxiety probably greater than had been caused him by any direct attack on his throne, should at long last have decided to make a move. He sent for Mr Hyde.

9

THE CONVERSION OF EDWARD HYDE

WRITING of it from memory long afterwards, Edward Hyde would have us believe, as he had no doubt come to believe himself, that this invitation to the Palace took him by such surprise that he at first thought the whole thing to have been a mistake, and that the King, who had never had any sort of contact with him hitherto, must have intended to summon another member of the same name. That was a becomingly proper attitude for the young barrister statesman to assume, but it would have argued an obtuseness very foreign to his nature if, in the depths of his being, he had not had a certain premonition of it.

Since he had come forward in his new rôle of Church defender, far from any overt attempt to crush him, he had found himself courted as never before by the revolutionary chiefs. He was now constantly being invited to those political dinners in Mr Pym's lodgings, in the little court behind Westminster Hall, where we may be sure that Hampden's most flattering blandishments were lavished upon him, and— we may be no less sure—received with a corresponding urbanity. What could be behind all this? For Mr Hyde, noting these phenomena with the barrister's instinct of looking to what lay behind them, could not fail to suspect that behind this feverish anxiety to lure him and his friends back into the fold, was something more than appeared on the surface.

After one of these dinners, which we must remember took place in the middle of the day, they had sat talking till the cool of an early summer evening, when one of the company, Nathaniel Fiennes, brother of Lord Saye and Sele, suggested to Hyde that the two of them should take a ride in the flat meadowlands that stretched between Westminster and the little riverside borough of Chelsea. As they rode together, Fiennes became extremely vehement, and wanted to know what inducement there could be for sticking so passionately to the Church, which, he said, could not be supported. His companion, impenetrably bland, pleaded reason and conscience, and even more blandly proceeded to enquire in his turn, what form of church government it was proposed to substitute for the existing one. This riposte seems to have been rather more than Fiennes had bargained for, for all he could find to answer was that there would be time enough to think of that ; and then, like many a badly rattled witness whom Mr Hyde could probably remember, he appears to have completely lost his head, for he launched forth into a violent tirade that went a good deal further than he can ever have intended, into language of open menace and sedition, threatening "as sharp a war as had ever been in England" if the King did not give up the Bishops.

This, though it produced no ostensible reaction, must have come as a shock even to Hyde. It was out now ! Never before, in the most intimate of their discussions with him, had any of the Parliamentary chiefs given away that they might be plotting rebellion—and yet that was the plain drift of Fiennes's harangue.

It was only two days after this that Mr Hyde was buttonholed in the Abbey churchyard by the queerest of all his extensive circle of Parliamentary acquaintances, Harry Marten, one of the members for Berkshire, and a gentleman of more than doubtful reputation, being a rake, a spendthrift, and even a suspected atheist, with a particular grudge against the King, who on one occasion had had him turned out of Hyde Park as "an ugly rascal" and a "whoremaster". Still, there seems to have been something likeable about the incorrigible Harry, who was certainly, as we should say nowadays, a character, as well as a bit of a lad, and we can imagine that the correct lawyer must have smiled a little indulgently when his friend started, in his usual impetuous style, warning him that he was on the way to ruin himself by going over to the side of the Court. Hyde was at no loss for his provokingly discreet answer, to the effect that he had nothing to do with the Court, but was only concerned with preserving the government and the law—and then, with his usual *flair* for turning the tables, asked Marten what *he* thought of the men who were governing the House. With disarming candour Marten replied that he thought them knaves, and added that when they had done what they intended to do, they should be used as they did others. Hyde would not have been the man he was had he failed to draw out whatever significance lay behind this rather cryptic verbiage. So he pressed Marten to say what he himself wanted. There was no reply for a few seconds, and then, with defiant emphasis, out it came :

"I do not think one man wise enough to govern us all."

Such words, up to a very recent date, if any one had dared to use them and they could have been brought home to him, would have entailed his certain and probably painful decease. As it was ... Mr Hyde could not help thinking of Marten's great wealth and influence in his own county ; and perhaps, to so devout a Churchman, the words may have occurred :

"From all sedition, privy conspiracy, and rebellion ..."

For that nothing less than this was working up, would have been apparent, by now, to a less shrewd observer than Ned Hyde. And I do not think it can have taken him altogether by surprise when, shortly afterwards, he was buttonholed in the lobby by a

Mr Percy,* with a command to attend on His Majesty that evening, and with as little advertisement as possible, if we may judge by the fact that at the appointed hour the messenger himself came to fetch him from his chambers to Whitehall, and conducted him for the first time along that great gallery through which he was so often to pass in after years as Chief Minister of England. When they arrived at the square room, or ante-chamber, his companion disappeared for a moment into the King's closet, and then returned to fetch him. As Charles and Clarendon looked each other in the face for the first time, and the young statesman bent dutifully over his Sovereign's outstretched hand, the courtier backed through the door, leaving them alone.

It is quite evident, from all that we know about their subsequent relations, that the two men at once and instinctively took to each other. Charles was an artist, and a stylist to his finger tips—fate had played him an ill turn in dragging him from the quiet of the studio and the study to wrestle with Philistines in the political arena. He was quick to recognize that in the man who had it in him to execute the most masterly series of character studies in English prose literature, he had found a kindred spirit. So well, in fact, did the King come to appreciate the fine points of Hyde's style that—with the connoisseurship for which he was so famous in detecting the authorship of pictures—he once, in their campaigning days at Oxford, offered to bet Falkland that he could never fail to detect Hyde's authorship of any unsigned piece of writing ; though Falkland did eventually succeed in catching him out with one of the contemporary news sheets in which a speech of Hyde's was attributed to Lord Pembroke.

The interview started conventionally enough with the King saying how grateful he was for the loyal stand the young opposition leader had made in the House of Commons, and particularly for his championship of the Church. Something in His Majesty's voice or manner must have moved Hyde out of his usual lawyer-like discretion, for he came out with the impulsively uncourtierlike remark that even if the King *had* commanded him to withdraw his affection from the Church, he would not have obeyed. Charles was delighted—here was no place-seeking politician, but

* Or so Clarendon, writing 28 years after the event, says. But it could not have been Henry Percy, the only M.P. of that name ; for he had fled the country before Strafford's death. Perhaps the old statesman's memory tripped over the identity of the messenger.

a true man ; and from that moment the ice was broken, and they were soon plunged into a discussion, without the least formality, about the situation in the House. That Root and Branch Bill— the bill that would practically have abolished the Church—did Mr Hyde think they could get it through ? Mr Hyde thought not ; or at least, that it would take them a long time. The King wanted to know whether Hyde and his supporters would be capable of holding up the bill until such time as he himself had departed on the progress he intended to make to Edinburgh, by which time the armies in the North would have been disbanded, and—as I think His Majesty clearly meant to imply—Mr Pym no longer had the Scottish Army of occupation to use as a black- mailing counter.

"I will undertake the Church," said the King, "after that time" (in other words, shall be in a position to refuse my Royal assent to such a bill).

"Why then," was the reply, "by the grace of God, it will not be in much danger."

That was enough to go on with, and the two separated with an understanding between them that was never afterwards broken. For besides their love of the Church, they had also in common a fundamental reverence and respect for the law, and that reign of law which those wealthy revolutionists who assumed to them- selves the style of "Patriots" and "The Popular Party", plotted to override by their own arbitrary will.

To the King, in familiar conversation, it would henceforth never be Mister but always Ned Hyde, and the time was not so far distant when it would be his regular habit to check up on any advice by asking if Ned Hyde were of that opinion. And, as for Hyde, we can let him speak of himself for himself :

"He had a very particular devotion and respect for the person of the King ; and did believe him the most, and the best Christian in the world. He had a most zealous esteem and reverence for the constitution of the government ; and believed it so equally poised that if the least branch of the prerogative were torn off ... the subject suffered ... and he was as much troubled when the Crown exceeded its just limits, and thought its prerogative hurt by it."

From that interview it may be said that a Cavalier, or Consti- tutional party dates, if not its birth, at least its conception.

IO

WRECKERS WHO WOULD NOT GOVERN

IT may very naturally be asked why, having got as far as sending for the leader of the Opposition, King Charles could not at least have sounded him on the possibility of himself and his friends taking over the key posts of the government—forming a ministry, as we should say nowadays. That is what it eventually came to, and that in the chaotic state of the administration it did not come at once, can hardly be accounted for except on the assumption that Charles was clinging, almost beyond hope, to his purpose of conciliating the still dominant party in the House. He had given them everything they had demanded, had allowed the Crown to be stripped of one after another of its ancient prerogatives and himself to be reduced to a position of utter helplessness and dependence on the controllers of Parliament—and that Parliament no longer answerable to the constituencies, but to itself and its bosses.

Charles, as we have seen, had been ready, and in fact eager, to accept the logical outcome of this situation, and allow the controlling faction to form a ministry of its own. It was Pym, and not he, who had wrecked the project. But the King was not so easily discouraged. To his clear and reasonable intelligence it must have seemed obvious that this was now the only possible thing to do. For Charles, we must remember, had not our advantage of access to shelf upon shelf of magisterial tomes, asserting with one voice that he was such an incurable plotter and double-dealer that the very reasonableness of any proposal emanating from him was reason for turning it down. All that we know, apart from what we have been taught to believe about him, shows him to have been not only a man of unswerving principle and honour, but unsuspicious, to a fault, of treachery and double-dealing in others. Even with these men who had called the invader into England, and had stuck at nothing to compass ends that from his point of view, at least, must have appeared the blackest treason, he would not give up hope of an accommodation. All through the summer he was clinging to this idea of a Pym government.

That the project must have come nearly to a head at the end of July is evident from two letters written to Admiral Sir John

Pennington, giving the names of the proposed appointments, and the second of which, from the Clerk to the Council, Sir Edward Nicholas—who, if any man ought to have known—names Pym himself for the Exchequer, Saye for the Treasury, Hampden for the Duchy of Lancaster, Denzil Hollis for Secretary of State, and Lord Brooke as Privy Councillor : the substance of a complete Pym ministry. But as once again nothing came of it, we can only assume that Mr Pym, for reasons of his own, was still adamant in his determination neither to govern nor let govern.

What reasons ? Logical enough, if we follow the bent of Pym's mind. If a perpetual Parliament, why not a perpetual Government ? Why allow the King to dismiss his ministers any more than to dissolve his Parliament ? If public opinion swung against Mr Pym, as it showed every sign that it might do, the appointment of an opposition ministry might have incalculable effects in rallying the people (that "dung", as Lord Brooke would have called it) to the support of monarchy. That was, at any rate, the direction in which Pym's policy was beginning to tend. Until such time as the King's ministers not only received their mandate from King Pym, but held it at his pleasure, there was to be no truce for King Charles, nor any question of his forming a coherent government.

Pym himself could not fail to be conscious of the way in which, in spite of all his successes, the tide was beginning to turn against him. But the genius of this great political strategist was never more conspicuous than when difficulties began to accumulate. With admirable resourcefulness, he set himself to check the drift to opposition, and to prevent the control of Parliament from slipping out of his hands. So far the opposition had centred itself upon this one issue of the Church, and the essential thing was to prevent it from broadening out into the support of the Crown.

Particularly important was it, at this stage, to prevent the conflict that had developed with the Upper House over the question of the Bishops, from developing any further. Nothing could be better calculated to bring back the Peers into line, than to appeal for their fraternal co-operation in circumventing the latest sinister design imputed to the King.

This was nothing less than the proposed Royal visit to Scotland. At first sight there might seem something a little inconsistent in the idea of the men who had been actively in collusion with two Scottish rebellions, and had been privy to introducing an invading army into England, working themselves, and trying to work the country, into a panic about this peaceful gesture. For what could have been more natural, or more timely, than for the King of these two unhappily contending countries to have signalized the termination of strife between them by a visit to his Northern capital, in order to show himself to his Scottish subjects, and do what only a King could to apply balm to the wounds left by these late, unhappy conflicts, and diffuse that atmosphere of goodwill without which no peace can be more than a hollow truce ?

This simple and charitable explanation of the King's motives is borne out by every detail of his actual conduct, nor is there a shred of serious evidence that he had any ulterior design, or that he was plotting anything whatever. But the assertions of Pym's propaganda on the subject have been reproduced with such parrot-like accuracy that it is very improbable that one student in a million of the history of the time dreams of doubting that Charles Stuart's Scottish treason against King Pym is as indubitably attested as Guy Fawkes's Gunpowder treason against King James. Even Gardiner refers to this unarmed visit of the Scottish King to his own realm as a "wild adventure !"

Perhaps it was that in effect ; though certainly not in any sense that Gardiner intended, or Charles could have envisaged. For however innocent his intentions, he was, from the standpoint of his opponents, committing the unforgivable sin. For it was a vital object with them to keep him from re-establishing himself in those affections of his people from which they had so long, and with so large a measure of success, striven to part him. What reckoning might not King Charles exact, with the loyalty of his people to back him ? What real plots and conspiracies might not be brought to light, once attention was diverted from these imaginary ones ?

But it does not follow that Charles was not committing a grave error of political judgment, though the sort of error into which only an honourable and plain dealing man would have fallen. He was giving his enemies, who had already shown that they would stick at nothing to blacken him, far too great an opportunity to do so. They had worked up public opinion to such an extent with scares about army plots, that it was only too easy to make out that the King was going to what was still the Northern front, either to put himself at the head of the bilked and humiliated English forces for a march on Westminster, or else that he was

about to employ his wily arts to commit the unspeakable treason
of inducing the Blue Bonnets from across the Border to support
him against Pym instead of *vice versa*. It is more than possible that
Pym himself may have credited him with what must have
appealed to his strategic instinct as just the sort of move that he,
in the King's shoes, would have elected to play.

And apart from the grist that it provided to Pym's propaganda
mills, the project was fraught with incalculable risks. If ever there
was a witches' cauldron of treasons, plots and stratagems, it was
Scotland at this time. The powers of anarchy, never very far
below the surface, had been strengthened and exacerbated by the
troubles of the past four years. And there were those who had only
too much interest in fomenting them, so as to get his Majesty
involved.

It would have been more prudent to have stopped at home.
But Charles could never forget that he was a Scot, born at
Dunfermline Castle, and had what Clarendon calls "an immod-
erate love for the Scottish nation", that repeatedly, in spite of
experience, betrayed him into a fatal and pathetic confidence in
Scottish loyalty, and had the effect of a blind spot on his mind.

However genuine Pym's alarm may have been over this
proposed move of the King's, he did not intend to let slip the
opportunity it afforded him of diverting the attention of the Houses
from the dangerous question of the Church. He accordingly drew
up a series of cunningly worded propositions to be discussed in
conference with the Lords and presented to His Majesty. These
constituted a masterpiece of insinuation. They started with a
request to the King to postpone his journey till the armies had
been disbanded—with dark hints about "persons ill affected that
may have designs on the army"—and then went on to suggest a
petition of both Houses to his Majesty to remove evil counsellors,
unnamed, and to appoint others in whom Parliament should
have cause to confide—and proceeded even more ominously, to
"divers particulars" concerning the Queen and "the wicked
conspirators" of her own religion by whom she was alleged to be
surrounded. It was all so non-committally phrased that no one
could pin it down to a definite intention of debarring the King
from the right to nominate his own ministers, or of singling out
the Queen as Strafford's successor in the rôle of chief public
enemy—and yet what else could all this rigmarole be leading up
to ? But it went through the Commons without opposition—

doubtless Hyde and his friends did not feel it to be a definite enough issue for them to challenge a division on—and the Lords accepted it with one or two trifling amendments to spare the Queen's feelings. Pym had scored a striking success, in both signally re-asserting his dominance of the Commons, and dashing whatever hopes the King might have had of obtaining support from the Peers.

I I

A QUEEN ON THE RACK

THE toils were now only too visibly beginning to be drawn round the frail person of the Queen. It was not that Mr Pym was a cruel man, or more fanatically intolerant than might be necessary in the way of business, but simply that he framed his political strategy with an entire disregard of human considerations. The man who from the beginning of his career had specialized in Catholic baiting, was not likely to be blind to the propagandist opportunities afforded by the very existence of a Popish consort, one moreover whose safety the King cherished with a devotion that might, in certain circumstances, lure him into a fatal blunder.

Poor Henriette was the last person in the world to be cast for a leading part in a drama of high politics. Least of all was it the part that she would have chosen for herself. She had, before these troubles had begun to accumulate upon her, done all, and more than all, that a Queen of England, in normal times, could have been expected to do ; and she would have been perfectly happy, as she had been ideally successful, as a wife, a mother, and the mistress of a court. The academic panjandrums who have written of her as if she were one of those managing and ambitious she statesmen who are never happy except when they are pulling all the political wires—such a one as her friend, Lucy Carlisle, or her countrywoman, Madame de Chevreuse—give one to doubt whether they can ever have made contact with any normal, feminine woman at all.

For indeed the trouble with Henriette was just that she had no more *flair*, or taste, for political management than a child of six ; she was a mass of impulsive loyalties, and being completely without fear, and—what almost invariably follows—lacking in the instinct of caution, she was ready to fly to the assistance of a husband, a faithful servant, a persecuted co-religionist, or even a little dog, without counting the cost. Moreover she was royal, and thoroughbred to the tips of her delicate fingers ; never did she forget that she was the daughter of the gay and gallant Henry of Navarre, who knew not, as she had said, how to fly, and who had also, as she did not fail to observe, been a Huguenot before he had been a Catholic, a circumstance little calculated to induce in her the austere attitude to heretics of a Mary Tudor. That after her husband had been publicly murdered and herself hounded into exile, the iron of intolerance did enter into her soul, is hardly to be wondered at, and affords no reason for doubting that in her happy days she had desired nothing better than to live in the exercise of her own faith and to let others live in theirs.

Naturally her all too conspicuous position as Catholic Queen of a realm that, though Protestant, had a considerable Catholic minority, could not fail to make her an object of those ceaseless political activities that for centuries have been the speciality of the Vatican. A succession of polite and sympathetic Papal representatives took advantage of the privileged position guaranteed to her personal entourage, and she chattered back to them with her usual impulsive frankness, not even troubling to conceal her distaste for such exuberances of godliness as the disembowelling of priests, and the savage execution of the penal laws against Catholics. One of the few items in the indictment against her that no one could possibly dispute, was that she had set her heart on securing what measure of tolerance she could for those who shared her faith, and that she tried to move her husband in this direction ; an easy task, since Charles, though as little inclined to become a Catholic himself as the hottest gospeller in his realm, was not of the stuff of which persecutors are made. But to imagine she had any serious designs of converting him, still less that she was harbouring some deep and subtle plan of reversing the verdict of the Reformation, is ludicrously to misconceive her nature.

When, however, she herself was singled out as the victim of a pitiless persecution ; when under the impact of disaster after disaster the foundations of her hitherto serene existence began to crumble beneath her feet, and she found herself, and those dear to her, faced with the prospect of utter ruin, she was not the woman to lie down like a frightened rabbit in the path of a stoat. Her fighting instincts were roused, and she looked about for the opportunity to do something—anything—to ward off the peril. There was little enough that she *could* do, but she was at least ready—only too ready—to explore all ways that might be suggested of retrieving the situation ; and it was only too easy for any plausibly loyal helper to obtain her ear for suggestions that a woman of greater political experience would have turned down as impracticable or tainted. It would no doubt have been more prudent for her to have sat with her hands folded and her lips sealed while her friends were destroyed, waiting for her own, and her husband's and her children's turn, but that was not the sort of wisdom bequeathed by the great Henry to his offspring.

She had nothing that could have been described as a policy, beyond a woman's desire to save her own by any means that might offer. She would have been quite as ready to come to terms with Pym as with the Pope himself ; she had in fact made a desperate effort to win the hearts of the Parliamentary leaders, in a series of midnight meetings, at the time when the project of their forming a government was first mooted. It is true that after painful experience had shown her that they were only concerned to involve her in deeper trouble, she had toyed with the idea of touching the Holy Father for the wherewithal to oil their palms— showing, it must be confessed, a lamentable failure to anticipate the lofty estimate of their motives standardized in the now current myth.

She would have had to be very much more politically conscious than she was, had she succeeded in grasping whatever subtle difference there might be between the political respectability of this Northern island and the Latin frankness of her own country, where the Crown, with the backing of armed force, was engaged in one long struggle to impose the terror of absolute sovereignty upon a centrifugal chaos of Leaguers, Frondeurs, and every conceivable permutation and combination of blue-blooded anarchs, engaged in their habitual practice of rebellion and conspiracy, and each playing openly and unashamedly for his own hand. She can hardly have failed to wish, sometimes, that her gentle husband would vary his policy of perpetually futile concession by a touch of the firmness that had served her father in such good stead, and which the Red Cardinal had applied with such brilliant success on behalf of her brother.

But whatever she may have thought, the last thing she had the least desire to do, was to take the political lead out of her husband's

hands. She loved Charles, and since the day, early in their marriage, when he had asserted his authority over her by turning her
suite of intriguing French attendants neck and crop out of the
country, she had learned to respect him. But his surrender of
Strafford, though she knew it had been done to save her, was the
sort of favour that puts a terrible strain on a normal woman's
faith in her man. If when the hunt was up for *her*, he were again
... she may have put the thought from her as disloyal, but deep
down in her soul she must have felt that there was one surrender
that would strain even her love for him to breaking point.

Meanwhile it must have been only too plainly borne in on her
that the hunt *was* up in deadly earnest, and that all the terrible
machinery of destruction that had crushed Strafford now had
her in its grip. She had already gone through fearful experiences.
Her flight from London at the crisis of Strafford's fate had been
pitilessly forbidden ; she had been held as Pym's hostage to
undergo the grim ordeal of that week-end during which she and
her children had been expecting at any moment to find themselves in the hands of a howling mob ; she had been the butt of
every vile slander that malice could devise against her, including
the filthy lie of her liaison with Jermyn, which—since her standards of chastity were as meticulous as those of her husband—
had driven her nearly to distraction.

Her being brave was no bar to her being also extremely
temperamental, and a less sensitive woman would have had her
nerves shattered by all this—had it been in our time she would
have been ordered a complete rest cure. But there was to be no
rest for her, or even respite ; the nerve-racking torture, far from
being intermitted, was maintained and subtly intensified. It is
true that the immediate threat from the mob was suspended, but
it must have been grimly obvious to her that it was only a
question of time before the hand that held her in its grip would
be ready to close and crush the life out of her.

What must have caused her as much pain as any threat to
herself, was the pitiless persecution of which her fellow-Catholics
were now the victims, and which she and her husband were
powerless to prevent. Her Capuchins were driven away ; her
confessor since the early days of her marriage, Father Philips,
was haled to the bar of the Commons on the charge of a Popish
plot, and made the object of an impeachment ; and there had
been the martyrdom at Tyburn of an aged Catholic Priest named

Ward, whose heart a brave French lackey had snatched from the hangman's fire and run through the streets with, until the mob pulled him down.

Hitherto she had had the beloved presence of Charles to comfort and sustain her, but she must have felt it the last straw when he proposed to set out on the unknown hazards of his progress to Edinburgh. For a lonely woman, with nobody to trust except the accommodating Lucy, to be left in the power of Pym was a grim prospect ; and indeed to Charles himself it had seemed unthinkable. Luckily there presented itself a means of escape that was also in strictest accordance with her royal duty. Her little daughter of ten, the Princess Mary, had, just when the Strafford crisis had been rising to its height, gone through the form of marriage with the fifteen year old Prince of Orange, an event whose political aspect at least was calculated to afford the liveliest satisfaction to the Parliament chiefs, to whom Calvinist Holland, in spite of its brutally unsentimental eye to the main chance in its dealings with England, was the spoilt darling of a Protestant foreign policy ; and who would have been more delighted still had they known that the issue of this marriage would be the second William the Conqueror who would impose, by foreign arms, the final triumph of their cause over that of monarchy in England.

An alliance with the royal House of Stuart was a distinct step up in the world for the still comparatively parvenu Stadtholders of the House of Orange, who were by no means too sure of maintaining their tenure even of that thankless office. So it was not altogether unnatural that the lucky young Prince, or his advisers, should have wished to cash in on their good fortune by receiving the person of the bride at the earliest possible moment, especially as recent experience must have convinced them that England was no safe place for a Princess to abide in. And they were ready to pay in good clinking guilders—so desperately needed by the almost penniless and bankrupt parents—for delivery of her.

Accordingly it was the most natural, and might have seemed the only human course, for the poor little bride, hardly out of the nursery, to be taken to what must at best have been a strange and alarming new environment, in charge of her mother. And it was an obvious opportunity for that mother to pay a visit to Spa, in the province of Liége, to drink its famous curative waters. Charles would have been a very different sort of husband from what he actually was, had he failed to welcome the chance that thus presented itself for his cruelly overstrained wife to withdraw for a little season into a place of safety and freedom from the unremitting terrors, insults and humiliations that were scoring her aspect of vivacious loveliness with lines of anxiety, and giving the first foretaste of that haggard hardness that we find in her later portraits. She did really need—and how much she needed—a rest !

But she must have been very naïve had she imagined that Mr Pym, of all people, would be minded to let her off so easily. For Pym, who anticipated so many other points of the Totalitarian technique, was fully alive to the importance of holding the family of a political opponent as hostages for his correct behaviour. The machinery of insinuation and suggestion was at once put to work. The blackest possible motives were attributed to her. She intended to take the Crown Jewels out of the kingdom and use them to raise men and money for who knows what horrific designs to subvert the religion and liberties of the realm. Also she would join the fugitive Jermyn—and the inference from that was obvious enough to those who had the minds to draw it.

But it did not occur to her that Parliament itself would seek to deny the Queen of England the liberty of travelling where she would on her lawful occasions. She would, she said, be prepared to obey the King, but not 400 of his subjects. Her baggage was packed all ready for departure, and she herself was due to follow a week later. To a Parliamentary deputation that had come primed with dissuasive arguments she replied—what she had also confided privately to the Venetian ambassador—that her own health and safety was the sole object of her journey. On this the controllers of Parliament determined to apply the screw with full rigour. They sought to blackmail her by turning on the army plot propaganda to full blast again, so as to hamstring her preparations by inquisitorial demands upon her servants responsible for them—with even more drastic measures of coercion to follow, if these proved insufficient.

At this she gave way, for what could one frail woman do against so overwhelming a concentration of force ? Little Princess Mary's bridal journey was, for the time being, cancelled, as it was no doubt a good thing for her that it should be. And the Queen, to oleaginous asseverations of tenderness to her health and readiness to further her satisfaction in all things, desired, with delicately barbed courtesy, to thank the Houses for their care of her health, of which "I hope", she said, "I shall see the effects," and she retired, for such safety as she could get, to her palace at Oatlands near Weybridge—that of Holdenby, in Northamptonshire, having been judged too far from London for her to be allowed to shelter there except under conditions too humiliating to be borne, and amounting to those of open arrest.

No wonder that the poor lady could write to her sister, the Duchess of Savoy, that she had been driven nearly insane at finding herself fallen from the utmost contentment into innumerable misfortunes of every sort :

"Imagine what is my state, on seeing his power taken from the King, the Catholics persecuted, priests hanged, those devoted to our service banished from us or hunted for their lives for having tried to serve the King, and I myself held here like a prisoner, when they will not even allow me to follow the King to Scotland, and with no one in the world to whom to tell my afflictions ..."

With her nerves stretched to this degree, there was only too palpable a danger that a sudden crisis might find her moved not to collapse, but, as is the way with such high-spirited natures, to the snapping of all inhibitions and some fatally precipitate outbreak into action.

Could this have formed part of Mr Pym's calculations ?

12

PYM MEETS HIS MATCH

ONE of the choicest of the many plums of unconscious humour to be extracted from the vast, stodgy surfeit contained in the eighteen tomes of the admirable Gardiner, is in reference to this proposed journey of King Charles to Scotland, which Mr Pym was quite obviously determined to make him postpone till such time, in an indefinitely remote future, as all risk of serious consequences to Pym himself and his friends could be absolutely ruled out—one of them being, in Gardiner's own words, that His Majesty might

"... ask for the surrender of that letter which might show that the Parliamentary leaders had invited to Scots to invade England in the preceding summer. With this proof of treason Charles might hope to bring his opponents within the meshes of the law."*

One can sympathize with the desire of even the most stainless patriot to prevent the written proof of his own treason from getting into the hands of his Sovereign—or the writer into the clutches of the law !

Pym therefore, whose way was never, when it could be avoided, to swallow in one bite where two would do, had caused Parliament to beg the King to postpone his journey till the 9th of August. The King promptly and graciously consented to do exactly as he was asked—August the 9th let it be ! On which Gardiner's comment is :

"Charles was indeed now prepared to make concessions, if only he could avoid any hindrance being thrown in the way of his journey to Scotland. It is indeed impossible to argue from any scheme which crossed Charles's mind, that he had any fixity of purpose to carry it out in action." †

Now it is just possible—though far from certain—that Pym may have been banking, in view of Charles's hitherto unbroken record of concession, on just such a view of his character as is implied in the last sentence. If so, no one can doubt that so realistic a student of human weakness must have revised his estimate when it proved that Charles was fixed like a rock in his determination to carry out his side of this bargain to the day and to the letter, let Mr Pym change his mind and raise his demands as he would ! Not so Dr Gardiner. With his accustomed conscientiousness, and frequent judicial headshakings, he proceeds to set down the black record of Charles's unbudgeability in face of all the massive pressure that Pym's technique could bring to bear on him. And even on going over his proofs it never seems to have struck the great Whig-Liberal historian that there was any occasion for the blue pencil‡ in respect of the sentence I have just quoted, which is a perfect specimen of the sort of thing that writers far less erudite and honest than Gardiner are in the habit of throwing off, with perfect impunity, on the subject of King Charles !

For Charles, as is the way with men of strong principles and conciliatory disposition, was apt to create quite a false impression

---

* *History of England*, ix., p. 410.   † *Ib.*, ix., p. 402.

‡ If he had one ! For I can believe it of Gardiner much more easily than of Shakespeare, that he never blotted a line.

of his own weakness ; and those who presumed too far on his gentleness were brought up against the discovery, made by Henriette in the early days of their marriage, of the toughness as well as the suppleness of steel in his nature. Except in that one extreme instance of Strafford, there was always a point—a point of ultimate principle—beyond which he was prepared to die rather than go ; and this his critics, who have committed themselves in advance to the dogma of his instability, are never able to understand. So having ruled out the obvious and honourable explanation of his conduct, they accuse him of incurable duplicity, of megalomaniac illusions, or even, with the good Gardiner, of being at once, and equally regrettably, fickle and immovable.

In his dealings with the Long Parliament, Charles had been perfectly consistent from the first. He had plainly seen that his position as a monarch in the Tudor tradition, conducting his own government in the way an American President does nowadays, could no longer be maintained. Whatever he may have thought of the methods by which the Parliamentary chiefs had gone about to engineer a constitutional revolution, he had evidently resigned himself to accepting it. He would not only allow them to carry out all their declared programme to the last detail, or, in the language of the time, to obtain full redress for their vast catalogue of alleged grievances, but he was ready, and in fact eager, to accept the logical consequence of appointing them, or their nominees, to the key posts in his ministry. It was they, and not he, who refused to accept this solution of the problem.

But when it became evident that they were determined to go to lengths never envisaged in their original demands ; when they aimed at taking the power of appointing ministers and of controlling his armed forces completely out of his hands ; when, above all, they aimed at subverting the Church—then he resolved to draw the line and stand firm on it at all hazards, even the most extreme, and from that determination he never wavered. And though he himself perished, that line which he had drawn was, in the event, maintained inviolate, and—as far at least as the law of the land, apart from constitutional practice, is concerned—so remains to this day.

Once this is grasped, it will be seen that the whole of Charles's conduct during this most critical time, was along with a patience and courtesy proof against all but the most outrageous provocation, marked by unwavering firmness and clear-cut decision of purpose. This question of his journey to Scotland had become a test case. Having conceded his opponents all that even they had demanded, not all their threats and persuasions, not even their attempt to blackmail him by holding the Queen a virtual prisoner, was going to make him give way another inch. His intentions were innocent—had they not been so, would he have dared leave her as security for them ?—and that the King of England and Scotland should not be free to journey on his own highway, or to show his face to his own subjects, was too much to be borne. And great was the consternation at the Patriot headquarters when it became evident that he regarded the matter as closed. What could he have up his sleeve ? And in face of what almost amounted to contempt of Pym—what was Mr Pym going to do about it ?

But that formidable personage had other cares thickening upon him. Even in spite of the temporary rally he had effected, things were conspicuously failing to go according to his plan within the walls of Parliament. Not only were the Peers proving utterly impracticable about allowing the Lower House to doctor the composition of their own by the exclusion of the Bishops ; but that terrific Root and Branch Bill, which had been designed to scrap the whole ecclesiastical organization in order to substitute God only knew what—for there was no agreement among men— was hopelessly bogged down. Mr Hyde had uttered no empty boast when he had assured the King of his capacity to block the bill at least till his return from Scotland. Nor had this capacity been underrated by Mr Pym, who, with his knowledge of all the fine points of Parliamentary sharp practice, laid his own plan for circumventing it. What could be more simple, or more plausible, than to have the distinguished barrister, who had already made a name for himself at such work, voted into the chair of the Committee to which the bill was referred ? That would muzzle him effectively, and deprive the opposition of its debating spearhead.

But Mr Pym had for once met his match. Mr Hyde understood only too much about the management of committees, and what can be done by a designedly long-winded and meticulously correct chairman whose object is not to expedite, but to obstruct and sabotage the business in hand by every possible means. The relish with which Hyde records these proceedings shows how thoroughly he must have enjoyed himself.

The promoters of the bill—and here one can surely detect Pym's hand—had themselves thought out a highly improper way of rushing it into law by getting the committee's proceedings each day reported late in the afternoon to the whole House, and voted through automatically when most of the members, except those supporters who had been specially whipped up for the purpose, were otherwise engaged, since, as Falkland dryly remarked,

"They who hate bishops, hate them worse than the devil ; and they who love them do not love them as well as their dinners."

However no one could deny that it was Mr Hyde's duty as chairman to report the motions passed by the committee to the House, nor could any one deny, though few could have anticipated, that Mr Hyde, being no longer in the chair, had the right, being once on his feet, to argue at length against every one of the motions he had to present, and so, as he says, "spent them much time". Nor was this the worst, for the motions, when they came to be presented, proved most often to be an unintelligible hotchpotch, since the chairman had shown the most super-serviceable zeal in getting every unconsidered proposition of every excitable enthusiast or committee bore framed as a motion, and voted on by the whole body, so that time and again he found himself under the sad necessity of reporting, to a bewildered House, two or three directly contradictory motions.

The result we ourselves may allow Mr Hyde to report to us :

"After nearly twenty days," he says, "spent in that manner, they found themselves very little advanced toward a conclusion ... and the King being resolved to begin his journey to Scotland they were forced to discontinue their beloved Bill and let it rest."

"Never again," exclaimed one of the revolutionary leaders, Sir Arthur Haslerigg, "will I hereafter put an enemy into the chair !"

Pym had been properly hoist with his own petard. This wrecking of his principal measure—for Root and Branch was not revived till the Civil War—was a resounding defeat for the revolutionary control of the House, and a loss of face that Pym could ill sustain. It was in vain that the extremists tried to retrieve what they could of the situation by devising a form of Protestant shibboleth, failure to subscribe to which would deprive a member of his seat in either House. The Lords threw it out ; and an attempt to jump the claim by circularizing the constituencies, led to an angry clash between the Houses on the question of privilege. Even an attempt to get rid of the Bishops by wholesale impeachment stood little chance of success with the Peers in their present mood.

But it was not only on the issue of the Church that the hitherto dominant faction suffered rebuff. They were openly determined to prevent the King from making that dreaded journey to Scotland, even on the date to which they had induced him to postpone it. The process of disbanding the armies was still far from complete, and whether or not Pym believed his own propaganda about the King's intention effecting a *coup d'état* with one army or the other, there is no doubt that his followers did.

It was on Saturday, 7th of August, that Charles made it plain that there could be no question of his breaking tryst with the Scots, or postponing his departure beyond the following Monday. When this was realized, something very like a panic ensued at Westminster—or perhaps was engendered, since there was little that Pym did not know about the technique of panic-mongering. According to the Venetian Ambassador, who took extraordinary pains to report full particulars of the crisis, the members heard this decision with the utmost fear and perturbation, and spent that night and the day following (not even the fear of the Lord being able to restrain them from so unheard of an affront to Puritan taboo as that of a Sunday session) in continuous and perilous attempts to devise ways and means of stopping the journey.

Perilous indeed when we consider that among the suggestions put forward—if we may trust this very capable informant, who could hardly have invented them—were the bringing up of a mob of 20,000 working men to intimidate the King, the putting of him under a guard, and even depriving him of his Crown and giving it to his nephew, the Prince Palatine, or the young Prince of Wales. This last, I cannot help surmising to have been the contribution of Marten.

The King was fully informed of these proceedings, but they did not make the faintest visible impression on him. The utmost he would consent to do, was to make the conciliatory gesture of postponing his departure by twenty-four hours. He did, however, readily consent to come down to Parliament on Monday. When he arrived he was greeted by an excited mob—not the 20,000 envisaged in the previous day's debate, but the few hundreds which was presumably all that Pym was able to whip up at such short notice on a Monday afternoon. These however did their best by loudly importuning His Majesty not to go to Scotland.

Charles was fully equal to the occasion. He made them a graceful little speech, expressing his gratification that they were as anxious to have him among them as his good subjects of Scotland, whom nevertheless he was pledged to visit, and sent them away perfectly satisfied. Pym had played his trump card, the mob, and Charles had taken the trick.

For this bout, Pym's game was up, though he was determined to have one last fling. A couple of Peers—one of them the Earl of Warwick—turned up at Whitehall in the name of Parliament, to make a last minute attempt to persuade the King to stop. But Charles had come to the end of his patience with this importunate nagging, and informed the two astonished noblemen, in a manner very different from that to which they were accustomed in him, that his mind was made up : he would give any one who laid hands on his horse's bridle cause to regret it.

That did settle the matter ; and punctually at noon on Tuesday the royal coaches, with only the Elector Palatine and a few Scottish Lords in attendance on His Majesty, were lumbering citywards out of the gate at Whitehall, on the way to join the Great North Road.

Mr Pym's feelings are not recorded. But no one who knew him could have imagined that he would—even if he had dared—lie down under this open humiliation. His trump card had been out-trumped, but the capacity of his sleeve was not so easily exhausted.

13

THE KING GOES NORTH

So they were gone, and a slowly moving cloud of dust marked the progress of the little cavalcade through the flat plain of Eastern England. The dread journey that all the resources of Parliament and the London mob had been mobilized to prevent, had actually materialized. The King was at large, with both armies in being. To those who had been fed with stories of his dark intrigues it must have been a matter of anxious speculation which of these armies would appear—and when—marching by way of Spital-fields upon Bishopsgate.

Meanwhile Parliament continued in Session for the good reason that the King could not, under Pym's Act, so much as adjourn it ; while, until the King and troops were safely out of harm's way, Pym dared take no chances. But now that the small-pox had come to join the plague in London, and both were claiming their hundreds weekly, attendances were getting thinner and thinner, and it was lucky if a fifth part of the Commons, or more than a beggarly dozen or so of peers, could be scraped up for a division. Under such circumstances, to maintain a steady control of the House had come to be fraught with more and more difficulty.

But difficulties and setbacks had merely the effect, on such a nature as Pym's, of calling all his reserves into play. He acted now with the utmost vigour. His first care was to plant on the King, in the name of Parliament, a deputation of Parliamentary commissioners—though the modern word that would be more descriptive is "commissars"—to dog his footsteps and hamper his proceedings in every way possible. How far Pym intended them to go beyond spying and snooping is one of his many secrets of which, in the highly improbable event of its having been committed to paper, all record has perished. But we can form our own conclusions from the fact that the little party of five included that same Nathaniel Fiennes who, as we have seen, was already revolving thoughts of rebellion and civil war, and the sleek millionaire, Hampden, the master wire-puller of the Commons, and one of those guilty men who knew that their necks might depend on keeping that fatal letter, inviting the Scots to invade England, out of the King's hands. Such a team did not go to Edinburgh, at a time when Pym could ill afford to spare them at Westminster, for the mere purpose of dancing ceremonial attendance. It is not impossible that Charles, on the appearance of these only too well-known faces among his entourage, may have been reminded of a passage from his favourite Shakespeare :

"Marry, this is miching mallecho, it means mischief."

Even so, he might not have realized what deep and subtle mischief had been implied in the very mandate of their com-mission. It was characteristic of the man who was called "The Ox," that the more gradually he could approach his objective, the better it suited him. This seemingly innocent and even loyal purpose of keeping Parliamentary touch with His Majesty, was effected by what seemed the equally innocent means of an Ordinance of Both Houses. An Ordinance—action, that is to say, taken by a Parliament that no longer consisted of King, Lords and Commons, but of the two Houses acting jointly, without assent or knowledge of the King, as a self-sufficient Sovereign Power. Viewed in this light it was a constitutional innovation even more audacious, because accomplished without the faintest pretence of legality, than that of cutting off Parliament from its constituents. There was no logical—nor would there prove to be any actual stopping place between appointing Commissioners, by ordinance of both Houses, to spy on the King, and setting up a mock tribunal, by ordinance of whatever might be left of one House, to murder him.

Such was King Pym's reply to the successful defiance offered him by King Charles, and such his bid to regain the political initiative that seemed to be slipping from his hands. It can only move our admiration of the master strategist whose hand is revealed in it. For it is clear that Pym perceived that the hour had struck for proceeding, with calculated expedition, to the next and clinching part of his programme. The sovereignty of the Crown having been effectually crippled, it remained to set about eliminating it. This, as nobody knew better than Pym, would, failing the actual consent of the Crown, have to be done by openly overriding the law. Hitherto he had always at least made a show of keeping within its bounds. But this way of proceeding by ordinance —or, in intention and effect, by his own ukase—was the first demonstration of his intention to proceed to all lengths, legal or otherwise, that might be necessary to consummate the revolution of which he was chief engineer. Perhaps he may have hoped that a demonstration would be all that was needed to bring the King to heel ; which it certainly would have been with a King resembling in the least degree the Charles of the accepted myth.

But he can hardly have counted on it. Pym was no fool or wishful thinker, but a realist. He may well have formed a somewhat juster appreciation of his enemy than that of his own posthumous *claque*, and he must have known at least as well as Fiennes to what path he was now committing himself. He who sets himself above the law, challenges the decision of the sword. He offered the King a plain choice between virtual abdication and civil war ; and all his policy is henceforth framed in energetic assumption of the latter alternative. Civil war, he must have reflected, would at least offer him incomparably better chances than those of an eventual treason trial with such evidence for the prosecution as the King might unearth at Edinburgh, held under the auspices of a Constitutional ministry, and on the crest of the royalist reaction that was already under way. And with all the forces at his command, he may well have looked to decide the issue before it could ever come to push of pike. Like the advocates of total war in our own time, he may honestly have believed that in war the most ruthless course is, in the long run, the most merciful.

By the issue of the first ordinance Pym had, in effect, unfurled his banner at Westminster just over a year previously to the raising of his rival's at Nottingham. And from henceforth his measures are measures of war, a war like that of the eleven months following Munich, waged by one party alone on a peace-clinging and almost passive opponent ; a war camouflaged by the forms of peace and comprising the most desperately energetic mobilization, manoeuvring for position, and seizure of vital points, so that when the time was ripe for the unloosing of the all-out offensive, there would be no battle, but collapse and surrender.

Those who are not blindly wedded to a preconceived theory will see that the actions of the revolutionary party, following each other like shot after shot of a controlled barrage, fit in precisely with this hypothesis and with no other. It is just as we should expect, that the plan of campaign should now concentrate, as its prime objective, on wresting the control of the armed forces out of the hands of their lawful Sovereign, and at the same time depriving him of his fortresses and stores of munitions. Four days after the King's departure a so-called Committee of Defence was set up in the Commons to take upon itself the supervision of these most essential of all the appurtenances of sovereignty—an encroachment never dreamed of until then.

At the same time every care had been taken to lodge the command of the forces in the hands of men whose treason could be guaranteed in the event of the plainly impending crisis. The King had not only complied with the demands of the revolutionaries to the extent of appointing Essex to the Southern command, but he had entrusted the Northern to Warwick's brother, the Earl of Holland, who had been the first president of the Providence Company, and who, like Essex, harboured a grievance against the King for refusing to oblige him by an act of jobbery—in this case the ennoblement of a certain person, from whom Holland had stood to pocket a commission of ten thousand pounds. And consequently this rather foppish and luxurious Patriot who, as Clarendon remarks of him, "did think poverty the most insupportable evil that could befall any man in this world", had, in his disgruntlement, become as steady as such a weathercock was capable of being, in his adherence to the King's enemies.

One would have thought that with all this vast edifice of precaution, Mr Pym would have felt himself reasonably secure against the effects of his failure to hold up those three or four royal post coaches on their journey northwards. And as a matter of fact, everything happened precisely as any one with a clear conscience and without plots on the brain, might have expected. There was not the least trouble anywhere, nor suspicion of it. The King passed through both armies, and was greeted with the loyalty that British troops are always ready, if left to themselves, to accord to the person of their Sovereign. But nothing more.

Both were equally in a mood to welcome him. The English, whatever cold feet they may have had at the time of the original invasion, were no longer stuffed up, but fed up, with the propaganda of the politicians, and the long boredom of hanging impotently about, while those traditional enemies, whom their ancestors had met and broken at Halidon Hill, at Neville's Cross, at Flodden, at Solway Moss, at Pinkie, and in many another engagement whose legend was still alive and lost nothing in the telling, were lording it as conquerors on English soil. If King Charles had only cared to put himself at their head, and let them show what they could do when they really meant to fight, his progress to Edinburgh might have developed on rather more colourful lines. But he was there not to lead but to review them, preparatory to their demobilization, and they could only put up as smart an appearance and give him as hearty a cheer on his way as possible.

As for the Scots, they also, though for different causes, were in a mood of exasperation with their Parliamentary allies and paymasters, that might at any moment have detonated an explosion. A blackmailer, even the most extravagant of whose demands has been jibbed at by his victim, is little apt to take it in good part. And now, to the refusal to Presbyterianize the Church, was added the offence of Parliament's frantic and hysterical attempts to keep the King from honouring his engagement with his Scottish subjects ; and His Majesty had put himself in correspondingly good odour by his firm and public refusal to disappoint them.

Perhaps Mr Pym would have had some reason to quake in his boots, if Charles had really been the Machiavellian schemer he was made out to be. For such a one, there might have been rich fishing in these troubled Northumbrian waters. But the simple fact was that Charles was not dreaming of any plots or stratagems at all, unless we are to designate as such his longing to win back the alienated affections of his dear Scottish people.

In spite of conditions more promising for a military *coup* than he could possibly have anticipated, he put out not even the most tentative feeler towards it. He would always have a warm place in his heart for soldiers, even when they were his mortal enemies, and he had something of the connoisseur's appreciation of a brave martial turn out. It must have been a welcome relief to him after the unceasing tension of his existence at Whitehall, to ride along these grave but friendly lines of Lowland peasants, with their blue bonnets and glittering pikes, and to be received at the headquarters at Newcastle with such a hearty Scottish welcome as must have reminded him of his coronation visit to Edinburgh— how many years was it ago ? And not the least agreeable feature to him, must have been the opportunity of making contact with the little crooked, leathery veteran who, the previous Autumn, had driven his forces in headlong flight from the Border to York, but who now was all loyalty and goodwill. This was the Commander-in-Chief, Alexander Leslie, whose reputation, won under the great Gustavus Adolphus, was European, and who had not given best even to so redoubtable an opponent as Wallenstein. He might have passed for just the type of blunt-spoken, downright soldier for whose company Charles would have been most delighted to exchange the smooth blandishments of the actual and potential traitors by whom he had so long been surrounded.

His Majesty may have been a little too much inclined to take at their face value the festivities and pageantry and demonstrations of loyalty he received at Newcastle. No experience could cure him of the uncritical affection which coloured his view of his beloved Scots, and ultimately proved a source of fatal weakness to him. It was not the last time that he would be the recipient of Scottish hospitality at this English town of Newcastle.

EDWARD
HYDE
EARL OF
CLARENDON

British Museum

LUCIUS
VISCOUNT
FALKLAND

QUEEN HENRIETTA MARIA

Meanwhile, during the month of August, the session of what was now no more than a skeleton Parliament dragged on wearily, pending such time as Pym would think safe to allow a recess. The stout hearted few who remained scattered about the benches, were rendered fewer still, not only by the fear of the plague, but by the necessities of Pym's propaganda, for a number of the most influential members were touring the constituencies "to propagate among the people", in the words of our Venetian observer, "ideas favourable to the Parliament but hostile to the King's service". At Northumberland House, the splendid residence of the head of the Percies, hard by Charing Cross, the chief revolutionary Peers, Essex, Warwick, and the disreputable Newport, Constable of the Tower, were observed to be resorting for prolonged conferences. Something ominous and sinister was evidently brewing, if not from the King's side, as Pym's propaganda was desperately concerned to have it believed, then from that of the King's enemies within the realm, who were so fervently pushing forward their preparations for ... what ?

14

PARLIAMENTARY FIASCO

WHEN it became apparent that the King had proceeded quietly to Edinburgh without the faintest attempt to give substance to the scaremongering about a military coup, it became apparent even to Pym that it was time to set an early day for the release of the plague-haunted Rump that continued to discharge the functions of a Parliament. On the 28th of August, therefore, the joyful news was proclaimed of the adjournment being fixed for the 8th of September. All the more reason, therefore, for Pym forcing the pace at all costs and by any means, of his drive against the Church !

A grandiose motion was accordingly produced in the Commons to prohibit every sort of practice calculated to offend Puritan susceptibilities ; crucifixes, pictures of the Persons of the Trinity, and so forth were to be taken away and abolished—which amounted to giving a *carte blanche* for indiscriminate vandalism upon Church property all over the country ; to make it an offence to bow at the name of Jesus ; to grant free access, by the removal of rails, for dogs to the Altar, and to permit of it being used as a hat stand and a depository for un-house-trained babies ; besides the imposition of a legal extinguisher on every form of enjoyment more strenuous than sermon-bibbing on the Jewish sabbath that, under the style of the Lord's Day, was now transferred from the seventh day of the week to supersede the Christian festival of Sunday.

This, as Gardiner hopefully maintains, might have got passed, if not *nem. con.*, at least by some sort of a majority, had not a too enthusiastic supporter jumped up in his place with the bright idea of rounding off the good work by a purge of the Prayer Book. This was a fatal blunder. That almost miraculous achievement of English prose composition, at a time when the rudiments of the art had hardly begun to be comprehended, had done more to transform the spiritual complexion of the country, than all the measures taken by her Sovereigns and statesmen to achieve her independence of Catholic Christendom. It was one thing to stoke up propaganda against the Bishops—but as late as the Twentieth Century it was proved, even when the impulse came from the Bishops themselves, that it is the counsel of Parliamentary prudence to leave the Prayer Book alone.

The opposition leaders saw their opening, and instantly passed over to the counter offensive. It was Colepeper, their hardest hitting debater, who cut in at once with a motion calling on the House to provide a remedy against those who vilified and contemned the Common Prayer Book. Though the House was thin, there was no blinking the importance of the issue. The challenge was taken up by a fighter on the opposite side as formidable as Colepeper himself, a choleric, red-faced, rather uncouth-looking squire from the East Anglian fen country, who had already come to violent loggerheads with Hyde on one of the many committees of which the latter was chairman, about the grievances of the poor fen-men, who were being pauperized in the course of the vast scheme of reclamation promoted by the House of Russell. This gentleman, it might have been remarked, differed from the hard-bitten politicians with whom he was associated, by the bull-headed intransigence with which he was wont to identify himself with causes, mostly religious, that by them were exploited from motives of political calculation. He was the member for Cambridge, Oliver Cromwell, a cousin of Hampden's, and as such, in intimate association with the extremist leaders, though whether they would have taken so emotional a firebrand into their innermost confidence may perhaps be doubted. But on this occasion he argued, with a common sense that ever seasoned his most impassioned pleadings, that after all there *were* things in the Prayer Book that grave and learned divines ... But with feelings roused to the pitch that they must have been by this sudden alarm of the Prayer Book in danger, it is most unlikely that anything said in debate would have turned a single vote. And when these came to be counted, it proved that Colepeper's motion had, in a House of no more than 92, been carried by a majority of 18, and a resounding defeat, on a major issue, inflicted on Pym. Such an event in a free Parliament would have provided obvious occasion for an appeal to the country. But not in the Perpetual Parliament. Pym had insured himself against that.

He had one last shot left in his locker. The adjournment was put off for one more day to give Pym the opportunity of saving face by a more high-handed act than any he had attempted hitherto, which was nothing less than the forcing through the Commons of a resolution empowering parishes to set up lecturers, or lay preachers, on their own responsibility. But this happened to be not only a flagrant usurpation of the royal prerogative, but also a direct challenge to the Lords, who though they might be got to connive at such usurpation by both Houses, drew the line when it was done by the Lower House without even a "by your leave". They accordingly retorted by enjoining the printing and publication of an order passed in the previous January, directing that services should be carried on according to the existing law ; and their Lordships refused, in spite of a protest lodged by half a dozen of the most revolutionary of them, even to communicate this resolution to the Commons. Thus Pym's attempt at a face-saving gesture had earned him a public snub and precipitated an open conflict between the Houses. So shaken was he, for the moment, by this latest reverse, that he seems to have completely lost his head, and even proposed sending a messenger after the King to get him to issue a proclamation revoking the Lords' order. But this was more than the Commons were prepared to stomach even from Pym, perhaps fortunately for him, as a snub from the Crown on the top of that from the Lords would have been the most that could possibly have been gained by so preposterous a *démarche*.

That was the end, as far as this Session was concerned ; and the forlorn Rump of members, we may be sure, lost not a single unnecessary moment in shaking off their feet the dust of disease infested London, and thanking God for their deliverance ; while Mr Pym, recovering his nerve, may have put up an even more fervent thanksgiving, on his own behalf, that this Parliament was after all perpetual and cut off from appeal to its constituents. But there was no recess for him. He stopped on in his Westminster lodgings to preside over a committee, another of his revolutionary innovations, that he had got appointed to keep the sovereignty of his perpetual Parliament continuously in being, and to act hand in glove with the other committee that under the leadership of his confederate Hampden, was dogging the steps of His Majesty up North.

Pym was no coward ; and even if, as the nights lengthened and the first Autumn mists spread their veil over the Abbey and the deserted Parliament House, his slumbers were at all disquieted, it was not by thoughts of the plague. But it is just conceivable that they may have been haunted, as the clock told the hours to morning, by almost audible reverberations of a remembered clatter of hooves, and cries of "His head is off ! His head is off !"

IV

Checkmate to King Charles

I

SCOTTISH TRAGEDY

ALL had been loyalty and goodwill on the King's progress
to Edinburgh, and the ancient city, which then bore more
the appearance of one very long street, had put on her
best face to welcome him. In the whole town, it was said, was
nothing but joy and revelling like the day of jubilee ; and in the
Parliament House a magnificent banquet was provided, in which
the King and Prince Palatine sat at one table, the heads of the
Scottish nobility at another, and the Lord Provost "like a plain
Dutch host bestirred himself bravely, drunk a health to the King,
the Queen, and the royal children, and afterwards insisted with
His Majesty to pledge ; and so in this Scotch familiar way ... bid
the King and Lords welcome with such hearty expressions as
served but for mirth and satisfaction."

Particularly pleased were his Scottish hosts with His Majesty's
gracious demeanour. There was not the faintest trace of resentment at the hard treatment he had received at their hands during
the past three years. He had come in no bargaining spirit, but
prepared to grant them the utmost they could possibly demand
in reason, and even beyond it. He was content to sit with pious
attentiveness in the great church of St Giles, at which all the
trouble had started, and listen to that redoubtable evangelist,
Alexander Henderson, thundering from the pulpit, like a second
John Knox, at his Bishops and ministers of state, in such downright language as a year previously would have been at least a
Star Chamber matter. And when Charles, in his innocence of
Presbyterian taboo, instead of facing up to a second sermon in the
afternoon, betook himself to the links at Leith for a round of what
was even then the Royal and Ancient game, he received, with
meekness, on his return, what the Lord moved Henderson to
impart to His Anointed on the subject of Sabbath breaking.

It is no wonder that, despite his having resigned himself to
parting with the utmost that might be demanded of his Scottish

prerogative, he should have taken the loyalty and enthusiasm of his reception at its face value, and that the melancholy that had weighed down his spirits since the death of Strafford should for the first time have been lifted. He gladdened the heart of the Queen in her loneliness and peril at Oatlands, by writing to her in a strain that was buoyant and almost optimistic ; though we may well believe that under such circumstances he may have felt it incumbent on him to paint the situation, for her benefit, in the rosiest colours possible.

The optimism may however have been genuine enough, since his love for his native Scotland had the effect of a blind spot in his usually lucid vision, and he had had no opportunity of acquiring his father's canny divination of what lay behind the romantic façade that she presented to the outward eye. Before he had been able to talk they had taken him from her, and his only subsequent contacts had consisted of one hectic visit of ceremony, and the framed up fiasco of a Border campaign.

Yet had it not been for that lover's and child's blindness of his, he might have thought twice before plunging into what the experience of centuries had shown to be the witch's cauldron of Scottish politics, now doubly bedevilled by the ingredients of a new fanaticism. He might have taken warning from the seven Stuarts who had gone before him, and of whom his father had been the first and only one to die peacefully in his bed—and that an English bed. And he might have guessed something of what was brewing from the knowledge that accusations of treason were being freely bandied among the rival magnates, and that the young Earl of Montrose, head of the Lowland House of Graham, was at that very moment confined in Edinburgh Castle, through the machinations of the most powerful and ambitious personage in Scotland, the Earl of Argyll, who had only recently played his part in the fight for Kirk and Covenant by turning loose the forces of his Clan Campbell to march looting and raping over the lands of their Lowland neighbours.

This is no place to unravel the tangle of plots and counter plots that is even to this day far from having been elucidated by the most laborious research into Scottish history. The point to be noted here is that it was a tangle in which the unfortunate King, in spite of all that he could possibly do to keep out of it, soon found himself inextricably caught. It was part of that hard luck which dogged him all through these latter years of his tragedy, that the one man who could conceivably have given him guidance and support was the imprisoned Montrose, who was not only devotedly loyal, but whose loyalty was founded on the reasoned support of a philosophic intelligence. For Montrose saw that a strong sovereignty was the thing above all others that Scotland needed to preserve her from chaos, since even the grim democracy of the Kirk was not enough to hold in check the power of the practically independent chieftains, who, having grown fat on the plunder of Church property, had acquired a vested interest in the Protestant cause.

At the present moment Montrose was lying in hopeless impotence, and imminent danger of his life, at the mercy of Argyll, who was just as much in the way to become uncrowned King of Scotland as Pym of England ; and though Montrose desperately sought to get into touch with the King and warn him of the treasons that were being hatched round him, Charles was so determined to keep clear of any sort of plotting, that he refrained from affording him encouragement.

But he had at his elbow a counsellor of very different calibre, the Marquis of Hamilton, whom he had brought with him from London, and who himself had been under some suspicion in the past of aiming at the throne of Scotland, to which, after the descendants of James I, he had the nearest claim. But Hamilton was not of the sort who play the grand game of treason ; he was merely a fool, and one might almost say a fool of genius, since he had just enough plausibility to pass himself off as a man to be relied on in all the innumerable conflicts of principle in which he got his talents for backstairs intrigue accepted by one side or the other, or more likely by both simultaneously. And it may be said of Hamilton that nobody ever relied on him on any single occasion without having reason bitterly to repent it, and that none of the combinations he effected or enterprises he undertook ever ended in anything but the most signal failure, until, having wrecked every cause with which he was ever identified, he finally succeeded in immolating himself.

Charles however, with that invincible constancy to a trust, once given, that justified Clarendon's description of him as the best friend in Christendom, had never wavered in his attachment to his kinsman, and one suspects there must have been a personal charm about Hamilton to account for his success in gaining from so many people a confidence that he never did anything to justify.

He had been allowed to make a characteristic mess of the King's affairs, both political and military, in the first troubles with Scotland, but this had proved no bar to his being the King's most intimate companion on this critical visit to Scotland.

Once there, he began to act true to form. Less from design than habit, he at once started intriguing, and was soon thick in confabulation with the sinister Argyll, a fact that caused Montrose from prison to write to the King warning him of his treachery, and a certain Lord Ker to present him with a challenge ; and though Charles succeeded in stopping the duel and even extracting some sort of an apology from the challenger, his patience was so far strained as to cause him to remark, to Hamilton's brother, Lord Lanark : "Your brother has been very active in his own preservation", which, on Charles's lips, meant more than most men's invective.

And indeed, there was bitterness in his heart. The gloom that had lifted for a moment in the warmth of his first welcome, now lay heavier upon him than ever. It was only too plain that however sincerely he longed to establish himself in those affections of his countrymen that had welled up so spontaneously at the first sight of him, there was no chance for confidence to strike roots amid these conflicting and malign influences that contended all around him for the mastery.

Edinburgh was not only a hotbed of intrigue, but swarming with armed men. Argyll and Hamilton between them were reputed to have 5,000 at their beck and call. And their enemies had retainers running into hundreds.

Meanwhile the Scottish Parliament, which was ready to dance to any tune of Argyll's piping, not content with the crippling sacrifices of sovereignty that it had demanded and obtained from the King, sought to drive him to the lowest depths of humiliation. It not only cancelled his appointments to ministerial offices almost before the ink was dry on his signature, but it actually made loyalty to him in the recent troubles a formal disqualification for any office whatever.

"There was never King so insulted over," wrote one observer, "it would pity any man's heart to see how he looks ; for he is never at quiet among them, and glad he is when he sees any man that he thinks loves him. Yet he is seeming merry at meat."*

So far Charles, by exemplary patience and restraint, had

* Gardiner, *History of England*, x, p. 21.

handled his impossible situation in such a way that he might reasonably have hoped to have returned from his visit with no loss of esteem and perhaps some gain of Scottish goodwill. But now he was overtaken by a misfortune that to this day is one of the unsolved mysteries of history, and is always referred to as the Incident.

Briefly it consisted in the sudden and sensational flight of Argyll, Hamilton, and Lanark, to one of Hamilton's country houses, on the afternoon of the 12th of October, when the King was on his way to the Parliament House, escorted by an armed guard estimated at about half the strength of a modern battalion. Ostensibly, at any rate, this flight was due to the discovery of a plot against their lives, and their unwillingness to precipitate a battle in the streets. But to the King it was an utter disaster, because although he was wholly innocent in the matter, his involvement, even by proximity, in so flaming a scandal, would, at a time when every action of his was certain to be malignantly misrepresented, have been bound to more than cancel out any good effects that might otherwise have accrued from his visit.

Certain it is, that whatever else may have accounted for this theatrical disappearance of the magnates who were believed to hold Edinburgh in the hollow of their hands, the King had not had the faintest inkling of their intention, much less been privy to any conspiracy to remove them. But when he arrived at the Parliament House to find the birds flown, he at once saw to what sort of interpretation the incident would lend itself. And as luck, or sinister contrivance, would have it, he had arrived accompanied by an escort drawn largely, it was believed, from the retainers of the anti-Campbell chieftains. It is easy to blame him after the event for allowing them to accompany him—but why should he have gone out of his way to suspect or snub so natural a gesture of loyalty? Charles, as has been said before, was unsuspicious to a fault.

He came into the Parliament House in a state of terrible agitation. Tears choked his voice as he spoke of his affection for Hamilton, and reminded them how years ago, when the Marquis had been denounced to him for aiming at the Throne, he had commanded him to sleep that night in his own bedchamber. And earnestly he pleaded with them that he should be given a chance to clear his name by an investigation conducted in the full light of publicity. Not only that afternoon, but for days afterwards he continued to urge this just and reasonable request, as he called it—surely the most modest ever made by a King to his subjects. "I must", he told them desperately, "see myself get fair play." It was the last thing that they had the least intention of conceding him. At last, baffled and humiliated, he gave over the attempt, and consented to the committee of investigation conducting its sittings behind closed doors.

Such an enquiry was not likely to bring to light anything that those who had reason for loving darkness preferred to conceal, and to this day the matter of the Incident remains wrapped in as impenetrable a mystery as that of the Iron Mask, or the murder of Sir Edmond Berry Godfrey, or the identity of Jack the Ripper. It requires little acquaintance with the state of Edinburgh at this time, or with the sentiments excited by the overweening power of the Campbells, to make it safe to believe that some sort of conspiracy was afoot on the part of his many enemies to get rid of Argyll ; though how far the sudden panic of that super-subtle chieftain may have been deliberately simulated for purposes of his own is another matter. But then, how came Hamilton to be associated with him, and what game was *he* playing ? Even those most deeply versed in the ramifications of Scottish history have never discovered an explanation that completely accounts for all the facts.

If I venture to suggest one hitherto unexplored line that might be worth following up, it is with the utmost diffidence. But in any such enquiry the question of motive must figure prominently. Who stood to profit most by the Incident ? And who as a matter of fact did profit by it ? It is at least not without a certain suggestiveness that Hamilton had already come under suspicion of having played a characteristically shady part, in collaboration with the English Parliamentary chiefs, in compassing the death of Strafford. Also that the Parliamentary committee, though Charles had done his best to hold it at arms' length, was now in Edinburgh headed by the millionaire wire-puller whose reputation for subtlety was hardly inferior to that of Argyll himself. I, for one, find it hard to credit Gardiner's assumption that Hampden would have been sent all the way to Edinburgh for no other purpose than to hang about as a shocked but passive spectator of His Majesty's proceedings. A word whispered in Hamilton's ear may well have had the effect of genuinely panicking him, or even of prompting him to engineer the scandal of set purpose. And if we are to trust our Venetian observer, it was freely asserted among the courtiers that the whole affair had been deliberately contrived by Hamilton and his associates for the purpose of discrediting the King and furthering their own ambitious designs.

Meanwhile the commissioners of Parliament, to quote the highly significant words of this secret and contemporary dispatch, "Anxious to establish their credit with the people, and render the name of their Prince more hateful to them, do not hesitate to take advantage of the opportunity and announce that carried away by ambitious thoughts of receiving for himself an absolute royalty, the King had not only laid these snares against the life of those who had courageously resisted his designs in their zeal for the welfare of the community, but that he is meditating fresh attempts in this kingdom also to the prejudice of liberty and the most active Parliamentarians." *

It appears then that the Stainless Patriot and his associates lost not a moment in putting into circulation this venomous and shameless libel on their Sovereign—for not even the most bitter detractor of King Charles would now dream of saddling his reputation with the guilt of conspiracy to murder—or in rushing off by express messenger this heaven-sent tit-bit of propaganda to Pym. It is certain, too, that Pym, on receiving it, knew exactly what to do about it, and displayed not a moment's hesitation in exploiting it to the utmost possible advantage for his own ends.

Such facts of the case amount to no more than circumstantial evidence—but against whom, and of what cogency, every member of the jury is free to decide for himself.

2

OFFENSIVE WITHOUT LIMIT

It must have been evident that the second session of Charles's Fifth Parliament, which opened on the 19th of October, was likely to be no less fruitful of dramatic interest than the first. Whatever Pym might like to pretend, there had ceased to be any question of the Commons functioning as one united body, without difference of opinion or party. Henceforth he would have to fight for his control of the House against a vigorous and well-led opposition, which, though it had taken shape in defence of the Church, could hardly

* S.P. Ven., xv, no. 273.

fail, especially under such leadership as that of Hyde, to extend its scope to the maintenance of the existing Constitution, as by law established, against the assault of these revolutionary wreckers who were only too plainly seeking to establish themselves through

Red ruin and the breaking up of laws

in a dominance over Parliament and people to which not even Henry VIII or Elizabeth, at the height of their power, would have dreamed of aspiring. Even such out and out Parliament men as Falkland, almost invincibly prejudiced as they were against King Charles, might prefer to retain him as Sovereign in constitutional leading strings, to handing over the controls of state to the directorate of the late Providence Island Company.

The Edinburgh committee's report had no sooner arrived than it was put into circulation, no doubt with the most lurid colouring that could be imparted to it. Even before the Commons met, on the following day, the lobbies were buzzing with it. Mr Hyde, pacing about in Westminster Hall taking the temperature of the House, came across the two potentially rebel commanders, the dandy Holland and the stolid Essex, in a state of dire perturbation about the Incident, and the danger in which "other men"—a category in which they certainly meant to include themselves—stood from a repetition of the dark design that had been formed against Hamilton and Argyll. There was a twinkle in Hyde's eye as he blandly expressed his surprise that they should be concerned about the fate of these two lords, about both of whom they had been wont to express themselves up to recently in a very different sense. Though they could not refrain from smiling back at this typical thrust of Ned Hyde's, one of them (surely Essex—one can almost hear the gravid thud of his syllables) did his best by remarking that the times and court had much altered since.

It can have come, then, as no surprise to Hyde, that the Speaker should hardly have been in the chair before Pym was off the mark, working up the Incident for all that could be made of it. Hyde was equally prompt in leading off for the opposition by advising the House not to take up fears and suspicions without any certain ground for them ; and—what probably troubled Pym a great deal more—he was followed in the same sense by Falkland, who was now for the first time taking his stand with the constitutional party on a political, as distinct from a Church issue. For there was no doubt now that such a party was in being, capable of opposing what was still the revolutionary majority on something more and more closely approximating to equal terms, and supported by a surge of popular feeling that only needed time to become overwhelming.

Time ! It was on that that the whole issue now depended. Could Mr Pym force on matters to a crisis while the balance of forces was still in his favour ? Or—best of all—could he find some means of turning that tide of popular sentiment *against* the Crown for long enough, at least, to enable him to weigh in with the knock out that should decide the contest once and for all in his own favour ?

How much he appreciated the importance of the time factor is shown by the whirlwind rapidity with which his blows now followed one another. It is probable that as yet he was tied to no fixed plan of attack, but was anticipating the Napoleonic tactic of testing his opponent's line along its whole length for a weak spot, before deciding on the point of decisive penetration. The Incident was only one of many pretexts for hitting at the King, though Pym turned it to account with characteristic resourcefulness on this first day of the session, by moving to have Parliament put under the protection of an armed guard of the Westminster Trained Bands, on whose support he well knew that he could rely. This was a singularly audacious move, as not only had neither Pym nor Parliament the remotest shadow of a legal right to give orders to a man of them, but the only violence that had ever been threatened to the Members had come from the mobs that had been Pym's supreme resource for paralyzing opposition. But Pym had already shown it to be his purpose to wrest the control of the forces, with or without law, from the King's hands, and this cunningly timed manœuvre was in fact, as it certainly was in intention, an important step on the road to open rebellion.

It is characteristic of Pym that when he had found an expedient succeed once, he should have made a point of trying it out again at the first convenient opportunity. The most successful of all his devices, in the final drive for the liquidation of Strafford, had been the bogey of an army plot, which he had cunningly refrained from producing until what he rightly judged to be the psychological moment. He had gone on harping on this same string for the rest of the session, though as Clarendon justly remarks, there was, in all the testimonies produced, so far from any proof of a design to bring up the army to overawe Parliament, that it was very evident that there had been no plot at all. By the end of the summer the thing had come to be less of a bogey than a bore, and Pym himself must have seen that in continuing to put all the forces of Parliament into motion against a few silly young officers, who had talked big in their cups, he was flogging a spent horse. But now that the time had come for throwing every available resource into the offensive against the Crown, a completely fresh army plot scare, coming on the top of the Incident, was obviously called for. And it is characteristic of Pym that though he had hardly any remotely plausible evidence to work on, he had been thoughtfully keeping up his sleeve the best that could be faked under the circumstances.

A certain Captain William Legge, an officer who like so many others had served his apprenticeship in the Swedish service, seems to have approached the King, some time in the late spring, with the draft of a petition to which he hoped to obtain signatures among his fellow officers.

This petition, after speaking of the work of Parliament in terms almost fulsome, offered the support of the signatories against such ill-affected persons as caused tumultuous mobs to beset Parliament and Whitehall. These persons were nowhere specified,* and if Pym or anybody else liked to fit the cap on to his own head, it would amount to an open confession of treason. The King, having glanced at the draft and found it couched in such unexceptionable terms, seems, perhaps a little indiscreetly, to have initialled it with a C.R., and passed on to other business ; nor is it likely that anything more would have been heard of the matter, had not Pym's ubiquitous spy service got hold of it, and Pym himself perceived what play might be made at the proper time with these unlucky initials. And incredible as it may seem, this palpable mare's nest has passed into orthodox history with the impressive title of the "Second Army Plot".

That was only one of the many expedients that Pym had in readiness for use against the crown. If a second army plot, why not an English Incident? Pym would hardly have been Pym if such an idea had not occurred to him. And sure enough, on the sixth day of the Session, before he had produced the plot from his sleeve, the Incident duly occurred. A letter adressed to him was delivered to the porter of the House by a mysterious horseman,

---

* Though Gardiner, a little more significantly than perhaps he intends, assumes them to be the "leading members" of Parliament.

British Museum

KING CHARLES I IN ARMOUR—from a painting by Van Dyck

PLAGUE·SORE:

Wrapt up in a *Letter*, and fent to Mr. PYM : Wherein is di
covered a Divellifh, and Unchriftian Plot againft the High Court of
PARLIAMENT, *October* 25. 1641.

The trueEf-
fige of M.I.
Pym, Efqu.

Burgeffe in
the High
Court of Pa
liament for
Taviftock i
Devonftire

Reade in this Image him, whofe deereft Blood
Is thoug't no price, to buy his Countries good,
VVhofe name fhall flourifh till the blaft of Fame
Shall want a Trumpet, or true worth, a Name.

Printed for *W.B.* Anno Dom. 1641.

JOHN PYM: "A DAMNABLE TREASON"

and handed to him in his place by the Sergeant at Arms in a way that must certainly have focussed the attention of the members. Every one therefore must have seen Mr Pym take the letter out of the envelope, and one can imagine the gasp that ran along the benches when there fell out of it, on to the floor, a bloody and filthy looking rag. Mr Pym, by no means put out of his stride, at once proceeded to inform the House that the letter appeared to be a scandalous libel ; whereupon business was suspended, while the Assistant Clerk of the House, who can hardly have relished the transfer, took the letter, with its enclosure, and proceeded to read it out at length, to the effect that the rag had been passed through a plague sore, that Pym was a traitor and bribe-taker, and that if this failed to get him, there was a dagger ready to do the business—which dagger, it may be remarked, never seems subsequently to have materialized. Of course it is impossible to prove that this episode, so dramatically staged and opportunely timed, may not have been from Pym's point of view an unpremeditated windfall ; but nothing but the hypnotism of the current myth would have sufficed to rule out the far more obvious explanation, that the whole thing was deliberately contrived by him, since it was so typical an application of his technique that it would have been little short of a miracle had he failed to produce something of the sort at this particular juncture.

All along the line the offensive against the Crown was being speeded up by every means possible, and each successive move can be seen to fit into the pattern devised by one master mind, that foresees and times everything with beautiful exactitude. Nowhere is this foresight more clearly exemplified than in the care that was taken to keep public hatred and fear of the Queen continually on the boil by fresh increments of anti-Papal dope, with a view to her eventual selection for that part in a political drama which is never played twice by the same actor.

This was more than ever necessary, because her little court at Oatlands had of late been resorted to by increasing numbers of the nobility, to whose chivalrous instincts her unhappy situation can hardly have failed to appeal. To what lengths the revolutionary bosses were prepared to go, beyond their customary form of harrying and persecuting the Catholics in her entourage and manufacturing evidence of Popish plots, is shown by the fact that when she had allowed herself the solace of a visit from her two eldest children, the revolutionaries had given peremptory orders to the children's governor, Lord Hertford, not to permit them to go near their mother in future. To such a pass had the Queen of England come !

It is not without its significance that about this time the disreputable Newport, whom the revolutionary control had managed to insinuate into the Constableship of the Tower, was reported to have been heard arguing, over his cups, to the effect that it concerned the Parliamentary chiefs far more to secure the persons of the Queen and Prince of Wales than to mount guard over the King in Scotland.* It was doubtless what others of his associates, who were discreet or sober enough to keep their mouths shut, had in their minds.

But the great, forward step that Pym designed to take on the road to revolution, was to get the majority that he still reckoned on commanding in the Commons to force through a manifesto that should constitute an open and violent attack on the Crown, magnifying every grievance, raking up every malicious insinu-ation from the beginning of the reign onwards, and embodying the whole in the form of a Grand Remonstrance which, though it purported to be adressed to the King himself, was—and this was the real point of it—intended to be printed and published so as to infect as large a proportion of the King's subjects as possible with detestation of his person and the will to rebellion against him. And this in spite of the fact that ever since this Parliament had met, the King had granted the whole of their demands, and spared no effort to earn their goodwill.

A committee was accordingly appointed to put this amiable document into shape with all convenient expedition. Things were plainly being hurried to a crisis. For Pym knew that what he had to do must be done quickly, if it was to be done at all.

3

CATASTROPHE IN IRELAND

FOR more than a month after the Incident the King lingered on at Edinburgh, and indeed he could hardly, with any seemliness, have terminated his visit before its ostensible purpose had been

* S.P. Ven. xxv, no. 318. When the matter got to the King's ears it is hardly neces-sary, to anyone acquainted with Newport's record, to say that he assumed an attitude of injured innocence. "I am sorry," said the King, "for your Lordship's memory."

fulfilled. But he must have known now that this unpredictable misfortune had utterly ruined the last chance he might have had of re-establishing the invisible bonds between him and his Scottish subjects that the Covenanting sword had severed. In vain had he parted with one sovereign prerogative after another, in form to the Parliament, but in fact to Argyll, who lost little time in returning from his self-imposed banishment to assume complete mastery of the situation, and to wield a power such as few of the lawful Kings of Scotland had ever possessed. Hampden, it is significant to note, judged that after the Incident his presence in Edinburgh had become superfluous, and leaving Fiennes to supervise the task of shadowing the King, hurried South to join Pym at their Westminster headquarters.

On the 28th of October, just over a fortnight after the Incident, the King was enjoying a round on the Leith links, when a messenger arrived bearing fearful tidings. A rebellion had broken out in Ireland ; throughout the whole of the Northern province of Ulster the peasantry had risen and were massacring the English and Scottish colonists ; the fate of Dublin itself was uncertain, and the rebellion was sweeping like a forest fire throughout the length and breadth of the island.

Fearful news indeed, and yet such as any intelligent student of recent events might easily have anticipated. Never had catastrophe been more wantonly provoked or engineered with such suicidal ingenuity. It was now barely a couple of years since Strafford had been forced to end his all too brief period of office as the King's deputy, in the course of which he had worked such miracles in cleaning up the Augean Stable of Irish corruption and putting the country on her feet both financially and economically, besides giving her what was most urgently needed of all, if order was to be maintained, a small, but excellently disciplined and appointed military force.

But when the Providence Island directors had joined forces with the Irish racketeers, who were the principal witnesses against Strafford at his trial, all his work was violently undone, and Ireland again became a pawn in an English political game. Not only was free rein given to the old corruption and anarchy, but the confusion was worse confounded by the fanatical intolerance of everything Catholic that Pym and his associates were playing up for all it was worth, and which naturally had the effect of driving even the Irish nobility into dalliance with rebellion.

But with civil war being sedulously engineered in England, no one had any time to concern himself about the fate of Ireland.

The Lord Lieutenant, Leicester, who was appointed to succeed Strafford, did not even bother to cross the sea to take up his post ; and to make the catastrophe absolutely certain, the regiments raised by Strafford, which were under suspicion of loyalty to the King, were disbanded by order of the Parliament bosses, who even objected to their taking service abroad under Catholic monarchs, so that the men were turned adrift among their fellow countrymen, to put their military training to a purpose that might have been foreseen.

If the Irish had been capable of organizing themselves efficiently the whole structure of English rule might have collapsed with the seizure of Dublin Castle ; but the two gentlemen whose business it was to arrange the surprise got gloriously drunk on the eve of the attempt and blurted out the secret. That was typical of the bungling and happy-go-lucky way in which the Irish leaders allowed a matchless opportunity to slip through their fingers. The miserably exiguous English garrisons contrived, for the most part, to hold out in the towns ; but in the Ulster countryside, where the Catholic peasantry fell in overwhelming numbers upon the Protestant farmers who had dispossessed them of their lands, deeds of atrocity were perpetrated, atrocities that were bound in any case to be magnified by report, and that it was the task of Protestant propaganda in England to inflate to the utmost limit of sadistic exaggeration. The few thousand or so of actual victims were multiplied by anything up to a hundred, to vastly more than the whole English population of the affected province.

But what had actually happened was dreadful enough, and the detailed accounts that lost nothing in the telling of the fate of helpless women, children, and old people, aroused a fury among the good Protestant folk of England comparable to that which was afterwards provoked by the horrors of the Indian Mutiny, or German and Japanese atrocities within recent memory. Henceforth every Catholic Irishman (not to speak of Irish woman) would be regarded by English Puritans with as holy a horror as a Jew used to be by the Nazis. They were shut out from the pale of human brotherhood and Christian charity, and a dreadful new application would soon be given to the text:

"The time cometh that whosoever killeth you will think that he doeth God service."

Such were the emotions with which simple folk in England reacted, and were encouraged to react, to the news from Ireland. But the level-headed politicians without whose masterly negligence the catastrophe would never have occurred, had long ago schooled themselves to eliminate the emotional bias from their calculations. What signified to them the fate of a few Ulster farmers more or less ? They were playing for heavier stakes, and were not like those amateur conspirators of Dublin, the men to let slip a decisive opportunity—least of all such an opportunity as now presented itself. For though Mr Pym's Irish chickens had come home to roost, yet—as so often happens in the metaphorical, if not in the literal sense—they had come home to roost in his rival's hen-house. Or say that he and his friends had run up the account and it was King Charles who, if they knew anything about it, would have to foot the bill. And whoever had to suffer for it, they would spare no pains to run up that bill to staggering proportions.

Let us see how the contending parties in the now plainly impending English civil war did actually react to that in Ireland. Since his Irish policy had been laid in ruins by the liquidation of Strafford, it was little enough that the now almost powerless King had been able to do to influence the course of events, or to arrest the drift to anarchy that was what the new masters of the situation stood for in default of a policy. There was one direction however in which what little influence he could exercise was continually exerted. Like Strafford before him, he was able to see that the ferocious intolerance and persecution of Catholics that had been Pym's political speciality, if it was folly in England, was sheer madness in Ireland. He knew that loyal Catholics there were asking, with some point, why they should be denied the same freedom to worship God in their own way that was accorded to Presbyterian rebels in Scotland. In his dealings with the Irish nobility, King Charles had never made any secret of his sympathy with their demand for toleration, a lapse that profoundly shocks the liberal soul of Gardiner :

"A mere shifty expedient," he calls it, "from which nothing good was to be expected, and the mere suggestion of which was certain to kindle hopes which could hardly be disappointed with impunity."*

Even more sinister, if possible, was the fact that the Queen was

* *History of England*, x, pp. 46-7.

likewise known to harbour a desire for the toleration of her fellow Catholics.

But the King was the one person in authority who, when the news came, acted with clear-cut decision. Whatever might have been his opinion on the toleration of the Catholics, the remedy of lawless violence was one he was not prepared to tolerate under any plea whatever. Isolated though he was, in this suspicious and intrigue-ridden Edinburgh, he went to the Scottish Parliament with the object of getting some of these still mobilized Covenanters —men who had recently been in arms against him—dispatched at once to the scene of danger. For once he commanded their whole-hearted support. They were ready to supply the troops, provided the English Parliament was prepared to co-operate, and advices were instantly dispatched to Westminster to this effect.

Three days before this arrived, the Commons had been apprised of the situation, and had evinced every apparent disposition to react to it promptly, since they had voted for the raising of 8,000 men and the borrowing of £50,000. But when the proposal from Scotland arrived it met with a very mixed reception, especially from opposition leaders like Colepeper and Falkland, who were inclined to a less detached view of Scottish co-operation than the King. However, all seemed to be about to straighten itself out in the normal course ; the House had resolved to accept the assistance of the Scots to the extent, provisionally, of 1,000 men, and was putting the message to that effect into final shape, when Pym rose to his feet and proceeded to fire off the most shattering bombshell that had come yet, even from his armoury.

After a certain amount of the customary eyewash about his being ready to risk life, honour and estate in his Majesty's service —as if it were a question of Pym exposing his portly form as a target for rebel bullets—he proceeded to move an amendment to the effect that unless the King would consent to remove his evil counsellors (that is to say any ministers that Pym might be pleased to specify) and appoint others approved by Parliament (that is to say, named by Pym himself as the controller of Parliament) they would hold themselves released from any engagement to give him (or the suffering Protestants) any assistance in Ireland at all.

Naturally this attempt to use the rising as a counter for blackmailing the King into virtual abdication brought Hyde to his feet, to bring home to the House the revolutionary nature of Pym's proposal ; and after Hyde rose a member with whom the House was more familiar as a poet than a debater, and who, unlike most poets, was a very wealthy man, Edmund Waller, owner of the beautiful estate of Hall Barn, just outside Beaconsfield. He, like Cromwell, was a cousin of Hampden's, and had started as staunch for their party as other members of his family, but since the trial of Strafford he had been drifting more and more away from them. Waller had none of the diplomatic finesse of Hyde, but blurted straight out what was in his mind, namely that the attitude Pym was taking in absolving himself from all duty to His Majesty, unless he could get his own way, was precisely that which had been imputed to Strafford as the deadliest count of the indictment against him...

He was not allowed to finish. Pym was on his feet vehemently demanding reparation for this plain suggestion that what had been good measure for Strafford would be equally so for him, and voices were heard from all quarters calling on Waller to explain himself. But the poet was unequal to riding a storm of this kind, and after what seem to have been some unconvincing efforts to qualify his remark, he was commanded to withdraw, and presently, after some angry debate, he was brought back and allowed to apologize, Pym being probably only too glad to let it go at that. None the less the Ox seems to have been badly put out of his stride, for the debate was adjourned, and no attempt made to revive his proposal in a form smacking so openly of treason.

But Pym was not the man to accept defeat. Three days later he returned to the charge with a new and enormously verbose "additional instruction", in which the same demand for the appointment of ministers over the King's head was repeated, and weighted with a threat—which in turn was masked by brazen assurances of continued reverence, faithfulness, service and obedience—that if His Majesty refused to toe the line, "we" would proceed on our own authority to make the appointments in question, and assume all necessary powers for dealing with the Irish situation. This astounding manifesto, which would have set Pym, through his control of the Perpetual Parliament, not only above the King, but—what no King of England had ever been— above the law, was carried through the Commons by a majority of 41. The vote had no sort of legal validity, but that did not prevent it from being in effect, as it was in intention, a declaration of war on the King in his realm, and as such, treason in the highest degree, far exceeding anything that had been even alleged against the unhappy Strafford.

But even if Pym and his confederates had wished to set a limit to the desperate game which they were now playing, they had—at least in their own estimation—gone too far to draw back. For they were not only playing for the Sovereignty, but for their own necks ; and Pym was the last man to take any chance where this latter stake was concerned. He must have known well enough what he would have done in the King's shoes, the moment he got the opportunity ; and it would have been plain to a much less subtle intelligence that this Irish outbreak presented a supreme opportunity for whichever side could seize it first. For not all the revolutionary legislation that even this Parliament had put on the statute book had done anything to detract from the immemorial right and duty of the King of England, in time of war or rebellion, to put himself at the head of his armed forces and crush force with force. And that Charles was in a mood to take this duty seriously, must have been suggested by the firm line he had taken on the first news of the outbreak.

But if Charles were to fulfil his duty, and the King's peace were to be imposed by the King's troops, under his own leadership or that of commanders whose loyalty to Pym could not be guaranteed—what then ? Among the most zealous advocates for seizing the power of the sword was that same member for Cambridge who, nine years later, and as the agent of Parliament, did at last succeed in imposing peace on the desert his victorious army had made of Ireland. Pym did not live to see what subsequent use that commander was destined to make of his army, and in any case Charles was not of the tough stuff of which Cromwell was made—but, with his knowledge of the account that stood to his name on King Charles's books, we can hardly blame Pym for a determination to go to all lengths to deny the creditor a chance of pressing for settlement.

The effect of the Irish revolt was therefore inevitably to precipitate the English rebellion. It was no new idea that the control of the forces should be wrested from the King. Pym had already in his deliberate way made the first tentative approaches towards this objective. But now the matter had become one of vital urgency. Public opinion would brook no delay in raising an expeditionary force for Ireland. But Pym dared not allow the control of that force, or consequently of any force, to rest with the

Crown. But unless the King could be persuaded or intimidated into parting with it of his own accord, there was no way of making him, except by levying war on him in his realm. That was the plain issue that henceforth overshadowed all others. In the textbooks it is called the struggle for the militia—a word that has quite different associations nowadays. In modern English, the question to be decided was, whether the King should surrender the command of his own armed forces into the hands of a political clique.

4

PROPAGANDA BARRAGE

PYM had every reason to congratulate himself on the new turn of events. If it had forced his hand, it had also immensely strengthened it. The stunting of atrocities that were sensational enough in themselves, was calculated to inflame to madness the militant anti-Catholicism of which he knew so well how to take advantage. He had now to drive that advantage home by every means in his power, so as to confront the King with a situation that on his return from Scotland, would leave him no choice but to surrender at discretion, or be crushed by overwhelming force. For no doubt Pym still hoped, as he would certainly have preferred, to force a bloodless decision by disarming his adversary. Hence we find the propaganda barrage quickened to drumfire intensity. Now was the time for bringing out of store that long cherished evidence about Legge's petition and the King's initials, and whipping up a majority to vote it proof of "a second design to bring up the army against the Parliament".

That was an obvious move, and one that had been held in reserve for months past. But this Irish windfall presented Pym with the opportunity for planting a new and far deadlier suggestion, on a mass consciousness worked up to a pitch of ideological hysteria no less acute than that which his political heirs of the next generation were to turn to such profitable account, through the good offices of Dr Titus Oates. The logic of it was simple. There was the unassailable premise that a Catholic populace had without warning made a concerted attempt to wipe out, amid every circumstance of horror, the Protestant minority in their midst. That this might be the last resort of men driven desperate by intolerable oppression, was an explanation against which the mind of every godly and patriotic Englishman was sealed in advance. What remained, but the enthusiastically congenial assumption that this could be nothing else than the result of a plot—a Popish plot? That stood, if not exactly to reason, at least to whatever is the substitute for logic in the mass consciousness.

But that logic had to be pushed a stage further to reach the desired conclusion. No sufficient purpose would be served merely by making Protestant flesh creep. A Popish plot implied a Popish plotter, and that, for Pym's purposes, could be no other than the most prominent Papist in the Kingdom. For as I have tried to show, ever since he had disposed of Strafford, Pym—whose way it was never to bring off a successful manœuvre without trying to repeat it—had marked down the Queen for his next victim. He had, in his unhurried way, been preparing the ground and biding his time. It was unthinkable therefore that he should let slip this opportunity of pillorying her as the prime agent in what Gardiner describes as "a great Popish plot for the extinction of Protestantism in the three kingdoms".

All the apparatus of rumour and panic-mongering that had been set to work to compass the death of Strafford was set in motion on the now familiar lines. There was that same Sir Walter Earle, who, at the time when the Perpetual Parliament Bill was being smuggled through the House, had started a wild and most opportune panic among his fellow members, by persuading them that they were all immediately about to be blown sky-high in a second gunpowder plot. This useful individual was now brought again into the limelight to give a fresh lease of life to the cock and bull story about a French invasion. With an invincible faith in the credulity of his audience, the good Sir Walter fixed on Portsmouth as once again being the destined port of entry. In proof of which he read a letter from an alleged correspondent whose identity he refused to disclose, to the effect that a secret post was passing several times a week between the Queen, at Oatlands, and the Governor, Colonel Goring, who had up to recently stood high in the graces of Parliament, for having turned Pym's evidence against the brother officers whom he himself had previously incited to accept his leadership in what was rather absurdly dignified with the name of the First Army Plot. This time, the advance guard of the invading army had materialized in the shape of "a Frenchman of the Romish religion brought in to be a chirurgeon of the garrison"—who was no doubt privy to Goring's construction of new forts commanding the town from the land side, while those intended for defence against invasion were allowed to go to ruin. No wonder that "the Papists and jovial clergymen thereabouts are merrier than ever."

At this same time a committee of the Commons, including both Pym and Hampden, was solemnly investigating the story of a certain tailor, who according to himself had overheard two men behind a bank expounding in detail the design of certain Catholics, at the instance of two priests, to murder 108 members on their way home from Parliament ; and since this awful design was said to have been hatched at the house of "my lord" (unspecified) a search was actually made of the houses of several Catholic peers.

So far Pym had not come into the open with a formal attack upon the Queen. But this intensive attempt to work up the country into a fever of appalled plot consciousness, was a repetition of the propaganda drive that had preceded the final assault on Strafford. The inference is obvious. Pym was not the man to put forth a supreme effort unless he hoped to obtain a commensurate result. Nor must we forget that he had yet to set the seal on his propagandist offensive—the necessary means of approach to his main objective—by forcing through Parliament that Grand Remonstrance, or manifesto against the Crown, which had been indicated as the chief business of the new session.

In respect of which we may cite the words of the faithful Gardiner : "There was doubtless a singular opportuneness in the circulation of the rumours which sprang up just at the time when the fate of the Remonstrance was at stake, *and it is quite possible that Pym and Hampden did not at this moment care to scrutinize so closely the tales which reached their ears as they might under other circumstances have done.*"* (The italics I have, perhaps superfluously, taken the liberty of supplying.)

Which is certainly a classic example of the way in which an honest advocate can reconcile his duty to his clients with the strictest regard for accuracy and even fullness of statement. It is what makes Gardiner so much more enduring a support of the

* *History of England*, x, p. 72.

Whig myth than the Macaulays, Forsters, and Greens, whose brilliance is dulled by no such cramping inhibitions. Though I suspect that Gardiner in this case is doing less than justice to Pym and Hampden, who were too consummately versed in the arts of propaganda not to scrutinize their ammunition with all necessary closeness.

5

REVOLUTIONARY MANIFESTO

AT long last the King had contrived to get himself free of what had now become the hopeless entanglement of his affairs in Scotland, to set his face Southwards to deal with the even graver crisis in England. He very sensibly resolved to suppress whatever might have been his real chagrin at the way in which all his efforts to win back the hearts of his Scottish subjects had been cunningly frustrated, and to accept with a good grace those wholesale sacrifices of his sovereignty that he could in no case have averted. Even Argyll, who was too canny to advertise a power of which he was content to have got the substance, received a step up in the peerage ; Hamilton's twisting was rewarded with ducal strawberry leaves, and that rough and tough old adventurer, Leslie, was set to look as plausible as he could in the dignity of Earl of Leven. All ended in a parade of loyalty and goodwill— Argyll was even ready to grant an amnesty to Montrose, a step he might afterwards have cause to regret. And Charles may perhaps have indulged himself with the hope that his invincible determination to earn the goodwill of his beloved Scots might yet, in due time, bear fruit. He was due in London on the 25th of November.

His arrival must have been awaited by the revolutionary leaders with a certain apprehension. For in spite of the almost unbroken series of defeats and humiliations to which he had been subjected, signs had not been lacking of a turn of the tide in the King's favour. Even in London itself placards had been appearing in public places denouncing as traitors and seditionists those Members of Parliament whose extremist activities had been most notorious, and similar manifestations had been reported from other parts of the country. A universal dissatisfaction, according to our Venetian observer, had even before the opening of this second session been openly expressed with the efforts of Parliament, which is hardly to be wondered at, when we consider that the country was groaning under the weight of such taxation as had never been known even in time of war, smarting under intolerable humiliation, and plunged from its dream of peaceful prosperity into a nightmare of wars and rumours of wars, of political vendetta and religious nihilism, and with the shadow of almost unimaginable catastrophe looming ahead. There must have been millions of inarticulate people up and down the country whose only desire was to get back, while there was yet time, to the peace and prosperity that they had enjoyed for so many years under the mild yoke of a constitutional monarchy.

No one can have realised better than Pym, who was the last man to flatter himself with optimistic illusions, that the new constitutional party that had come so near to wresting from him the control even of his once unanimously submissive House of Commons would, if something were not done to arrest the threatened landslide, soon command such an overwhelming backing of popular support as would sweep away even the artificial barrier of his Perpetual Parliament Act. The appeal from England drunk with ideological fanaticism and doped with continual injections of propaganda could not be much longer delayed. And then ... ?

But it might be delayed just long enough for the revolutionary junta to put its control of the country on such an impregnable footing that the people themselves would be past the power to bring about a constitutional restoration. For to talk as if the balance of forces had already tilted against the revolution would have been premature. In the centres of population, and particularly London, the ideological ferment was at work more powerfully than ever since the quickening it had received from Irish atrocity reports and propaganda. Tendencies indeed were beginning to manifest themselves that might have wakened the gravest apprehensions in the Parliamentary chiefs, had they found time to look beyond the immediate issue. The common people, no longer content to pull the chestnuts out of the fire for the plutocrats or to accommodate themselves to the iron shackles of a Presbyterian discipline, were beginning to go all out for the full Protestant claim of every man to own no religious superior other than his

Maker, and of every two or three men who liked to gather themselves together in a congregation to be their own church with an
unlimited right to choose their own mode of worship and behaviour. And if Jack were to set up as his own master in a spiritual
capacity, what was to prevent him from deducing that "the
poorest He that is in England hath a life to live as the greatest
He?" Which was hardly a conclusion likely to be palatable to
such great "He's" as Lord Brooke and Squire Hampden.

But I do not think that Cromwell himself, who, with his
championship of the fenmen was their only associate who had
evinced the slightest practical sympathy with the common people,
had as yet any forevision of Independents or Levellers snatching
the control of the revolution out of the hands of its starters and
imparting to it a really democratic urge. Their whole attention
was concentrated on the desperate game they were playing not
only against the King, but against the clock. Something—anything—had to be done to swing back popular sentiment to their
side.

The time was therefore ripe for launching the appeal to the
nation against the Crown, that had been in preparation since the
beginning of the Session. It was plainly Pym's intention to get
this endorsed by Parliament so as to present the King with it on
his arrival from Scotland, and to get the printing presses instantly
to work so as to confront him with a situation in which he would
have no choice but to make a second and final surrender to the
threat of mob law.

That enormous document—it contains 204 clauses—is cited
in every textbook under its name of the Grand Remonstrance,
as one of the landmarks of English constitutional liberty. But I
cannot help wondering how many, if any, of those who assume
such familiarity with its purport have ever been to the labour of
reading it through. For whatever it may have been to the ostrich-
like digestion of a seventeenth century public, to the modern
reader it is about as unreadable a production in proportion to its
size as has ever been put into print.

Such fragmentary record as we have of the process by which
the Remonstrance was put together suggests that while its
essential clauses were no doubt drafted in advance, its extraordinary bulk and diffuseness were largely the result of individual
contributions and amendments in the course of its passage through
committee, on the principle that any point scored off the King

was helping on the good cause. Largely it consists of a long, rambling recital of whatever events were alleged to have occurred during the past sixteen years, that either had been, or could be, worked up into "grievances" ; much of it is no more than insipid cataloguing of events with which everybody must have already been familiar ; much of it malignant or impudent travesty ; sometimes it wanders off from attack into apology and self glorification, including such heroic attempts to put a favourable complexion on the least defensible proceedings of the Remonstrators as is contained in the clause dealing with the military blackmail levied by the Scots on the nation through their agency, to enable them, in their turn, to blackmail the King :

"... All that we have done is for his Majesty, his greatness, honour, and support, when we yield to give £25,000 for the relief of the Northern counties ; this was given to the King for he was bound to protect his subjects."

Which is certainly one way of putting it !

But interspersed with the vast uncompounded hotchpotch of garbled history, of assertion, argument and declamation, were items in which the veneer of loyalty is dropped, and in which the attack on the King is pushed to the point of open insult and sedition. This would be even more apparent had we before us the text as it emerged from committee. A statement, for instance, issued in his own name by the King, was characterized as "false and scandalous" ; a deliberately scurrilous reference was made to his not having"bread for his head "except by "the bounty of his people"—in other words, by favour of the Parliamentary chiefs ; and there is something not far short of an incitement to regicide in the statement, that appears to have been made in the original draft, that the persecution of the former extremist leader, Sir John Eliot, had been committed "by the King's own hand", and that his blood still cried to heaven for vengeance.

Informing this vast accumulation of verbiage is an implied purpose of unmasking a malignant conspiracy to extirpate the Protestant religion and destroy all the liberties of the realm. The authors and promoters of this conspiracy are nowhere specified, but the implication is plain that its prime source is the Vatican, and that its agents include the most prominent Catholics in the country—not excepting the most prominent of all, the Queen— that the Bishops of the Anglican Church are either party to or actively sympathetic with it, that everybody known to be loyal to the King is more or less tainted with it, and that the King himself, on the most favourable estimate, is its passive instrument.

The only remedy, therefore, is to take all power out of the King's hands and transfer it to those of the patriotic and godly men who speak with the voice of Parliament ; to give these men absolute control of all appointments in Church and State, and— the threat, is explicit—in the event of His Majesty's refusal, to bring the whole machinery of government to a standstill by the refusal of supplies. Incidentally, the Church is to be completely purged and reconstituted on lines as yet undisclosed, except that in no case will there be the least tolerance of dissent.

Thus the Remonstrance had a double purpose : to present the King, on his return home, with a demand for his immediate abdication of all but the trappings of sovereignty ; and simultaneously to broadcast among the people a seditious libel, calculated to render him an object of detestation and contempt, even in the capacity of figurehead.

The time factor, the appreciation of which constituted no small part of Pym's greatness, was all important. The King was on his way south, and at all costs must be prevented from taking advantage of that mounting indignation of the people with the proceedings of their new masters, which might, in a short time, develop into a counter-revolutionary landslide. The chaotic drafting of the Remonstrance itself bears witness to the precipitation with which its clauses must have been rammed through the committee ; and on Saturday, the 20th of November, when His Majesty was already well on his way, it was proposed to rush it whole through the House, in the course of an afternoon's debate, in much the same way as Pym had dealt with the Perpetual Parliament Act. But in the present case he had reckoned without the opposition, which under Hyde's leadership put up so solid a resistance to this arbitrary proposal that even Pym had to give way so far as to allow the debate to be put back to Monday, and the Remonstrance to be debated clause by clause. When one considers that there were no less than 204 clauses, one realizes what was implied in the determination to get the whole thing disposed of in the course of a single sitting ! But on that Pym was adamant. By Monday His Majesty would already have passed through York. A day's delay might make all the difference.

6

REMONSTRANCE   AND   COUNTER-REMONSTRANCE

THE effect of the attempt to rush the issue had thus been merely to awaken the opposition to its importance, and unite it in a passionate determination to fight the Remonstrance to the last ditch. Few debates can ever have been awaited with more anxiety, and none, in all the long history of the Commons, was more worthy of record. It is proportionately to be regretted that our knowledge of it is no more than we can piece together from all too fragmentary references in the diaries and memoirs of those who took part in it. There was no Hansard in those days. What is certain is that from midday to midnight the fight went on without a pause, the opposition contesting every point with indefatigable persistence.

The backers of the Remonstrance had been determined to carry it intact, and would appear—at least in so far as we may judge by some impatient remarks made after Saturday's adjournment by Cromwell to Falkland—to have counted on a merely perfunctory debate. If so, they had reckoned without Hyde. The qualities that had made his reputation at the bar stood him in good stead in fighting a case like this. With a never failing command of his temper, and a persuasive candour in conceding the truth of those parts of the Remonstrance that were mere narrative padding, he proceeded for hour after hour to fasten on its many inconsistent, dangerous, and seditious items, with what must have been deadly insistence. He had behind him a party that was at last enthusiastically united in the cause not only of the Church, but of the law and constitution. There was Colepeper, with his sledge hammer debating blows, and Falkland, pleading with a gentle insistence that having obtained everything they had asked for, it would be better to cover the unhappy past with an Act of Oblivion.

But there also was Pym, holding his now precarious majority in hand with massive persistence, equally determined not to yield a point more than necessary. We can only catch a faint echo of the tones with which he must have held the attention of the House to variations on the theme of Popery and plots, plots and Popery—all projects were rooted in Popery—had not a Lord Treasurer been a Papist ?—a Secretary a Papist ?—all plots and designs were thrust home to the Court—it was time to speak plain English, lest posterity should say England was lost and no man dared speak truth. Pym knew the mood of his followers, and such tub-thumping was no doubt better calculated to sustain it than the most statesmanlike oratory would have been.

Candles had been called for early in the November afternoon, and must have burnt down near to their sockets before the debate showed any signs of flagging. Some of the weaker spirits had trailed off, including, most unfortunately, our leading authority, the diarist Sir Simonds D'Ewes, who was in the first stages of a cold. But the protagonists stuck to their work with a concentration that appeared to be proof against fatigue, and it would seem that the opposition did succeed in forcing the promoters of the Remonstrance to tone down some of its more openly offensive items, including the "bread to his head" sneer, and the sentence invoking vengeance on the King, by name, for the blood of Eliot.

To what extent the fight put up by the opposition was successful in drawing the claws of the Remonstrance is a matter on which, failing the text of the committee's draft, we have but barest scraps of direct evidence. But that the promoters, contrary to their original intention, were fain to lighten the Remonstrance by submitting to considerable amendments, sometimes without a division, we do know ; and also that Hyde was well satisfied with his success in getting "many clauses and unbecoming expressions cast out". He had reason to be. For twelve hours on end he had fought his delaying action against the greatest of all masters of Parliamentary tactics and a majority ruthlessly determined to get its way, and he had succeeded in converting what was meant to be a walk over into what would, at most, be a Pyrrhic victory.

When, after midnight,* and in an atmosphere of tense excitement, the Remonstrance, as amended, was finally submitted to the vote of the House, Mr Pym must have cast anxious eyes over the now noticeably thinned benches. With this leakage of voting strength—for even Pym does not appear to have evolved a technique of efficient "whipping"—could even a majority be taken for granted ? If the Remonstrance should be defeated ! Cromwell, at least, had envisaged this possibility, and afterwards admitted that if it had materialized, he and others of his party would have packed up and cleared out of the country. They might well have judged it too hot to hold them !

* Sir Philip Warwick puts it as late as three in the morning.

It was, as Wellington would have said, a damned near run thing, but when the votes came to be counted, it proved that the Remonstrance had just scraped through by a bare eleven. This, if not an open defeat, was a result far more shattering to Pym's prestige than the King's. It was an advertisement to the whole nation that his control of Parliament was slipping through his fingers. A majority that had shrunk in a few months from one of the whole House to a beggarly eleven on a vital issue, was now all that stood—for how long ?—between him and ruin.

Under such circumstances we can only admire the nerve of men who in face of such a rebuff and at such an hour, could persist in their determination to keep the House sitting until they had carried through their essential purpose of turning the Remonstrance from what it purported, into what it was intended to be.

Hardly had the result been declared, when one of the most fanatical of the Puritan wild men, George Peard, was heard moving that the Remonstrance be put into print. The intention of this was obvious—it was no longer a question of remonstrance, but of open incitement to sedition. Hyde and Colepeper, who had no doubt anticipated such a move, instantly and vehemently begged leave, if it should be proceeded with, to dissociate themselves and their followers from it by the hitherto unheard-of means of a formal protest. This, though couched in characteristically discreet terms, was as plain a declaration of war on the revolutionary control as the Remonstrance had been on the King. But by this time it must at last have become apparent even to Pym that, with tension so near to breaking point, it would be madness to accept the challenge. This dance, as Sir Robert Walpole was to put it on a hardly less memorable occasion, would no further go.

The Speaker was accordingly just about to leave the chair, without anything decided, when one of the opposition members, Geoffrey Palmer, carried away by the excitement of the moment, jumped to his feet and—repeatedly as it seems—started to insist on the protest being registered then and there on behalf of himself and his fellow members. That detonated the explosion. A roar went up, with cries of "All ! all !" predominating—members waving their hats and even unslinging their swords from their belts ; and though none were drawn,* there was the chance that

* A point missed in the highly coloured conventional account of the incident. No man who meant business would have unslung his sword ; he would have drawn it.

some fresh provocation might have precipitated a bloody fracas, when Hampden, whose skill in the management of his fellow-members was never more conspicuously displayed, brought them back to earth by asking how Palmer could possibly know what was in, other men's minds. That was hardly fair to Palmer, and the question might more logically have been adressed to his supporters, but it gave the excuse that most of the shouting mob probably wanted for getting out of the *impasse* with whole skins, and dragging their weary limbs to bed.

A more humiliating fiasco could hardly have been conceived. The terrible Remonstrance, instead of exploding like a mine beneath the throne, had fizzled like a damp squib. "After numerous debates", as the Venetian Ambassador reported in cipher about a week later, "they have decided to abandon the idea of sending it to the Upper House for approval or to have it printed. They have merely decided to present it to His Majesty."

7

THE KING'S HOMECOMING

IT must now have been evident to all parties concerned that the King's return ushered in the decisive phase of the constitutional struggle. The issue was clearly defined : the Tudor Constitution, under which England had thriven so gloriously for a century and a half, had been revised so as to give Parliament a complete stranglehold on the Crown—this the King had frankly accepted, and there was no serious question, in any quarter, of putting back the clock. The real question to be decided was whether he were to be given a fair chance of carrying on his own government within the framework of the revised constitution, or whether the Parliamentary chiefs were to tighten the stranglehold so as to crush the last vestiges of sovereignty out of him.

The Grand Remonstrance had made it plain that nothing less than this latter solution would suffice for Pym and his associates. Until they had gathered all sovereign power into their own hands, and confirmed it by law, they could not feel safe. But to those who had eyes to see, it was becoming equally plain that the King, in conceding the utmost of all that they had originally demanded of him, had carried concession to a limit beyond which not even death could move him. He had the law, he had the immemorial practice of the constitution, and, as he must have felt in his innermost conscience, he had the right on his side ; and if they were determined to ride roughshod over all three, he owed it to his people no less than to himself to maintain his right and theirs to the uttermost of his kingly power. It was a quarrel in which he might well hope to have the people on his side. And if Pym were determined, as he only too plainly was, to force the issue by any means, constitutional or otherwise, then the country was being rushed, with appalling speed, into the civil war that not one in a hundred of Englishmen could have envisaged without the utmost horror, and yet none of them had any means of averting.

At any other time, the remedy would have been simple. All the King would have had to do, after the fiasco of the Remonstrance, would have been to have dissolved Parliament, and appealed to the country. The result of such an appeal must, at the lowest estimate, have been to convert Pym's already precarious majority into a minority capable of being voted down on any decisive issue ; and what then would there have been to prevent him and his associates from being called to as strict an account as they themselves had called Strafford ?

But this was the very danger that Pym had foreseen and provided against, months before, in his Perpetual Parliament Act. As long as he could hang on, even by the narrowest margin, to his shrinking majority in the Commons, so long could he cut off the King from any peaceful way of appealing to his people, or the people from rallying to the support of their King.

But for how long would that hold good ? For long enough, perhaps, to drive the revolution through by the instant and ruthless exploitation of such chances as still remained—the Popish terror—the London mob—the Queen. Most of all, perhaps, the Queen !

But there was a spirit abroad even in London almost incredibly different from that which had prevailed during the siege of Whitehall by the mob six months before. The King must have been astounded by the welcome he received when, accompanied by the Queen, who had been graciously allowed to meet him at Theobald's in Hertfordshire, he arrived at his capital. There had been nothing in the whole course of his reign to compare with its warmth and enthusiasm. The new Lord Mayor, Sir Richard

Gurney, a whole-hearted loyalist, who had been elected, after
a stiff fight, in that explicit capacity, had spared no pains in
organizing the most splendid reception that the resources of the
city could furnish. The nobility of England, in their orders ;
five hundred of the most prominent citizens with their chains and
liveries ; the sheriffs, the trumpeters, the Lord Mayor himself
bearing the sword of state, formed part of the splendid pageant
that wound its way from Moorgate to the Guildhall, with the
city companies lining the route, the houses—the lovely timber-
built houses of pre-fire London—hung with costly tapestries,
every window packed with welcoming faces, dense crowds all
along the way vociferating "God bless King Charles and Queen
Mary !" The very conduits ran red with wine. Then after a
splendid banquet, at which his Majesty knighted the Lord
Mayor's newly married son-in-law, the procession was reformed,
and proceeded by torchlight past St Paul's, where the choir were
drawn up in their surplices to chant a specially composed anthem,
and thence through Ludgate and past Charing Cross to Whitehall—a way that so many of these cheering thousands must have
taken last May on a very different occasion. His Majesty, as he
rode with one commander designate of a rebel army just in front
of him and the other following behind the Queen's coach of
State, can hardly have failed to recall the welcome he had lately
received at Edinburgh—and its sequel.

But he had not come to town to play the part of a pageant
dummy. In reply to a loyal address, he had made a speech in
which he had declared his intention of governing according to
the law, and maintaining the Protestant religion as it had been
established by Elizabeth and his own father, "and this", he said,
"I will do at the hazard of my life, and all that is dear to me."

There was the ring of an unmistakable challenge in these words.
It was an intimation, to all whom it might concern, that the King
had come back prepared to take his stand on the law, and that
he had done with the policy of unlimited concession by which he
had so vainly hoped to appease the revolutionaries. Even before
he had left Edinburgh he had taken the significant step of making
a batch of appointments to vacant bishoprics, admittedly of
excellent men, but which had involved the promotion of two of
these Prelates whom the junta had marked down for impeachment, and "what was serious", as Gardiner somewhat naïvely
complains, "was the intention to nominate bishops as he had

nominated them before ...", to proceed, in fact, on the assumption, that he, and not Pym, was Supreme Governor of the Church.

This same determination, from which he never afterwards receded, to oppose his "thus far and no further" to the revolution, was indicated by his prompt dismissal on his return of the guard that had been illegally appointed in his absence by Parliament for the ostensible purpose of its own protection, and the substitution of one provided by himself under the command of the loyal Earl of Dorset. Though it was the King's obvious responsibility to furnish Parliament with whatever protection it might happen to need, this was taken as a grievance—as it perhaps was, for reasons that could not very well be avowed.

Six days after his return, the King's attitude became still more clearly defined by his reception of the Commons' deputation bringing the Grand Remonstrance. This already vast compilation had been rendered still bulkier by a verbose and mostly redundant petition that Pym had succeeded in getting tacked on to it, and which besides repeating the demand for transferring the appointment to all public offices from the King's hands to those of "Parliament", requested his connivance in depriving the Bishops of their votes in the Lords, and also in a wholesale confiscation and share out of Irish land by which it was hoped to turn the rebellion and its suppression to profitable account for Patriot capital.

When the deputation, headed by Pym, arrived at Hampton Court, where the King was, he received them with his usual courtesy, and submitted patiently to having it all read to him from beginning to end, only relieving the monotony with one or two such dry comments as "We must not [in Ireland] dispose of the bear's skin before the bear is dead," or [when the Catholic conspiracy was on the *tapis*] a double-edged "Devil take him, *whoever he be*, who has a design to change religion !"

Having then intimated that he supposed they would not require a present answer to so long a petition, he handed them over to the care of the Controller of his Household with instructions for them to be entertained for the night with the best cheer the palace could provide. It was too royally done even to constitute a snub. It was merely an anti-climax.

This was the last time Charles and Pym were to meet face to face. One would like to think that the last look that passed between these redoubtable opponents was one of chivalrous appreciation ;

but they were too differently constituted, in every respect, to render such a supposition tenable. It may however have begun to dawn on Pym's realistic intelligence that he had come up against a will as unyielding as his own. Whatever hope he might have taken to Hampton of a second Whitehall surrender, could hardly have returned with him to Westminster. The constitutional way to his goal was barred. But with public opinion shifting against him, the Lords passively obstructive, and his own prestige no longer what it had been, to plunge into naked treason and rebellion would be the surest way of rallying a decisive majority of Englishmen to the King's support. And yet with even his control of the Commons on its last legs, it would be safer to dare the uttermost than even to pause in his offensive.

The King, who had thus far played his hand with masterly restraint, had only to remain quietly on a now almost impregnable defensive, in order to force Pym to put himself suicidally in the wrong by attacking him in defiance of the law.

But suppose that Pym, out of the resources of his genius, could find a way of forcing the King's hand, to the extent of making him throw away all those advantages with his eyes open ?

The thing might not appear possible. But to genius it is hard to fix bounds of possibility.

8

THE MOB COMES BACK TO WESTMINSTER

FROM the moment that it became apparent that the King was finally determined to stand firm against any further abridgement of his sovereignty, the Parliamentary struggle ceased to be significant except as a manœuvring for position in the civil war that had become the only possible way of resolving the deadlock. It is true that so long as Pym retained his narrow majority in the Commons, there would be no slackening of the revolutionary drive ; but the Upper House, with that solid block of episcopal votes that was now his chief bugbear, still declined to co-operate in legislation designed to alter its own composition, or to bring about the subversion of either the monarchy or the Church.

There was, therefore, a certain unreality about the Commons' debates ; and even when a bill was introduced to take the whole control of the forces out of the King's hands, it had no other effect than that of producing a violent scene in the House with shouts of "Cast it out ! Cast it out !" from the Opposition ; and though a motion to refuse it a hearing altogether was defeated by the unexpectedly large majority of 33, it was not thought worth while to proceed with it further, since even if it could have been got through the Commons there would not have been the faintest chance of passing it into law.

The Parliamentary way was, for the nonce, blocked, and must be cleared by violence before the revolutionary programme could go through. The demonstration on the King's return had not in the least discouraged Pym and his supporters from bringing the mob into play ; it had only stimulated them to greater efforts. Dorset had not been appointed to his command a moment too soon, for his guard had not been on duty for a couple of days before Palace Yard was filled, as at the time of Strafford's trial, with a surging crowd armed with swords and cudgels, shouting "no bishops !" and endeavouring to terrorize members into pledging their votes to this effect. Dorset handled the situation with vigour, and was alleged to have given an order to fire, though it appears likely that nothing more was meant than a demonstration, since the sight of the levelled muskets was all that was needed to send the crowd bolting for safety. None the less there was serious talk of impeaching Dorset for high treason !

The fact that the mob were now playing so accurately into Pym's hands by concentrating on the mitred obstruction that was now the main obstacle in his path, would alone be sufficient reason for suspecting that their activities were not wholly spontaneous. And out of the fog of oblivion that has fallen on the inner political workings of this time, emerge one or two unmistakable indications of the way in which the business was being engineered. It was, for example, reported that a certain John Venne, one of the burgesses for the city, and a future regicide, had been heard at a shop in Cheapside telling the prentices :

"You must go to Westminster with your swords, for that party which is best for the Commonwealth is likely to be outvoted."*

Again we hear of a petition being got up in the city for the removal of the bishops and Catholic peers from the Lords, and of a mercer named Hobson, described as "a dangerous and factious

* S.P. Dom. 2/12/41.

man", summoning his fellow parishioners, with the aid of a constable, to his house in Ave Maria Lane, and telling them that if they refused to sign they were neither good Christians nor well affected to the Commonwealth ; the same procedure being adopted in the next ward by "Deputy Taylor of the Hen and Chickens at Paternoster Row"—in short it would seem that there must have been a highly organized system of such propagandist coercion at work.*

Things were obviously boiling up to a crisis, and unless it was the King himself, there can hardly have been any one on either side who seriously imagined that hope remained of a peaceful solution. But for a few uneasy weeks the crisis delayed to materialize. And though every day's delay was strengthening the King's position, to throw off the mask and hoist the standard of open rebellion, in the teeth of the law, was too desperate a venture even for Pym to undertake, unless he could first contrive to swing public opinion back to his side, by displaying the King in the light of the aggressor. To this his matchless skill in the arts of propaganda had hitherto been equal. But now the old stimuli of French invasions and army plots were dulled by repetition ; the long catalogue of exploitable grievances had been redressed to demand ; and there was every sign of moderate opinion all over the country rallying to the King's side—provided only that he contrived not to alienate it by any ill-considered step. And ever since the death of Strafford, the King had played his difficult hand with an admirable blend of patience and conciliation, tempered increasingly with firmness. To imagine that he would now go out of his way to put himself in the wrong by some wanton act of aggression, would have been wishful thinking indeed. And to credit Pym with the power of forcing him to do so would have seemed fantastic to any one who had not—and who had ?— gauged the extent of Pym's resourcefulness.

One error of judgment the King did certainly make in the middle of the month, when the Lieutenancy of the Tower fell vacant by the resignation of Sir William Balfour, an honourable soldier, according to his lights, but one who had notoriously been holding the royal fortress not for but against his King. Even Pym stopped short of openly contesting the King's right to appoint a successor, and Charles must have felt that under the circumstances, the one chance of denying this great stronghold and

* S. P. Dom. 9/12/41.

arsenal to the revolution was to put in command the toughest fighting man on whose loyalty he could rely. Such a man was Thomas Lunsford, a fiery-headed, limping squire, of an old Sussex family, who certainly qualified for the part as far as pugnacity was concerned. Unfortunately, an exuberance of this quality had brought him into trouble, some years before, with Star Chamber ; first for poaching deer on the estate of his kinsman, Sir Thomas Pelham, and then, when he had been adjudged to pay compensation, leading an assault on Sir Thomas himself. For this he had been outlawed, and had spent some years knocking about on the Continent in the French service ; but had eventually got his pardon, and done good service for the King in the Border campaigns. Charles would have been well advised at this juncture to have refrained from giving his enemies the least handle for misconstruction, but he can hardly have been prepared for the concerted howl that went up on Lunsford's appointment. It was assiduously put about that the new Lieutenant was capable of any villainy ; that he was not only in the habit of eating babies, but that he had actually been guilty, on campaign, of neglecting divine service. Amid all this propagandist clamour no one noticed (nor has to this day) that the Constable of the Tower, who would have been Lunsford's second in command, and who was so much in the good books of the revolutionaries that they were urging him to usurp the Lieutenancy, was that same Earl of Newport, who had volunteered to oblige them, in case of need, by murdering his prisoner, Strafford, in cold blood, and whose record was not that of a swashbuckler, but to borrow a phrase from Cromwell—of a corrupt, unjust person.

It is by this that we can appraise the sincerity of the holy horror aroused by Lunsford's appointment. But Charles had made a tactical error, and one that he had the sense to recognize by promptly cancelling the appointment, and giving it to Sir John Byron, as tough a fighting man as Lunsford, but of unimpeachable respectability. He closed the incident by compensating Lunsford with a knighthood, and purging the Tower of Newport.

But he had given his enemies just the opportunity they had wanted for reviving the activities of their ally, the mob, which had taken nearly a month after the sharp lesson it had received from Dorset, to put in a fresh appearance at Westminster. But now a new stimulus was applied by reports that were circulated among the apprentices to the effect that Lunsford's appointment covered horrific designs on the part of the Court, or the Catholics, or both ; and so effective had this been that the Lord Mayor had actually warned the King that the lads were prepared to storm the Tower unless Lunsford was dismissed. Such projects are not conceived spontaneously.

By the time that Parliament had reassembled after Christmas, the ostensible grievance had been removed, but the mob had been worked up into a mood reminiscent of that which had prevailed during the Strafford trial. It was back at Westminster as soon as the members themselves, thronging the approaches, and setting on to the bishops, with the obvious intention of cancelling their inconvenient vote by a crude anticipation of the technique of Pride's purge. Archbishop Williams, in particular, who had been promoted from Lincoln to the Archbishopric of York, came in for some very rough handling ; and about 500 of the rioters burst into Westminster Hall, where they were unlucky enough to find a party of a dozen officers, including the redoubtable Lunsford himself, who promptly proceeded to set about them, chasing them about the Hall, and smacking them with the flat of their swords—for they were careful not to use the points. They then proceded to drive them down the street, until the crowd having been swollen by fresh additions, and the odds being now more than 50 to 1, the adventurous twelve were forced to retire by showers of stones.

Next day only two of the bishops dared turn up to run the gauntlet ; whereupon the mob, for want of other sport, burst into Westminster Abbey in order to wreck the organ and altar, which were successfully defended by that plucky old Welshman, Archbishop Williams, at the head of a few servants and volunteer helpers. The Lords, thoroughly alarmed, were pressing the Commons to join them in a declaration condemning these open attempts to terrorize Parliament, but Pym now carried his majority with him in refusing to lift a finger to stop it :

"God forbid," he is reported to have said, "that the House of Commons should proceed in any way to dishearten the people to obtain their just desires in such a way."

The mask was off now with a vengeance ! It was no longer a question of secret plotting under the forms of constitutional liberty ; Pym and his followers were openly determined to stick at nothing whatever in order to force their will upon King and

Parliament alike. It is no wonder that people in London were beginning to act as if war had already broken out ; citizens closing their shops and everybody going about the streets armed.

"There is no doubt", as we read in one letter, that has been preserved of many like it that must have gone out from London at this time, "that if the King do not comply with the Commons in all things they desire, a sudden civil war must ensue, which every day we see approaches nearer."*

But the situation differed from that of the Strafford crisis, in that the mob was neither so formidable in itself, nor in the same unchallenged mastery of the situation. On the former point, it is impossible to adduce positive proof, but we have at least no evidence of anything like the tremendous surge of popular passion —however induced—that might have been said to have brought up all London, at that memorable time, first to Westminster, then to Whitehall, and lastly to Tower Hill. One's impression is that these after-Christmas mobs consisted of not much more than the few hundred fanatics, chronic desperadoes, and rowdy apprentices† that Pym's extremely efficient organization, working at full pressure, was able to shark up, and that even these were not keyed to any more dangerous enterprise than that of manhandling a few helpless old bishops or indulging, up to the limits of safety, in pious sacrilege. On every occasion fight was shown them, they stampeded like a crowd of ragging undergraduates at the appearance of a proctor.

And there was now every prospect that fight would be shown. The swing of public opinion away from the revolutionaries had gone far enough to place the germ of a fighting force at the King's disposal. Whitehall was no longer in the helpless state it had been early in May. Such steps as could, had been taken to make it defensible, and the King had ordered the courtiers to carry arms.

The palace naturally acted for a focus for the numerous disbanded officers who had gravitated to London, in hope partly of getting employment from His Majesty in the Irish campaign, and partly of getting the pay that was still due to them from Parliament. A number of those who had been successful in obtaining appointments had been entertained in the Banqueting

---

* Sir Robert Slingsby to Admiral Sir John Pennington. S.P. Dom. 30/12/41.

† And the spirit of these young fellows may be judged from the fact that they had been just as ready to hang Praisegod Barebones from the sign of his own shop, which he had made a noisy nuisance, by turning it into a conventicle, as they had been to tear the gown off the shoulders of Archbishop Williams.

Hall, and some seven or eight* had happened to stroll out to take the air. Here they attracted the attention of a hundred or so perambulating bishop-baiters, armed with swords and clubs, who first called them redcoats and Papists, and then started to throw dirt at them. This last was too much for the officers, who vaulted over the railings and came at them with drawn swords, though with no lethal intent, since those few of the mob who started to fumble with their own swords were promptly disarmed and speeded on their way with the toe of a boot. Some forty or fifty were said to have been injured, most, presumably, in the region of the pelvis.

One effect of this incident was that next day 500 gentlemen of the Inns of Court volunteered their services to the King as a guard. It must have been apparent to everybody that open hostilities between the defenders and the subverters of the Constitution might come any day now, and that this time there was going to be no walk-over for Pym.

9

THE KING'S HAND IS FORCED

WHEN the bells of the London steeples were heard ringing in the year 1642, the same thought must surely have come to the mind of every hearer. Long before the end of the year England would again, as in that unforgotten time of troubles when White Rose had contended with Red, be a house divided against itself—a self-created shambles. It was the horror of all others that had been most deeply seared into the English soul. Even Pym, in his lodgings at Westminster, must have regarded the prospect with apprehension. Nature had not made him a man of war, nor even a man of blood ; he would no doubt have far preferred to arrive at his goal in what he himself would have described as a Parliamentary way. But having once set his face towards it, neither remorse nor scruple would turn him aside. Though the steeples themselves should be silenced, he at least would see this year out with his head on.

---

* Estimates vary—one puts it as high as 15 or 16. Even that would suggest an average of nearly three kicks per officer.

Meanwhile in Whitehall, with its improvised guard house and its informal garrison, King Charles must have been listening to the same sounds with an even keener anxiety, in proportion as he lacked his rival's unimaginative toughness of fibre. To him, with his almost feminine horror of violence, the prospect of civil war must have been more bitter than that of death itself, of which he was never to show the least fear. But in these last months he had come to realize that for him too the die was cast. Nothing of all that he had conceded, nothing that he ever could concede short of the trust that he held for his people, could satisfy these few who were banded together to make their will law for the rest of the community.

And yet it would seem that in the dawn of their New Year, he could not abandon all hope of finding some honourable means of averting this unthinkable catastrophe—a solution by reason and conciliation and not by the sword. That such thoughts must have been passing through his mind is clear from the fact that he chose that very day for making one last desperate effort to give his enemies all that they demanded of him short of the actual over-throw of the Constitution. For the last time he offered to govern the realm through a ministry of their own choice and composition —a Pym ministry.

Of the form in which this offer was made, we are even more in the dark than we are about the two previous occasions, but that it *was* made seems beyond all reasonable doubt, and it is equally certain that Pym turned it down out of hand. We can well believe that his suspicious mind scented a trap in the invitation to take up an office from which his Sovereign retained the right to dismiss him at will. And in any case, it seems certain that he and his friends were now determined to go through to the last item with their programme of revolution, which envisaged a perpetual government in control of a perpetual Parliament. And Pym, conscious of the trump card that he had been keeping all this time up his sleeve and was now ready to produce, can have been in no mood for compromise. Why—we can imagine him putting it to himself—walk into the King's trap, when the jaws of his own trap were ready to close on the King?

Did the King realize what Pym was about to spring on him? And did Pym divine that he realized it? In the light of subsequent events the overwhelming probability would seem to be that they did, both of them.

Certainly the King seems to have decided that the last hope of appeasement had vanished, and that the time had come for countering his enemies' offensive by action as firm as their own. It is significant that up to now, in spite of every provocation, he had refrained from closing the door on a settlement by putting the key offices of his administration into the hands of the opposition leaders.

Now he could hesitate no longer. New Year's Day was time enough to waste in the final futile negotiations. The morrow was Sunday, and after morning service it was the King's custom to preside over a session of his Council. At this he announced that he was conferring on Colepeper the Chancellorship of the Exchequer that he had offered to Pym, while Falkland, whom it had taken all Hyde's efforts to persuade, was to take over the Secretaryship of State made vacant by the recent dismissal, on more than sufficient grounds, of that elderly twicer, Sir Harry Vane.

The King had wished to complete the arrangement by getting rid of Oliver St John, who was undisguisedly functioning in the interests of his enemies, from the post of Solicitor General, and conferring it on Hyde. But the real leader of the constitutional party, in spite of all that the King, backed by the Queen, could do to persuade him, positively declined to take office—as yet.

He pleaded that he would, for the present, be able to do better service without being tied to an official post. He remained, in effect, an unattached minister, head of a little cabinet of three, in as close touch with his Sovereign as with his two colleagues, and becoming more and more, as time went on, the directing brain of the royal administration.

This prompt action of the King was none the less calculated to infuriate the revolutionaries, from its having been the result of their own refusal to take office. Instead of the surrender to which they had meant to drive him, he had gone quietly ahead and challenged them, by implication, to do their worst. And he must have known them well enough, by now, to realize that the challenge would be accepted.

Some days must needs elapse before the two new ministers, who were quite without administrative experience, would be ready to take over their departments, and by that time the whole face of the situation was destined to be transformed. For on Monday, the third day of the year, the Attorney General, Sir

Edward Herbert, appeared before the Lords, to present, in the King's name, articles of impeachment for treason against Pym, Hampden, and three others of the extremist stalwarts in the Commons, Haslerigg, Denzil Holles, and Strode, as well as one of the Peers, Lord Kimbolton.

IO

INDICTMENT FOR TREASON

It was an amazing and, to those not in the secret, must have seemed an unaccountable move. It is certain that the King's new advisers had had no part in it, and they can hardly have failed to regard it with consternation, since they must have realized to what an extent it was calculated to frustrate all their efforts, and to give the game, in which their Constitutional party had built up for itself a position of winning advantage, into the hands of Pym and his extremists. But the fact that none of the trio, not even Falkland, did what might have seemed the obvious thing, and retired from the service of a master who had to all appearance let them down so hopelessly, suggests that they may have had a more discerning insight into his motives than that of the conventional version in which he figures as a crowned villain plotting to establish his absolute power by eliminating the noblest champions of his peoples' liberties. The truth was not so crudely melo-dramatic.

Not improbably the person who was least surprised at the news, was Pym himself, who must have felt all the satisfaction of a chess player who has forced his opponent to make a fatal move. Paradoxical as it may seem to characterize him as the prime mover in getting himself arraigned by the highest legal authority in the land on the most heinous charge known to the law, we have only to regard the matter from what must have been his standpoint, to realize that this offered him his only way of escape from otherwise practically certain ruin. He had committed himself to destroying the King, and the King had entrenched himself in a constitutional position from which, so long as he sat quiet, there appeared to be no means of dislodging him, before the not distant date when the forces gathering to his support had rendered him strong enough to turn the tables on his assailants.

It had come to this. The only person who could defeat the King now was the King himself. Once let him quit his secure defensive to launch out with some premature counter-stroke, and the revolutionary forces in the field, with public opinion rallied to their support, would have him at a fatal disadvantage. It is true that the King had hitherto not shown the faintest disposition to oblige his enemies in this way, and that with Hyde at his elbow, he would be even less likely to do so now. But what if his hand could be forced? What if means could be found of compelling him at the last moment to throw patience to the winds, and to rush, with suicidal precipitation, into the trap prepared for him?

Anyone who had followed Pym's strategy up to this point would have seen that such a design was its necessary culmination. For it had been his invariable principle to repeat every once successful manœuvre as nearly as possible to pattern when the next opportunity occurred. The former great royal surrender he had forced by bringing all his pressure to bear on the King's most vulnerable point, which was constituted by his love for the Queen. In the even more difficult and delicate operation he had now to perform, Pym could not fail to exploit the same weakness. He would force the King to move, by a threat to the Queen. He would confront his opponent with the choice between attacking him, and sacrificing her. Or what was equally to the purpose, bluff him into thinking so.

The more closely we study his proceedings, the more surely shall we realize how, with the unhurried persistency that had earned him his nickname of "the Ox", he had stuck to this line ever since the removal of Strafford had rendered it *her* turn to fill the essential rôle of propagandist bogey in chief. It is improbable that he had any more hatred for her than a chess master has for his opponent's queen, or that he was primarily concerned with her actual elimination. Checkmate to the King was his object, and if this could be compassed by a mere demonstration against his Consort, both his artistic and whatever human feelings he may have possessed would no doubt have been gratified. But the game was all in all, and personal feeling had nothing to do with it, one way or the other.

This time there had been no need for a lightning swoop, like that which had just, by a matter of hours, enabled him to forestall Strafford. For months he had waged a war of nerves against her, and through her, against her husband. He had played cat and mouse with her. Every time she had tried to escape, even for a respite, out of his invisible clutches, she had been drawn back with just sufficient firmness. Her feelings had been played upon with that gentle skill which modern progress has prescribed for its technique of the Third Degree. Her love for her children, her sympathy for her persecuted co-religionists, her sensitiveness to calumny—never for one moment had she been allowed the least respite from a menace that was all the more nerve-racking from the fact of its always lurking just out of sight behind the forms of fulsomeness and loyalty. Meanwhile opinion in the country was being exacerbated against her in every conceivable way—the ordinary man was being conditioned to associate her with Army plots, Popish plots, and now with the monstrous libel of having been accessory, before the fact, to all the horrors of the Irish rebellion. So firmly was this impression planted that these associations—as I think most readers can testify for themselves—cling to her memory to this day.

At the dawn of the New Year the time was judged ripe for the *coup* for which Pym had so long and carefully prepared. So great had become the tension that at any moment now the situation might get out of even his power to control. Pym was forcing the pace in a way that could not be sustained. He had just proceeded to the most extravagant of all his measures. Twelve of the bishops, headed by Archbishop Williams, had presented to the King what seems an obvious, though not necessarily a diplomatic, protest, to the effect that while they were prevented, by organized terror, from attending at their places in the Upper House, the proceedings were not free, and as such invalid. Pym's reply had been to have the whole twelve of them impeached for this on a charge of nothing less than High Treason, and the unfortunate old gentlemen were haled off to the Tower, where they might keep their heads on their shoulders, for all Mr Pym cared, so long as those heads were not counted on a division.

It was now an open secret that the extremists were about to fly at even higher game. On the last day of the year, a Friday, it had been proposed that a committee of the Commons should sit over the week-end behind closed doors in the city Guild Hall, to deliberate over the safety of the Kingdom. What lay behind this may be gathered from the coded report of the Venetian Ambassador :

"These persons, supplied with arms, proceeded publicly to the destined place, giving every one the impression that there was a plot against the liberty of Parliament. By this device they redeemed their credit generally and won back the affection of ignorant people. Shut up there in long secret discussions, they persuaded themselves that the King's action [in appointing a guard for the palace] and his resentment were due to the advice of the Queen. Accordingly they decided to accuse her in Parliament of conspiring against the public liberty, and of secret intelligence of the rebellion in Ireland. When their Majesties learned this they decided to put aside all dissimulation, and denounce to the Lower House as guilty of high treason five members of the Lower Chamber and one of the Upper, of the most powerful and factious individuals."*

Even if we did not know, specifically, that the committee was open to any member who liked to attend, it is incredible that intelligence of its dire intent can have failed to get through to the King almost at once. Nor can we doubt that this was just what Mr Pym wanted, since such a master in the arts of concealment would never have chosen this theatrical way of wrapping up his bombshell unless he had meant to advertise it. And that such warning was conveyed to the King, probably on Friday night, may be inferred from his desperate last minute attempt to come to terms with Pym on the Saturday, and the energy with which he acted on the two following days.

For the thing that of all others he must have feared was now upon him, and to his troubled conscience it may well have seemed the Nemesis of Strafford. For it had been his love for the Queen, and assuredly no fear for either his life or his Crown, that had induced him to make that fatal compromise with his honour. And his mind may have travelled back to that other failure of his from which it had all started ; when at his urgent request, Strafford had come up to London to confront the then all-powerful Parliamentary leaders with the proofs of their own treason ; and how he, Charles, had by his failure to appreciate the urgency of the situation, succeeded in delaying his minister's stroke for just the few hours required to enable Pym to get in with his framed up impeachment, and thus keep out of court and publicity the evidence of the real treason that would have branded its perpetrators with a stigma as ineffaceable as that of Guy Fawkes.

And now the same hand that had struck down his friend was

* S.P. Ven. 17/1/42.

lifted to strike down his wife. Behind those doors at the Guild-hall another charge of treason was being framed up. Parliament was resuming its sittings on Monday, and Pym was not the man to let the grass grow under his feet. At any moment he might be expected to rise in his place to read out the list of charges, drawn up with all his proved skill in denigration ; and then the Sergeant at Arms, followed by the trained bands, would arrive at the palace, to conduct her through the insults of the mob away from him and her children, to eat her heart out in some gloomy chamber of the Tower until she left it to mingle her dust with that of two other Queens of England beneath the floor of St Peter's Chapel.

On that previous occasion it had been through no disloyalty that he had failed Strafford, He had not realized—and who has to this day !—what sort of an opponent, in Pym, he had had to deal with. But if he were to fail again in the same circumstances and through a similar hesitation to grasp the nettle—what excuse could he plead ? This time there should be not a second's delay in getting the true charge brought home to the real traitors. So he must have thought ; and so Mr Pym must have known, and counted on his thinking.

But *were* the circumstances the same ? Are they ever, in life ? There was one difference that the King may have failed to notice. Last time, Pym had taken very good care that his victim should not have the least warning of what was in store for him till the moment of his arrest. This time he positively went out of his way to warn him in advance—all the more by that ostentatious make-believe of secrecy. Pym was not likely to act in this way without some sufficient motive.

If Charles had been playing political chess with the same cold calculation as his opponent, it might have occurred to him that just because the threat to the Queen was being made with such ostentation, it was his game to ignore it. But this was more a matter of the heart than of the head with him. And that, I think, accounts for the fact that he went ahead without pausing to take the advice of his new counsellors, who, just because of their loyalty, would have taken a more detached view than his own. Perhaps he may have divined, in his innermost soul, the sort of advice he would have received from Hyde :*

"Have no fear, Sir. Pym is desperate, and you can safely dare him to do his worst. It is to the last degree unlikely that he will

* I have, of course, put it into modern English.

go to the length of moving an impeachment against Her Majesty. That he could get a majority for it in the Commons is at least doubtful ; that he could ever get the Lords to condemn her is unthinkable. Pym is no fool. Even if he could get her as far as the Tower, he knows that she would be safer in the care of Sir John Byron than she would at Whitehall. And the spectacle of its Queen in distress would rally nine tenths of the nation, in its present mood, to your support. Be advised, Sir ! Hold your hand for a very little longer and all will be well. But give Pym the opportunity he is seeking, to transfer the issue to one of Parliamentary privilege, and you give him the one chance he has left of turning the tide against you."

That would, I believe, have been not only a just appreciation, but one that Charles, if he had felt himself free to do so, would have been the first to endorse. A masterly restraint had been the keynote of his policy during all these months, and now that he was just about to harvest its fruits, why should he wish to jettison it unless it was that policy had to give way to honour ? Rather than run the slightest risk of harm to the Queen, he was ready to forgo any advantage to himself. And the bitter repentance, that haunted him to the scaffold, for his surrender of Strafford, had planted in him a resolve, from which he never wavered, that his loyalty even to the humblest of his followers—and how much more to the wife he adored—should be unconditional, and unswayed by prudential considerations.

And if this had not been enough to spur him to action, there was the indignation that he must have felt against these men who were striking down right and left his ministers, judges, and bishops, and were now preparing to strike down his Consort, on charges of treason so impudently unsubstantiated that an impeachment had come to signify, in effect, a proscription for loyalty. Whereas they themselves ...

But let us examine the charges one by one on which he had directed Sir Edward Herbert to proceed against them.*

1. *That they have traitorously endeavoured to subvert the fundamental laws and government of this Kingdom ; and deprive the King of his regal power ; and place his subjects under an arbitrary and tyrannical power.*

A more modestly worded, or historically correct, description

---

* I have stated the case as it refers to the two principal accused, Pym and Hampden. How far the rest of the six were actively or merely passively collaborating is a question of minor importance.

of the aims unswervingly held by Pym and his associates, from the days of the Providence Island Company and their Broughton Castle caballing to those of the plot against the Queen, it would be hard, even now, to frame.

2. *That they have endeavoured, by many foul aspersions upon His Majesty, and his government, to alienate the affections of his people and to make His Majesty odious to them.*

Not only endeavoured, but largely succeeded, owing to Pym's consummate mastery of the arts of propaganda.

3. *That they have endeavoured to draw His Majesty's late army to disobedience to His Majesty's command and to side with them in their traitorous design.*

To what other purpose had been their endeavours to place it under the command of their own stooges, to prevent it taking the least step to oppose the invasion or interfere with the occupation of English soil, their relentless proscription of all officers suspected of disloyalty to their faction, and now their open conspiracy to wrest the control of it out of the King's hands altogether and lodge it in their own ?

4. *That they have traitorously invaded, and encouraged a foreign power to invade His Majesty's Kingdom of England.*

Their most ardent supporters have not denied the substantial truth of this.

5. *That they have traitorously endeavoured to subvert the very rights and being of Parliament.*

What milder description could be applied to their Perpetual Parliament Act and the means whereby it had been jockeyed through Parliament and forced on the Crown ?

6. *That ... they have endeavoured ... by force and terror to compel the Parliament to join with them in their traitorous designs, and to that end have actually raised and countenanced tumults against King and Parliament.*

Notoriously and consistently, and Pym had recently gone out of his way openly to applaud and justify such tumults.

7. *That they have traitorously conspired to levy and actually have levied, war against the King.*

By foreign invasion, by terror of the mob, and now—though it had not yet got beyond the stage of conspiracy—by civil war.

I have set down the terms of this brief indictment in order to show that every item of it is as indisputable a statement of historical fact as that England was conquered in 1066, or that Queen Anne died in 1714. Nor are they, in point of fact, any more disputed, the invariable line of justification being that even if these things were done, provided they were done by men like John Hampden against a King like Charles Stuart, they *must* be justified, and that to count them as treason is one of those things that are not done. But even so, it seems a little hard on the King to blame him for being too biased to have anticipated this convenient standpoint.

To those not capable of thus transcending the issue it will seem that the error of Charles was one less of justice than of judgment. His case may have been irrefutable, but to press it at this time and in this way offered him no chance of getting a verdict, or even a hearing. The accused were determined, for the most cogent of reasons, to go to any lengths rather than face the publicity of a trial, and if anyone had been capable of forcing them into the open, and carrying through the affair, once embarked on, with a strong hand, it would not have been Charles. Confident in the righteousness of his cause, he was determined to proceed openly within the strictest limits of the law. It did not even occur to him to secure the persons of the delinquents by having them arrested quietly in their beds, which would have been the first thing that would have occurred to any one with the least instinct for lawless or underhand methods.

He preferred to ask for their arrest openly, through the mouth of his Attorney General, never doubting, in his innocence, that the Peers would take the necessary steps. The only police measure he authorized on his own responsibility was to prevent them from making away with the evidence of their own guilt ; and this he only sought to effect by having their rooms and trunks sealed, instead of the locks broken and the papers impounded.

A man inhibited by this exaggerated delicacy of scruple was ludicrously incapable of bringing off what—had it succeeded at all—would have been a *coup d'état*, even if a lawful one. The hard-bitten and ruthless politicians to whom he was opposed, and whose lives were at stake, saw at once that their manœuvre had succeeded, and that the King had placed himself at what, if they acted with sufficient energy, would be an irrecoverable dis-advantage. For Charles, in his frantic urge to shield the Queen at all costs, had committed a whole series of tactical blunders. He had put the Lords against him (at the very time that Pym had crippled his voting strength there by removing the twelve Bishops) by the ill-advised last minute inclusion of one of their own number in the indictment. He had allowed Pym to shift the issue from one of treason to the ground most favourable to himself, that of Privilege, the remotest suggestion of a threat to which was enough to set the Commons buzzing like a hive of disturbed bees. And finally, though he could plead precedent for his mode of procedure, the legal grounds of it were not so clear as to be undisputable. The question was whether the Crown had any way whatever of bringing even the most notorious treason, when committed by such powerful and privileged persons, legally to justice.

In any case, a few hours were sufficient to make it apparent to Charles that his indictment had been set at naught with open defiance and contumely. The Sergeant at Arms was sent to break the seals on the doors and trunks of the accused, and the Commons, with the accused themselves in control, had hastened to approach the Lords on the ground that their common privileges were at stake, and had openly characterized the King's accusation as a "scandalous paper". And it goes without saying that Pym did not neglect to take all necessary steps to advertise the Lord Mayor and citizens of London of the sinister and violent designs that were being hatched at Whitehall.

I I

SUICIDE BY COMPULSION

MEANWHILE within the palace itself there was an atmosphere hardly less tense than when Strafford's fate had hung in the balance. It was now evident that Pym and his associates were determined to resist, as a breach of Parliamentary privilege, any attempt to bring them to account, and that they were likely to have the support of one, if not of both Houses, in their attitude. Under these circumstances it might have seemed the only course for the King to have desisted from his hopeless attempt, and stomached his humiliation with such grace as the circumstances would have permitted. And this is no doubt the course that his judgment would have recommended—had it not involved abandoning the Queen to the vengeance of these men who were known to be engineering her destruction. We have only the most uncertain and fragmentary evidence of what was taking place in the night and early morning, but it is certain that the King and Queen were in anxious consultation, and that the Queen at least was determined that come what might, there could be no question of a second Whitehall surrender.

Let us not forget, in trying to appreciate her point of view, the nerve strain to which she had continuously, ever since the time of Strafford's trial, been, of set purpose, subjected—a strain that would reduce any average woman to a debilitated wreck. But the daughter of Henri Quatre was no average woman but, as she repeatedly showed, courageous to the point of recklessness. And the effect of nerve strain, prolonged to breaking point, on such a nature, was not likely to be collapse, but a snapping of all prudential bonds, in the spirit of that very gallant fallen angel of Milton's :

> "My sentence is for open war. Of wiles
> More inexpert I reck not, them let those
> Who will, and when they will, contrive, not now."

Also it must never be forgotten that Henriette was, by her intensely feminine nature, as little inclined to political activities as any woman that ever lived. But if it were a question of her husband being dethroned, her children disinherited, and herself cast for the rôle of a second Mary Queen of Scots, then she meant to fight, and she expected her husband to fight too. Loyal as she was to him, she had seen how he had condescended to the shame of abandoning Strafford, and though she understood and appreciated that he had done it to save her, such sacrifices are not calculated to enhance any woman's subconscious appreciation of her man—and if that man should, the next time there was a demand for surrender, begin to toy with thoughts of abandoning *her*, it was likely to be the last straw.

And just because the Queen was so innocent of politics, was the reason that she tended to confide in friends to whom she was attached on personal grounds, and whose advice might only too probably be unwise—or even worse. There was that ineffable fop, Lord Holland, who, along with Essex, had been actually designated as one of Pym's army commanders. There was the genuinely loyal George Digby, an extraordinarily handsome and accomplished young man, who, though he had been a personal enemy of Strafford's, had been so shocked at the outrageous farce of the proceedings against him, that he had chivalrously risen in his place in the Commons to protest against them, thereby becoming a marked man for the vengeance of Pym. But unfortunately Digby's brilliance was without ballast. He was recklessly impetuous and quite undependable—the most fatal adviser such a woman as Henriette could have had at this crisis, for it was certain that George Digby's advice would be to go right ahead and damn the consequences.

Finally, and worst of all, there was Lucy Carlisle who, whether or not she was Pym's whore, was certainly his agent. And we can imagine with what advice Pym would have instructed Lucy to ply her victim, advice that would have come all the more glibly if, as is commonly believed, Lucy's polyandrous affections had previously been bestowed on Strafford. For Pym, who had some appreciation of the consequences, was even more concerned than Digby himself to see that Charles damned them, and went through with it.

We can imagine only too well what Charles, to his horror, must have come to realize before the morning—that his wife was now utterly beyond reason or persuasion, and determined that this time there was to be no surrender, no drawing back. Utterly convinced as she was that now or never was the time for him to put everything to the test, for his sake no less than for her own, we may well believe that any suggestion of a retreat was enough to precipitate an angry explosion. These traitors had chosen to defy the King in the eyes of the whole nation, had thrown back his indictment of them contemptuously in his face. What was he to do now? Swallow the insult, and in so doing, hand them, in effect, *her* head upon a charger? Or else—what Digby, or Lucy, or both, saw so plainly to be called for—assert his authority once and for all by going down to the House itself and making the arrest. Privilege? What privilege could stand against treason? That, Henriette must have felt, was the spirit in which her father would have acted, and what she had the right to expect from her husband.

Such advices were not without support. The palace was swarming with high mettled gentlemen who had been inflamed to the last pitch of exasperation by the reign of terror that Pym's mob had sought to establish at Westminster as well as Whitehall; and they had seen the mob run like hares whenever two or three of them had challenged its proceedings. After all that they, as well as the King, had had to endure at the hands of the politicians, it may well be believed that not many of them would have stood too nicely on points of constitutional etiquette when the opportunity presented itself of settling a long overdue account.

The King was on the horns of a most cruel dilemma. Anyone who is inclined to judge harshly of him for not having taken from the first a line of clear-cut decision, should ask himself, "What would I have done in his case?" It is easy to say he should have put his royal veto, in no uncertain fashion, on a project that he himself must have seen to be suicidally insane. But it is in the last degree improbable that he doubted for a second that this would, in actual fact, involve the sacrifice of the Queen; for I see no reason to believe that it ever crossed his mind that Pym may have been bluffing. And even if he had *thought* so—would he, or would any man worthy the name, have been ready to stake not his own, but *her* life on the chance of it? Especially as it must have been only too clearly borne in on him, that to do so would involve, at the very least, the loss of her love, that had become to him the most precious thing in life. For what woman *would* consent to be offered as the sacrifice in a political gambit?

The mythical notion of Charles as an overbearing tyrant, determined to cast aside all restraints and perpetrate a deed of bloody violence in his own Parliament House, is ludicrously opposite to the truth. Any man so disposed would have recognized that his only chance to carry through such a venture would be by the utmost swiftness and secrecy. The *coup* would have had to come as a complete surprise, unless he could imagine that Pym and the rest of them would kindly sit still until he arrived to arrest them; or that even if they did, he would enhance his chance of their coming quietly by giving the House full notice of his intentions. But the morning went by without any action being taken, though not without the news getting about everywhere— and we can only too easily guess by what channel—that the King was about to come down to the House with sinister and violent intent. In the early afternoon, crowds had begun to assemble on his expected route from Whitehall to Westminster. From the House to the City, which was already seething with excitement and where the shops were being closed, went messages demanding armed aid—though for once, thanks probably to the Lord Mayor, none seems to have materialized. The House was adjourned at noon and assembled again at half-past one—and still nothing had happened.

The "tyrant" was, in fact, holding out desperately against the pressure that was being brought to bear on him, though in the state of expectancy to which the palace garrison had allowed itself to be worked up, it is a wonder that some of them had not broken bounds, and attempted some stroke on their own behalf. It was about three before the long expected event happened.

It would seem, according to the most probable story, that the King had gone for the last of many times to his wife's apartments and found her—with Lucy Carlisle. So he drew her aside into her own closet, and started to break to her that he had reluctantly decided to yield to necessity and abandon the attempt. She faced him with her dark eyes flashing, and flung at him two terrible words, in her native French :

"*Allez, poltron !*"*

And from her ! It does not matter what else she did or did not say in her excited mixture of French and English. He turned and went out, through the long gallery and down the stairs, probably too stunned to feel. There was no need to issue orders. The spectacle of the King leaving the palace was enough to set the whole expectant throng in motion. There happened to be a coach standing before the entrance. Into this the King stepped, followed by the only other male Royalty present, his nephew, the Elector Palatine, who had trailed about negligibly after him for months ; and so the drift, rather than the advance, to Westminster began.

Much unprofitable ink has been spilled to determine who first dispatched the news in advance of him to Parliament. Lucy Carlisle of course lost not a moment in slipping out of the Presence and scribbling off a note to Pym. The French Ambassador who, in spite of his master being the Queen's brother, was playing the unvarying cold game of French power politics and was only concerned to reduce England to a European cipher, was equally prompt in dispatching the news by one of his own suite. But if neither had done so, intelligence that the long overdue cavalcade had at last got under way would not have taken more than a minute or two to get across to Westminster. And incredible as it may seem, it appears to have taken something more like half an hour for the King to cover the few hundred yards from the palace entrance to the door of what had once been St Stephen's

* *Poltron*—coward !

Chapel. During that time Pym and his four colleagues had stepped into the boat that was waiting at the steps below the Parliament House to take them to the City. One of them, Strode, made a theatrical gesture of refusing to flee, but allowed himself to be bundled into the boat by a fellow member.

Nothing can have less resembled the usual course of tyrannical proceedings than this royal *coup d'état* at less than the pace of a state funeral. It is evident that nothing had been organized or planned, since the only person with power to issue orders had been trying, up to the last moment, to prevent the attempt from ever being made at all. As far as we can judge of Charles's mind by his actions, and still more by his inactions, he was as one who feels himself impelled by a merciless destiny to tread the path of his own ruin, and is only concerned to get to the end as soon as possible.

Nobody, even at the time, seems to have had any clear notion of whom, or of how many, the King's following consisted. Probably the only organized body comprised the few scarlet halberdiers of the guard who would have fallen in round the coach. The rest were a mere mob of officers, courtiers, and possibly a sprinkling of casual volunteers, spies and sightseers. It is difficult to see how the whole body can have mustered a couple of hundred at the outside. Perhaps some part of the inordinate time it took for them to arrive at their destination may have been consumed by the procession in trying to marshal itself in some sort of order.

It cannot in any case have been a quick business forcing a way through the crowd, with the coach lumbering in the rear, and the bottleneck of the two Gates to be negotiated. According to the Queen's confidante, Mme. de Motteville, proceedings were still further delayed by the King's stopping to listen to each one of the humble petitioners who pressed round the windows of his coach—quite a unique departure, one would think, from the ordinary paths of tyranny.

No wonder that when he had at last alighted in Palace Yard, His Majesty found Westminster Hall already full of officers, many of whom were using it for the deposit of their heavy cloaks. A considerable party had already overflowed into the lobby leading to the House of Commons.

The King, who was plainly determined to limit to the uttermost the mischief of this undertaking in which he could hardly have hoped to succeed, strode through them with that rapid gait characteristic of his family, while they parted to right and left ; and on reaching the lobby he gave orders that no man, in peril of his life, should follow him. Then, accompanied by the Elector, he passed through the door that no King of England had ever entered since the time when St Stephen's had been a chapel in fact as well as name. His orders were obeyed, but one of the Scottish lords, who had presumably held the door open, took the natural precaution of keeping it so, by putting his back against it.

On entering, if we are to believe Macaulay, Charles "darted a look towards the place that Pym usually occupied," and according to Gardiner "his glance, perhaps involuntarily, sought the place." One would have imagined from this that Charles had been an old Parliamentary hand, instead of entering the packed assembly for the first time and gazing on a bewilderingly unfamiliar scene ! So determined are the mythologists to fit all things into the framework of their own preconceived melodrama, with the King in the part of villain, executing his audacious plot, and fully prepared to turn the House into a shambles rather than be balked of his prey.

It is more than doubtful if he had come down with any plan at all, except possibly to overawe the House by the assertion of his personal authority into conceding what he considered his just demand. Even if the accused members had been in their places and had openly defied him, the last thing anyone acquainted with his character can imagine is that he would have ordered those cavaliers in the lobby to rush in, with sword and pistol, and fetch them out. Quite likely he had never intended this irregular retinue to accompany him at all. From the moment of his getting into the coach, the situation had taken charge of itself.

The Commons, whether or not they had expected the visitation, retained enough presence of mind to rise and uncover—thus making it a more than ever difficult task to spot any given five of them. The King passed between the benches to the dais in which stood the Speaker's chair, and courteously asked him for the loan of it, though it does not appear that he actually sat down. He was hopelessly embarrassed and conscious of the falsity of his position. He stammered out a few almost apologetic sentences about the purpose of his coming, and then, after looking around in vain, he asked, Where was Mr Pym ? Where was Mr Holles ? Eliciting no response, he turned to the only human being likely to answer him. Was Mr Pym there? Speaker Lenthall, whose capacity rivalled that of the Vicar of Bray for swimming with the stream and avoiding trouble, displayed it on this occasion in such masterly fashion that his reply has become a classic of evasion—he had neither eyes to see nor tongue to speak but as the House was pleased to direct.* Poor Charles was reduced to the thankless task of casting his own eyes round the silent rows of faces. At last, failing to distinguish any of those whom he sought, he said with that idiomatic turn of phrase characteristic of him :

"I see all the birds are flown."

And then, anxious to terminate the scene, he made a few more remarks into the silence, and assured them on the word of a King—what was certainly true—that he had meant no force, but to proceed in a fair and legal way, and also that he had not the least intention of going back on any of the concessions he had already made.

Then, descending from the dais, he strode rapidly out of the House, where some of the hardier spirits had found time to assail his ears with cries of "Privilege ! Privilege !" before he passed out of earshot into the lobby, where his followers were waiting for him, thoroughly fed up and disillusioned, if we may judge by some of the soldierly grouses recorded with portentous solemnity as evidence of the direst intent.

"A pox on the House of Commons !" one of them had been heard to say, and another—a halberdier guardsman, surely—"Zounds, they [the Five] are gone, and we are never the better for our coming !" or as his modern equivalent would have put it, "What in ———'s name did he —— well expect the ——s to do? And why the hell he wants to bring us out on a job like this ..."

Meanwhile the Queen, having carried her point, had been in a state of exaltation awaiting her husband's return. "Rejoice," she had cried into the sympathetic ear of Lucy, "for within an hour the King, I trust, will be master of his realm !"

Too late, when he arrived baffled and humiliated, did she realize what she had done by her uncontrolled impetuosity. But this man whom she had goaded with the taunt of cowardice into taking the irretrievable false step, put her protestations of

---

* One of the regicides, Scott, at his trial, after the Restoration, found that Lenthall had the tongue to speak with lethal effect about what he professed to have heard in the Chair, when it was a question of turning King's evidence to save his own neck.

repentance gently aside. Never, either then, or as the tragic consequences of that step began to be revealed, did she hear one syllable of reproach from his lips, or mark the least failure of the sweet tenderness and consideration he habitually lavished on her. Never again would she be tempted to waver in her loyalty to him or esteem him less than "the worthiest gentleman, the best friend, the best husband, the best Christian", and—may we not add ?—the most chivalrous lover on earth. And for that, might he not have accounted crown and life well lost ?

12

FLIGHT FROM WHITEHALL

THE long and doubtful struggle within the walls of Parliament between King Charles and King Pym, or, as it had become, between the Constitutional and the Plutopuritan-Revolutionary parties, had ended in a clear-cut decision. Not only was Pym the victor, but it was a victory that could only have been pulled out of the fire by the suicidally false move that the King, with his eyes open, had been constrained to make at his adversary's dictation. For even now it is hard to see how, under the circumstances Pym had created for him—and granted there were some things he would never have done under any circumstances—Charles could have avoided the trap. It was the triumph of a finesse hardly paralleled in the annals of political warfare.

The whole patient work of the past seven months, which had seemed about to be rewarded with the defeat of the revolutionary conspiracy, and establishment of what, in the phrase of our own time, might have been called a new constitutional deal between King, Parliament and People—all this had been shattered beyond repair between the morning of one day and the afternoon of the next. The deadly indictment that had been impending over the heads of Pym, Hampden, and their confederates ever since Strafford had come up on his last journey to London, had been launched prematurely. They had successfully, and finally, contrived to keep the case out of court. With the damning evidence of their treason they were now no longer liable to be confronted. Henceforth they would be able to stand, literally for centuries, in the eyes of the nation as heroes and patriots— champions of those very liberties that they were in league to suppress, of that law which they had trampled underfoot, and of those Parliamentary institutions that they had reduced to a camouflage and a mockery.

Not only that, but they had so handled the matter that the King himself had been pilloried, for an equal period of time, as the false tyrant who but for the Grace of God, would have turned these patriots into martyrs.

The King faced up with admirable courage to the situation created by that ill-starred visit to Westminster. Knowing that the delinquents had taken shelter within the confines of the City, thither he proceeded in state on the following day in the forlorn hope that the known loyalty of the Lord Mayor, and of the crowds that had greeted him in his recent return from Scotland, might yet be relied on to secure their surrender to justice. But though his reception at the Guildhall was by no means one of unqualified hostility, it was evident that the state of public opinion had been so fatally altered to his disadvantage that they might as well have been in the moon for any hope there might have been of effecting an arrest. And on his way back, Pym's crowds were out in the street in greater force and uglier spirit than ever. The King might esteem himself lucky to get back to Whitehall without being actually mobbed. As it was, some fellow had had the audacity to come up to his coach and fling in a paper on which was inscribed "To your tents O Israel !", which to a Bible-reading populace constituted a plain appeal to revolt in arms and depose King Charles as Israel had deposed Rehoboam.

Pym with his prestige now immeasurably enhanced and his control of the Commons for the time secure, was in complete mastery of the situation. But he was in no hurry to end his own, and his companions', Hegira to Coleman Street in the City, before the spectacle had been staged of Parliament unable to sit at Westminster for fear of some tyrannical outrage, and until all was ripe for him to be brought back in triumph as the people's champion by the whole united force of London in arms. A test mobilization, stimulated by the now familiar technique of panic-mongering, was carried out on the night of the 6th, and though the Lord Mayor was not to be bluffed into calling out the trained bands to defend the City against the royal *coup de main* that was alleged to be imminent, they were mustered without his authority, and reinforced by all and sundry who could arm themselves with weapons of any sort ; and though the alleged number of 140,000 all told—more than five times as great as any army that took the field in the Civil War—is frankly absurd, it is evident that the turn out must have eclipsed all previous records. Even more ominous was the arrival from Buckinghamshire, the county where Hampden had his vast possessions, of armed levies, several thousands strong, in the ostensible capacity of petitioners, just as the retainers of Warwick the Kingmaker and other territorial anarchs had rallied to their support in the bad old days.

The return of the Five to Westminster was timed for Tuesday, the 11th of January, exactly a week after their flight. By this time it had become apparent to Charles that it would be madness to linger on at Whitehall, where at any moment now he might find himself hopelessly caught in his adversary's toils. To the Queen the danger was even greater ; for what was to prevent Pym from signalizing his return by instantly moving that impeachment which had been impending when the King had launched his desperate counter-stroke ? And the overwhelming forces that he could now bring up would be amply sufficient to render resistance or escape hopeless.

On Monday intelligence must have reached the King that decided him to get himself and his family instantly out of London, without warning or ceremony, before the way of escape was closed. If anything could have proved the necessity of this step it would have been that Lucy Carlisle (which was as good as to say Pym) joined with Essex and Holland in seeking for means of dissuading him. Nobody, however, could be found hardy enough to approach him directly.

It had not been a moment too soon. As it was, the little cavalcade, escorted by thirty or forty loyal officers, had had to force its way through menacing crowds, most of whom had in their hats papers bearing the propaganda slogan of "Liberty". When they arrived at Hampton Court, which was their destination, so little were they expected that nothing had been prepared for them, and the royal couple were forced to pig it for the night with their children, in one bedroom and a couple of beds.

Whatever joy Pym may have felt in his triumph must have been considerably dashed by the discovery that the King had stolen a march on him. For nobody can have realized better how essential it was for his purpose to secure the person of at least one of the royal pair, and preferably of the whole family. For in so doing he would have gained all the fruits of a victorious civil war without the necessity of fighting it. And there was a further consideration that Pym may or may not have realized : that it was only by winning the war without a fight, or by a swift and easy victory, that its fruits could be harvested in the barns of those who had sowed the seed. All wars, if sufficiently prolonged, have a way of resembling that between the frogs and the mice, with the spoils of victory and perhaps the combatants themselves, swallowed by the eventual owls.

For once, the master strategist had been caught by surprise. The swiftness and suddenness of His Majesty's escape to Hampton had given him the first trick in the civil war, or rather—as one would say at fives—it had put him in. For he was now free to make in arms the appeal to the country that Pym had denied him at the hustings.

The following day saw King Pym at the culmination of his career. He and the other four were rowed back in state to Westminster stairs, amid scenes of delirious enthusiasm ; with the trained bands out in their thousands under the *de facto* monarch's newly appointed commander, Philip Skippon, a ranker veteran of the German wars, with little book-learning, but an abundance of rough and ready godliness and—what mattered more than anything—a born trainer of infantry. The mob filled all the streets and open spaces round Whitehall and Westminster, deliriously acclaiming the triumph of the new dictator. Pym, however, was not the man to be lifted above himself by these intoxicating ebullitions. We may grant him to have been human enough to congratulate himself on the success that had so magnificently rewarded his long, patient evolution of the strategic plan that he had framed months before with such forethoughtful penetration of his opponent's weakness, and to which he had adhered in spite of every possible setback and discouragement. But to so great an artist, no success can be satisfactory that is lacking in one final, and essential element. Pym—if we may guess at what was hidden beneath his shaggy exterior—was less elated by the sight and sound of the crowds, than by the thought that this great mobilization and march of armed London to Westminster had been a blow in the air. Whitehall was empty. The royal birds had flown.

13

DRIFTING TO WAR

FROM henceforth, the proceedings in the Parliament House at Westminster became devoid of the interest even of a debating society, since the assembly had become little more than the passive instrument for registering the decrees of Pym and his associates. The time for effective talk had gone by ; such negotiations as went on, at voluminous length, during the next few months, have a merely propagandist significance. The plain fact of the matter was that what Pym required of the King was nothing less than the unconditional surrender of all but the mere formalities of sovereignty, and that in case of refusal, he would stick at no extreme of violence and illegality in order to extort it.

Just how far it would be necessary to go was probably more than Pym himself could have said—as yet. Like the master strategist that he was in his chosen field of politics, he preferred to attain his ends with the utmost economy of means. He had certainly no love of war or bloodshed for their own sakes, and no man was ever a greater adept in producing the maximum effect of terror with the minimum of frightfulness. I have not the least doubt that during these next eight months he clung to the hope that by bringing steady, remorseless pressure to bear on the King, and by depriving him in advance of the means of waging successful war, he would break down his will to resistance without the necessity of plunging the nation into a blood bath, with all the risks and drawbacks involved. Only if all other means failed to compass the end in view, would this be justified.

But Pym, though he may not have realized it, had come up against a will as inflexible as his own. King Charles was still willing to go to all lengths of conciliation that did not involve the surrender, for all time, of those fundamental rights of the Crown that had descended to him from his ancestors, and that he held in trust for his heirs and for his people. He would even have been willing—he put out feelers towards it—to staff his army, as well as his government, with persons agreeable to the Parliamentary leaders, provided this were done as of grace, and without prejudice to his prerogative. But to make over the keys of sovereignty to the leaders of a faction, was a thing that no violence or pressure would—or ever did—induce him to consider. Pym on the other hand neither would, nor dared, consider anything less. He knew now what charge the King had to bring against *him*, and he knew that his only safety lay in keeping it—as he had succeeded in doing hitherto—out of court.

It was a direct, head-on, collision of armed wills ; a situation—that is to say—of war. And in fact it would be technically correct to say that a state of war had existed at least from the moment that Skippon had been illegally appointed to organize and command what was openly designed to be a revolutionary militia. The first act of war followed almost immediately ; for having now got the rest of London under his control, Pym felt it essential to get the citadel, or Tower, out of the King's hands. A demand was accordingly made that its commander, Sir John Byron, against whom no fault was even alleged but that of loyalty to his Sovereign, should be replaced by one of the nominees of the faction, and when this was denied, Skippon proceeded to mobilize a sufficient number of his levies to lay siege to the fortress. There was no need for bloodshed, since the old soldier was easily able to reduce the garrison to terms by blockade, and Byron was set free to fight another day. But to starve the greatest stronghold in the land into surrender constitutes every bit as much of an act of war, or rebellion, as a pitched battle.

Charles's position, in spite of his escape, must at this time have seemed desperate, for he had only a handful of followers, and there was no apparent prospect of his getting military support, on any sufficient scale, in any part of the country. Nor did he feel himself in a position to strengthen his own hands, until he had set them free by getting the Queen shipped out of harm's way overseas, and this, strangely enough, Pym no longer sought to prevent. He designed to deprive the King's recent *démarche* of any ostensible justification, by brazenly denying that there had ever been any plot to impeach her. A deputation from the Commons was actually sent to persuade her that the idea of anything of the sort having been contemplated was a malicious libel ! But even Pym could not simultaneously adopt this pose and insist on detaining her as a hostage.

Most likely he reckoned that the King, once her strengthening influence was removed, would cease to kick against the pricks, and would sign anything that was put before him. In any case the journey to Holland with her daughter, which had been so strenuously and successfully opposed in the summer, was now free for her to take, and the King, bypassing London by way of Greenwich, went down with her to Dover, to which—as they must sadly have reminded each other—he had ridden over seventeen years ago to clasp her in his arms for the first time, a laughing bride of fifteen.

As the ship bearing her away sailed up the Straits, he kept pace with her on horseback along the Downs towards the South Foreland.

"It is not", she wrote to her sister, "the fear of death that has made me depart, but of a prison, which, by parting me from my lord the King, would have been harder than death to bear ; for it would have ruined all our prospects, and I hope that now I am at liberty, I shall be in a position to serve him."

And from the depths of her gay and gallant soul, she meant what she said. However disastrously her ill-timed impetuosity might have compromised her husband in the past, she was determined, to the best of her ability, to make up for it in the future. She had learned to honour him now as unconditionally as she loved him ; and whatever trials lay before them, she would endure with him to the end. If it was to be war—and she at least had no doubt that it was a fight to a finish with organized conspiracy—it would be seen what part the daughter of Henri Quatre could play !

14

"BY GOD ! NOT FOR AN HOUR !"

It was on the 23rd of February that Charles parted from his Queen, and on the 26th he was back at Greenwich with his hands free and his mind made up. The Commons, now merely a sounding board for the voice of Pym, were overwhelming him with requests to surrender the controls of state into their hands, and when he refused, seizing them in defiance of the law. It would have obviously been even more to their purpose to have secured the person of the King himself, and even if Charles had not realized how dangerous was his stay in the vicinity of London, their emphatically expressed desire for its continuance would have been enough to convince him. As it was, they were only just prevented from making a hostage of the Prince of Wales, by the fact that his Governor, Lord Hertford, was loyal enough to put the King's orders before theirs, and send his pupil from Richmond to Greenwich. Even thither he was followed by certain members charged to bring him to London, but luckily his father arrived from Dover in time to send them about their business. Henceforth, turning a deaf ear to Parliamentary solicitations, he kept the boy closely at his side. "Now that I have gotten Charles," he said to Hyde, who was helping him draft his answer to the latest Parliamentary demand, "I care not what answer I send them."

As he had previously arranged with the Queen, he intended, with all convenient expedition, to proceed North, and make his headquarters at York. It was only too plainly evident that no conceivable concession, short of abject surrender to the Parliamentary bosses, would be of the least avail. He had offered to go the whole way in staffing the army with their nominees, but this offer, since it involved no surrender of his legal right, had been voted a refusal, and they had proceeded to levy open rebellion by nominating Lords Lieutenant in order to usurp the control of the army through their agency.

When the King had got as far as Newmarket he was overtaken by a Parliamentary deputation headed by the Earls of Holland and Pembroke, the latter a person peculiarly unwelcome to him on account of his notorious loose living. Having obtained an audience, they proceeded to read him a manifesto of such scurrilous insolence as plainly to betray the fury of its authors at his success in evading their toils. It was something more than insinuated that he had formed "a great design, for the altering of religion, the breaking the neck of your Parliament ... that the Pope's Nuncio hath solicited the Kings of France and Spain to lend your Majesty four thousand men apiece to help to maintain your royalty against the Parliament."

Other items in this precious document were plainly intended to convey that the Queen was at the bottom of the Irish rebellion, that the King had intended to have massacred and destroyed the members of the Commons, and that he was ready in pursuit of his dark designs to become a Catholic.

No man was slower to anger than Charles, but as he listened to these shameless slanders, which were more than even the tribunal eventually convened to do him to death would dare allege against him, it is no wonder that he was no longer able to contain himself. "'Tis a lie !" he interrupted, and "That's false !" and when Holland had at length finished reading it :

"I could not have believed," he exclaimed, "Parliament would have sent me such a one, if I had not seen it brought by such persons of honour."

He proceeded to draft an answer, in terms of burning indignation :

"What would you have ? Have I violated your laws ? Have I denied to pass any Bill for the ease and security of my subjects ? I do not ask you what you have done for me. ...

"God do so with me and mine, as my thoughts and intentions are upright for the ... preservation of the laws of this land, and I hope God will bless and assist these laws for my preservation."

When he delivered this answer, on the following day, they had a last try at him—but it was no reed shaken with the wind that they had come out to see. When they demanded that he should put himself into their power by retracing his steps to London he retorted :

"I would you had given me cause. But I am sure this declaration is not the way to it."

Pembroke rather feebly suggested that the King should let them know what he wanted.

"I would whip a boy in Westminster School", was the contemptuous rejoinder, "who could not tell that by my answer."

Headed off from this line, Pembroke thought up a hopeful suggestion—why could not the King allow them to have the army just for a time ?

"By God !" cried Charles, who must have been moved beyond all measure to allow such an expression to cross his lips, "not for an hour ! You have asked that of me was never asked of any King, and with which I would not trust my own wife and children."

And so they went back, with that clear defiance ringing in their ears, to those who had sent them. Not even Pym could imagine now that there was going to be any question of surrender. And meanwhile the King, taking his time, and taking it more freely than wisely when every moment counted, proceeded on his way to York. He rode in through Fishergate Bar on the 19th of March.

15

DECISIVE HESITATION

"PYM and his friends", says Gardiner, in one of those passages in which his honesty of intention bursts through the shell of his indurated prejudice, with shattering effect on his main thesis, "had been driven ... to uphold the doctrine that Parliament and not the King was supreme in England. How could they hope to make it good unless the votes of Parliament embodied the national will? Yet it was perfectly evident that this was no longer the case."* That was the whole point. Parliament was already—what Cromwell was to call it eleven years later—no Parliament.

For by the time Charles rode into York, Parliament had ceased to be representative of any will except that of Pym and his plutocratic caucus. After the fatally premature launching of the indictment for treason, into which Charles had been forced or bluffed by the threat to the Queen, the prospect of capturing Parliament for the constitutional reaction had vanished. The debates in the House had ceased to have the least importance ; it was almost literally as much as a member's life was worth to put up resistance to Pym. The leaders of the opposition, with the exception of Hyde, who had remained behind in London, to his own imminent peril, as the King's unofficial representative, had followed him up North, and there was a steady trickle of loyal members of both Houses after them. The resistance of the Lords, which had been the main stumbling block in the way of the revolution, had now, by dint of terror and absenteeism, been broken down, and England was in fact, as she was to become in form seven years later, under single chamber government, and that of a chamber raised by statute above the will of its former constituents and passively responsive to that of its controllers.

In the Parliamentary sense, therefore, the King was debarred from his right of appeal to the country. There were to be no more elections until such time as King Pym might be graciously pleased to appeal to the country himself. And the more the country wanted to get Pym off its back, the less likely would Pym

* *History of England*, x, p. 184.

be to afford it the chance. As much as Louis XIV, in the next generation, he had committed himself to the principle, "The State am I."

That being so, he must have realized, too late, what a mistake he had made in allowing the King to slip out of his clutches to York. For now, in spite of the Perpetual Parliament Act, the impeachments, and the militia ordinances, it *would* be open for the King to appeal to the country, if not by votes, then by force of arms. For the vote is after all no more than an artificial and civilized substitute for war, and if the vote is denied, the social contract—as a certain Thomas Hobbes would have called it— is broken ; and the argument of the sword resumes its ancient supremacy over that of the polling booth.

It would have been well for King Charles if he could have realized the clear-cut implication of his journey to York. It was an act of war, the first move in a campaign. It ought to have been plain to him that, short of virtual abdication, there was no possible way of appeasing his opponents. They knew now what he knew about them, and they can have harboured no doubt in their own minds of what he would do to them, if they ever gave him half a chance. The voluminous documents and manifestoes with which they continued to bombard him were no more than manœuvrings for position in an offensive in which—as Pym well knew—the propaganda weapon might well be decisive.

But to Charles the idea of war within his own realm was too fearful even now for him frankly to accept and act upon. He still refused to abandon hope that some way of conciliation might be found ; and while he hoped, he continued to hesitate. But to hesitate was, as so often in war, to invite defeat. For even before the armies had taken the field, the scales might be so tilted against him as to make his cause practically hopeless. He had already scored one essential point in getting himself and his family out of the clutches of his enemies, and establishing himself in the fortress city that had come into being as the base of the Roman defence of the North. But to the strategic eye, there was a more important point to be secured than York itself, in its sea port Hull. Not only was the possession of practicable sea ports a crying need for the King, since the chief of these were notorious focuses of revolutionary influence, but Hull had served as the munitioning base for the unfortunate army that had been mobilized to resist the Scottish invasion, and whose resistance had been hamstrung by the treasonable connivance of the Westminster bosses with the enemy. The result was that Hull had become stocked with a sufficiency of unexpended munitions to provide either side generously for the short and swift campaign that no one doubted would decide the issue, if it came to blows, between the King and his rebels.

The issue therefore that dominated all others, to those who understood the situation, was—who was going to have Hull? So far as the law, or immemorial practice of the constitution counted for anything, the King had it already. The fortress was his fortress, its munitions belonged to the Crown, its Governor was the King's officer. To deny it to the King and usurp the command in the name of Parliament, or any other, was an act of treason and rebellion as gross as could be conceived. Naturally such considerations were not likely to deter Pym, who was determined to get Hull at all costs, and—what mattered more— with all speed. The King himself was quite aware of the importance of securing the port and munitions, but he, unfortunately, was thinking in terms not of war, but of law. As early as the 11th of January he had secretly instructed the Earl of Newcastle, a great and gifted territorial magnate against whom no conceivable objection could be advanced except his known loyalty to the King, to take over the command. But the King's orders were betrayed, even before they were despatched, to Pym's ubiquitous spy service; and Newcastle found Pym's man already in possession, in the person of Sir John Hotham, member for Beverley, and an old campaigner of the German wars ; a person of unpleasing manners, ungovernable temper, and no very decided allegiance except to the main chance, which for the moment inclined him towards Pym. But as a big local landowner, he was the most formidable person who could have been installed at short notice, and it is characteristic of the furious haste with which Pym could act on due occasion, that within an hour of receiving the news he had sent off Hotham's son riding as hard as Dick Turpin himself up the North Road to get ahead of the King's messenger.

It was by no means certain, however, that even so, Hull might not have been saved by firm and prompt action. The King's authority still carried weight, and there was reason to hope that a wobbler like Hotham might be bribed, or overawed, into coming down on the right side of the fence. But the longer he had to think about it, or be got at by the other side, the less likely he was to comply, and the squat Tudor bastions and battlements were not to be forced without a regular siege, for which the King had neither the men nor the resources.

There was one person who grasped the situation as clearly and vigorously as Pym himself, and that was the Queen, now safely, if not too comfortably, installed at the Hague, where she was hard at work furnishing her husband with the all important sinews of war by pawning the Crown Jewels. Henriette had not the foggiest comprehension of politics, but she was her father's daughter, and her fighting instincts were sound :

"When you come to York," she wrote to her husband, "if you find the country well affected, Hull must absolutely be had ; if you cannot, you must go to Newcastle, and if you find that is not safe go to Berwick, for it is necessary to have a sea port. ..."

It was how the great Henri, or her cousin Condé, would have reacted to the situation. But it was not in Charles's nature to throw away the scabbard, or even to draw the sword in a quarrel with his own subjects, so long as he could persuade himself that there was the faintest chance of making the voice of reason prevail. Above all, he was determined not to take the initiative in a civil war. He accordingly let his chance of taking Hull slip through his fingers, because he was not thinking of winning the war so much as avoiding it. He was far too long in getting to York, and having got there, he delayed unconscionably in dealing with Hull. So confident was he in the righteousness of his cause, that he must needs send a remonstrance to Parliament against the outrageous illegality of Hotham's appointment, in which he quoted words spoken by Pym himself about the law being that which puts a difference between good and evil ; the argument was unanswerable—if the man with whom he was dealing had been amenable to argument.

The Queen, meanwhile, who saw only too surely what was likely to be the effect of this unrequited scrupulousness, was in a state bordering on distraction :

"Everybody", she wrote, "dissuades you concerning Hull from taking it by force unless Parliament begins—is it not beginning to put persons in it against your orders ?...For you having Hull is not beginning anything violent, for it is only against the rascal who refuses it to you."

"The longer you wait," she wrote in another letter, "the worse it will be."

The Queen was not alone in urging action. A number of loyal Yorkshire gentry petitioned the King to the same effect. Even so, Charles was determined to proceed by law and reason rather than by violence. On the 22nd of April—more than a month after his arrival at York—he tried to sound Hotham's attitude by sending his young son, the future James II, with the Prince Palatine, to visit the town, where they were loyally entertained. The next day Charles himself followed them, with about 300 horse. As usual, Pym's spy service betrayed his plans, and also took care to persuade Hotham that the King, once he got Hull, was determined to hang him. Even so, the unhappy governor was in such a state of indecision that it is very probable that he might have allowed the King to ride straight into the town, had not His Majesty halted the cavalcade about three miles off, and sent a reasoned request for admission. That gave Hotham, who no doubt decided that it was better to fill the cup of treason to the brim than be hanged out of hand, time to screw up his resolution to the point of having the drawbridges raised ; and he must have cut a sufficiently ridiculous figure, kneeling on the walls and protesting undying loyalty to the Sovereign he was thus defying, while the King's troopers shouted to the garrison to throw the fellow over the wall. The King was forced to content himself—for what else could he do ?—with having Hotham proclaimed a traitor, and with getting the two young Princes out of what was now their perilous position, a matter that itself took some hours to negotiate. He then rode back to York.

Even now, there might have been a chance of saving Hull. Hotham continued to wobble, and later in the summer actually got to the point of signifying his intention of letting the King into the fortress if he would only be good enough to put up the show of attacking it. But again Charles failed to take the swift and violent action that might have done the business, and by the time he was at hand to take possession, Hotham, who was probably afraid of being lynched by his own garrison, had wobbled back again. This time, the garrison sallied out and attacked the King's retinue, handling it very roughly. Hull was lost, and with Hull, a large percentage of whatever chances there might have been of a constitutional victory in the Civil War that had now started in good earnest—for at Manchester, too, blood had been shed in dispersing an attempted muster of rebel militia.

16

DIEU ET MON DROIT!

ON the 2nd of June, what was left of Parliament had dispatched to
the King what was, in effect, a declaration of war. This consisted in
a series of nineteen demands so brutally extreme that it is impossible to imagine that even Pym, whom we may assume to
have been their real author, could have dreamed that the King
would have considered them for a moment. Every military and
civil appointment under the Crown was to be made by, and held
at, the discretion of Parliament—which to all intents and purposes
signified Pym himself. Not a single function of sovereignty was to
be exercised by the nominal Sovereign, who was besides to be
deprived of the elementary rights of the humblest subject ; for
the education of his own children was to be taken out of his hands,
nor were they to be allowed to marry or even to be courted—under
the direst pains and penalties—save with the explicit sanction of
the same omnipotent authority. The King was even to be denied
the right to have a bodyguard. Especial provision was made for
enabling Parliament—or Pym—to pass what it might choose to
call justice on any persons it might choose to cite before it, in
other words to wreak arbitrary vengeance on political opponents—
the King's right of pardon being of course debarred. To make
sure of their control of the Lords, the votes of Catholic Peers were
to be taken away, and no Peer made in future by the King was to
sit in the Upper Chamber except by explicit sanction of "Parliament". The King was actively to assist in any settlement of the
Church that his masters might be pleased to dictate. And Pym
would not have been Pym had he neglected to make special
provision for tightening up the persecution of Catholics. It was
the most elaborate scheme of tyranny ever devised in England,
and would, if carried into effect, have formed the enabling act for
the dictatorship of Pym, and through Pym of that wealthy clique
of which Pym was the controller.

There have been few monarchs who, on being presented with
such a document, would have deemed it worthy of any answer,
except with the sword of justice, and it is proof of Charles's
extraordinary patience that he should have condescended to a

long, reasoned reply, in which his attitude is defined with a truly prophetic finality.

"We should be unworthy of the trust reposed in us by the law, and of our descent from so many great and famous ancestors, if we could be brought to abandon that power which only can enable us to perform what we are sworn to in protecting our people and the laws ... although not only our present condition (which it can hardly be) were more necessitous than it is, and we were both vanquished and a prisoner, and in a worse condition than ever the most unfortunate of our predecessors have been reduced to by the most criminal of their subjects."

It would come to that, in course of time, but never—not even on the scaffold—would Charles budge an inch from the stand that he had here taken.

There was still voluminous correspondence to come, but it must have been quite obvious to everybody concerned—even Charles himself—that it was so much waste paper. Only the sword could decide now.

If the King were so fortunate as to have any sword to defend himself with ! For even after his arrival at York, this had been by no means to be taken for granted. The prospect of civil war was so atrociously horrible to all those quiet and non-political Englishmen to whom the King would have to look for his chief support, that at first it seemed doubtful whether he would have even the nucleus of an army. Even in Yorkshire opinion appeared to be divided, and it was only gradually, after the rebels, as they had now openly declared themselves, had begun to proceed from outrage to outrage, culminating in Hotham's treason at Hull, that it began to be apparent that at least North of the Humber, popular sentiment was overwhelmingly and militantly in favour of the King and Constitution.

Oddly enough—in view of the fashion of alluding to the King's government as "tyranny" and Pym's supporters as "the popular party"—it turned out that it was just among the common people, outside a few centres of capitalist enterprise, that the sentiment of loyalty burnt with the purest flame. Most of all in the North : not only because, through the good offices of Pym and his fellow Patriots, the people had been subjected to the humiliation and extortion incidental to many months of foreign occupation, but also because the abolition of that alleged instrument of tyranny, "The Council of the North", had left the poor man without any-

one capable of maintaining his right against those rich and powerful neighbours against whose oppression the courts of Common
Law had no remedy to offer to the like of him.

It was however only to have been expected that among those
same magnates, opinion should have showed much less approach
to unanimity. An enormous mass meeting had been convened by
the King on Heyworth Moor, near York, and the mere fact that
its numbers were estimated in the neighbourhood of 80,000 is
sufficient indication of the way things were beginning to move.
Though the whole affair seems to have been organized in the most
amateurish way, for the King had not even begun to study Pym's
technique of mass conditioning. There seems no doubt at all that
his reception by the crowd was as hearty as he could have wished,
but the proceedings were somewhat marred by the presence of a
small and evidently carefully organized opposition. As the King
rode through the cheering crowds, an extraordinarily handsome,
youthful gentleman thrust his way to his side, bearing a rebel
petition. The King recognized him as Sir Thomas Fairfax, a
scion of one of the proudest of the county families and one
notoriously hostile to his cause ; for he refused to receive the
document, and when Sir Thomas had the audacity to thrust it on
to the pommel of his saddle, let it fall to the ground. The two
were destined to encounter one another again, and next time
Fairfax would not be so easily put off.

From henceforth it began to be apparent that the rebel forces,
now openly mobilizing under the command of that heavy
personage who bore the ominous name of Essex, were at least not
going to be granted anything like a walkover. The King's hands
were being strengthened every day. Help was beginning to come
in from all sides, help not only in men, but in that of which he was
in equally desperate need, the material and financial sinews of
which he had been so fatally deprived by the loss of Hull. He had,
however, taken the Queen's advice to the extent of securing the
next best thing in the way of a port—Newcastle, which was
occupied by its own Earl. Nor was the gallant little woman
behindhand in showing the uses to which a port might be put,
for she lost no time in shipping over all the culverins, demi-
culverins, bullets, pistols, saddles, etcetera that—as if her vocation
had been to serve as minister of munitions—she had been able to
purchase with the proceeds of those outward adornments of
royalty for which there was now no more use. And it soon became

evident that the King would command devoted support from the overwhelming majority of those of his gentry who lived on the fruits of their land, and did not, like the Hampdens and Warwicks, seek to make fortunes in that fluid and impersonal sort of wealth which was the strength of the new plutocracy. One of these, the Earl of Worcester, whose rent roll amounted to something fabulous, furnished the King with a princely contribution, that made all the difference to him now that most of his usual sources of revenue were cut off.

Meanwhile loyal members of both Houses were beginning to arrive at York in increasing numbers. This was not surprising, since it was quite evident that Pym intended to treat any one who was not prepared to throw himself heart and soul into the rebellion, in the light of a traitor. As early as March, a majority of the Kentish Grand Jury, who had presented Parliament with a moderately worded petition in favour of maintaining the constitutional *status quo*, had found themselves arraigned as criminals. As matters began to move towards a crisis, the determination of the revolutionaries to go to all lengths became more and more clearly defined. A proclamation was actually issued in the name of the Lords and Commons denouncing "all such persons as shall upon any pretence whatever assist His Majesty" as "traitors to His Majesty" and threatening them, as such, with condign punishment ! At the same time every member of Parliament was required to take an oath to live and die with the rebel commander, and one unfortunate gentleman who had asked for time to consider his answer was subjected to such an awful wigging from the Speaker that, in terror, he faltered out his assent, and then was told that it was too late for his Aye to be accepted. Westminster had ceased to be any place for a loyal subject, and such of the constitutional party as could get away hastened to do so. Neither the Lords nor the Commons constituted a free assembly in any sense of the words ; their debates, such as they were, had ceased to be of the least interest to anyone—even themselves. They were, and were intended to be, Pym's mouthpieces.

While the King at York still hesitated to act as if a state of war existed, and continued to confine himself within the strictest limits of the law, at Westminster all pretence of legality was dropped, and one act of arbitrary tyranny followed another. The judge at the Maidstone assizes, merely for refusing to publish the ordinance for levying war against the King, was dragged from the bench to a cell in the Tower, where he lay for two years without any pretence of a trial. All up and down the country similar arrests were taking place of any one whose treasonable intentions could not be guaranteed. And it is a strange comment on that perpetual grievance against the Crown of Tonnage and Poundage, that when the King refused to sanction the bill for its continuance, the Parliament first proceeded to denounce the direst pains and penalties against any one who presumed to collect these duties, and then proceeded—in open defiance of the law—to make an exception by levying, or (to put it plainly) stealing them on its own behalf.

It is no wonder that under these circumstances the King's preparations were far less advanced than those of his enemies. Essex, with the whole resources of the capital at his disposal, was beginning to form his army in its neighbourhood, with an advanced headquarters at Northampton, while the King's forces at York, supported by casual and irregular contributions, were still numbered in hundreds. Under these circumstances a good deal of pressure was brought to bear on the King to sit tight where he was, and trust to the loyalty of the Northern counties to supply him with an army. But Charles, whose respect for the law by no means implied a lack of military enterprise, at once saw that to write off his books the greater and richer part of England, would be to commit himself in advance to certain defeat. He therefore formed the bold decision to thrust as far South as he could, even with his mere handful of men, though with superior enemy forces gathering round him, this was to risk being rounded up and captured. His forces indeed, though repulsed from Coventry, did succeed for a time in occupying Leicester.

The King was not with this adventurous spearhead, but remained at Nottingham to perform the great symbolic act that he had put off as long as there was the faintest hope of a peaceful accommodation. It was on the evening of the 22nd of August that he paraded his little force, that consisted only of his personal body-guard and a few local militia, on Castle Hill, overlooking the Trent. It was a miserable day, with a northerly wind blowing gusts of rain before it, damping the men's spirits as well as their uniforms. But there was no lack of enthusiasm when the huge standard was hoisted by no less than twenty men, under the command of its bearer, Sir Edmund Verney.

"God save the King !" was shouted by all present, and "Hang up the Roundheads !"

The King had now at last, in spite of the Perpetual Parliament Act, made his appeal to his people.

That night the wind rose to gale force, and in the morning the Royal Standard was found blown over prone on the ground. Those who wished best to His Majesty augured no good from the circumstance.

V

Appeal to the Country

I

THE PREDETERMINED ISSUE

THE Civil War that was formally proclaimed with the raising of the King's standard at Nottingham, and of which the final decision—final even so only in the military sense—it took nine years to reach, presents, at a first view, a spectacle of sheer chaos. It seems to be less of one national split than a hundred separate local contentions, with hardly any more connection than the common circumstance of their being fought between the King's party and that of what called itself Parliament. Each county has its own civil war, the history of which is sometimes recorded in substantial tomes. A big house was perfectly capable of sustaining a series of sieges, or forming a focus of offensive action. The actual armies in the field, that kept swelling and melting away with the fitfulness of mountain torrents, must have included at any one time but a minor proportion of those who, with any arms from cannon to pitchforks, were more or less involved in lethal activities against their local opposite numbers.

Nevertheless, if we have patience to look a little deeper, and to concentrate on the essentials of the struggle, we shall see that the prospect takes on an aspect of extreme simplicity—to such an extent that, barring unpredictable accidents, one is tempted to say that the result was a foregone conclusion from the first. So decisively, in the long run, were the odds weighted.

Not however because those who were loyal to the King were inferior in numbers, still less in valour, to their opponents. It is a strange, but undoubted fact, that as the struggle proceeded, the more the balance of military force was tilted in favour of the revolution, the more decidedly that of popular sympathy swung over to the support of monarchy. If the Cavaliers and Roundheads could have met together and fought it out under approximately equal conditions, the chances of a royalist victory would, to put it mildly, have been greatly enhanced. But the conditions were not equal.

For one thing, the rebels started with a vast material advantage, and one that was bound to go on increasing, as time went on, till it became overwhelming. For it was no accident that the chiefs of the conspiracy to wrest the controls of the state out of the hands of its lawful Sovereign, should have first come, and learned to act. together in one of those wealth-making ventures to which we should now attach the name of capitalist. And it will be found that the chief material strength of the revolutionary drive is drawn from this new, fluid sort of wealth, and the kind of economic activity with which it is associated. Wherever you have a centre of nascent capitalist enterprise, there you are pretty certain to find a focus of rebellion—the chief seaports, brisk manufacturing towns like Coventry or Manchester, such thriving areas of the cloth industry as those in East Anglia and the West Riding of Yorkshire, with their easily tapped resources, and above all, London. Generally speaking, it would be true to say that capital fought against the King ; and even in the seventeenth century, the business of war was one that demanded the backing of capital for its successful conduct, unless it could be carried on from hand to mouth, so to speak, as it was by the freebooting armies in Germany living on the country. And of this there was happily no question in England, except in a very minor way.

From the first, then, the rebel armies had a tremendous pull, the effects of which were realized in all kinds of ways that seldom get recorded in history books. A soldier who draws his pay and rations regularly, who has confidence in his weapon and—what counted for almost as much in the seventeenth century—his defensive armour, has confidence in himself and in his officers, and is far more amenable to discipline.

It is true that the heads of the rebellion—not excepting Pym—being civilians without military knowledge or instinct, but with an incurable addiction to predatory finance, and a scurvy record of bilking the soldier, allowed a good deal of this advantage to run to waste—there were times when the Roundhead armies, with good cause, became discontented to the verge of mutiny. But the advantage was there all the time, and nothing could be more certain than that if the war were sufficiently prolonged, the side that had the means would find ways of using them to create the well-found, professional force that would do the business. And that side was not the King's side.

He, in the military sense, was forced to live all the time precariously on irregular and wasting assets. His army was doomed to be an amateur and out-at-elbows army. His one chance was to snatch a quick win—a surprise knock out. But was there, except by a miracle, such a chance at all ?

For he had against him that literally immense factor that had been decisive in every civil war fought in England. London was under the control of his enemies. And the side that is in effective control of London is to all practical intents and purposes unbeatable, except by such a professional army as the King had no means of raising.

The one and only time that we know for certain of London having fallen to direct assault (we may rule out more or less collusive penetrations by mobs like those of Wat Tyler and Jack Cade) was in its early days as a Roman colony, before the hordes of Boadicea. Even the Conqueror, fresh from Hastings, had side-stepped from the walls, and preferred to persuade it to voluntary surrender by indirect means. In the previous great Civil War, the army of the Red Rose, which had swept down from the North, killing the Yorkist claimant and driving the Kingmaker in rout from St Alban's, had stuck fast in its own tracks, and not dared to hurl itself against the walls of a Yorkist London. A precisely similar refusal was that of Prince Charlie's Highlanders, a century after the Great Rebellion, to take the opportunity they had won by brilliant marching and manœuvring, of a clear run on the capital from Derby. So insoluble was the problem of reducing London by military force that no solution had even been attempted in all these centuries.

And yet this was the inescapable problem that from the first stared King Charles and his staff in the face. Unless they could get London, they might spin out time for years, they might cover themselves with glory, but by no conceivable possibility could they force a win. And unless they could force a win, it was only a question of time before the material balance against them became overwhelming. The very best that they could hope for was for war-weariness behind the front to drive the rebel chiefs into making a compromise peace. But as long as such desperate leaders as Pym and Hampden maintained their control, it might be taken for certain that—whatever pretence of negotiation might be put up for military or propagandist reasons—nothing less would be accepted than a royal surrender that was practically unconditional.

And London had never been so formidable an obstacle as now. For one thing, it was the greatest port in England, and the revolution had the command of the sea. By a bitter irony the navy, the royal navy, which has lasted from that day to this, and of which King Charles may justly be described as the father, had been seduced from its allegiance and was now under the command of the piratical Warwick. It would thus be impossible to reduce London by blockade without the fantastically difficult operation of closing the Thames below it, while operating against it from the West. London at that time had still its ancient walls and massive gates, and there was ample labour available to surround it with a ring of earthwork fortifications on a wider perimeter. And Charles's little field army could not run to the luxury of an effective siege train.

Even supposing, for the sake of argument, that by some prodigy of valour it were possible to break through all obstacles and march in triumph up Cheapside to hoist the Royal Standard over the Guildhall—what then? What could a few thousand men do, swallowed up in that vast labyrinth of streets, and liable to be set upon at any moment by numbers vastly exceeding their own of the men of whom the trained bands were composed, and whom it would be impossible effectively to disarm? And Skippon's training had rendered London's Puritan militia a force by no means to be despised, under conditions ideally favourable to themselves.

If Charles had possessed the military genius of a Napoleon, with a Marlborough or Montgomery for his chief of staff, it is difficult to see how, with the means at his disposal, he could have fulfilled the minimum requirements of victory.

And over and above these material and strategic disadvantages, there was a psychological factor more difficult to assess. It may be doubted whether under the most favourable circumstances the landed gentry, who were the mainstay of the Cavalier cause, would ever have provided the King with the leadership of such a military organization as eventually crushed both Crown and Parliament, and imposed a tyranny on the country that was neither royal nor plutocratic, but a dictatorship of the sword. For even in the high days of the Elizabethan age, the weakness of that class had been its utter unamenability to discipline. And the extreme Protestant ideology of Calvinism was—whatever else there may have been to be said about it—about the most efficient instrument of discipline, military or industrial, ever forged. It had provided the stiffening element of what, so long as he had survived to lead it, had been the invincible Swedish army of Gustavus Adolphus. And among Essex's amateur colonels there was one with the makings in him of a Puritan commander and trainer of troops, in no way inferior to Gustavus. Such an artificer, even supposing him to have arisen on the Cavalier side, would not have found the necessary material to his hands.

Reckoning up the odds that there were from the beginning against the King, it speaks enormously for his own leadership and that of his nephew, Prince Rupert, as well as the strength of the popular loyalty he had to draw upon, that he should have kept up his end for four continuous years, and even at one time have looked as if he were getting the better of it.

2

PRINCE RUPERT SETS THE PACE

IF the Earl of Essex had possessed the energy of a competent commander, it is probable that he could have ended the war before it had got fairly started. When he arrived at Northampton accompanied by his coffin and winding sheet, by way of demonstrating his willingness to lay down his life for the cause, he soon found himself in command of round about 20,000 men. Charles, when he made his bold advance to Nottingham, less than sixty road miles away, had nothing fit to be called an army at all. It was believed in Essex's camp that a swift advance would have resulted in the King being captured ; and even if he had got away by a headlong flight into Yorkshire, he could have been followed and rounded up. But it was not the Earl's way to act with such undignified precipitation. His movements in the field were as sluggish as his mind, and, in spite of the coffin, he was far from having reconciled his conscience to the task of going all out to smash the King, to whom he still professed as undying an allegiance as he did to the Parliament. And thus, though he went about his work with as staunch a heart as the circumstances permitted, he did so—like not a few of the magnates who found themselves compelled to take one side or the other—with decidedly cold feet.

Essex, then, let slip his opportunity, and in doing so, that of winning the war for King Pym. And that season of overwhelming advantage, during which the King was reduced to bluffing in the face of the rebel army without any of his own to speak of, was destined to be short-lived. This was largely due to the attitude of Pym himself, for it is fair to assume now that the voice of Parliament and that of Pym were the same. At the time he hoisted his standard the King had sent a desperate and heartrending appeal to the Houses—"our very soul is full of anguish, until we may find some remedy to prevent the miseries which are ready to overwhelm this whole nation by a civil war"—imploring them, in the most conciliatory terms, to enter into negotiations, while there was yet time, for a peaceful settlement, safeguarding the Protestant religion, the law of the land, and the privileges of Parliament.

The reply was as prompt as it was decisive. Parliament—or Pym—was not prepared to listen to any overtures or consider any compromise whatsoever. And it went beyond anything hitherto dreamed of, by declaring that the rebel army would never lay down its arms until His Majesty should explicitly abandon to its mercy every one who had embraced his cause, in order that every penny of war expense alleged to have been incurred, should be recouped out of the property of these delinquents. The reply to the Royal Standard had thus been the hoisting of the Jolly Roger.

Truly might it have been said of this *démarche* of Pym's that it was not only a crime, but a blunder—perhaps the one major blunder that can be brought home to him. But we must remember that this way of making war pay for itself was one that the powerful financial interests behind Pym had already adopted in Ireland, where the suppression of the rebellion was to be conducted in the spirit of a huge land-grabbing speculation. And in fact, the chronic addiction of the Patriots to "ways that are dark and tricks that are vain" where money was concerned, was sufficiently powerful, on occasion, to overbear considerations of elementary prudence. Pym had, in fact, done more than all conceivable appeals and standard hoistings and commissions of array, to raise an army for the King. Loyal gentlemen who had been shrinking on the brink of the abhorred abyss now saw themselves faced with the choice between open treason, and being marked down for plunder. They hesitated no longer. Followed by those they could enlist of their neighbours and dependents, they flocked to his standard.

But this was not the only thing that had happened to enable the King to look Essex in the face on something like even terms. King Charles's horsemen—not more than a few hundreds to start with—suddenly seemed to have developed a capacity of turning up everywhere out of nowhere. And soon, wherever the soldiers got talking together on either side, one name was pretty certain to form the theme of discussion, that of the King's nephew, recently arrived from overseas—the diabolical Prince Rupert, or Robber, as he soon got to be dubbed by the Roundhead camp fires. And the fire of military genius was imparted to what would otherwise have been depressingly uninspired proceedings.

This youth of twenty-three was the brother of that singularly unpleasant Elector Palatine in exile, to whom Charles had for months been more like a father than an uncle, but who judged that the time had come to detach himself from the King's failing fortunes—probably because he was playing up for the chance of being adopted as Parliamentary candidate for the throne, in the event of his Uncle's deposition. Anyhow, his departure overseas at the nadir of the royal fortunes had been followed closely by the arrival of Rupert, accompanied by a still younger brother, Maurice, both of them thirsting for a fight against any odds there might be. Rupert, in spite of his age, had already achieved in Germany the reputation, not only of a born cavalry leader, but of a tactical innovator—for he had from the first determined to make full use of the mobility of the mounted arm, by training his horsemen to charge home at the gallop, without halting to fire off their pistols, as had hitherto been the accepted practice. And this was not just the blind outcome of a hot-blooded young fellow's instinct, but was entirely characteristic of one of the most remarkable minds even of an age so prolific of inventive genius. For Rupert was incapable of turning his attention to any subject whatever, without setting the stamp of his originality upon it. He was not only an innovator in arms ; he became one of the pioneers of electrical discovery, and if not the inventor of mezzo-tint, he at least ranks among the pioneer founders of that fascinating art. He even, with no previous experience of the sea, contrived to figure without discredit in the capacity of Admiral. Since the days of Leonardo, there had arisen no more plausible candidate for the title of universal genius. In all the fantastic character distortions of the accepted myth, there is none more preposterous than that of Rupert to the likeness of a feather-brained thruster. He may be proved wrong in this or that action of his career, but it is extraordinary that any one with a knowledge of his record, or even with the image in mind of his chiselled, thoughtful profile, could credit him with taking any action whatever except for what appeared to him the most cogent of reasons.

It is strange too that he should have been misunderstood by his admirers quite as much as by his detractors. For Prince Rupert must have figured as the idol and daydream of romantic maidenhood for many generations. But few men have had less of the romantic in their composition. He had neither the time, nor the inclination, for dalliance. He devoted himself with austere concentration to whatever field of activity might afford present scope for his genius. At the time with which we are concerned, his whole heart and mind and strength were devoted exclusively to cultivating the art of war. And in that he has a curiously exact counterpart in his great French contemporary, the Prince of Condé, though Condé's, unlike Rupert's, was through life the one-track mind of a soldier and had none of Rupert's versatility. Even so, there was one side of the ideal soldier's make-up that Rupert conspicuously lacked. He had none of that faculty possessed by the great Duke of Marlborough, of tempering his martial zeal with the arts of the diplomat. He had no patience with sluggards and could not suffer fools gladly. Consequently he was not only at perpetual loggerheads with the King's civilian ministers, but what was much worse, was seldom able to get that whole-hearted co-operation from other commanders, that may make all the difference between success or failure in the field.

None the less, a more heaven-sent acquisition could hardly have been imagined to the King's cause at this particular juncture. For if Rupert was a thruster, a thruster was just what was needed. Assuming there to be a chance at all of a Royalist victory, it lay in a whirlwind offensive before the rebellion had time to bring into play its potentially overwhelming resources. The King's hope therefore lay in his mobile arm, then, as in all conditions of open warfare, that of decision ; and if there was a man who could at short notice create an irresistible cavalry out of the splendid human and equine material provided by the country estates, it was this already leading European exponent of shock tactics.

Moreover Rupert, alone of all royalist commanders, was out to smash the enemy, with no political afterthought or qualification whatever. As a soldier, his business was to impose peace, not to ingeminate it.

But this was far from being the attitude of his uncle. Not Falkland himself, that agonized pacifist, regarded the prospect of this unnatural war with a more fearful horror than King Charles. He would have gone—he had gone—to all possible lengths, short of abject surrender, to come to terms with these men who were now openly banded together to make their will the law of the land, and who had the face to demand his co-operation in setting up a reign of terror and confiscation of which his most devoted friends were marked down for the victims. But even with Pym's latest manifesto staring him in the face, the King could not bring himself to follow the example of Hampden—according to the expressive phrase of Clarendon—in throwing away the scabbard. He could not bring himself to believe that these men, who never ceased to interlard their most intransigent defiance of him with the humblest professions of duty and devotion, would so harden their hearts against the voice of conciliation as to insist on plunging the nation into this blood bath, that not a single individual on either side who did not feel his own neck or fortune to be at stake, regarded with anything but horror.

Hence, even at the expense of compromising his own chances, he was determined not to give the remotest handle to those who wished to put him in the wrong. And in consequence, his being the first to recognize the genius of this fiery nephew of his did not prevent him from cramping his military style in a way that must have been maddening to Rupert. Not that the Prince would have stood for frightfulness or plunder of the kind with which he must have been only too familiar in Germany. He was far too good a soldier and—we may add—too honourable a gentleman to encourage his soldiers to run riot. It was hard enough to discipline them without that. But when Essex's disorderly levies were helping themselves to everything they could lay hands on belonging to their opponents, and above all, to Catholics ; when plunder and arbitrary arrest were systematically practised on reputed loyalists everywhere the rebel power prevailed, and when arbitrary impositions were being laid on to his Majesty's subjects in a way of which the worst monarch would never have dreamed, the young Prince did not see why he should not lighten the King's desperate need for money by applying, in a moderate and orderly way, what was then the universal custom of war.

Thus while the King had been parading his bumpkins at Nottingham, and Essex had been sitting importantly in the midst of his overflowing legions at Northampton, Rupert had dashed forward at the head of the few hundred miscellaneously equipped horsemen that constituted his whole command, and by sheer impudent audacity possessed himself of the important town of Leicester, the half way house between the two armies, and a focus of rebellion. Naturally he realized that his stay there was limited by the time it would take Essex to get his ponderous forces and mind into motion, but there was time to collect, through the agency of the Mayor, what must have struck the Prince as the reasonable contribution of £2,000, which, if it did not go into His Majesty's pocket, would pretty certainly find its way into that of his enemies. His Worship was determined to strike a hard bargain, and—no doubt to his great relief—His Highness allowed him to call it quits for a quarter of the sum, cash down. But the Mayor had still a shot in his locker, and doubtless knowing the nature of the tyrant for whom Rupert was acting, sent off an urgent and indignant demand to His Majesty for a refund. He got it, on the nail. Charles was horrified at his nephew's proceedings, which, he said, "we do utterly disavow and dislike." Rupert's comment is—perhaps fortunately—not on record. But doubtless it was to the expurgated effect that such is not the way in which wars are won in this indelicate world.

3

THE KING TAKES THE OFFENSIVE

IT would be a mistake to imagine that because Charles hated war, he had therefore no *flair* for its conduct. War was an art, like any other, and he was an artist to his finger tips. But his only experience of it had been of one farcical campaign on the Scottish Border three years before, and it would have been as absurd to have expected him to blossom out all of a sudden into a military genius, as it would be to expect a man handling a paint brush for the first time to dash off a masterpiece. Especially now that he had to improvise his whole military organization from the bottom upwards, a task to tax the resources of the greatest commander that ever lived.

But apart from the way in which he allowed himself to be handicapped by moral and constitutional scruples not shared by his opponents, nothing can be more remarkable than the quickness with which he adapted himself to his new rôle. He divined, almost at first sight, that in this amazing nephew of his he had got a commander worth all the solid and steady veterans of his entourage put together. And he saw, or allowed Rupert to persuade him, that as a commander of a later war was to put it, clubs and not spades were trumps. It was a choice between a quick win and spinning out time to an inevitable defeat. And whether uncle or nephew was its originating spirit, between them they hit upon a strategic plan as daring as it was subtly conceived.

It was that the King should break up his headquarters at Nottingham and retire westward in the direction of Shrewsbury and the Welsh Border, where, thanks largely to Pym's predatory manifesto, he might safely count on attracting an army to his standard out of the loyal West and North, that would enable him to confront Essex with a force equal in numbers and superior in morale. Then, after the two or three weeks necessary for hammering this force into some semblance of fighting trim, he would, while the campaigning season still held, march hot foot by the directest practicable route upon London, disposing of Essex on the way. Then, having arrived before the rebel command had had time to organize the defence, he might bank on the support of a Fifth Column in the City, the chapter of accidents and the fortune that favours the bold, to give him back his capital, and with it his place in the Constitution. One of several assumptions on which this scheme was based was that Essex would kindly refrain from interfering, until the army had been formed to deal with him. But Essex was not the man to do anything in a hurry, and Rupert could be trusted to find ways and means of slowing down still further any activities of which he might be capable.

The whole venture, as any professional soldier could have demonstrated, was a blind gamble. To count on a scratch force which, even if it could be formed, there would be no time properly to equip, staff, or discipline, fulfilling a programme of this ambitious nature, was sanguine indeed. But the wildest gamble was preferable to a delaying policy that, in the long run, offered no chance at all. If the King *had* a chance, it was by staking everything at the outset on a surprise capture of London ; because however hard a nut it might now be to crack, in a few months' time it could be rendered uncrackable. And not to get London was to lose everything.

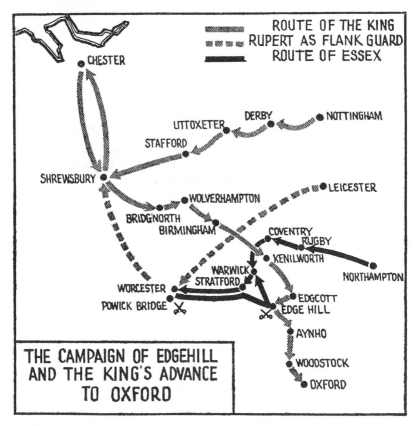

THE CAMPAIGN OF EDGEHILL
AND THE KING'S ADVANCE
TO OXFORD

It was on the 13th of September that Charles broke up camp at Nottingham, and it took him just a week, proceeding by way of Derby and Stafford, with his forces continually swollen by the accession of the local gentry, to reach Shrewsbury, which he entered without opposition. Three days later he made himself master of the fortress town of Chester, which, like York, had from Roman times been one of the strategic keys of England, and commanded the Northern approaches to Wales, which was henceforth to provide the King with his most fruitful recruiting ground.

Rupert meanwhile, well out on his left to the South, had been acting the part of screen and flank-guard, in a way that was already beginning to render his name legendary, and to cause him to be regarded among his adversaries as something more or worse than human. Even his dog Boy, a beautiful white poodle that he had been given when a prisoner of war in Austria, and who accompanied him everywhere, came to be regarded as his familiar spirit. These lads of his, who had come together without any experience of discipline, and to whom there had been no time to impart it on the parade ground, were receiving their training in the course of this strenuously active service, and in an incredibly short time came to acquire a confidence in themselves and their leader that it only needed blooding in the field to translate into an assurance of being able to charge home and rout their opponents at almost any odds. Nor was that experience to be long delayed.

Essex, mystified and blinded by these bewildering tactics, made not the slightest attempt to interfere with the King. When at last, six days after Charles had left Nottingham, he did get on the move, it was not in the direction of the enemy, but on a parallel course due west to Worcester, with the idea, presumably, of barring the way to London. His was not a force too easy for any commander to handle. At Nottingham it had been on the verge of mutiny, owing to the characteristic failure of the revolutionary chiefs to provide the soldier with his pay. And once on the march, the men were continually breaking the ranks in order to plunder and poach on the estates of suspected Royalists and Catholics, while the Puritanism, with which they were kept indoctrinated in perpetual sermons by a great company of attached preachers, expressed itself in acts of sacrilegious vandalism and such antici-pations of Nazi technique as parading an aged clergyman in derision about the streets of Coventry. It is only fair to say that Essex did all in his power, by threats and persuasion, to put a damper on this holy ruffianism.

Meanwhile all over the country the flames of civil war had broken out ; and in the South things had been going badly for the King. The great naval base at Portsmouth had already fallen ; its commander, that roystering Judas, George Goring, who had played traitor to both sides in succession, having left his garrison in the lurch in order to make good his own escape by sea to Holland. Nor was Sir John Byron, the dispossessed Lieutenant of the Tower, able to maintain himself even in the loyal university of Oxford, but taking with him such of the student volunteers as could provide themselves with horses, he had retired while the going was good and got into Worcester, whither Rupert had been directed to join hands with him and bring him off. This service the Prince performed, right in the path of Essex, with his usual energetic efficiency, and it provided him with just the opportunity he needed of demonstrating his new shock tactics in action.

For scouting forward in the direction of Powick Bridge, over the Teme, he waylaid a superior force constituting Essex's cavalry advance guard riding down a narrow lane, and quite unsuspicious of his presence. Only a few of Rupert's men were provided with the body armour that was considered essential for the seventeenth-century trooper, but His Highness was not the man to be put off by trifles of this kind.

"Whom are you for ?" he called to their commander, Colonel Sandys.

"For King and Parliament," replied that probably still unsuspicious officer, in the accepted rebel formula.

"Not for the King alone ?"

"No"—it must have been beginning to dawn on the Colonel now.

"Then," thundered Rupert, "in the King's name, have at you !"

On which probably prearranged signal his cavaliers crashed into them. It was a complete surprise, and the Roundheads, jammed in the lane, never stood a chance of recovery. But they lacked nothing for pluck, and it was only after strenuous sword and pistol work, with perhaps some assistance from musketeers lining the hedges,* that the brilliant little victory was consummated. Shortly afterwards the rebel survivors, some with swords still drawn and some without their helmets, came galloping into the headquarters town of Pershore as if the devil were at their heels, though all pursuit had ceased four miles back ; and the panic spread even to Essex's life guards, who were turned out to support them, and started a *sauve qui peut* on their own account. The result of this first action of the Civil War was thus to establish a complete temporary moral ascendancy of the royalist cavalry. The gallant Sandys, who had fallen mortally wounded into Rupert's hands, and was carefully tended by his orders, died—according to the surely reliable evidence of Falkland—expressing bitter repentance for his treason.

* Either loyal townsmen or drafts from Byron.

When Essex at last lurched forward with his unwieldy command to Worcester, he found the crumbling walls undefended, and Rupert and Byron vanished into the blue. Still there could be no better place to sit down and await the attack that the King could no doubt be trusted to make in due course. And Pym's propaganda organs were soon thrilling all London with accounts of the glorious victory won by the Parliament horse over the robber Prince.

Meanwhile Shrewsbury had become a scene of such furious activity as that sleepy old town had probably not experienced for centuries. These three weeks of grace that My Lord Essex had so kindly conceded, were taken full advantage of. Something like 20,000 men were now at the King's disposal, from splendidly caparisoned young bloods of ancient houses, to little dark Welshmen, scantily clad, armed with nothing but knives or clubs, but with an inbred faculty of supplementing their resources with any removable commodities that might be in their neighbourhood.

How to provide arms for so many at so short a notice was a problem indeed ; but the King had done the best he could towards solving it by impounding the arms of the trained bands of the counties through which he had passed, and whose allegiance, as they were largely recruited from the towns, was at best doubtful. Fortunately he had available quite a number of officers who had served their apprenticeship in the Dutch or Swedish service on the Continent, and these were kept strenuously employed in sorting out the army into brigades of cavalry, and tertias, as they were called, of infantry, and instilling into them at least the rudiments of discipline. But when you come to consider that the drill of the professional pikeman or musketeer in those days was of a complexity far exceeding anything known on the barrack squares of our own, you can imagine what sort of an army it was that the best efforts of the commissioned and non-commissioned officers could get on the march, in three weeks, for what was meant to be the decisive campaign. And even granted that their opponents were in little better condition, military history records few instances of decisive success being achieved by half-baked mobs.

The King had at least not only materially but morally immensely strengthened his position since the hoisting of his standard. It is impossible to imagine a more striking contrast than that of his repeated and urgent pleas for peace, accompanied by his solemn protest of his willingness to abide by the law and honour to the uttermost the privileges of Parliament, with the blustering insolence and rapacity with which every one of these overtures was flung back in his face. The climax came when a London lawyer, called Fountaine, refused to contribute to a forced loan levied in the name of Parliament, on the plea that Parliament's own Petition of Right had expressly debarred this hated form of imposition. The Parliament of Pym and Hampden replied to this assertion of the liberties of the subject, by flinging its author into jail, on the plea, defined with his usual candour by Marten, that the Petition was only intended to restrain Kings !

Meanwhile Essex, for want of anything better to do, had been putting out feelers for his Majesty's reception of a Parliamentary petition that he should abandon his army and supporters and give himself up to the rebels at London, when all would be well. If we may trust Clarendon, one of the conveyors of this modest demand was to have been Hampden, "who, they thought, would have skill to make infusions into many persons then about His Majesty." But His Majesty had had too much experience of being spied on by Hampden in Edinburgh to dream of allowing him, of all people, to come snooping round the camp at Shrewsbury. He therefore politely intimated that he was ready to receive any messengers who were not lying under a charge of treason. This, except for some furious invective at the King's daring to object to any messenger sent him by Parliament, was the last that was heard of this not too ingenuous snare spread in his sight.

He was, however, more than willing to oblige by coming to London ; for on the 12th of October his still half-equipped but enthusiastic new regiments got the eagerly expected order to set out on what, taking all circumstances into consideration, must rank among the most daring marches ever undertaken ; and it speaks volumes for the work of Charles's improvised staff, that his army of raw recruits, with only such an apology for a commissariat as could have been scraped together locally in the three weeks, made what for a professional force would have been quite creditable marching time—an average of over 10 miles a day.

Essex was still confidently expecting him to offer battle under the walls of Worcester, and Charles kept him under that illusion by directing his first day's march on Bridgnorth. But Rupert had, with his cavalryman's eye for country, noted the unsuitability of the enclosed orchard lands of the Severn valley for the shock tactics on which he was relying, and he was determined to draw Essex into the open terrain of the Midlands. The King therefore side-stepped to Wolverhampton, and taking in his stride the insignificant townlet of Birmingham, but avoiding the Roundhead strongholds of Coventry and Warwick, he proceeded to climb the great limestone escarpment that runs diagonally across England above the valley of the Avon, and bivouacked on the 22nd, at the village of Edgcott, a name of ill omen, since it was here that in the last Civil War King Edward IV had been surprised and put to ignominious rout by the treachery of the Kingmaker Warwick.

Thus in ten days' marching the King, without encountering the slightest opposition, had covered more than half of the distance to London. But had done more than he knew ; for that night, as he was arranging to give his men a well-earned Sunday rest, a report came in from Rupert to the effect that the King's quartermaster, scouring the country for forage, had run into his opposite number of the enemy engaged on a precisely similar mission, and having, in the brisk encounter that followed, secured a few prisoners, had learned of Essex's arrival at the little town at Kineton, seven miles away slightly to the north of west, and still down on the plain. Thus the King had got in between the Roundhead field army and London. But Rupert was not fool enough to counsel a march on the capital with Essex following intact at their heels, to crush them between hammer and anvil. He had got the Earl now exactly where he wanted him for the decisive battle, and his urgent advice was for the King to march with all speed to his support on the height of Edgehill, looking steeply down on the enemy and blocking his road to the South. And the King, after Rupert had taken some ridiculous offence about receiving instructions from Secretary Falkland, patiently autographed :

> Nepheu,
> I have given order as you have desyred ; so I
> dout not but all the foot and canon will be at
> Eggehill betymes this morning, where you will
> also find
> > Your loving oncle and
> > > Faithful frend
> > > > CHARLES R.
> 4 o'clock this Sunday morning.

After which we may hope that His Majesty contrived to turn in for an hour or two's sorely needed sleep.

4

AMATEUR ARMIES CLASH AT EDGEHILL

THE crest of which Edgehill forms part had, some millions of years before, formed the edge of a sea tenanted by fantastic monsters inconceivable to the contemporaries of King Charles. Below spread an almost level plain that must at this time have consisted principally of open stubble, and on which, with one of those new-fangled prospective glasses or even with the naked eye, it was easy to observe the movements of any considerable bodies of men on either side of the road that cut across it towards the roofs and church tower of Kineton. Though a cheerless day in what, by our reckoning, would be early November, visibility was good ; for there was an astringent wind blowing out of the North quarter, and chilling the bones of Rupert's men on the heights which they had occupied without opposition first thing in

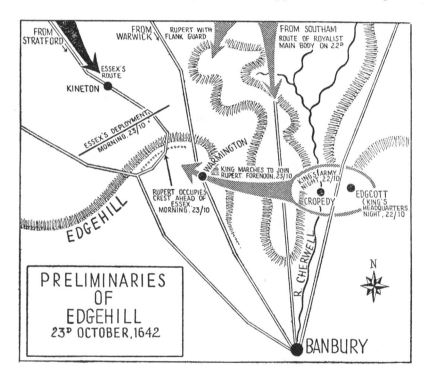

the morning. They must have awaited with some anxiety the arrival of the King, for if Essex had been off the mark at daybreak, his heavy columns could easily have driven the cavalry screen off the crest before the main body marching from Edgcott had got up out of the valley of the Cherwell. But Essex as usual let slip his opportunity ; the King was as good as his word, and some time in the forenoon the Royalist army, horse, foot, and artillery, was drawn up in an ideally favourable position, waiting for the enemy to climb the hill.

But Essex, slow though he was, had learnt too much about soldiering to be lured into playing his adversary's game. If he must accept battle, let it be at no disadvantage of ground. His own concentration was not yet complete, for Hampden, with his Buckinghamshire greencoats escorting the baggage train, had not arrived at the rendezvous at Kineton. So the Roundhead army formed up out of range of the Royalist artillery, and awaited events.

In so doing they had forced the King's hand. He could not possibly stay where he was. With Essex on his front, the strongly garrisoned Roundhead town of Banbury on his right rear, and with no base of supplies in an unfriendly country, his army would have broken up in search of food. A council of war, hastily convened, decided that there could be no question of marching *away* from Essex. "I shall give them battle," decided the King, "it is the first time I ever saw the rebels in a body." So early in the afternoon orders were given for the army to descend the hill and deploy in battle formation at the foot. This, if Essex had known his business, might have given the whole game into his hands. He had had ample time during the morning to complete his own deployment, and an instant offensive, vigorously pressed home, would have caught the Cavaliers with the infantry scrambling anywhere they could down the hill face, the cavalry threading along the only practicable road, and the guns being hauled painfully down, with most of the teams roped behind to brake them. But sudden offensives were not in Essex's line, and he allowed the King to marshall his host without making the slightest attempt to hurry him. Each side seems to have mustered something in the 14,000 neighbourhood, though the Royalists were superior in the decisive cavalry arm.

The marshalling conformed to the accepted pattern of the time, which differed in no essential respect from that of Cannæ, or Zama, sixteen centuries previously. The infantry of each side were drawn up in the centre with the cavalry on the flanks. The infantry would become locked in a clinch, while the side whose cavalry could succeed in driving that of the other off the field would, if it could keep a sufficient number of its own in hand, bring them to bear upon the flanks and rear of the enemy infantry with annihilating effect. The classic model of this was displayed in the Prince of Condé's victory, that shattered the military power of Spain, less than a year later, at Rocroi. But Condé, it must be remembered, was operating with a highly trained professional cavalry, and not raw levies, like those of Rupert, to whom there had been no time to teach any lesson except that of charging hell for leather straight at the enemy. That he should even have taught them that was something that only Rupert could have accomplished in the time.

The King rode from regiment to regiment, speaking words of encouragement :

"Let Heaven," he said, "show its power by this day's victory, to declare me just ; and as lawful, so a loving King to my subjects."

They received him with loyal huzzas, and he would certainly have taken his place in their midst beneath his standard, had not the whole body of his commanders insisted in his retiring to a point of vantage, probably on the side of the hill, saying that if he exposed his person, they could not get the men to advance. The King very unwillingly gave way—a disastrous concession, since it put it out of his power to co-ordinate the movements of his various units just when it was most essential. For Rupert, who could never endure to have his style cramped by a stonewaller like Lord Lindsey*, hitherto commander-in-chief, had persuaded the King to make the cavalry an independent command, whereon Lindsey declined any responsibility whatever except for his own regiment ; so the command had been turned over at the last moment to Lord Forth, a fine old Scottish veteran, well stricken in years and liquor.

It was about 3 o'clock in the afternoon, when barely two hours of daylight were left to fight the action that both sides were agreed in hoping would settle the quarrel for good and all, that proceedings commenced with a noisy interchange between the few

---

* Who, as Lord Willoughby, had been unfortunate enough to be saddled with the command of the ignominious and abortive final attempt to relieve La Rochelle, in 1628.

cannon on either side, which, when it had gone on for some time without much damage, gave place to the serious business of the day. Rupert had galloped from one end of the line to the other, giving his commanders final instructions and then, taking personal charge of the right wing, having led his squadrons in a wide sweep so as to take ground well outside the enemy's flank, wheeled in and blew the charge. As the pace quickened to a gallop, a strange thing happened. A troop of the enemy's horse detached itself from the main body, discharged its pistols on to the ground, and then wheeled round as if to attack its own comrades. Which was indeed its intention ; for these men had been raised by Sir Faithful Fortescue to fight for the King in Ireland, but had found themselves, to their shame and indignation, conscripted to commit treason against him. But Sir Faithful, true to his name, had bided his time and got into touch with Rupert—and this was the result. Unfortunately in the excitement they forgot to divest themselves of their orange, or Essex scarves (for the sides were distinguished from each other in this way like a couple of hockey teams) so that several of them got cut down by excited cavaliers. For at the first shock, almost before you could speak of a combat, the thing had become a rout ; the whole mass of horsemen, blue scarves and orange, were mingled together, galloping in the same direction over the fields towards Kineton ; Rupert's men

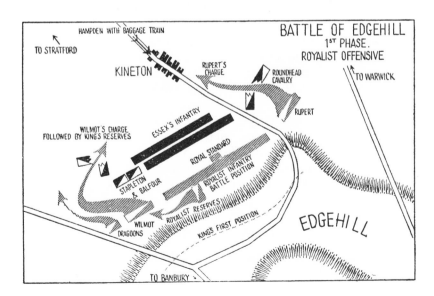

shouting, and cutting at everything orange, the Roundheads bent over their horses' necks and riding for their lives. Under such circumstances it is not too easy for a probably unskilful swordsman to inflict much damage on a man in steel helmet and cuirass riding as fast as himself; and a stout fellow, who keeps his sword and his wits, will probably not be in too great danger. We may surmise that the majority of the pursued were more frightened than hurt; but it would be some days before the whipped squadrons could be got together again as effective fighting units.

On the Royalist left, the cavalry had been commanded by a person of very different calibre from Rupert, Henry Wilmot, one of those irresponsible young officers who had been involved in the "army plot". Wilmot, though no fool, was no reliable officer, either in the personal or the military sense, and in the one combat he had fought in the present campaign, had anything but distinguished himself. He had a more difficult task than Rupert, in that there was some broken and enclosed ground on his left; but his business was to dispose of the Roundhead cavalry on that wing—and instead of doing so, after the preliminary dragoon work of clearing his flank, he rode at the easiest target,* some horse to his front, and drove them from the field, sweeping away some infantry at the same time. But there were two substantial bodies of Roundhead horse, under the ex-Lieutenant of the Tower, Sir William Balfour, and Sir Philip Stapleton, with which he made no attempt to deal. This might not have mattered so much had the King kept his cavalry reserve in hand, but this reserve was under the incurably hot-headed Byron—"Bloody Byron" as he came to be called—who, blind to all considerations of prudence and commonsense, galloped off after Wilmot. And to make the picture complete, the King's personal guard, composed of some of the richest young men in the country, either got or took permission to gallop off after them.

The position was thus one of the most unique and paradoxical ever recorded in the annals of war—something that only *could* have happened in a battle of amateur armies. The King's horse had swept everything in wild confusion before it, and yet the cavalry fight had all the effect of a victory for the rebels.

---

* The explanation, though not the excuse, seems to have been that Essex's army had been drawn up in two lines, and Wilmot had ridden round and struck at the right of the rear one. Such things will happen with amateur leadership.

Because the only cavalry left on the field were two intact formations of Roundheads, perfectly in hand, and available to be
flung into the scales of the infantry combat. This, if the
Roundhead horse had been up to the form they subsequently
attained, would have ended the war. As it was, it came very near
to it.

To the King, surveying the field from his commanding view-
point, it must at first have seemed as if everything had prospered
beyond his most sanguine expectations. He could see his horsemen of both wings, now mingled together in one indistinguishable
crowd, hunting the enemy like hares over the plain towards
Kineton. He could see his new infantry "tertias", with his
standard in their midst, pressing hard upon the enemy line—
things had in fact, been going so desperately against the rebels
that Essex himself, abandoning his duties as commander-in-chief,
had seized a pike and was fighting on foot among his men. And
then, away to the left, the King saw a new body of horsemen
swing out and charge home upon the flank and rear of his struggling infantry. Now, with fearful suddenness, the whole aspect of
the situation was changed. His line was crumbling—it was being
rolled up from the left. The masses of enemy infantry were now
surging forward, confident of victory and drawn towards the
standard as by a magnet. It swayed above the fight, the pole

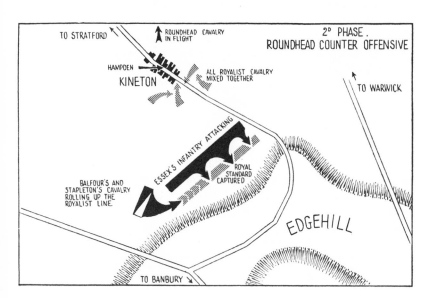

grasped in the hand of Sir Edmund Verney, an intransigent Puritan, and one whose political sympathies were all with the other side ; but, as he had recently confided to Hyde,

"My conscience is only concerned in honour and gratitude to follow my master. I have eaten his bread, and served him near thirty years, and will not do so base a thing as to forsake him ; and choose rather to lose my life (which I am sure I shall do) to preserve and defend those things which are against my conscience to maintain and defend."

That time had now come. The standard fell ; the precious silk was torn from the staff,* which lay on the ground, still grasped in one severed hand—which was all that was ever found of Sir Edmund Verney. When Charles saw his standard fall he could hesitate no longer. The place of the King of England was where that had been, and he made all haste to take it.

Nothing could have been more timely than his arrival. The situation seemed desperate. The raw regiments on the left which had never seen a shot fired before, under this terrific mauling had lost all semblance of cohesion. Those in the centre were in little better condition. The gallant Lindsey had gone down with a mortal wound, and was in the hands of the enemy ; his son, Lord Willoughby, fighting over his body, had been captured with him. But tough old Forth survived, and, what was even more to the point, another veteran, Sir Jacob Astley, the commander of the infantry, one of those born leaders whose presence in the field has a stiffening and a tonic effect upon the soldier. It was he who, before leading his men down to their battle stations, had clasped his hands in front of them all, and as if speaking for each one of them, had prayed aloud : "O Lord, Thou knowest how busy I must be this day. If I forget Thee, do not Thou forget me !" and then, changing to his heartiest parade ground voice : "March on, boys !"

He and Forth were busy enough now. Luckily the two stoutest regiments, the Prince of Wales's and the Duke of York's, drawn in from the right, were still intact, and these they succeeded in planting where the standard had been, like a breakwater in the spate of shouting, struggling combatants, horse and foot, few of whom can by this time have been swayed by any motives what-

---

* It was brought back by a young Catholic officer, Captain John Smith, who put on an orange scarf, strolled into Essex's camp, demanded the standard in his name, got it, and walked out with it.

ever save each man's blind urge of self-preservation or fury. That was the situation when the King arrived, and the effect of his presence in the midst of these last reserves, with the balls whistling round him—one only just missed him—cool and debonair as on a review, may well have been decisive at this supreme crisis. To the two young princes, whom he had left at his vantage point, it must have looked as if their father were at every moment about to be surrounded and overwhelmed in the mellay. But the two regiments—*their* regiments—were standing like rocks. The crisis, if they had known it, was really past. Essex had shot his bolt. His last reserves had been thrown in ; his punch—even that of his cavalry—had no more power to back it.

Meanwhile what of the Royalist cavalry, who had left the field in that mad ride to Kineton ? Typical of the stereotyped account of the matter is the remark of Gardiner :

"Little recked Rupert of how the battle fared behind him !"

What means Dr Gardiner had of diagnosing a state of blind imbecility that would be hard to account for in a responsible commander except by some intensive roystering before the battle, is a secret that has died with him. Doubtless if the Prince had had the advantages of an Oxford Don's education, instead of picking up his soldiering in the rough and tumble of the field, he would have known at once how to halt and manœuvre a galloping mob of excited lads, many of them probably unable to stop their own horses, all units mixed up together, especially after the converging spate of Wilmot's command had joined with his own, and all these mixed up with orange scarves galloping in the same direction. Rupert may or may not have succeeded in keeping his trumpeter at his side, but the fellow might have blown his lungs out into the wind for all the effect it could possibly have had. If Rupert had drawn rein himself, the crowd would merely have swept past and left him derelict.

The art of stopping cavalry, that had crashed into their enemy at the gallop and gone in pursuit, was one that even the hard-bitten mercenary commanders of the Thirty Years' War had never properly mastered. The good old German word "plunder" was so basic to their mentality that once out of the strictest control of their officers, they galloped straight off for the nearest available loot, and were as much lost to their commanders as if they had been killed. That was the compelling reason for the slow and sticky cavalry tactics that only King Gustavus, whose devout

Swedes made "some conscience of what they did," had dared—
and that but partially—to modify. Rupert, when he committed
himself to hundred per cent shock tactics, or rather had them
forced upon him by the fact that his men were only half found in
either body armour or firearms, was thus setting himself a
problem that even with the best trained veterans—and how much
more with the amateur officers and raw levies at his disposal !—
had proved well nigh insoluble : of how, having driven the
opposing cavalry from the field, to keep enough of his own in
hand to bring to bear on the infantry for the decisive blow. Only
one man did find the solution in this war, and he had human and
material resources not available to Rupert.

His Highness must have perceived that the magnet that was
attracting all these scattered individuals was the conspicuous
landmark formed by Kineton. Even the Cavaliers must have
realized that this was the enemy field base, and would contain
whatever fruits of victory there might be for the reaping. Short of
that it would be hopeless to think of rallying them. But the gallop
of a couple of miles or so across heavy champaign, some of it
plough, and with riders carrying so much weight as the average
trooper of those days, must have been terribly hard on a scratch
collection of horses that had probably been both overworked and
underfed in these last ten strenuous days. There was probably
little charging capacity left in those of the Cavaliers who began to
straggle up in twos and threes to where the road broadened out
into the street of the little market town, now packed with the
waggons of the just arrived convoy. These offered a tempting
prize ; but with them were Colonel John Hampden's green
Buckinghams. And Hampden, if he knew nothing of soldiering,
was a master in the management of men.

Probably the attempt to rush his laager by leaderless groups of
tired horsemen was not pressed very seriously once it was apparent
what reception it was likely to get. And Rupert certainly would
have been the last man to encourage it. His trained eye, and even
his ear—though the wind was the wrong way—must have
apprised him that all was not going according to plan with the
main body. A desperate and stationary fight was evidently in
progress, with continuous smoke of firing banking up against the
side of the hill. The Prince must surely have felt in his bones that
his uncle must be breathing something equivalent to, "Rupert
or night !"

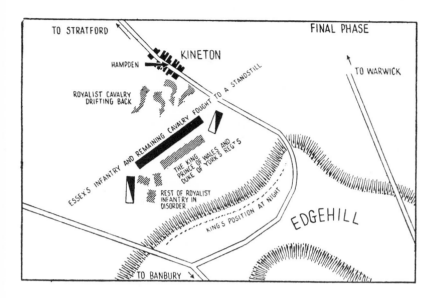

The check at least afforded the commanders the opportunity of calling their men off and leading them back, though at a very different pace from that at which they had come, towards the main action. They found His Majesty, surrounded by a few of his nobility, still maintaining his post on that corpse-piled plot of earth over which his standard no longer floated. The situation remained anxious in the extreme, for what was left of Balfour's cavalry was still hovering about threatening to charge again.

"But," says Clarendon, "though most of the officers of horse were returned, and that part of the field still covered with the loose troops, yet they could not be persuaded or drawn to charge ... the officers pretending that their soldiers were so dispersed that there were not ten of any troop together, and the soldiers that their horses were so tired that they could not charge." Officers were without their men, and troopers without their officers, and neither willing to come up to the scratch without the other. Even Wilmot, who of all men might have been expected to set an example, had developed cold feet :

"My Lord," he said to Falkland, who had urged him to make one last effort, "we have got the day. Let us live to enjoy the fruits thereof."

From that time forward, Rupert never had the least use for

Wilmot. With such men to work with, there was nothing that even he could do.

Under these circumstances, panic might easily have developed, and there were already those around the King who were again importuning him to leave the field—though whither, no one could imagine. But the King, though this was his first battle, was the coolest person there, and taking calm stock of the enemy, he observed, to those who were urging him to this act of ignominious insanity :

"They do not look as if they thought themselves conquerors."

Nor did they. For they, too, had had enough for one day, and were as little minded as the Cavaliers to be brought up again to the assault. So, as the early darkness was now beginning to fall, the action petered out by common consent.

Soon the King was sitting with Rupert beside a camp fire, while the cutting North wind blew over the field, chilling and freezing the unhappy wounded who lay out under the stars, but perhaps saving many a wound from developing fatal gangrene. And nothing had been decided—except that the war was to go on indefinitely.

There was another interview which, though it cannot be dated for certain, probably took place that night.* Colonel John Hampden, who had every reason to be satisfied with his part in the day's work, must have been benevolently relieved at the tempestuous irruption at his quarters of his cousin, Noll Cromwell. It is to this day a matter of conjecture what precise part Cromwell, with his troop, had played ; but he must have seen the way in which Rupert and Wilmot had made hares of the greater part of his fellow cavalrymen, and he was almost apoplectic with indignation.

"Your troops" ... he stormed, "old decayed serving men ... tapsters ... such kind of fellows ... do you think that the spirits of such base and mean fellows will ever be able to encounter *gentlemen,* that have honour, and courage ... you must get men of a spirit ... take it not ill what I say, [the elder man having evidently showed signs of restiveness] I know you will not ... of a spirit that is likely to go as far as gentlemen will go, or else you will be beaten still."

---

* Not after Powicke Bridge unless—which has never been suggested—Cromwell had been there. Only the battle-drunkenness of a man fresh from the field could have engendered such blind fury—even in him.

The millionaire was accustomed to his cousin's tantrums, and knew how to manage and use him as he did other men. But it must have caused him some secret amusement to watch Noll, of all people, laying down the law about military matters. Still, Noll being Noll, it was no more than one might have expected of him.

5

THE THRUST FOR LONDON AND THE
UNFOUGHT DECISION

ALL that night the two armies—the King's having pulled back after dark to its position on the crest—remained in face of each other ; and if Continental analogy had been anything to go by, would have been only waiting for the light to bring the interrupted battle to a decision. But these were not professional soldiers, but unconditioned civilians, who had never bargained for such a frightful experience as that of the struggle beneath the hill, and had had just about as much of it as either army was prepared to stand. Besides, though most of Essex's cavalry had disappeared, the King's infantry was in no condition to take the offensive, nor could even Rupert have persuaded his cavalry, without support, to fling themselves against the bristling pikes of the Roundhead foot, now reinforced by Hampden's two fresh regiments.

All through Monday, then, the two armies remained looking at each other, without either making a move ; and on Tuesday, Essex, who was getting into more and more difficulties with his supplies, abandoned the field and fell back upon his bases at Warwick and Coventry to reorganize, leaving the King, for the time, master of the situation, with nothing between him and London.

It was now debated whether they should instantly march on the capital by the nearest way, which would have been by Aylesbury and Berkhamsted ; and it seems that Rupert and Forth would have been ready even for this. But it is fantastically impossible to conceive of that army, disorganized as it was, with most of its ammunition shot away, arriving in a fit condition to take on the greatly superior numbers of the trained bands, and to storm and hold London. It was above all things necessary for the King to have a base from which to operate ; a fixed point, as Napoleon would have said, round which to manœuvre ; and the ideal place for this was Oxford, two days' march to the South, the most loyal of all English towns to the King,* and giving command of the Upper Thames Valley. And indeed the approach to London by Oxford was only a matter of about six miles, or half a day's marching, longer than the other. To occupy it therefore was a sequel to Edgehill both obvious and necessary. The retreat of Essex also enabled the King to mop up the Roundhead garrison of Banbury, and secure that essential member of the ring of strategic outposts by which Oxford could be secured.

So far, so good. But now everything depended on whether the King could seize the opening that Essex had given him and get to London before the Roundhead field army had done pottering about in the Midlands, and had arrived to interpose itself between the King and his main objective ; also before its citizen defenders, realizing their danger, had had time, by their united labour, to throw up field works that should turn it into an impregnable obstacle. The King lost this time, and in so doing lost his only real chance—if there was a chance at all—of winning the war.

It was not till the 29th, six days after Edgehill, that the King completed the two days' march to Oxford, which he entered without opposition ; and even then, when every hour was of importance, he does not seem to have made up his mind whether to march on London or not. It would seem that certain of his advisers, who included Hyde, thought that he ought to have gone into winter quarters and husbanded his resources for a spring campaign. Rupert, with his usual untamable energy, was scouring the country—but at first in the wrong direction, that of Aylesbury, another keypoint in the outer ring of Oxford defences, which he occupied but could not hold. He then turned south east along the line of the Thames, and bursting through the Goring gap in the chalk hills, occupied Reading, blazing so plainly the path to London as to end all hesitation, and to bring the main body marching at his heels. "But alas," as one of the King's officers, Lieutenant Bulstrode, complained, "the King

---

* Though not wholly so. There was a considerable suppressed Puritan element among the townsmen.

retarded his march, of which the Earl of Essex, taking hold, got between the King and London."

For Essex, who had been in no hurry to shorten the process of re-conditioning his army at Warwick, had received an S.O.S. from Pym that not even he could ignore. The terror inspired by Rupert's visitations, and the knowledge that the road to London was now open to the King, had created a panic. Crowds of citizens, with women and children joining in, were working like beavers to fortify the approaches. For it was firmly believed, on the strength of Pym's propaganda, that "Prince Robber", once he got into the City, would give the whole place to the sack, in the heartiest German tradition.

It was essential for the rebel chiefs to slow down the King's advance until the field army could be brought back, and it was characteristic of Pym that he should have sought to entangle him in negotiations, thus achieving the double object of gaining vital time, and taking the edge off the agitation for peace by demonstrating Parliament's willingness for an accommodation. That the purged remnant that still called itself Parliament would have been allowed, or prepared, to offer any terms whatever short of the King's complete surrender and abandonment of his followers, there was from first to last not the faintest hint. In fact Pym himself, in a speech at the Guildhall, made it plain enough—though he camouflaged it with his usual ponderous rhetoric—that what he really understood by a reasonable peace treaty was one to be drafted by the rebels and presented to the King for his signature.

Moreover Pym and his confederates had just been up to their old trick of trying to persuade the Scots to invade England on their behalf ! Men who had thus piled treason on treason were not likely to consent to any settlement that would afford their Sovereign, who had already once striven to call them to a lawful account, the remotest hope of doing so in the future.

But it showed shrewd psychological insight to play up to the King's still passionate desire for peace. For as long as there appeared the least chance of an honourable settlement, he might safely be counted upon not to push his offensive with that ruthless expedition that alone would give him the remotest chance of success. Even the business of receiving their envoys, and drafting his replies, was hindering him from taking advantage of every hour of a mild spell of November weather to urge his columns

along the Bath Road in the final stages of their march Londonwards.

He wasted two days at Reading before deciding that one of the
Parliamentary commissioners, being a proclaimed traitor, could
not, in defiance of an express stipulation he had already made to
the contrary, be admitted to his presence. This though the rebels
had marked down all the most prominent of his own supporters
for their vengeance as delinquents, was received with a howl of
indignation as a breach of Parliamentary privilege. But the
negotiations went on, and a new deadlock was reached on the
conditions for the necessary armistice ; since the King had
suggested his being allowed to occupy his palace at Windsor, and
the rebels, who had just repulsed an attempt of Rupert to seize it
by a *coup de main*, were not unnaturally—from their point of
view—indisposed to let it go.

All this was the merest eyewash, for so long as Pym and Hampden remained in control, the farce of negotiation signified nothing
but an attempt to brake down the royal progress. And, whether
from sluggishness, indecision, or an invincible hope of avoiding
further bloodshed, what really mattered was that the King
arrived at what ought to have been the scene of decisive action
just about a week behind the time he might have taken if, after
disengaging himself at Edgehill, he had proceeded by forced
marches, with every available man, horse, and gun, by way of
Oxford on London. But it is easy for us, who know nothing of the
difficulty of his officers in reforming their regiments, or quarter-
masters in providing commissariat, to talk as if war were simply
a matter of shifting flags on a map. Let us put it that from one
cause or another the King, in the relevant modern phrase, had
missed his bus. Essex, taking a circuitous route through Bedford,
had turned up with enough of his Edgehill infantry to impart
just the stiffening that was wanted to old Skippon's unblooded
militia.

The little Royalist army, cutting the chord of the great loop
that the Thames makes to the South below Windsor, was thrust-
ing itself into a more and more perilous position with every mile
it advanced. It had a river line on its flank, with the crossings
held by the enemy, and an army with every advantage of numbers
and position forming on its front. Already Essex's staff were
urging him to thrust a strong force across the bridge at Kingston
to cut the Royalist communications, and though the thought

must have been profoundly disquieting to that sluggish intelligence, there was no saying how soon it might not sink or be driven in. No wonder that in such a position the Parliament leaders would have given anything to bamboozle the King into delaying his advance in hope of an armistice. For the powerful influence that was being exerted at headquarters to ginger up Essex into a pincer movement whose jaws should close behind the King, was—significantly enough—said to be that of Hampden.

But in that case Hampden had reckoned without Rupert. He, with the Royalist advance guard, came up on the 11th of November against the last of the minor river barriers in their path, that of the Brent at Brentford. This was occupied by one of the notorious Five Members, Denzil Holles, with his own regiment of redcoats, closely supported by Hampden's greens. The conditions, with an early morning fog lying over the little town, were ideal for a surprise, and Rupert was not the man to let slip such an opportunity. He had his work cut out, for the Redcoats rallied from the first shock and made a grand fight of it. But there arrived one of the King's regiments of Welshmen, who, probably from being armed with no more than knives and clubs, had done badly at Edgehill, and who now, having something more effective in their hands, went to it in a way that Welsh infantry have, and had soon cleared the whole place ! It was a brilliant and complete little victory, and the bitter complaints that went up about Rupert's unseasonable pugnacity are still echoed faintly from the pages of textbooks.

The King having come up with the main body, and the last physical obstacle on the road being surmounted, it now only remained to fight the decisive battle that should clear his path to Whitehall. "Prince Robber's" storm of Brentford had by this time thoroughly alarmed the City, and enabled the revolutionary chiefs to mobilize all its resources. The army of Essex barred the King's path at Turnham Green, and it was swollen by the whole force of the London trained bands, who were drawn up in serried columns, marshalled by Skippon, and armed with all the best weapons that the wealth of the capital could produce. In contrast to the King's hungry and footsore soldiers, they had their dinners brought out to them by their own families ; for the parade had something of the picnic atmosphere of a peace time review, with enormous crowds of sightseers, who tended to panic at any sign of a Royalist move.

The King's army was duly deployed in attacking formation, with Rupert's now almost legendary squadrons conspicuous on the flanks. The cannon were unlimbered, and the booming detonations caused anxious tremors in many a heart within sound of Bow Bells. The King, with Rupert and his staff, must have been plainly visible to the prentice lads who stood, grasping their pikes, waiting for the royal order for the assault to be delivered. But that order was never given. The same conviction was being forced on King Charles as on Queen Margaret before him, and Prince Charlie after him—that London was too formidable an obstacle to be assaulted with any hope of success. To have

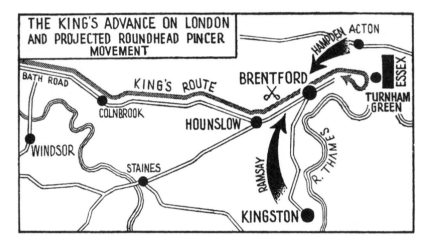

launched a frontal attack on that army in position, at odds of less than one against two, would have been suicidal. Even if, by some miracle, he had forced their lines, his situation, with London in front and fresh forces closing in behind him, would have been desperate. He looked at them all day, and then decided to recognize the inevitable, and retire into winter quarters round Oxford.

If Hampden had had his way, the King would not even have been able to do that without cutting his way out. But Mr Pym, at Westminster, must have heaved a great sigh of relief. He knew now—what he had probably felt all along—that with London in his grasp, he was unbeatable. How long it might take to win, and what might prove to be the ultimate price of victory, was another matter.

6

CAVALIER GRAND STRATEGY

Now that the King had missed his first spring at London, it was almost impossible to see how he could ever hope to get it ; for never again was he likely to have so favourable a chance as that which he had rightly judged desperate in the late Autumn of 1642. For abundant labour power was now available to construct the perimeter lines that would, with proportionate numbers to man them, turn London into an impregnable fortress. With the coming of spring, Puritan burgesses turned out in their thousands to throw up fieldworks and construct entrenchments ; infuriated, but undeterred, by the song that the supressed loyalist element could not be prevented from singing, of

"Cuckolds, go dig !"

But whether he could win or not, the King was far from beaten, and no man could say how long it would take to beat him. As month followed month, the prospect of a rebel victory waxed more remote. Not only was it revealed what strength of popular support the King had behind him, particularly in that most virile section of the country that was least affected by the new industrialization, but it also became apparent that for the time being, the rebel command had nothing in brains or energy to set against that which went to the planning of the Royalist strategy.

The first thing, of course, was for the Cavaliers, as it was for the Roundheads, to secure their main base of operations. Oxford was both in size and position hopelessly inferior to London, but there was nothing better available anywhere south of York, and the King's staff were resolved to make the most of it. They decided to make the clay plain of the Upper Thames basin into one fortified area, with the centre at Oxford and the circumference marked with a ring of strong, garrisoned points : Oxford, Banbury, Brill, Abingdon, Wallingford, and, as soon as they could be reduced, Marlborough and Cirencester, with access to the Lower Thames secured by the advanced post at Reading. The system was not perfect, for it ought to have included Aylesbury, the loss of which had created a dangerous dent in the most vulnerable sector.

Meanwhile no effort was spared to make Oxford itself

impregnable. The householders, the students, even the dons, had to turn out and put their backs, like those of the London citizens, into the work of constructing fortifications. And so well did they go about it, that there was soon no question of reducing it by anything but blockade. King Charles had secured the essential fixed point round, and from, which to manœuvre. He even did what he could in the way of improvising munitions works in the neighbourhood.

Upon this indispensable foundation he had to base his plan of offensive strategy. For, no doubt owing to the dynamic force of Rupert's personality, the Cavalier commanders had grasped that it was their cue to force the pace from the start with uncompromising energy. Every month that passed without a decision was tilting the already crushing balance of material advantage still more in favour of the side that, whether or not it was right in annexing God to its support, had certainly the overwhelming preponderance behind it of the power of Mammon. Valour and loyalty may perhaps snatch a quick win in defiance of material odds, but in a war of attrition the material pull of one side, continually increasing, will become in time so nearly irresistible as to put even the chance of a miracle out of practical consideration.

Clubs then, not spades, having been declared trumps, the King and Rupert were well advised to go out for a quick decision, regardless of odds. And a decision meant one of two things. Either the King's forces would master such a large area of the country and achieve such striking success in the field, as would enable the perhaps numerical majority of Englishmen behind the rebel lines, who favoured a constitutional settlement on the basis of the existing law, to make their influence prevail. Failing that, the only hope for the King—who desired nothing more and would stoop to nothing less—was to force the conclusion of such a peace by an all out military victory. And that, translated into practical terms, could mean only one thing : the capture or surrender of London.

Now to bank on the hope of a compromise peace, tempting though it might seem, was to pursue a will-o'-the-wisp. For the will to compromise had to be not only bilateral but present in those highest quarters from which will is translated into action.

But nothing can be more certain than that so long as the men who had engineered the rebellion remained in the saddle, there could be no peace on any terms that stopped short of the full revolutionary programme, accurately defined by Denzil Holles as being,

"To destroy and cut off not a few ... to ruin the King ... alter the government, and have no order in the government nor power in the state over them,"

in other words, for the King to surrender unconditionally into the hands of "Parliament"—which is to say, their own—the whole effective sovereignty of the realm.

And these men, having once got the controls into their hands, were able to maintain them against the supporters of any peace movement, as easily as we have seen the Dictators of our own age doing so before their military overthrow.

Whether he liked it or not then, the King's whole strategy had to be concentrated on the one end of bringing about the fall of London at the earliest possible moment. Even if there should be only one chance in a million of doing this, his only sane alternative to throwing up the sponge would be to stake everything on it.

Granted that, the plan he adopted dictated itself. From his main base at Oxford, he calculated on operating with a field army sufficiently powerful to keep that of Essex fully occupied until the time came for approaching London by way of the Thames Valley. For the support of this Oxford army he sought to muster and draw upon the West (exclusive of the South-West) of England, and most of all his infantry recruiting ground of Wales. He also proposed to form two other armies operating from widely divergent flanking areas. One of these, commanded by Sir Ralph Hopton, was to be formed in Cornwall and, if all went well, might be expanded into an army of the South-West. The other, based upon York and under the command of the Earl of New-castle, was to be recruited from Northumbria, and especially from Yorkshire, which its first task would be to bring under control.

Having established these three armies, it was the King's object, by a grand converging movement on exterior lines—that is to say from points on a circumference towards a common centre—to bring them to bear on London. It is not known, and perhaps had not even been decided, whether they were to unite, in the first place, in some area of concentration in the neighbourhood of Oxford, or whether the idea was for the King to advance on London by his original route along the Thames valley, while

Hopton swept up through Kent to seize the South bank below
London, and Newcastle, coming down from the North, appeared
on the opposite bank to join hands with him, and all three
united to form a siege and blockade of the capital.

It was a grandiose scheme, but, given certain conditions, it
might not have been altogether hopeless. Such highly trained and
disciplined professional armies as actually existed in Germany,
and as the New Model in England eventually became—armies
that could be relied on to go anywhere and do anything, under

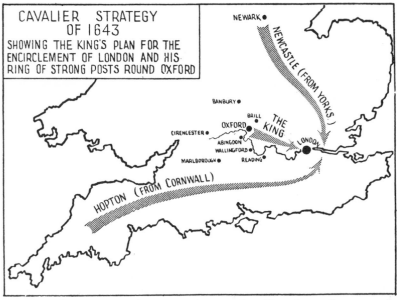

CAVALIER STRATEGY
OF 1643
SHOWING THE KING'S PLAN FOR THE
ENCIRCLEMENT OF LONDON AND HIS
RING OF STRONG POSTS ROUND OXFORD

commanders accurately responsive to the directives of a central
command—might conceivably have been combined in this way.
Even so, a scheme that required so many conditions for its
fulfilment, was lacking in that large simplicity that characterizes
the strategy of the great masters.

But the Royalist armies, being improvised and amateur, could
not be relied on to go anywhere or do anything they did not
want to ; and even their commanders were only too frequently
possessed of wills of their own which they were by no means
prepared to subordinate to that even of the King himself. And
they were not only amateur, but local armies, any one of which
might be prepared to fight it out to the death in its own district,
but saw no necessity for leaving it ; particularly when this

involved leaving behind such unreduced strong points of the enemy as Hull in the North and Plymouth in the West, with garrisons capable of sallying forth and harrying the countryside in the absence of its fighting manhood.

If only the King could have succeeded in forging his three armies into disciplined and manœuvrable units, or of combining them into one body sufficiently strong in numbers and equipment to have undertaken, with any chance of success, the reduction of London, then—and then only—would he have had a chance of achieving peace on the basis of the constitutional *status quo*. But neither on the material nor the ideological side, were the means at his disposal for conditioning men to fight like devils and work like machines ; men who—as Cromwell expressed it—made some conscience of what they did.

It is merely otiose to blame it on to the King that he did not make a New Model out of his own army, or Rupert, that he did not succeed in training his cavalry to manœuvre like Ironsides. Nor do I think that Charles, even if it had been open to him, would have been prepared to purchase military victory on terms that—at least to his way of thinking—would have involved the sacrifice of his own soul and the soul of his people.

"All these things will I give thee if thou wilt fall down and worship me." It was the way of King Charles to test the spirit whether it was of God, and not to seek the Lord night and day until he had yoked his conscience to his interests. He had precedent for his answer and a straight course to hold, for which, even if it should prove to be the way of martyrdom, there was likewise precedent.

But Colonel Cromwell, who had the Lord in his pocket, and Mr Pym, who kept Him up his sleeve, might view the matter from a less Quixotic standpoint.

7

"YOUR SHE MAJESTY GENERALISSIMA"

WHATEVER might lie in the future, during the opening months of 1643 there was no sign of the Roundhead armies finding either the means or the spirit to get the whiphand over those of the King. Almost everywhere the Cavalier cause was in the ascendant, and there was a dash and decision about the operations of the King's forces of which there was little enough sign among those of his enemies.

The fact is that the inner ring of the Parliamentary bosses, who had once formed the directorate of the Providence Island Bubble, though they would have had nothing to learn from Machiavelli himself in the arts of political intrigue, had no more talent for military than they had evinced for colonial enterprise. The only one of them who gave the least sign of it was Hampden, to the extent that he possessed the instinct of going all out to win, though without the technical knowledge of how to go about it. Pym was indeed a tower of political strength ; but he understood more about the raising of mobs than the conduct of armies. And meanwhile the command of the main Roundhead army remained in the inert hands of Essex.

On both the extreme flanks of the King's far-flung grouping for the envelopment of London, things were starting brilliantly. In Cornwall, the overwhelmingly loyalist sentiment of the people had found leadership in Sir Ralph Hopton, a cavalier gentleman of the finest type, and Sir Bevil Grenville, the worthy scion of a famous fighting stock. In Yorkshire, the Earl of Newcastle had made himself master of the greater part of the area, though the clothing towns of the West Riding and, worse still, the port of Hull, remained unreducible. The fortified zone round Oxford was being consolidated without interference from Essex, while Rupert, darting hither and thither with incredible rapidity, was instilling the fear of his cavalry far and wide into the forces of the rebellion.

"It is," complained some indignant Parliamentarian during that winter, "summer in Yorkshire, summer in Devon, and cold winter at [Essex's headquarters] Windsor."

Meanwhile, the Queen, having spent a year strenuously collecting weapons and money in Holland, judged that the time had come for her to rejoin her husband. It was a bold decision, since the long threatened impeachment had now at last begun to materialize ; which meant that if she got into the clutches of Pym, she would either be butchered outright, or her life would be made the price of the King's surrender. But Henriette was as fearless as her father, and the peril of death only had on her the effect of a stimulus. Of this she was soon to give proof. For putting forth on the North Sea in early February, she ran into one of the worst winter gales, which wrecked two of the ships of her little fleet, and it was only after nine days tossing off a lee shore that her own flagship succeeded in getting back into a Dutch port. The crew had almost, and her ladies quite, given up hope ; but the one person on the ship who was gaily unperturbed was this heroic little lady, who had hitherto been accustomed to all the luxuries of court life, but who now was tied into her bunk in conditions of almost unimaginable discomfort, since all the filth in the ship was washed about the cabins, so that when she landed she was said to be almost unapproachable owing to the stink of her garments. But she succeeded not only in enduring, but thoroughly enjoying the experience, and was in fits of laughter when she heard her ladies bawling out the dying confession of their most intimate sins into the ears of Capuchin Fathers as seasick as themselves. She bade them cheer up—Queens of England, she assured them, never get drowned !

One would have thought that after this, it would have been a long time before she wanted to quit *terra firma ;* but in nine days she was at sea again with her fleet and its precious cargo, and this time she succeeded in making the indifferent harbour of Brid-lington, by Flamborough Head, and had barely landed when a rebel squadron, that had just failed to intercept her, stood in close to the shore with the high tide, and sent shell after shell crashing into the houses of the little port. The Queen and her ladies were forced to turn out of their beds and get such shelter as they could in a ditch ; but then Henriette remembered that she had left an old, ugly lapdog, of which she happened to be particularly fond, in her bed. Nothing would stop her from leaving her shelter, and going back, through the hottest fire, to rescue this Mitte of hers. Even when she got back, one near miss of her shelter sent the earth all over her !

"I never till now, dear Heart," wrote the King, on hearing of her arrival, "knew the good of ignorance, for I did not know the danger that thou wert in ... for indeed I think it not the least of my misfortunes, that for my sake thou hast run so much hazard, in the which thou hast expressed so much love to me, that I confess it is impossible to repay by anything I can do, much less by words ; but my heart being full of affection for thee, admiration of thee, and impatient passion of gratitude to thee, I could not but say something, leaving the rest to be read by thee out of thine own noble heart."

Noble indeed ! if we may believe the story that is told of her, that she actually rescued from the gallows one of the commanders of the Roundhead ships, who had fallen into the Cavalier hands, and been awarded the rope by court-martial, for having deliberately trained his cannon on Her Majesty.

"I have forgiven him," she said, "and as he did not kill me, he shall not be put to death on my account."

Is it any wonder that the grateful seaman became there and then one of the King's most loyal supporters, and persuaded a number of his shipmates to follow his example !

The Queen now put herself at the head of a substantial force of Cavaliers that Newcastle had dispatched to act as her escort on the dangerous journey to York. As confidently as if she had been Rupert himself, she assumed the command of her little army ; she rode at its head in all weathers, took her meals among her men without the least ceremony, and talked like a comrade with all of them. She had the satisfaction, as they struck across the Yorkshire wolds, of actually capturing a town, Malton, in which she took good care to leave a garrison. So it was in the highest spirits that "your She Majesty Generalissima", as she described herself to Charles, arrived at York with her invaluable reinforcement of money and munitions for the royal cause ; though it would be some months before it would be practicable for her to march right across England for the eagerly awaited reunion with her husband.

She was only thirty-three !

8

A RAID AND ITS SEQUEL

ALL through the first half of 1643, amid the indescribable complications and vicissitudes of what was less one war than a hundred local wars all over the country, the balance of advantage continued to incline in the King's favour. The spirit of Rupert seemed to have infected the whole of the Cavalier operations ; leaders like Hopton, Grenville and Byron displayed—if one may coin a phrase—a top-doggedness to which there was as yet nothing visibly corresponding on the other side, where the leaden example of Essex lay heavy on the souls of the other army commanders, with the possible exception of Sir William Waller, the sound but pedestrian head of what we might call the Roundhead Army of Wessex. The political magnate whom some people had thought of as a possible successor to Essex, that same Lord Brooke who had characterized the people as dung, had had his account settled by one of them, a poor deaf and dumb fellow who served a cannon on a tower of Lichfield Cathedral, which, during a temporary occupation, the Puritans had desecrated by sacrilege abominable, even for them !

Nobody, as yet, among the innumerable cavalry skirmishes that were being fought all over the country, saw any special significance in one on the rolling country near Grantham, where Colonel Cromwell, commanding no longer a troop, but a regiment of his own training, reversed the usual procedure by accounting very neatly and completely for a body of Cavalier horse.

In the West, Hopton with his Cornishmen had easily mopped up every rebel force as far as the Tamar, but then the hopeless difficulty had commenced of getting these local patriots to follow him beyond their own borders, and the King's cause had had to mark time for half a year until a small but mobile field force could be organized, that started operations by an amazing victory in which, without even artillery, it attacked in position, and wiped out, the main Roundhead army in the South-West, commanded by another of the Parliamentary bosses, Lord Stamford. Sweeping on through Devon and Somerset, gathering support as it went, and strengthened by Cavalier reinforcements from Oxford, it came up against the formidable opposition of Waller, who awaited it on those heights above Bath which some have thought to have been the scene of the last great victory, and death, of King Arthur. Nothing daunted, the Cornishmen proceeded to storm the hill, and by the time that Waller had retired grimly before them into the town below, the best part of the victorious army, including the gallant Sir Bevil, was, like that of Arthur, "dead upon the down". And soon Hopton, with his depleted numbers, and himself confined to his bed by the blowing up of a wagon containing his last ammunition, was standing siege by Waller in the town of Devizes, while Prince Maurice, Rupert's brother, rode post haste with the cavalry to Oxford to fetch relief.

Meanwhile in the North, though with many vicissitudes, the King's cause had been steadily gaining momentum. Here the commander was the Earl of Newcastle, who, to a superficial judgment, might have seemed to embody the quintessence of chivalrous nobility. A cultured and magnificent *grand seigneur*, of unquestioned physical courage and personal honour, he had, from the first, put his services and vast wealth at His Majesty's disposal. And as long as things continued to go well with him his operations in the field were marked by a stately competence. But there was something wrong about Newcastle's leadership that only came out when—as always happens sooner or later in war— things ceased to go smoothly to plan. To put it bluntly, Newcastle might have qualified for an epithet coined by the famous General Tucker of "a satin-bottomed ✶✶✶✶✶✶." He was a fair-weather commander without guts. And what was worst of all, there was reason to suspect him of being so fond of the authority and prestige that he enjoyed in the North, where he reigned like a little King, that he was by no means in a hurry to co-operate with the Oxford command's grand strategy, and march South to play a subordinate part in an arduous combined operation. And thus, though Newcastle did at last succeed in mastering the opposition of the West Riding clothing towns, and scoring a smashing victory over Sir Thomas Fairfax—who was more and more coming to be recognized as the fighting hope of the Northern rebels—at Adwalton Moor, and though Byron, at Chester, was strong enough to secure his flank on that side, Newcastle never did show the least serious inclination to get a move on London- wards, or to take advantage of the invaluable advanced base that secured the passage of the Trent at Newark.

There was always Hull, of course … and even if there had not been, there is seldom wanting an excuse, to those who seek it, for putting off decisive action.

In the main theatre, it was April before Essex was at last induced to bestir himself, to the extent of moving forward against the dangerously isolated Cavalier outpost of Reading. This was induced to capitulate with such suspicious facility that the commander, Colonel Fielding, was actually court-martialled and sentenced to death, and the King, who had been horrified that some of his loyal subjects who had deserted the rebels had been handed back, under the articles, to their vengeance, was determined to have the sentence executed. But the boy who was one day to become Charles II, and who even in those early days was on the side of leniency, contrived, at the instigation of his

Cousin Rupert, to soften his father's heart to the extent of sparing the Colonel's life—though not of restoring him to his command. There was a sort of baseness for which Charles had no tolerance.

Hampden would have had Essex follow up this success by an offensive against Oxford, but so bold a move was far beyond the scope of that commander, who now shifted his weight to the right and sought to infiltrate from his base at Aylesbury into the rich country north of the Chilterns, chiefly for the purpose of exploiting it as a recruiting ground. And in this Hampden himself, with the influence secured by his vast possessions, would be well-fitted to co-operate.

But so leisurely and diffuse an operation was foolhardy to undertake in the neighbourhood of Rupert. And perhaps there were some who were not altogether surprised when on an afternoon in mid-June, the loyal folk of Oxford were treated to the spectacle of a long column of Cavalier horsemen, jingling and clattering over Magdalen Bridge, followed by a picked detachment of light infantry—perhaps the only serious face among them all being that of the Prince himself, riding at the head of his blue lifeguards, his dark brows bent in pondering the business on which he was engaged. Plainly something quite out of the ordinary was in contemplation.

The ostensible objective was, in fact, a rich convoy, reported by spies to be coming up through the Chilterns by way of Wycombe to Chinnor, bringing arrears of pay to Essex's almost mutinous troops. But that, I think, was only an excuse. Rupert could hardly have counted on warning of his coming failing to outstrip it ; and even if he had surprised the convoy, it is most improbable that he could have brought it back to Oxford. But he could count on penetrating deeply behind the enemy's lines, creating all the mischief and dislocation possible, and getting away before any considerable force could be concentrated to deal with him.

Which is just what he did. Marching and riding all night by a circuitous route, his little force completely wiped out, at dawn, the unsuspecting garrison of Chinnor. But reconnaisance along the road through the hills to the South revealed no sign of the waggons which, if they had got past Wycombe at all, had presumably taken advantage of any by-lanes available, to find cover in the bosky beech woods. Rupert had no time to play hide and seek. The hue and cry was up, and if he was to make good his retreat, there was not a moment to waste.

The vital point to reach was the bridge over the Thame at Chiselhampton, and it was in the open cornfields, a few miles short of this that, having sent his infantry ahead to secure it, he turned to deal with the bodies of Roundhead horse that were now swarming round him like disturbed bees. He could have desired nothing better than this opportunity of catching them in the open, and giving them a lesson they would remember. "This insolency," he cried, "is not to be borne !" and started the proceedings in characteristic style by jumping his charger clean over a hedge into the middle of them.

What he did not know was that he had in front of him no less an opponent than Hampden himself, who had been pursuing his recruiting activities in the neighbourhood, and had pluckily enough attached himself as a volunteer to the first detachment he came across. The Cavaliers did not fail to note, afterwards, that this was the very place where Hampden had first committed open treason by raising troops against his Sovereign.

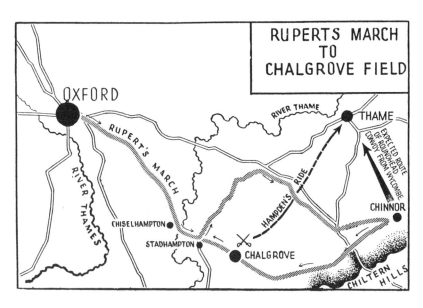

The rebels put up a stiff resistance, but they were no match for Rupert, and it was not long before their commander, Colonel Gunter, was dead, and the survivors in flight, Hampden among the first of them, bowed over his horse's neck with a pistol ball in

OLIVER CROMWELL—from a painting by
Robert Walker

PRINCE RUPERT—from a miniature by
John Hoskins

JOHN HAMPDEN: (inset) HAMPDEN BEING CARRIED, MORTALLY WOUNDED,
FROM CHALGROVE FIELD

his shoulder.* Rupert quickly reformed his squadrons—which shows what progress he had made in training them since Edgehill —and after bivouacking on the home side of the bridge, made his leisurely way, on the morrow, back to Oxford, with a few score of prisoners and the loss of no more than a dozen men, having given a classic example of the successful use, by a cavalry commander, of a mixed force.

How successful he did not, as yet, realize ! He had no idea of the arch rebel being accounted for. Hampden, who was cut off from access to the nearest of his many mansions, rode painfully North, some six or seven miles across country to Thame, where according to tradition he found a bed in the Greyhound Inn. With modern surgery, and taken in time, it is unlikely that his wound would have been more than a temporary inconvenience ; but during the ride, or in the process of extracting the bullet, the germs of mortification, or perhaps of tetanus, had had time to get planted. The medical opinion of his own time laid much stress on the supposed acrimonious condition of his blood, due to an unpleasant skin disease that disfigured his countenance with scurf. But I hardly think a modern doctor would regard this as relevant to the diagnosis.

Hampden died of his wound, and that is all we can really say about it. Though Macaulay in a famous essay, that has literally made history, has recorded how the dying patriot, with his intellect unclouded, lay, murmuring faint prayers :

" 'O Lord, save my country. O Lord, be merciful to————'
In that broken ejaculation passed away his noble and fearless spirit."

The great Whig historian, who seems to have experienced no surprise at the extraordinary prescience of Mr Hampden's deathbed plagiarization from Mr Pitt, had copied this from what purported to be "A true and faithful Narrative of the Death of Mr John Hampden," that had appeared for the first time in the *Gentleman's Magazine* sixteen years before, and "though accepted as genuine by Hampden's biographers, is" as Sir Charles Firth in *The Dictionary of National Biography* is unkind enough to record, "an impudent forgery ... containing many words and expressions not in use in the seventeenth century," but good enough for

* Or else his own pistol had burst. His pious biographer, Lord Nugent, went to the length of digging him up to settle the point, which he subsequently dropped, when it transpired that the body he had resurrected had not been Hampden's at all.

Macaulay,* whose gift of John Hampden to the nation was, and is, felt to be too precious an asset for merely factual scrutiny.

When the King heard of Hampden's wound, he laid aside all personal animosity against this most malignant of his enemies, the envenomed saboteur of every overture he had made for peace ; and, in what most people would call the spirit of a great, Christian gentleman, he sent Dr Gyles, rector of Chinnor, and a personal friend of the patient, to enquire after him, and to offer him the services of any of the royal surgeons ; and this is how Hampden's latest biographer records the incident :

"He [Dr Gyles] had been sent by the King to enquire whether Hampden was dead."†

About what other character in history than King Charles, or in mythology than Hampden, could even the most up-to-date biographer hope to get away with such a sentence ?

It would seem that such details as could be spared of Colonel Hampden's command were told off to attend at his funeral, and these men are actually said to have taken part in the singing of the 90th Psalm. This event, that really may—and, one would think, must—have occurred, is, in all orthodox biographies of Hampden, made the theme of such reverential eloquence that I should deem myself lacking in respect were I to pass it by in silence.

9

CAVALIER ZENITH

It was in the midsummer of 1643 that the King's fortunes, in the Civil War, were at their zenith. The elimination of Hampden had, in itself, counted for more than the capture of many convoys, and for the time being the terror of Rupert's cavalry had stricken Essex with paralysis. The Cavaliers now felt themselves capable of taking any liberties whatever, and only a few days after the great

---

* Good enough still for that indomitable Hampden worshipper, Mr John Drinkwater, who though he admits Firth's objections on the score of diction and orthography to be "on the whole" convincing, hopefully suggests that "the narrative, although it was doubtless put on paper at some later date, may still have been arranged from contemporary notes in the writer's family" (*John Hampden's England*, pp. 294-5). At this rate there ought to be no difficulty in proving that anybody at any time wrote anything that ever ought to have been written.

† *John Hampden*, by Hugh Ross Williamson, p. 329.

raid, Colonel Urry went one better than the Prince by riding through the Chilterns and mopping up Wycombe itself, and not even a scathing letter that Pym caused to be sent in the name of Parliament to Essex had any effect except that of getting him to offer to resign his command, which—as there seemed to be no possible successor—he had to be pressed to retain.

As far away as Berkhamsted the terror of these raids extended, if we can trust to local legend; for it is said that one of the Roundhead soldiers had offered to guide the Cavaliers through the surrounding woods to surprise the rebel cantonments in the valley; and being detected just in time, had been hanged in the gloomy hollow that is to this day known as Soldier's Bottom. It seemed as if Essex's army would soon consist of no more than a few scattered and demoralized bodies of men, incapable of combining for any military purpose.

One result of this paralysis of the Roundhead main army was that it was now open to the Queen to undertake the perilous journey to Oxford, bringing with her a second convoy of munitions (the first she had successfully dispatched after her arrival at York), and a small army commanded, under herself, by the faithful Sir Henry—soon to be made Lord Jermyn. She knew by this time what she had to expect were she to fall into the enemy's hands, for she was now being formally impeached, by the traitors in London, as a traitress. Though before proceeding to this step, Pym, along with Hampden, Saye, and one or two others of their confederates, had had the almost incredible effrontery to make a secret approach to her, in order to persuade or intimidate her into procuring her husband's surrender. This is a little too much to stomach even for Gardiner, who, for once forgetting his brief for the Patriots and his bitter prejudice against the Queen, is moved to comment, almost adequately:

"If Pym expected to obtain Henrietta Maria's consent to a treaty on his own terms, or to delude her into the belief that Essex could march against Oxford if he wished, he little knew the woman with whom he was dealing."*

He had, however, not taken long in realizing that she was only concerned to hold him in play, while she pushed on more vigorously than ever with her preparations to join the King. But though her person would have been a winning counter in the game—one that Pym would have known only too well how to

* *History of the Great Civil War,* I, p. 133.

play—Essex, no longer with Hampden to ginger him up, made not the faintest effort to secure it. The Queen, proceeding from one loyal garrison to another, was safely contacted by the inevitable Rupert with an escort from Oxford, and effected the joyous, and last, reunion with her husband, who, accompanied by her two eldest boys, met her on the battlefield of Edgehill—and we can imagine with what zest the lads must have pointed out to her where their father had fought and Verney fallen in that famous fight.

Her arrival in triumph at Oxford was greeted by a royal demonstration, Great Tom leading a delirious carillon from all the spires and towers, with town and gown and court all shouting and waving together to welcome the little Generalissima of the flashing eyes. One eloquent, but most inopportune effect of that reunion, was the announcement, in due course, of her ninth pregnancy.

Meanwhile the men who had so vainly spread a net in her sight, not being able to gratify their spite on her person, relieved their feelings as best they could by wrecking her chapel and persecuting her Capuchin Fathers.

She had brought luck with her ; for glorious news came to Oxford swift in the wake of her arrival. The indomitable Hopton, shut up in Devizes and conducting the defence from his sick bed, had come to the end of his ammunition, and Waller had fixed the 13th of July for the final assault. But gallant young Maurice, who had ridden off for help to Oxford, had not failed his tryst ; the assault on that day was delivered by the Cavalier horse, thundering at the charge over the springy turf of Roundway Down, with Hopton's Cornishmen joining in with a will from below ; and by the nightfall little more was left of Waller's army than Waller himself, who effected a timely and solitary getaway, to be received in London—thanks to Pym's excellent propaganda service— with triumphant honours.

But this was not the last, nor the best of it ; for Rupert, always hot foot to exploit a success, followed up his brother's annihilation of the rebel army in the South West by going straight for Bristol, the second city in the Kingdom. He had been repulsed in a previous attempt, but he knew what the prestige of success can do, and he also knew that the man in command was Nathaniel Fiennes—one of the Broughton Castle gang—the same who had tried to seduce Hyde into treason in that ride over the Chelsea meadows. Nathaniel was better at plotting than fighting, and the piercing of his outer defences at the first assault was followed by his ignominious capitulation. He was, of course, brought before a Roundhead court martial, which sentenced him to death ; but as it would obviously never have done to shoot a Fiennes, he was allowed to disappear, with a pardon, till the scandal had blown over.

This splendid capture on the 26th of July was the greatest thing yet that had happened for the King, and it must have seemed to the Cavaliers that their cause was on top in all theatres of the war, and that now was the time to clinch the business by that grand converging march on London to which it was all supposed to be leading up. But there was no sign anywhere of it getting started. Even Hopton's victorious levies were obsessed with the existence of an unreduced Plymouth in their rear, and though Newcastle, if he had been a commander of a different stamp, might possibly have contrived to contain or ignore Hull, he showed not the least inclination to do so. The King had indeed only just missed getting this all-important base delivered over to him by that interesting couple, the Hothams, who after some anxious wobbling, had decided to double-cross their associates in treason but were laid by the heels just in time, and a very different father and son installed in the shape of the Fairfaxes. Thus the whole Royalist plan was held up for the interminable process of reducing two fortresses that could neither be stormed nor blockaded.

And this month of July, so glorious for the Cavaliers, had not passed before an incident had occurred, whose significance, if they could only have appreciated it, was of fatal import to them. Newcastle had at least done his best to prepare for the eventual advance Londonwards by operations in Lincolnshire, and his field army had been trying to secure another crossing of the Trent, besides Newark, at Gainsborough. But this county, so ominously placed on the flank of any advance Londonwards, had been the scene of exceedingly active operations by the forces of the Eastern (or, as we should say, East Anglian) Association, one of a number of county groupings by means of which it had been proposed at once to propagate and decentralize the revolutionary cause. And East Anglia, being not only the home of a wealthy cloth manufacture but also, perhaps on account of its Dutch connections, a hotbed of Puritanism, was coming to acquire a military importance hardly second to that of London itself—and most of all, as a recruiting ground for that well paid and godly disciplined force of cavalry which, as the Lord had revealed to His servant Oliver, would be the decisive factor of the war.

This force, still no more than a strong regiment, was the spearhead of one detailed to relieve Gainsborough ; and it had come up against the best of Newcastle's cavalry, under an extraordinarily handsome and promising young leader, a cousin of his, Charles Cavendish. In the action that followed, Cromwell, starting with the disadvantage of ground, had given a consummate exposition of the new technique, which might be described not so much of shock as of push tactics. In close formation, he had pressed back his opponents from the first clinch till they had lost cohesion and dissolved, and he had held back enough of his own force from the pursuit to account for their reserves—young Cavendish himself was forced into a bog and killed, and his command scattered to the winds. It had been a neat and complete success at the expense of the hitherto dominant Royalist cavalry arm, and it was immediately followed by another that was an even more exacting test, for when the relief force unexpectedly found that it had run into Newcastle's main army, Cromwell, with his tired horses and troopers, succeeded in covering its retreat by a series of calculated withdrawals, and without the loss of a man.

But perhaps even Cromwell did not yet realize that this minor and not even victorious operation signified the appearance on the scene of a force that, rightly applied, would prove unbeatable.

And if to the possession of the insuperable obstacle in London, the revolution were now to add that of the irresistible force— what hope could there be for the King ?

10

"GIVE US THAT DOG PYM !"

WHATEVER spirit might be stirring among the dour Puritans of East Anglia, in London itself, which had hitherto been the focus of the rebellion, the King's victories had had a profoundly depressing effect. Probably only a minority of extremists had ever wished it to come to war against the King ; and now that there appeared to be no chance of a speedy decision, the desire for peace became passionate. There had been negotiations at Oxford in the early part of the year, but these had never stood the faintest chance of success, as Pym and his associates would never have dreamed of offering the King any terms short of complete surrender, while the King was quietly determined to take his stand on the law and Constitution, and had not the least intention of conceding anything to revolutionary violence. That was the attitude that he would maintain even when he was a helpless captive ; and now that his armies in the field were everywhere in the ascendant, he was even less likely to modify it.

It was an attitude whose reasonableness could not fail to impress moderate men, and indeed there had been growing up a peace party even in the purged and dragooned remnant of the Perpetual Parliament. There had already been one dangerous conspiracy in which the poet M.P., Edmund Waller, had been involved, to rid the capital of the tyranny of the war-mongering bosses, which was discovered and suppressed only just in time. Perhaps the elimination of Hampden, the most bitterly intransigent of them all, had now given the voice of reason a chance to assert itself in despite even of Pym. It was believed that Essex, though as a soldier he considered himself bound to render unconditional obedience to the cause he had embraced, would gladly have seen the termination of hostilities on such terms as both parties might have been prepared, without loss of principle, to concede. And we may be sure that such passionate pacifists as Falkland, and loyal Parliament men as Hyde, would have come more than half way, from the King's side, to meet any genuine overture, though it was the frank opinion of the Queen that so long as the Perpetual Parliament succeeded in perpetuating itself, any overtures whatever from its chiefs would be a treacherous farce. And it is by no means certain that she was not right.

So far from Pym having the least idea of exploring the possibilities of a settlement, his energies were now diverted from the struggle with the King to an even more desperate endeavour to crush, with all necessary violence, the longing, among the people he was supposed to represent, to come to such terms with their Sovereign as would at least put an end to this nightmare and blood-bath of civil war, and—even if there was no chance of a return to the prosperous times of the "tyranny"—enable the government of the country to be carried on without the ferocious

exactions of Pym's tax-sweaters, or the activities of his impress-
ment agents, or the ever-mounting toll of youthful lives. Pym
himself was by this time a sick man ; the cells in the lower part of
his abdomen had started to proliferate with mortal virulence ; not
a day can have passed without gnawing discomfort in his huge
frame—but his will power was as inflexible and his brain as
unclouded as ever. And perhaps the feeling that his time might
be short may have spurred him to even grimmer exertions to
ensure the victory in this great game, that had become for him the
whole of what was left of life.

Did he realize, now, that anything short of a speedy victory
over the King would be worse than none for the faction that he
represented ? That the spirits he had raised for the limited
purpose of putting the controls of state at the disposal of a ring of
rich men, it would soon be impossible to lay ? That instead of
Parliament controlling the "militia", the "militia" might come to
control not only Parliament, but the rich men themselves, and the
whole country with them ?

We can only guess at his thoughts ; his actions were those of
the intransigent extremist he had been all along, who is determined
to force the pace at all costs, because he knows that his time is
short.

His powers were soon put to a stern test. At the beginning of
August the desire for peace had become so urgent that even the
picked puppets who usurped the name of Parliament—though
the King had ceased to recognize them as such—could no longer
be withheld from yielding to the general desire. The Lords
sanctioned a series of propositions to be presented to the King,
the effect of which would have been to restore the *status quo ante
bellum*, to have brought back to Parliament those members who
had fled or been expelled for their loyalty to the King, to have
disbanded the armies, and to have allowed a general amnesty for
all political offences on either side since January 1642. And this
simple and common-sense way of securing peace with honour
was not only approved by the Lords, but—what was far more
remarkable—the Commons voted by the surprisingly large
majority of 29 for taking it into consideration.

Passionate indeed must have been the desire for peace to
cause even this dragooned and disciplined herd to assert a will
counter to that of its masters. But Pym was not the man to stand
for nonsense of that kind, and he and his fellow extremists were

SIR JACOB ASTLEY

KING CHARLES I ON HORSEBACK—from a Van Dyck sketch

determined to go to all lengths to avoid a consummation which, whatever relief it might have brought to the country, would have involved the frustration of all their designs and—as they certainly imagined—have endangered their own necks. Pym had hurried, therefore, at the head of a Parliamentary committee, to Essex's headquarters, and having made sure that no interference was to be apprehended from him, proceeded to put in motion all his now familiar technique of intimidation. Within a few hours of the Commons passing their pacific vote, a meeting had been called in the city presided over by a certain Isaac Pennington, who had been illegally jockeyed into the office of Lord Mayor on the expulsion of the loyal Gurney ; and at this it was resolved to proceed to open violence against the peace party, and if necessary to arrest its leaders in both Houses. On the next day, being Sunday, a great company of preachers was working at full blast in their several conventicles, to generate in the name of its Prince a hatred of peace and all its advocates ; placards were everywhere posted up inciting the mob to proceed to Westminster on the morrow and terrorize Parliament ; a lying report was carefully disseminated that 20,000 Irish Catholics (the successors of Pym's equally mythical French army) were about to invade England. As a result of these efforts, a sufficient number of rowdies was induced, on the morrow, to throng the approaches to Parliament, howling accusations of treason at its unhappy Members, and converting the Commons' majority for peace into one of 7 for rejecting all terms.

But the day after, a very different sort of crowd made its appearance—one of women, driven desperate at seeing the cup of peace thus dashed from their lips. "Peace, peace !" they cried, "give us these traitors against peace ! Give us that dog Pym !" This was not the sort of mob that Pym was wont to encourage for fear of disheartening the people. The soldiers on duty were soon firing their muskets, at first with blank—some attempt, it was alleged, having been made by the women to pelt them. Reinforcements were hastily sent for, and some cavalry, survivors of the recently returned Waller's command, arrived on the scene. This was an enemy easier to tackle than Prince Maurice, and Roundway Down was soon gloriously avenged.

"The remedy", says the Parliamentary diarist, Sir Simonds D'Ewes, "used ... by the procurement of John Pym and some others, who were enemies to all kinds of peace, was most cruel and barbarious ; for not content to have them suppressed by the ordinary foot guard, which would have been sufficient, there were divers horsemen called down, who hunted the said women up and down the back Palace Yard, and wounded them with their swords and pistols with no less inhumanity than if they had been brute beasts, of which wounds some of the poor women afterwards died."

One innocent maidservant passing by was shot dead by a trooper who, it was said, had a spite against her father, but though the man was known, no redress could ever be got against him.

King Pym had his own totally democratic way of dealing with pacifists, and no one could deny its effectiveness. But such was not—even by the allegation of his worst enemies—the way of King Charles.

I I

THE CAMPAIGN OF NEWBURY

A TICKLISH problem was now presented to the Cavalier staff. The two pincer claws of the decisive movement on London were clutching ineffectively at Plymouth and Hull, and pending the fall of these places, could be counted immovable. But the main Oxford army, with its brilliant record of success behind it, and its whip hand of Essex's spiritless and crumbling forces—what was that to do ? There was one person who had no doubt, and that was the "She-Generalissima", whose fighting spirit had no patience with the endless delays and half measures that must inevitably result when a multitude of civilian and military counsellors, some of them playing for their own hands, some with only half a heart in the business, some verging on senile decay, and all claiming to have a finger in the pie, were intriguing and disputing against each other. All her love for her husband could not prevent Henriette from sometimes being driven nearly to distraction by that invincible patience and gentleness with which he persisted in weighing every man's opinion, instead of asserting his own in the way that her father would have known how to do.

In this case she at least had no doubt of what was called for. London was the objective—to win that would be to win the war. Time was against them ; the summer days were already beginning to draw in. Nothing stood between them and its defences but Essex, and if Essex liked to stand and fight, so much the better ! So reasoned Henriette, and it is no wonder that she looked for the support of the irrepressible Rupert. And if Rupert had been anything like the headstrong fool of the myth, she would not have looked in vain.

But Rupert, when he was bold, was bold on principle ; and he had, beneath those dark brows of his, the calculating brain of a scientist. War was, at present, his science, and though he knew it to be the King's game to play for the highest stakes, he was not prepared to gamble against a certainty. It was not a question of beating Essex in the field—where he was extremely unlikely to challenge a decision—but of forcing the now completed and fully manned fortified lines covering London, and having done that, of storming and holding the City. Rupert knew that the Oxford army had not the power behind its punch to do this. If it had recoiled from the attempt at Turnham Green, it had even less chance now.

What then ? Willy nilly, the main offensive must hang fire until Newcastle in the North, and Hopton and Maurice in the West, had done their business. But meanwhile there was the important nodal point and garrisoned town of Gloucester, directly in the rear of Oxford itself, and a standing menace to the loyal district of South Wales. Rupert believed, with some reason, that an all out offensive might account for this in as short a time as had sufficed for the far more formidable obstacle of Bristol. And when even Rupert's imperious voice was added to those who were for turning the King's back on London, what could Henriette do ? But it would be a long time before she could forgive her nephew.

To a long-sighted intelligence such as I believe Rupert's, or Charles's to have been, there might have appeared a more subtle reason to be urged for this move. If Gloucester were not to fall to the first assault, would "Parliament" dare to suffer the loss of face that would accrue from its standing passively by while that eminently godly city was starved into surrender ? Would not Essex be forced to march to its relief, and even if he succeeded, could he not then be brought to battle with Oxford on his rear, and annihilation the penalty of defeat? After which, with the best of the Roundhead army destroyed, a dash on London might, conceivably, be worth trying.

This Rupert at least was capable of appreciating, and that he kept his lips shut about it is no evidence that he had failed to do so. Naturally, on the principle of a bird in the hand, he would have preferred to storm Gloucester out of hand as he had Bristol, but when by one of those maddening half solutions incidental to councils of war, it was decided to sit down in front of it, he refused to have charge of the siege, and went off in a huff to Oxford. Which is just where, if his eye had been fixed on Essex, he would have chosen to be.

Everything fell out as might have been foreseen. The King's army was ill equipped for a siege. Gloucester held out with all the invincible stubbornness that Puritanism was capable of engendering in its elect. Pym and his fellow extremists, who had now re-established themselves in control of the Parliament and capital, saw that the time had come for a supreme effort. To have left the servants of the Lord to perish in their distress would have been more than even their authority could have survived. A tremendous effort was made to mobilize all the spiritual and military resources of London. The preachers thundered from their pulpits, and the pick of the trained bands left their benches and counters to fall in for the great adventure under the leadership of their adored old drill-master, Skippon. Essex, to whom the command of the relieving army was entrusted, was soon at the head of a formidable force, and for once in his career rose to the occasion. It was a straight, unimaginative task such as he knew how to perform. Making his final concentration at Aylesbury, he chose a line well to the north of Oxford through Bicester and King's Norton, his London lads making surprisingly good marching through a country swept bare of supplies. First Wilmot, and then, after Stow-in-the-Wold, Rupert himself, hung on their flanks with the Royalist cavalry, but these redoubtable troops seem to have done little seriously to hinder their progress. One cannot help suspecting that Rupert could have done more if he had been really trying. Perhaps he may have been well content that Essex should accept the gambit by relieving Gloucester—the capture of the enemy field army would be better than the sacrifice of a fortress.

On the 5th of September the King raised the siege and side-stepped north-east to Evesham, so as to be in the best possible position for getting across whatever line of homeward march Essex might choose. Whether or not Charles and Rupert had planned this trap for Essex, they were determined that he should not escape from it. The Earl was quick to see his danger, and

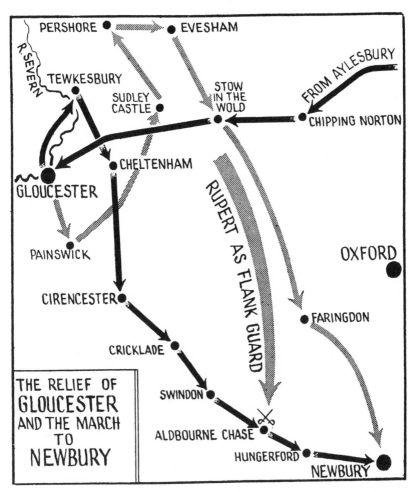

THE RELIEF OF
GLOUCESTER
AND THE MARCH
TO
NEWBURY

manœuvred with a swiftness and skill foreign to his usual nature. He first feinted at a northerly sweep, and then doubled back South to strike the Bath Road at Hungerford. The King, as soon as he had penetrated his intention, raced him on a parallel course, and about a day's march behind, to intercept him at Newbury. Essex had one rare stroke of luck, for with his army in danger of dissolving

through starvation, he surprised a Cavalier convoy at Cirencester ; and he might just have got past, had not Rupert, following
hard on his heels, pinned him down by a brilliant delaying action
at Aldbourne Chase. And so, when Essex approached Newbury,
he found the King in possession of the town, with the royal army
drawn up in position across his route to London, and his own
supplies again practically at an end. It was a desperate situation—
though the tables might have been turned with a vengeance had
Waller, who had another Roundhead army forming in the
neighbourhood of Reading, chosen to cut in on the King's rear.
But Waller had no love for Essex, and stopped where he was. So
there was nothing for it but for Essex to force his way, by an
immediate frontal attack, through the King's army in position.

The battle that followed, on the 20th of September, was the
most desperately contested of the whole war. It is obvious that the
King's army, resting with its right flank on the Kennet and its
left on a little stream called the Eri, had nothing to do but to sit
tight, and allow Essex to break his teeth on it. On all but the
southern part of the battlefield, it was enclosed country, with
thick hedges, unsuitable for cavalry, but ideal for defensive
tactics. On the King's left, however, there was open heath country,
and here Rupert, with the flower of his cavalry, was confident of
sweeping all before him and, eventually, of rolling up Essex's line.

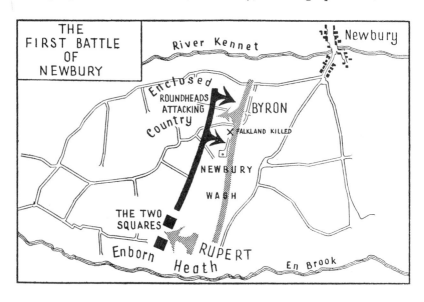

But on the right and in the centre, where a defensive game was called for, the undisciplined enthusiasm of Cavalier thrusters like Bloody Byron impelled them into trying to force the pace, and a murderous struggle ensued, from hedge to hedge and field to field, in the course of which Falkland threw away his life, which he seems to have had no desire to keep, for with his sensitive nature and weak will he was incapable either of mastering or enduring the part for which fate had cast him. Rupert meanwhile, on the left, with his Cavaliers so burning with enthusiasm that some of them actually flung away their armour, struck the opposing cavalry and scattered them like chaff. And then occurred one of the most significant episodes of British military history. There were also, on this flank, a couple of trained band regiments —London prentices, under the command of old Skippon himself. These boys, though it was their first taste of powder, and though they had been left thus unsupported to bear the full brunt of Rupert's attack, formed square, as their descendants were to do at Waterloo—and with the same result. Amazed at this "insolency", and determined not to be denied, Rupert's squadrons, whom he had evidently kept in hand, charged and charged again right up to their pikes, and in the intervals the scratch collection of Cavalier guns was brought into play to shatter their cohesion. But all in vain. The two regiments, manœuvring with the coolness of war-hardened veterans, drew off in perfect order to where the enclosed country gave them respite from the incessant charges. They had taken the sting out of an offensive that might otherwise have struck a mortal blow at the flank or rear of what was left of Essex's line.

Nevertheless, when darkness put an end to the fight, Essex had done nothing of what he was bound to do, if he was to escape destruction. He had not forced the King's position at any point, and the Royalist army lay unbeaten across his road to London. What then must have been his relief, and that of his men, to discover at dawn when they stood to arms for a last effort at a break through, that there was nothing in front of them ! The King's army had drawn off during the night in the direction of Oxford. The road to London was open.

Look at it what way you will, this withdrawal was a cardinal, and a fatal blunder. The cold-footers at headquarters had got their way—with of course the usual excuses, ammunition exhausted, and so forth—as if Essex, without any depot behind him, had not shot away just as much of it as the King. A Stonewall Jackson or a Wellington would have hung on astride of that road, if he had had nothing but sabres and pikes to do it with. Rupert, who seems to have been with his troops on the alert all night, can hardly have been responsible. But whoever had given the advice, the King cannot escape the responsibility for yielding to it, and thus allowing this supreme and last opportunity to slip through his fingers. It was in vain that Rupert, following hard behind and choosing his moment, cut up Essex's rearguard. In vain, too, that the King's forces, shepherding the retreat, repossessed themselves of Reading. The ovation that the tired London boys received from the crowds that lined the streets to welcome home the saviours of Gloucester and heroes of Newbury, was richly deserved. Nor can we grudge even Essex his laurels. He had done yeoman service on this occasion. The tide of success had been turned, though it had begun to flow in a direction which—had Essex only known it and lived to see it—would have proved as obnoxious to him as to the King himself.

For meanwhile, on the distant Northern front, events had been taking place that, though they attracted far less of the limelight, were of even profounder significance. That essential operation of the siege of Hull, which the magnificent Newcastle had been conducting at leisure, had been thrown out of gear by a visit from General Cromwell, bringing supplies and munitions to the garrison from the other side of the Humber. And on the 11th of October, this now much talked of commander had put the seal on his Lincolnshire operations by an even more resounding cavalry success than that of Gainsborough. This action, which Cromwell, whose horses were dead beat, had sought to decline, was fought at Winceby, near Horncastle. His men had chanted a psalm as they had trotted in close formation at the enemy, and for the third time, this new force proved itself irresistible. The result was to establish the Roundheads in effective mastery of Lincolnshire, on the flank of any possible advance from Newark on London.

The day following, Newcastle, who had found the siege of Hull a troublesome and thankless business, especially since the garrison had taken to flooding his trenches and capturing his guns, threw up the sponge and moved off with his customary dignity. The newly created Marquis was not the man to go on sullying his fine fingers with dirty work like this. Thus the King's grand strategy for the reduction of London was tacitly abandoned—and what other conceivable chance had he of forcing a decision ?

And now still further to the north, a dark cloud that had long been hanging over the Border, was about to burst—and the whole face of the war to be transformed.

12

KING PYM PLEDGES HIS COUNTRY

For a full year after the hoisting of the royal standard at Nottingham, the war had remained an exclusively English quarrel. England might indeed have been Robinson Crusoe's island, as far as any risk of Continental interference was concerned—thanks to King Charles's blessed determination, to which he had unswervingly adhered so long as he had been in control of his own foreign policy, to keep her at all costs from being rushed into the frightful and futile Continental struggle that was to prove the source of woes innumerable to subsequent generations. Nor had there so far been any active interference from beyond the Border. Edgehill and Newbury might have been incidents in a general election, which since Pym's Perpetual Parliament Act had abolished the method of voting, had to be conducted not by counting heads, but by breaking them.

This isolation had been no fault of the revolutionary chiefs. They had already engineered one invasion of England by her traditional enemy, Scotland, and they had been intriguing ever since the beginning of the contest to bring the Scots into England again on their side. It is true that the King, on his visit to Edinburgh, had conceded to his Northern subjects everything they had demanded, and had received in return the assurance of their most devoted loyalty. They could pretend no imaginable grievance against him. But a Scotland dominated by the Marquis of Argyll in alliance with the Presbyterian Kirk, was not likely to wait for a grievance, if it could succeed in striking a hard enough bargain to make its intervention worth while. But this time it would have to be a very hard bargain indeed. The ease with which, through the agency of her own "Patriots", the larger kingdom had been sweated for blackmail, had infected the Scots with something like megalomania. They had, even on that former occasion, made it plain that they expected England to submit herself body and soul to the same spiritual yoke that John Knox and his successors had imposed on Scotland. But to deliver a once merry people into that black bondage, had been too large an order for even the Pyms and Hampdens to undertake. Now, however, with the King's armies in control of half the country, Mr Pym might be inclined to take a more accommodating view of the matter.

Those who knew Scotland, and knew Pym, had no doubt that it was only a question of time before the terms asked for would be conceded. To bring the Scottish army into the field had become so urgently necessary for the revolutionary leaders, that they would probably have pledged themselves to anything. The arrangement had only one disadvantage from the Scottish point of view. *Their* part in the contract was to be fulfilled first, and payment made in blood down ; whereas it was only after the intervention of this new ally had put Pym and his associates in undisputed control of England, that there could be any question of handing over that country, as nominated in the bond, to the rigours of Presbyterian discipline on the Scottish model.

Whether, when the need for Scottish assistance had passed away, it would be quite so easy to get the bond honoured, remained to be seen. England herself might have something to say in the matter.

King Charles's advisers had been under no illusions about the way that things were shaping in Scotland. Montrose himself, the one man who in that murk of crooked intrigue had been playing a straight and loyal game, made his way to the King's camp before Gloucester to warn him of the treason that was being plotted against him. Montrose himself had been approached with an invitation to take command of the army that was being got ready for the invasion of England, and he begged the King to allow him to get in the first blow by taking the field at the head of all the loyal forces that the Highlands and Lowlands could be made to yield. But with what Gardiner calls "that strange[!] reverence for legality that never forsook him", King Charles would not hear of drawing the sword against his own subjects in order to forestall such action against himself. Even if it meant— as it did mean—throwing away his last chance of averting his own ruin, he would go into the fight with clean hands. A strange reverence indeed, and one that caused him to tread, of deliberate choice, the path to the scaffold, rather than meet his opponents on their own level. For not even the most Liberal hagiographer—not even Dr Gardiner himself—has dared to speak of King Pym the Martyr,* or the good Marquis of Argyll.

Some weight must be allowed to that pathetic trust, of which no experience could cure King Charles, in the love and loyalty of his Scottish fellow-countrymen. He was quite incapable of grasping that the heads of the Presbyterian Kirk appraised him with a sort of fanatical detachment ; if, and only if, he himself were to subscribe to their original Covenant of rebellion, would they consent to use him for what he was worth in the nominal capacity of the Lord's Anointed. Still less was he capable of appreciating that, in the event of his failure to toe this line, these hard-headed compatriots of his would be capable of disposing of his very person for what it would fetch, cash down.

Accordingly he cold-shouldered Montrose, and again allowed his Scottish policy to be swayed by the advice of that most fatal of all counsellors, the newly-created Duke of Hamilton. It is only fair to say that Hamilton himself seems to have had no hope of doing anything more than delay the entry of the Scots into the war, but he argued—not without some plausibility—that to authorize a *coup* by Montrose would merely put the King into the wrong for nothing, since Montrose would stand no chance at all in the Presbyterian Lowlands, and the Highlanders (as indeed it proved) being out for plunder and nothing else, would disperse to their glens as surely after a victory as after a defeat. Hamilton therefore—whatever may have been his own motives—counselled the King to do, from expediency, what he would have done in any case on grounds of principle ; and so, if he could not indefinitely postpone the crisis, at least do nothing to precipitate it.

Pym was a dying man in a hurry, and perhaps for that very reason the Scots were determined to take their own time to run up the price of their intervention. But there was Ireland as well as Scotland to be considered, and the situation there was furnishing timely grist for Pym's propaganda mills.

Naturally England's difficulty was Ireland's opportunity. In spite of all the indignation that had been frothed up about the atrocities alleged to have been practised on the Protestants in

---

* Though I would not put it past some of them to have applied this epithet to Hampden. It has a familiar sound, though I cannot put my hand on the quotation.

Ulster, none of the Parliamentary chiefs, who had successfully laboured to paralyze all the King's efforts to suppress the rebellion, were minded to divert a man or a penny from their rebellion against *him*, to relieve their suffering brethren. These could stew in their own juice until such time as, the Crown having been disposed of, forces could be diverted to the exploitation of its heritage overseas.

The result of course was that the Irish had it all their own way in repossessing themselves of their own country. Except for a strip along the East coast, and an area round Cork, all that remained to the English power was a few isolated garrisons. The King's commander, the loyal Marquis of Ormonde, was in a hopeless position, since the forces that were fighting the Irish were also fighting against one another. There was a Scottish Presbyterian army, under a general called Monro, operating in the North and distinguishing itself by appalling atrocities, that was just as ready to attack the King's garrisons as it was to fight the Irish. There was a force in the South that had tried, with equal ruthlessness, to carry out the plan of the Parliamentary leaders of making the war pay for itself by becoming a gigantic speculation in land robbery, coupled with the expulsion or extermination of the peasant owners.

Under these circumstances it was no more than elementary sanity for the King to take any opportunity that offered of calling a truce to the Anglo-Irish phase of this three-party war. The Irish themselves professed to have no other desire than to approve themselves his loyal subjects ; they asked for no more than the free exercise of their own religion and a free Parliament, and their utmost demands were moderation itself compared with those which the Scots had been abetted by their English Parliamentary allies in pressing on the King at the sword's point. Even so, Charles had no intention of conceding to the Irish a political independence, like that of the Scots, still less a Catholic supremacy over the Protestants. But he had not the least desire to treat the Irish as pariahs in their own land, or to persecute them on account of their religion. And for that, English Whig and Liberal opinion has never been able to forgive him.

The first thing was to get the fighting, that under the circumstances could only result in futile bloodshed, stopped. Charles accordingly authorized Ormonde to conclude an armistice—or "cessation" as it was called—with the Irish, on the only possible basis, of each side remaining in possession of the territory it actually controlled. This naturally did not protect or restrain Monro, who was actively engaged in aiding and comforting the King's enemies, and promptly proceeded to storm his garrison at Belfast. The negotiation of a permanent settlement was left till later.

But this common-sense and humane arrangement was worked up by the rebel propaganda in England, and denounced in Scotland, as a measureless outrage, a betrayal of the Protestant cause and part of a royal conspiracy to subject all three realms to a Popish tyranny of the most horrific description. And no doubt there was a certain amount of genuine apprehension lest the King should be able to obtain some counterpoise against the Scottish army that was even then being got ready to deal him a mortal stab in the back. He would not only be able to avail himself of a proportion of his English troops who had been tied up in Ireland, but some at least of his commanders were hoping to make use of the fine fighting material that a comparatively loyal Ireland would be able to furnish to what would be his hopelessly outnumbered and under-equipped armies. The Welshmen, who were now the flower of his infantry, were proof enough of what Celtic valour could do under competent leadership.

But we shall have to resort to analogy with our own time if we wish to understand in what way the typical Puritan zealot had been conditioned to regard the bare suggestion of Irish aid being invoked against English rebels. A Catholic Irishman was, in his eyes, what a Jew or a Pole was in those of a Nazi. If anything, this understates the case, because the Nazi was little enough inclined to bother about the religious aspect of the case, but the Puritan had not only taken over the view that the English were a sort of Herrenvolk, with unlimited rights to enslave, exploit, and if possible to exterminate, a breed of sub-human savages ; but the mere fact of an Irishman being a Catholic constituted him a mortal foe, in membership of a perpetual and super-national conspiracy to bring back the Lord's people into the Egyptian bondage. And this latter terror, which it had been Pym's lifelong speciality to inflate, had just enough substratum of truth to render it ideal propaganda. No doubt Rome was at the head of a vast international organization, partly open and partly underground, to re-unite Europe under her sway. The Jesuit international was every bit as pervading a reality as that of Communism, and more so than that of Fascism, in our own times.

But the substratum of truth bore a small and diminishing proportion to the actual facts of the case. The ideological crusade from which England had only just been saved by the miracle that scattered the Armada, was out of date. The religious motive had come to count for less and less in the bloody chaos of European power politics—the grand enemy of what remained of the Counter Reformation in arms was no longer a Protestant hero, but a Cardinal of the Church. The great English Catholic families were no longer the actual or suspected Fifth Columnists of Elizabethan days, but practically without exception, the King's most loyal supporters. As for Ireland, she had not yet, in spite of the fearful treatment to which she had been subjected, lost the tradition of a civilization as ancient as, and by no means inferior to, that of England. Catholicism there had none of the proselytizing intolerance of the Spanish Inquisition or—for that matter—of the Scottish Kirk. And the worst of the horrors perpetrated in the first wild fury of a dispossessed peasantry turning on the despoilers of their lands, paled into insignificance before the cold, calculated, covetous, and godly atrocities perpetrated over a long period of subsequent years by the avenging armies of the Lord on the hapless Irish.

But these are not facts that any good English Protestant was allowed to suspect. The bargain of blackmailer and bilker that brought about the unprovoked attack of the Scottish army on its King (and no man had been more fervent in his protestations of future loyalty than its commander-in-chief, the newly dubbed Earl of Leven), is represented as the result of a holy and democratic idealism. Whereas the bare suspicion that the unspeakable Charles was "intriguing" to grant the Irish some limited measure of toleration, in return for the support which monarchs normally consider themselves entitled to claim from their subjects against open rebellion, is enough to brand him a perfidious tyrant, for whom beheading was, if anything, too good.

Part of the English expeditionary force—about the equivalent of a modern brigade—was indeed shipped back from Ireland in the Autumn as the result of the armistice, and put under Byron's Chester command. In spite of the fact that Pym's propaganda organs stunted this as the abomination of desolation set up in England, only an insignificant portion of these troops were

Catholic Irish at all, and in fact many of them were of such doubtful loyalty as to render them more of a liability than an asset to the royal cause ; and they barely lasted into the New Year, when Fairfax made a swift march from Yorkshire and scuppered the entire force at Nantwich, after which a significant proportion turned coat and took service with their captors. A genuinely Irish element had, however, attached itself to them, consisting of a number of women camp followers, whom the devout London press was clamouring to have massacred out of hand, preferably by tying back to back and drowning. Fairfax however, whose piety was diluted by the instincts of a gentleman, would have nothing to do with this, and let them go. The servants of the Lord would know how to rectify such weakness on future occasions.

It is interesting that the first, though by no means the last, recorded employment of torture in this hitherto gentlemanly contest (as wars go), had been by the Puritan government at Dublin on a certain Colonel Reade who, in June, had fallen into its clutches when bearing to the King a message assuring him of the loyalty of his Irish subjects.*

Those who are capable of purging their minds of the hundredth-hand propaganda that they have been brought up to take for gospel, will see that Charles, so far from dallying with any idea of a Popish conspiracy, allowed his style, in dealing with the Catholic Irish, to be cramped by an almost morbid scrupulousness. If he could only have brought himself to have frankly conceded their demands for freedom of worship and a free Parliament—demands that appear to stick somewhat surprisingly in Liberal gizzards— he might have had the whole of Catholic Ireland enthusiastically behind him ; and his cause could hardly have suffered worse damage in England than it actually did by dint of incessant organized misrepresentation. As it was, he never went further than putting out very cautious feelers in the direction of tolerance. For Charles, to his dying day, was as staunch, though not as Totalitarian or unchristian, an opponent of Rome, as any of his traducers.

But like other simple-minded and straight-dealing men, his very innocence of the arts of propaganda allowed him to be pilloried as the exact opposite. It is probable that Pym—who would have been ready to pledge England to the delivery of the

* Gardiner, *Civil War*, vol. I, p. 113.

moon, if necessary, on the morrow of a Roundhead victory—would have succeeded in bamboozling the Scots into playing his game for him, in spite of anything that Charles could have done, or refrained from doing. But there can be no doubt that the Irish armistice, and the vast structure of lies and suspicions erected on this foundation about what the King was plotting to do, and what the Pope was doing, and what the Queen had done, was not without its effect in oiling the wheels of what, in every sense of the word, was a tricky negotiation.

By September the thing was practically settled. The formal act of submission and vassalage was gone through ; the stooges who still remained at Westminster to keep up the pretence of Parliament, were made to bow their necks to the yoke of signing the Solemn and Scottish League and Covenant. An assembly of hundred-per-cent Protestant divines was entrusted with the task of giving outward and orthodox form to the Kirk of England—a task that Mr Pym may perhaps have reflected was safe to outlast *his* time. In the exchange of words and promises for Scottish blood and iron, there was nothing that the English negotiators were not ready to sign away.

There were other considerations, of course, of a more substantial nature. The Scots—who had some experience of this sort of extraction—were determined to make the English pay through the nose for their services, the destined payee being the English taxpayer, so far as "Parliament" was able to get at him. On the principle that illegal taxation becomes no worse by being done thoroughly, "Parliament" was fully co-operative, engaging to pile on to their victim's already crushing burden of war expenses the swingeing sum demanded for the services of the Scottish ally. To what extent the Scots would succeed in securing delivery—and by what means—would appear in the sequel.

VI

8th of December, 1643

8TH OF DECEMBER, 1643

THE negotiation of the Scottish alliance, which was to be decisive of the Civil War, but which he was never to see in action, had been the culminating achievement of Pym's career. But until the beginning of the next year, the Covenanting army would not be ready to take the field, and then only if a sufficiency of money had been soaked out of the larger kingdom, which had already been squeezed nearly to the limit. It was a gloomy and depressing Autumn for the rebel cause, since after Newbury, paralytic inertia had resumed its sway over Essex's command, and he and Waller had come to oppose each other almost as stoutly as they did the enemy. Never had there been more urgent need for the inflexible purpose and organizing ability of Pym, to prevent the now desperate desire of all moderate folk for an accommodation from getting the upper hand before relief could arrive.

And Pym stuck to his task, in spite of the deadly complaint that now had him in its grip. Happily it seems to have assumed a merciful form. The tumour that had formed in the humblest part of his anatomy, appears to have given him little actual pain, though, of course, it was undermining his whole system, and he must have been feeling a very sick man. But his ruthless will power was as capable of driving himself as others, on to the end. His capacity for work remained unimpaired. On the 8th of November, when he had exactly a month to live, he added to his other functions that of Lieutenant of the Ordnance, the nearest possible equivalent to minister of munitions. He must have felt that he was the only man who was capable of coping with the chaotic shortage of which Essex was bitterly complaining, but which Parliament, with all its resources, seemed incapable of remedying.

Pym was no longer in the old Westminster lodgings he had shared with Hampden. He had taken up free quarters in the stately town house of Lord Derby, who was serving the other King—they would get his head before they had done, as well as his house. The change was doubtless a pure matter of convenience; Pym was not the man to be bitten by the love of ostentation. The master chess player is probably quite unconscious, as he ponders his next move, whether he is sitting on a tapestried chair or a plain deal one.

The collapse came with the bursting of the growth. The system and the brain itself were now mastered by the poison, and Pym, it is recorded, fainted repeatedly. He could only take to his bed and wait for the end, which was mercifully swift.

He must have realized, during those dark days of early December, how little chance there was of his seeing the dawn of a New Year ; but as he lay there, with his hold on life gradually failing, it is unlikely that he was spiritually moved either to agony or exaltation. Though he had always specialized in the religious side of politics, he was not of the stuff of which pious enthusiasts are made. He would have been incapable of understanding the torturing doubts of the dying Cromwell as to whether or not he was in a state of grace ; and it would be impossible to imagine him rising to the triumphant serenity of King Charles's "I have a good cause, and a gracious God on my side." One is inclined to look with a certain scepticism on the death bed speeches that are put into the mouths of celebrities, but there is a matter-of-factness about that fathered on Pym that renders it at least plausible :

"If I live, I will do what service I can ; if I die, I shall go to that God whom I have served, and who will carry on His work by some others."

From which we might fairly deduce that even on his death bed, Mr Pym wanted to voice the appropriate sentiment, and not give himself away more than he could help. Also, that he was not troubled by introspection, but that up to the last he was the master player, with his mind absorbed in the game.

That I feel sure, in so far as we can penetrate behind the curtain of secrecy with which he had always shrouded his real thoughts, must have monopolized his attention so long as the pain and the gathering mists would allow him to fix it on anything. There was nothing else in the world that it would much concern him to leave. That there was any creature who loved him, or whom he loved, we have not the faintest reason to believe ; very improbably his quite uninteresting sons—least probably of all, Lucy Carlisle !

Perhaps he may not have been altogether sorry to be going— and going, as he may have found a certain grim satisfaction in reflecting, with his head on. He was at the height of his achiev-ment, with a power and prestige such as few, if any, Englishmen, and certainly no Commoner, had enjoyed before him. It was in no ironical sense that men had come to talk of King Pym. For what crowned King had succeeded, like him, in making Parliament his mouthpiece and the law his footstool, in levying taxes and raising armies and calling in the foreigner to his support—nay more, in infusing masses of men with fury and panic serviceable not to *their* ends but to *his ;* making them see with his eyes and think with his thoughts against the evidence of their own senses ?

He had so far been equal to every occasion, and found the solution to every problem. And yet—as he may have reflected—he was no nearer a final solution than when he had started. Every difficulty overcome had unmasked greater difficulties behind. Every present call that he had met, had piled up greater liabilities for him in future.

This masterstroke of calling in the Scots a second time would make the defeat of the King sure—in the long run. Yes—but how long a run ? Even after the inevitable and ultimately decisive overwhelming of the Royalist cause in the North, how long would it take such commanders as Essex and Waller, with such armies as they more or less commanded, to drive home that victory against the military genius of Rupert, and the indomitable obstinacy of the King ? What if the war were to peter out, through sheer inertia, into one of mere attrition, an indefinitely prolonged stalemate ? That would not do. Public opinion—and Mr Pym knew only too well how desperately unpopular the war had grown even in London—would never tolerate it. Either a victory would have to be forced within a measurable time or—anything might happen. It had taken all his skill and all his ruthlessness to prevent the civil war from being called off by mutual consent, and the constitutional way resumed. Only let the war-weariness and frustration go on long enough to strain human endurance to breaking point, and that issue would be raised again. The devil might even put it into the King's head to stipulate for referring the dispute to a new and freely elected parliament. And even Mr Pym's propaganda could not go on concealing forever that His Majesty was merely taking his stand on the law—and the law as amended by the now Perpetual Parliament up to the utmost of even Mr Pym's original demands. All the immense catalogue of alleged grievances had been remedied as fast as legislation could be rushed through the Houses. The King had been fully co-operative, and did not now ask to put back that clock by a single second. But he was not prepared to surrender unconditionally what was still left of his trust for his people into the hands of Pym and his associates ; and he would die rather than abandon to their vengeance and plunder all those gallant gentlemen who had rallied to his standard—and Pym could accept nothing less.

Even if he had dared—and how dare he wait for the record of his treason to penetrate the consciousness of the people with whose enemies he had conspired and whose liberties he had betrayed ?—it was not in his nature to do it. Mr Pym was an elderly and an obstinate man ; a man who for all his subtlety and resourcefulness, had essentially a one track mind. For a quarter of a century now he had, without the slightest deviation, though with unhurried patience, played this great game that had only gradually developed into one against the King—and not even yet into one literally, as well as politically, *à outrance*. And yet—as Mr Pym may have begun to ask himself during those last spells of a lucidity which, just because it was the last, may have been mercilessly lucid—to what other end *could* it be tending ? Could the world be any safer for Pym, in the long run, with a living Charles, than with a living Strafford ?

If only that infatuated Sovereign would observe the logic of the game ! Gladly would Pym have allowed him to save face and crown by a timely resignation of sovereignty. It would have suited his purpose and inclination far better. Pym was not of the stern and reckless stuff of which regicides are made. But Charles was of that impossible composition which, with a certain checkmate in prospect, will go on and compel an opponent to inflict the *coup de grâce*. He was not playing by sane calculation, but on some principle to which victory and defeat were irrelevant. Rather than sacrifice *that* he would sacrifice the King himself—himself the King. In a more primitive state of society, unknown to either of them, such self immolation, on due occasion, for the sake of his people, had been an accepted part of a King's duty. How if Charles should, in the last resort, offer himself as the sacrifice in a truly royal gambit ? Would Mr Pym accept it ? Or rather—would he dare to refuse ?

I do not say that the dying man can have thought it out as clearly as all this. But he may well have breathed a sigh of profound relief to think that the problem of how finally to dispose of Charles Stuart would not be presented to him for solution. For I do not believe that Pym could have been guilty of the ineptitude of imagining that "stone dead" would answer for his case, as it had for Strafford's. With a Strafford, one could fight it out to a finish, according to the known laws of political duel. It had been my head or yours—that had long been understood, even if it had not been spoken, between them. But with King Charles, King Pym had no common ground, even of hostility. Their minds moved on different planes.

It was just because he could not understand Charles that there could be no question of coming to terms with him. Nothing that Pym and his associates could have offered to make it worth his while to stand in with them, no threat that they could bring to bear upon him even if they had him at their mercy, would avail with a man who had not his price, to whom force was no argument, but who, having gone to the limit of concession, had now taken his stand, with gentle obstinacy, on the law of the land and what was left of his own constitutional right. And if the law of the land were suffered to prevail—how long would it be before His Majesty had that law on those who had trampled it underfoot and violated it in the most heinous degree ?

Mr Pym could have no doubt on the point himself, and consequently had never been prepared to come to a compromise that left the King with the least substance of power—whether or not he could afford to leave him with the shadow, or even with his own life. The King's unconditional defeat—no man could answer for his surrender—was at least necessary, in the shortest possible time ... a clean knock out ... which meant ... what did it mean ? Something more than Essex, or even Essex plus Leven, could be guaranteed to bring off.

Mr Pym was no soldier ; he had shown none of the talent of a great, or even a competent war minister. But he was before all things a realist—enough to know that for total victory in the minimum time you have got to go all out, or, as we should say nowadays, to wage total war. And by total war is meant the mobilization of all material and spiritual resources, and their employment to the limit. A very different sort of war from the leisurely and amateur proceedings of the Parliamentary commanders up to date, conducted by the same sort of men as had staged the Providence Island adventure, and likely to degenerate into as sorry a fiasco !

Ah yes—but that was just the point ! Mr Pym, after all, stood for the Providence Island clique, the Broughton Castle ring ; it was to put the sovereignty of the country into their hands, and hands like theirs, to make England a Providence Island indeed for her rich and noble adventurers, that this war was being waged. And so far they had kept it well under their control. The Essexs and Wallers may not have been brilliant soldiers, but they were —again to adopt a phrase as yet uncoined—eminently sound Whigs.

But this new sort of war, that was required for the quick knock-out—under what sort of commanders would that have to be waged, and by what sort of armies ?

Mr Pym as he lay there, taking farewell stock of the situation that he had so long dominated, must have cast his mind's eye anxiously up and down the theatre of war. There was one portent by which it could not fail to be arrested ; one man who, in contrast to these stick-in-the-mud commanders, had developed the gift of victory under all circumstances ; one unit that had proved itself capable of pulverizing literally everything that had stood in its path—at Grantham ... Gainsborough ...Winceby ... —and after that ? Might it not be Rupert himself?

John Hampden must often have talked to his colleague about that uncouth nephew of his ; and the two may well have smiled a little over the story of those wild words spoken on the night of Edgehill. But the words may have stuck in Mr Pym's mind for all that. He was a realist, above all things. Noll Cromwell may have talked as if he were drunk, but he was a man with a plan ; he was all out—as these other commanders were not—to smash the King, and he believed he knew the way to do it ; a way that he had now tried out, on three separate occasions, with total success. It was, in fact, the way of total war.

To mobilize the whole material and spiritual resources available had been his plan from the first. His unit was the best found and best paid in the whole army—very different from Essex's skimped and half mutinous levies. And his men were not only the best disciplined, but the most godly and devout. They made some conscience of what they did—but it was conscience on a sound economic footing. No man can serve two masters, as Colonel Cromwell very well knew ; but a twinkle may have come into Mr Pym's now glazing eye as he thought how much better it would pay to make oneself master of two servants—God and Mammon ! A man who has discovered that secret will go far.

Let the war drag on for another year and nothing could stop this man from taking it in charge—brushing aside those worthy old soldier-politicians, and making his plan that of the whole rebel army, an army refashioned on his own new model of efficient sainthood. Then indeed would the Cavaliers become as stubble to their swords—and His Majesty——?

Total war is no respecter of persons, or principles. It would remain to be seen whether Noll would prove as able to stop himself in pursuit of a broken foe as he was to stop his troopers. Or as willing, when he made the discovery that even single-handed and disarmed, this foe was not prepared to make the slightest concession to the argument of force?* The royal gambit that Mr Pym would have been too wary to accept under any but mortal compulsion ... he knew something of Noll's explosive temper, and his afflatus for cutting any knot that he was incapable of untying ... thank God it would be none of his, Pym's, business to push total logic to its conclusion ! A conclusion that might yet darken total victory with the shadow of total defeat !

And even granting that the victory could be achieved, and consolidated—how if it should prove to be defeat in another and worse form for the cause for which Mr Pym and his friends stood ? He had never bargained for a long war, or a total war—least of all had he bargained to win it with an army that made some conscience of what it did—a conscience of its own, and one not, like that of the London mob, for Mr Pym to turn on and off as he chose.

For a new spirit was at work in this unique soldiery that was utterly alien from anything that Pym had sought to promote under the name of the Protestant religion. A sufficient leaven of these men had taken the Protestant principle naked and undiluted, and pushed it to lengths of which Calvin had never dreamed—of which perhaps only an Englishman, in those days, *could* have dreamed. They believed that a man in a state of grace (in which they all fortunately happened to find themselves) was in very truth not only God's image, but as directly God's representative on earth as any Pope had claimed to be. For the quintessence of Protestantism is for every man to become his own Pope, and—by grace—his own infallible authority in matters of faith and

---

* It does not fall within the scope of this volume to explain the refusal of the captive King to come to a deal with a junta of generals on terms that, however speciously drafted, they had no shadow of right—let alone the power or even the intention—to honour.

conduct ; and for every two or three men who freely elect to congregate together, to constitute themselves a spiritual law unto themselves. In this idea of Independency, as it was called, was implicit the principle of liberty of conscience, and underlying that, the even more pregnant idea of the equality of man. Combined with that of total militarism it might present a phenomenon unique in the experience of mankind.

This was the flat negation of all that Pym and his friends had worked and plotted and fought for—these men who had deliberately fixed on Providence Island because the colonists on the American mainland had been too independent and democratic, and who had broken down every restraint upon the tyranny of wealth and privilege here in England. It was seldom that Mr Pym betrayed anything like emotion, but if anything could move him to intemperate expression, it had been the bare suggestion of his condescending to tolerance in any shape or form. He was as great a believer in conformity—though to a different standard—as Laud himself, and in enforcing it his little finger would be thicker than Laud's loins.

And now, as the price of Scottish intervention against the King, he had in the most explicit terms engaged to subject the country to a spiritual yoke in which new Presbyter would be old priest writ large. There would be no nonsense under that regime about free congregations, or free conscience, or freedom of any kind— even of England to determine her own spiritual destinies according to her own faith and conscience.

But how if it turned out that the war after all had to be won by an army that was well and truly leavened by this new spirit of Independency—an army that made some conscience of its freedom ?

What would happen should an army of this kind, flushed with victory, be ordered by a Parliament—every one of whose members had already been made to subscribe to the Scottish Covenant— meekly to conform to the new Kirk of England ? And were Parliament to embitter the pill by persisting, as it certainly would—Mr Pym knew the men he was leaving behind—in its rooted addiction to bilking the soldier of his pay when his services were no longer required. What would the army, and such an army, do about it ? And what would then be the prospects of the Perpetual Parliament, and what survived of the Broughton camerilla ?

It had always been Mr Pym's forte to see the game several moves further ahead than other people. For such an intelligence as his, reinforced by whatever latent faculties of divination may be quickened in the dying, some inkling of these things can hardly have failed to penetrate as he lay there with the grey tide of oblivion rolling in upon him, wave upon wave. A certain contentment must have stolen over him as he thought how soon his responsibility would cease for whatever might lie ahead. It had been, more than anything else, by timing that he had achieved the unbroken record of successes that had marked his rise from a petty government post, to become the only subject in the realm to whom his countrymen had ever been fain to accord the name of King. But nothing in that career had been so consummately timed as the leaving of it. He had found the answer to every demand with which fate had presented him, but always by piling up heavier liabilities in the future. And now, whatever the future might have in store, nobody could—or at any rate would—blame it on to him. Rather would they say that the master hand being withdrawn—such and such had been the result. Though—who could tell ?... the Scottish irruption might yet do the business— the King *might* collapse, and England be made safe for the right people, before the situation had passed beyond the control of the inner directorate, with the half-baked armies of its tame generals in the field, and its well-sifted old guard in the Houses who could be relied on to make no conscience of any orders they might receive. Though what sort of control the Sayes and Warwicks and the rest of them would be capable of exercising without him and John Hampden to combine their predatory instincts into intelligent team-work, was a matter on which Mr Pym might prefer not to speculate.

One could only hope. All might yet go according to plan— or again ... either way, Mr Pym's reputation was safe. *He* would go down to history, not perhaps at his own valuation, but at the valuation of his own propaganda. Though at *that*, the world would never know his real greatness. Perhaps it was as well. It had never been Mr Pym's plan to give his real self away—even to posterity.

But the grey tide of oblivion was near the flood, and the waves were over his head. His grip, unrelaxed for a generation, on this great game that had absorbed his whole life for the past quarter of a century, was beginning to loosen. Everything was flowing together—becoming blurred. The war ; the Scots ; the clatter in the street and cries of "His head is off !" ; the boat at Parliament steps and the King coming down to the House ; the mob packing the approaches to Whitehall and shouting ... "Give us that dog Pym !"... no, not that mob ... but now one could no longer see the mob ... something had got between—rank on rank of iron-helmeted cuirassiers, with set faces and only the sound of hooves, pawing in the bitter January weather—a wall of iron between the people of England and their King ...

And hard by, the royal Abbey at Westminster, a grim shell, with the glass stripped from the windows and the organ silenced ; and on the north side of the choir a tomb, a plain slab, massive and austere, with new-cut lettering, bearing the name of the latest joined of England's Sovereigns :

JOHN PYM.

*   *   *   *   *   *   *

It is not there now.

Appendix

A NOTE ON SOURCES

MANY of the sources cited in the Appendix to *Charles, King of England* are good also for the present volume, and need not be cited again here. In the space at my disposal I shall merely indicate a few additional authorities and points of outstanding importance.

What we need most of all to realize in this, as in every period of history, is not only what we have, but what we have not got to work upon. How tantalizingly inadequate is our record of Pym, who, on any estimate of him, was essentially a Parliament man ! It was on the floor of St Stephen's converted chapel that his greatest triumphs were achieved. And yet how little even the most exhaustive research has vouchsafed about these Commons' debates ! The official journals, the one or two "perfect" or other accounts that were allowed to be published, the meagre gleanings of Cobbett's *Parliamentary History*, merely have the effect of sharpening our regret that nothing corresponding to the modern *Hansard* had come into being, or indeed would have been tolerated on grounds of privilege. The nearest approach is contained in the notes jotted down by one of the members, Sir Symonds d'Ewes, and edited—with all other relevant material —for the second session of the Long Parliament, by Professor Notestein, in a volume that is a masterpiece of its kind. But even Sir Symonds is as far short of verbatim as those snappy summaries of debates that appear in the modern popular press ; and he has maddening gaps—the all-important debate on the Grand Remonstrance, for instance, which he left early with a cold.

We have only fragmentary specimens of that massive debating style with which Pym dominated the Long Parliament, though of his decisive speech in the Short Parliament there are at least two fairly elaborate versions—probably heading summaries. Of Hampden's Parliamentary style, I doubt if there survives anything authentic longer than an occasional interjected sentence. A number of speeches that they *ought* to have made have, however, been put into their mouths at various times, and duly embodied in the accepted myth.

An even graver deprivation is the absence of documentary evidence about the inner activities of the formidable group of financier politicians of which Pym was the directing genius. Engaged as they were in what legally at least, constituted a treasonable conspiracy, they had a vital interest in covering up their own traces. If they kept any minutes of their confabulations, none has come to light, nor have we diaries or memoirs to fill their place. We are therefore left to infer their motives and plans from circumstantial evidence, though such evidence is capable, as the experience of the courts shows, of proving the most conclusive of all.

A sequence of brilliantly timed and co-ordinated moves in a political game may sufficiently enable us to dispense with the written word in penetrating the design of the master player. Moreover there is the direct evidence cited in the preceding volume, that long before the opening of the great Parliamentary offensive in 1640, the somewhat oddly styled Patriot chiefs had formed the habit of working in close combination for ends that were, to say the least of it, not free from suspicion.

A contemporary source of unique value is comprised in the secret dispatches of the Venetian Ambassador to his government, translated and decoded in the Calendar of State Papers (Venetian Series). This provides a running commentary of inside information by an expert observer, noting with Machiavellian detachment the unfolding of a design to transfer the effective sovereignty of England to a plutocratic oligarchy closely resembling that of his own Venice.

No other individual source is of comparable value to those I have mentioned, though taken all together they constitute a mass of miscellaneous material that it would take too long to catalogue, let alone sift and appreciate. Notable are the various series of State Papers ; numerous, but all too fragmentary gleanings from the reports of the Historical Manuscripts Commission ; the two miscellaneous collections of Rushworth and Nalson, and whatever bears on the time out of the *Somers Tracts*, *The Harleian Miscellany* and the *Camden* series ; and of course the tracts and manuscripts in the British Museum and Public Record Office.

The habit of memoir writing was not developed in England to the extent it was in contemporary France, and with the exception of Clarendon himself there is none of the protagonists in the drama who has left us his personal impressions of his part in it, unless we are to count the brief opening chapters of King Charles's *Eikon Basilike*—and this again would raise the disputed question of authorship, which I hope to deal with in a later book.* What would we not give for the intimate diary of Pym, an *Apologia pro Vita Sua* by Hampden, or Prince Rupert's commentaries on his own campaigns ! If some document would only come to light revealing what Argyll, or Hamilton, or perhaps Hampden, really knew about the unsolved mystery of the Edinburgh "Incident" !

We must do the best we can with the testimony of comparatively obscure witnesses, which besides helping to fill up many of the gaps in the story, is indispensable in giving the atmosphere and spirit of the time. Particular mention is due to the memoirs of Sir Philip Warwick, the best type of cavalier gentleman, a member of the Long Parliament who became one of the King's most trusted servants, and in whom, as in Clarendon, personal contact with his master engendered an affection almost idolatrous. Sir Philip had nothing of Clarendon's psychological subtlety or literary genius, but in what is on the whole rather a flat production he has his great moments, as in his account of the scene in the Commons after the vote on the Grand Remonstrance, and the best of his pen portraits, which are drawn with a firm and convincing stroke.

Far more pretentious are the *Memorials* of Bulstrode Whitelocke, another member of the Long Parliament, who ròse to be Keeper of the Great Seal under Cromwell. Whitelocke's reputation was posthumously inflated by the fact that he was run for some time as a Whig rival to Clarendon, but his book is characterized by Sir Charles Firth as "a compilation, put together after the Restoration, consisting partly of extracts from newspapers, partly of extracts from Whitelocke's autobiographical writings, and swarms with inaccuracies and anachronisms."† None the less, its very size gives it a certain value as a quarry.

For Memoirs of the Civil War to the end of 1643, we have the accounts of a fair number of those who took part in it on both sides, though it is even harder in this than in most wars to get a clear idea of even the major actions from the impressions of those

---

* Perhaps I ought to add that a brief record of the Queen's impressions was communicated long afterwards to her friend, Madame de Motteville, and sandwiched by the latter into her own Memoirs.
† *D.N.B.* Whitelocke, Bulstrode.

who fought in them. It cannot be too clearly emphasized that the customary confident and detailed statements of numbers engaged and elaborate battle plans, with the units of the opposing formations spaced out with parade ground neatness, are the product of sheer guesswork, or doubtful inference masking as certainty. This is most emphatically the case about the opening stages of the war, when it was so largely a glorified election fight of armed mobs marshalled by territorial magnates and politicians turned generals, with a leaven of dug-outs from the German wars. In the later stages, when a professional Roundhead army had taken the field, we have a progressively clearer account of its proceedings.

In the opening phase, at least, we are left guessing at almost all the things a soldier wants to know. How on earth did Charles and Rupert manage in three weeks' time, at Shrewsbury, to arm, train, staff and provision an army out of practically nothing, and bring it, at quite a creditable professional rate of marching, all the way to Edgecote, and there wheel it about and present it intact in battle formation between the rebel main army and its base ? Taking all the circumstances into consideration, it must rank among the most amazing feats on martial record, but who was responsible and how it was done we can only surmise. From most accounts one would gather no more than that the Cavalier team turned up somehow on the ground for the fixture at Edgehill, and that the only proceedings worth recording commenced from the order to charge.

Even so usually competent a military historian as John Buchan is betrayed, presumably, by the lucidity of his own maps, into explaining how the King (or perhaps Rupert alone) ought to have annihilated Essex by a flank attack at dawn ; though how such an operation could conceivably have been staged with the material and in the time available—even given the necessary knowledge of the enemy's dispositions—he does not stop to explain.*

Again, one would give a great deal to know the exact state of the King's army after the battle, and whether the admittedly fatal delay in advancing on London were not imposed by circumstances beyond the power of any staff to control. If we had the Quartermaster-General's account of the matter, it would tell us more than volumes of picturesque description.

* *Oliver Cromwell*, p. 151.

I should like to add that by far the most illuminating account of the Civil War that I, at least, have come across, is contained in Capt. C. F. Atkinson's article on the Great Rebellion in the 11th and 14th editions of the *Encyclopaedia Britannica*. As a strategic analysis it is masterly, but of what would now be known as the logistics by which strategy is conditioned there is, as far as I have been able to discover, no precise account at all, nor detailed evidence to base it on.

Of what has been written about the events and persons of the time by the historians of subsequent generations I need add little to what I have said in the Text. A portentous and almost staggering phenomenon that awaits elucidation in respect of our own time, no less than that of Herodotus, Livy and their peers, is that of the gradual overlaying and transformation of history by whatever myth may have struck root at those deep levels of common subconsciousness that lie below individual personality.

And the amazing thing is that the myth, once thoroughly established, is capable not only of outlasting, but actually of feeding upon the research and documentaton on which the modern age so justly prides itself. At least I am sure it is so with that of *The Tyrant versus the Patriots*, which long after Macaulay's rhetoric has been deflated and the Whig-Liberal heroics of the High Victorian Age have ceased to be readable, remains rooted like an oak, adding to itself a new ring of prejudice every year.

Index

ABINGDON, 335
Anti-Catholicism, 11-13, 63, 77, 98, 105, 200, 230-31, 235, 239
Apprentices, London, 54, 126-7, 361-2
Argyll, Earl (later Duke) of, 33, 56, 222-5, 233, 242
Army, 33, 36, 54-5, 99-100, 127, 195, 236-9
Arundel, Earl of, 36, 109
Astley, Sir Jacob, 55, 324
Attainder, Bill of, 92-7, 105-6, 109, 138-9, 141, 147-9, 152-3
Aylesbury, 330, 335, 345

BANBURY, 318, 335
Bath, 343
Battles and engagements : Adwalton Moor, 344 ; Aldbourne Chase, 360 ; Bath, 343 ; Brentford, 333 ; Bristol, 350 ; Chalgrove Field, 346-7 ; Chinnor, 345 ; Edgehill, 316-27 ; Gainsborough, 351 ; Grantham, 343 ; Nantwich, 369 ; Newburn, 59 ; Newbury, 360-62 ; Powick Bridge, 313-14 ; Reading, 344, 362 ; Roundway Down, 350 ; Winceby, 362 ; Wycombe, 349
Bedford, Earl of, 9, 57, 68, 86, 96-7, 98
Bishops, the, 187-9, 246, 253-5, 265
Brentford, 333
Brill, 335
Bristol, 350
Bristol, Earl of, 96, 109-10
Brooke, Lord, 35, 57, 187, 194, 343
Byron, Sir John, 257, 313, 342, 344, 361

CALVINISM, democratic nature of, 23, 26 ; as instrument of discipline, 36, 304-5
Capitalism, 302
Carlisle, Lucy, Dowager Countess of, 173, 273
Catholics, 11-13, 77 ; and see Anti-Catholicism
Cavalier Party, 192, 303-5, 336
Cavalry, 307, 313-14, 324-5, 340, 347, 352
Cavendish, Charles, 352
Charles I, King of England and Scotland : Scottish policy of, 20-25, 28 ; Scottish coronation, 22 ; Edict of Revocation, 21, 24 ; new prayer-book

Charles—contd.
for Scotland, 24-5 ; sends Hamilton to Scotland, 30-31 ; tries to raise army for Scottish campaign, 35 ; financial difficulties, 33-5 ; lacks support of nobility, 35, 41 ; his army, 36-7, 41 ; Scottish campaign, 37-8 ; signs Scottish treaty, 39 ; low ebb of his Government, 41 ; calls in Wentworth, 42 ; summons Parliament, 45 ; is denied Army subsidies, 49-52 ; dissolves Short Parliament ; 52 ; war finance, 57-8 ; takes command of Army, 58 ; summons Lords to York, 65 ; saddled with Scottish indemnity, 65 ; summons Parliament, 65-6 ; death of Anne his daughter, 75 ; curtailment of his revenue, 79, 184 ; assent to Triennial Act, 83 ; conciliatory policy towards Opposition, 85-6, 97 ; self-control of, 133-4 ; his deliberateness of judgment, 135 ; contrasted with Cromwell, 136 ; disloyal Ministers of, 143 ; consents to Attainder, 152-3 ; his Government hamstrung, 173-4, 176-7 ; his conception of monarchy, 175 ; his appointments controlled, 177, 181 ; deprived of Customs duties, 184 ; sends for Hyde, 188, 191 ; Scottish visit, 192, 194-5, 203-5, 208 ; calls halt to appeasement, 205-6 ; 252, 262 ; travels North, 209-15 ; attended by Parliamentary Commissioners, 210 ; Scottish welcome, 221 ; involved in Scottish politics, 223-6 ; ill-served by Hamilton, 223-7 ; fails to reconcile Scots, 233 ; his reaction to Irish rebellion, 236-9 ; return to London, 242 ; increased popularity, 242-6, 251-2 ; reception of Grand Remonstrance, 253 ; asks Pym to form Ministry, 261 ; forms Ministry, 262 ; impeaches Pym and others, 262-3 ; his reasons, 263-70 ; Commons' reactions, 271 ; leaves London, 281 ; sends Queen to Holland, 284-5 ; goes to York, 287 ; fails to win Hull, 289-91 ; loyalty of the North, 294 ; occupies Newcastle, 295 ; raises Standard, 297 ; his amateur Army, 302-3 ; the odds

Charles—*contd.*
against him, 301-5 ; his horror of civil war, 309 ; military competence of, 37-8, 310-11 ; his strategy, 311-12, 336-8 ; occupies Shrewsbury and Chester, 312 ; at Edgehill, 322-4 ; delays march on London, 330 ; makes headquarters at Oxford, 330, 334-6 ; requisites for his victory, 339 ; rejoined by Queen, 340-42, 349 ; military success, 348, 350-51 ; obstacles to his grand plan, 351 ; its abandonment, 362-3 ; rejects Montrose's advice, 364-5 ; Irish policy, 366-9
Chester, 312, 344
Chillingworth, William, 171
Chinnor, 345
Church of England, 169, 186-8, 189, 194, 253
Civil War, approach of, 260-61, 284, 288, 292 ; hastened by Irish revolt, 238
Coal, 63
Colepeper, Sir John, 170-71, 188, 216-17, 247, 249, 262
Commissioners, Parliamentary, 227-8
Constitution, the, 211, 250
Conway, Lord, 59
Cornishmen, 340, 343
Council of the North, 80, 284-5
Court of High Commission, 80
Covenanters, 28-9, 31, 35, 40-41, 56, 59-60, 62-3, 168
Coventry, 302, 316, 329
Cromwell, Oliver, 6, 7, 216, 328, 343, 352, 362, 378
Customs duties, 184-5

DEFENCE, Committee of, 212
Devizes, siege of, 343, 350
Digby, Lord, 94-95, 110, 272-3
Dorset, Earl of, 253, 255

EAST ANGLIA, 351-2
East India Company, 57
Eastern Association, 351
Equality, 379-80
Essex, Earl of, 36, 57, 96-8, 178-81, 212, 215, 272, 295, 297, 305, 312, 314-16, 318-19, 329, 331, 340, 344, 348-9, 358-60, 373
Evesham, 358

FAIRFAX, Sir Thomas, 295, 351, 369
Falkland, Lord, 73, 170, 188, 228, 247, 262, 353, 361
Fiennes, Nathaniel, 223, 350-51
Forth, Earl of, 320, 324

GAINSBOROUGH, 351, 352
Gloucester, siege of, 357-8

Goring, George, 101-3, 114-15, 118, 240-41, 313
Grand Remonstrance, 241, 244-50
Grenville, Sir Bevil, 340, 343
Gustavus Adolphus, 305

HAMILTON, Marquis (later Duke) of, 30-32, 37, 223-7, 242, 263, 365
Hampden, John, 6, 7, 52, 194, 210, 233, 315, 318, 326, 333, 340, 345-8
Haslerigg, Sir Arthur, 263
Henrietta Maria, Queen of England, 34, 86, 102-3, 114, 143-5, 176, 196-203, 231, 240-41, 264-5, 271-6, 284-5, 291, 295, 340-42, 349, 353
Herbert, Sir Edward, 262-3, 268
Historical sources, 385-9
Holland, 201, 284-5
Holland, Earl of, 36, 38, 212-13, 272, 286-7
Holles, Denzil, 82, 194, 263, 333, 337
Hopton, Sir Ralph, 338, 340, 343, 350
Hotham, Sir John, 290-92, 351
Hull, 289-90, 339, 351 ; siege of, 362
Hyde, Edward (later Earl of Clarendon), 52, 97, 169, 188-92, 205-6, 228, 247, 249, 262, 288, 330, 353

IMPEACHMENT, 142, 263
"Incident", the, 225-8
Inflation, 57
Ireland : rebellion in, 233-8, 365-8 ; Puritan attitude to, 367-8 ; Catholicism in, 368 ; Parliament of, 46

JAMES I, his Scottish settlement, 20-21, 30
Jermyn, Sir Henry, 103, 115, 349
Judiciary, the, 141-2, 184
Juxon, William, Bishop of London, 58, 148-9, 174

KIMBOLTON, Lord, 263
Kirk, Scottish, 20-24, 26-32

LANARK, Lord, 224-5
Laud, William, Archbishop of Canterbury, his policy in Scotland, 21-4 ; unpopularity, 54 ; arrest of, 75 ; his social conscience, 186-8
Law, the Common, 183-4
Legge, Captain William, 230, 239
Leicester, Earl of, 234
Leslie, Alexander, Earl of Leven, 35-8, 56-7, 59, 61-2, 247, 368
Lincolnshire, 351
Lindsey, Lord, 320, 323
London, 61 ; strategic importance of, 303, 312, 334, 336-8 ; fortification of, 335
London, mob, 61, 67, 98, 109, 114, 117-19, 126-7, 255-9

Lords, House of, 116, 187-8, 194, 206-7, 217, 254, 288, 354
Lunsford, Sir Thomas, 60, 257

MACAULAY, 5
Mary, Princess of England, 108
Maurice, Prince, 343, 350
Medici, Marie de, 34, 150, 177
Military Government of Cromwell, 5, 15
Militia, struggle for the, 238-9
Monarchy, function of, 174-5
Monro, General, 366-7
Montrose, Marquis of, 37, 222-3, 364

NANTWICH, 369
Navy, Royal, 52, 304
Newark, 344
Newburn, 59-60
Newbury, campaign of, 358-62
Newcastle, 55, 295
Newcastle Earl of, 338, 340, 344, 351, 362
Newport, Earl of, 140-41, 215, 232, 257
No-Dissolution Bill, 113, 116, 131, 147, 160-61, 251
Northumberland, Earl of, 58
Nottingham, 312

OLIGARCHY, the, 41, 56-7, 61, 64, 131, 174
Ordinance, the, 211
Ormonde, Marquis of, 366
Oxford, 330, 335-6

PARLIAMENT, 14-15, 63, 65, 78-9, 113, 131, 160-61, 211
„ the Short, 45-53
„ the Long, 66-80 :
    intransigence of, 66-7 ; its proscriptions, 76-7 ; invades Royal Prerogative, 78-9 ; triennial principle, 78-9 ; burden of taxation under, 84 ; subservience to Pym's party, 161, 171, 283 ; made perpetual, 116, 131, 147-8, 152-3 ; adjournment of, 217-18 ; second session of, 227 ; unrepresentative, 211, 288
Parliamentary Opposition : to the Crown, 46-47 ; exploits Scottish rebellion, 61-5, 66-7, 69, 99-100
Parliamentary Opposition, to Pym's party, 165, 169-71, 188, 227-9, 246-9
Peace, desire for, 353-5
Peace, party, 353-5
Pennington, Isaac, 355
Petition of Right, 50, 55
Petitions, 104-5, 114

Plague, 182, 210, 215
Plutocratic groups, 14-15
Plymouth, 101, 339, 351
Poll tax, 168
Portsmouth, capture of, 313
Prayer-book, 24-5 ; 216-17
Prerogative, the Royal, 50, 78, 86, 217, 238, 246, 283
Prerogative Courts, 183-4
Privilege, 271
Privy Council, 85-6
Propaganda, 45-6, 53, 63, 104, 110, 118, 176, 195, 239-41, 255-6
Proscriptions, 76-7
Protestantism à outrance, 12, 379-80
Providence Island project, 14
Pym, John, 6, 7 ; "the Ox", 8 ; character, 8-10 ; returned to Parliament, 9 ; expert in procedure, 11 ; exploits anti-Catholic animus, 11-13 ; attains leadership of Commons, 47, 50 ; indicts the Crown, 48-9 foments mob-violence, 54 ; treasonable conduct of, 64 ; electioneering campaign, 66 ; builds up case against Strafford, 48, 66, 71 ; attacks Strafford in Parliament, 72-3 ; exploits Scottish rebellion, 52-3, 83-5, 192 ; refuses office, 86-7 ; his fear of Strafford, 87, 89 ; Attainder of Strafford, 92-7 ; audience with the King, 97 ; use of mob-suggestion, 54, 98, 110, 117-18, 143, 239-40 ; subverts Constitution, 112-13, 116, 147 ; gains control over Lords, 116 ; his campaign against the Crown, 160-61, 165-6, 172, 176, 183, 211, 230-31, 236-8, 245-6, 283 ; his control of Parliament, 161-3 ; refuses to form Government, 163, 193-4 ; lack of constructive statesmanship, 162-4 ; insecurity of, 164-5, 167, 182 ; Parliamentary opposition to, 165, 169-71, 188 ; terrorizes judiciary, 184 ; attacks Church of England, 186-8, 215-17 ; reasserts dominance over Commons, 196-7 ; sustains Parliamentary defeat, 206-7 ; the Ordinance, 211 ; prepares for civil war, 211-12, 229, 236-9 ; further defeat over Prayer-book, 217 ; army-plot scare, 230-31 ; engineers Grand Remonstrance, 232, 241 ; challenges Prerogative of ministerial appointment, 236-8 ; bids for control of militia, 236-9 ; aims at Charles through the Queen, 240-41, 264-5 ; dwindling majority, 249, 254 ; heads Remonstrance deputation, 253 ; meets Lords' resistance, 254 ; attacks the Bishops, 253-6 ; 265 ; inflames the mob, 255-60 ; refuses to form minis-

Pym—*contd.*

try, 261 ; impeached, 263 : intention to accuse the Queen, 266 ; escape to the City, 275-6 ; restored dominance, 280-82 ; raises militia, 282, 284 ; arbitrary rule, 296-7 ; rejects peace overtures, 306, 315 ; intransigence, 336-7, 353-4, 377 ; sickness, 354 ; suppresses peace-party, 354-6 ; enlists the Scots, 363-70, 373 ; Lieutenant of the Ordinance, 373 ; last days and death, 373-5

READING, 330, 335, 344, 362
Religion, 368
Richelieu, Cardinal, 34, 40-41
Root and Branch Bill, 188, 206-7
Royalist army, character of, 338-9, 343
Rupert, Prince, 307-10, 313, 319-20, 324-6, 330-31, 333, 336, 345-7, 350-51, 357-8

ST JOHN, Oliver, 53, 64, 85, 142, 262
Savile, Lord, 56-7
Saye, Lord, 35, 107, 178, 194
Scotland, 20-22 ; power of the Kirk, 20-23, 26-7 ; Edict of Revocation, 21-4 ; new prayer-book, 24-5 ; St Giles' riot, 24-5 ; No-Popery, 23, 27 ; the Covenant, 28-9 ; revolutionary government, 28 ; Kirk Assembly, 31-2, 39-40 ; campaign in, 36-8 ; progress of revolt, 40-41 ; mooted French alliance, 40-41 ; Customs union proposal, 168 ; anarchy of, 196, 222-3 ; " the Incident ", 225-8 ; Argyll's dominance in, 233
Shrewsbury, 312, 314
Skippon, Philip, 282, 284, 304, 358, 361
Solemn League and Covenant, 370
Star Chamber, Court of, 79-80
Subsidies, 167-8
Suckling, Sir John, 100-103, 114

TACTICAL innovation, Rupert's, 307, Cromwell's, 352

Taxation, 63, 65, 84, 99, 167-8
Total war, 378-9
Trained Bands, 54, 229, 281-7, 304, 333, 361
Triennial Act, 78-9, 83
Tromp, Admiral, 41
Turnham Green, 333

USSHER, Bishop, 151-2

VANE, Sir Harry, 45, 51-3, 70, 91, 262
Verney, Sir Edmund, 322-3

WALES, South, 357
Waller, Edmund, 237, 353
Waller, Sir William, 343, 350, 360, 373
Wallingford, 335
Warwick, 316, 329
Warwick, Earl of, 215, 304
Welsh infantry, 336, 367
Wentworth, Thomas, Earl of Strafford, recalled from Ireland, 42 ; his policy, 42-3, 75-6, 112 ; Earl of Strafford, 45 ; raises expeditionary force in Ireland, 55 ; his sickness, 55-6 ; joins King at York, 58-9 ; is Opposition target, 48, 64, 66-9, 71-3, 87-9 ; returns to London, 71-2 ; is impeached and imprisoned, 73-4 ; trial, 88-95 ; urges assent to Attainder, 111-12 ; his situation hopeless, 140, 145 ; executed, 154-5 ; Hamilton's suspected share in his death, 226 ; his Irish settlement undone, 233
William, Prince of Orange, 108
Williams, Bishop, 138-9, 146-8, 258, 265
Willoughby, Lord, 320 *note*
Wilmot, Henry, Lord, 321-2, 327, 358
Worcester, 312-14
Worcester, Earl of, 296
Wray, Sir John, 110
Wycombe, 349

YORKSHIR E, 340